Ilman & Pilbrow Sc.

DEMOSTHENES

THE

OLYNTHIAC

AND OTHER PUBLIC ORATIONS

OF

DEMOSTHENES.

TRANSLATED, WITH NOTES, &c.,

BY

CHARLES RANN KENNEDY.

IN TWO VOLUMES.

VOL. I.

NEW YORK:
HARPER & BROTHERS, PUBLISHERS,
FRANKLIN SQUARE.
1860.

CONTENTS.

PAGE

PREFACE TO THE TRANSLATION i

CHRONOLOGICAL ABSTRACT OF EVENTS DURING THE LIFE OF DEMOSTHENES xx

ORATIONS:—

The first Olynthiac 37
The second Olynthiac 45
The third Olynthiac 52
The first Philippic 60
On the Peace 73
The second Philippic 81
On Halonnesus 89
On the Chersonese 100
The third Philippic 115
The fourth Philippic 132
On the Letter 149
(The Letter of Philip) 156
On the Duties of the State 164
On the Navy Boards 176
On the Liberty of the Rhodians 189
For the Megalopolitans 204
On the Treaty with Alexander 217

APPENDICES:—

I. Olynthus 227
II. Athenian Money and Mines 253
III. The Thracian Chersonese 262
IV. The Property Tax 306
V. The Trierarchy 311

PREFACE TO THE TRANSLATION.

My principal aim in undertaking this work is to produce a readable version of Demosthenes, adhering to the original as closely as is consistent with the primary object. Brevity and simplicity of style, together with the choice of apt and forcible words, are the most essential elements of a good translation.

It is sometimes asked, and there seem to be various opinions on the question, whether a translation should be literal? It depends, I say, upon the object which you propose to accomplish. If you are composing a translation to be used in the Hamiltonian method of teaching, or as a mere help to the idle student against his day of examination, then you must be literal. And to perform such a task is not very difficult. But if you seek to accomplish a higher purpose, it is not to be done in this way: a work of another order becomes necessary.

The primary object of a good translation is, that it may be read with pleasure, or at least without difficulty, by your countrymen; and secondary to this is the assisting of the student in his perusal of the original. It is true, that for both these purposes a certain degree of closeness is necessary: but the first of these can not be attained by a literal version, on account of the varying idioms of languages; whereas the second may be accomplished by a good readable version.

Nor does the matter rest here. I say that the classical student will derive much greater benefit from a readable version than he could from a literal. I speak of the real and self-improving student, not the cramming idler, nor yet the mere school-boy. Let us only see what his wants are.

Such a person, in studying a Greek author, is not to look to a translation for a perfect analysis of the construction of sentences. This he should find out independently, from those principles of grammar wherewith his mind has been long storing itself, from glossaries, notes and commentaries. A translation which undertook to solve all the student's grammatical difficulties, would be nothing more than a long note; having indeed its use, but not performing the service of a good translation.

The student, looking elsewhere for a thorough explanation of the syntax, may fairly consult the translator as an exponent of the true meaning of every sentence. And this is one piece of service which the translator renders him. But he has a right to look for much more than this; viz. good English, choice words, and all the other elements of good writing; in short, the full sense of the original expressed in such a way as an Englishman would have expressed it himself, allowing for unavoidable discrepancies.

No man will deny the importance of these things. One of the objects of studying foreign languages is, to obtain a more perfect mastery over your own. And a translation, either in prose or verse, may in this respect be made a useful medium of instruction, testing the powers and capabilities of your own tongue in comparison with those of another. Lord Brougham very truly observes:

"Even to scholars the experiment is not without interest of trying how far the two languages can be used, so as to render in the one the thoughts couched originally in the other; and even to scholars the comparative trial of the structures of the two, their resemblances, their differences, and their contrasts, is very interesting."

To attain the advantage here proposed, it is manifest that the version must be thoroughly English; or there can be no comparison at all. But I must turn now to another view of the question.

While it is the translator's duty to produce (if possible) such a work as, placed side by side with the original, shall be in point of style and composition not unworthy of it, he must be sure to preserve all needful accuracy in regard to the sense and meaning. The term itself implies that he must do this. A translation is different from an imitation.

He must adhere to the original. He must be accurate. But, how closely must he adhere? what degree of accuracy must he observe? are questions that naturally occur, and can not well be answered except practically, by examples. I will give just now some examples to illustrate my views; but will first endeavor, so far as I am able, to express my opinion in general words.

It is the business of the translator to express the full sense briefly, simply, forcibly; to add nothing, omit nothing; never to amplify or exaggerate. He should not servilely imitate constructions, or follow the order of words, yet not depart even from them unnecessarily. The production of good English he will regard as essential; to this every thing must give way but the sense of the author. Within the limits of these two conditions, faithful interpretation and good writing, he may turn and twist his sentences with a considerable degree of latitude and freedom. But these limits will always preserve him from unreasonable vagaries. While he does not affect to teach grammatical rules, they must be the guide to his own version, or he can not translate faithfully, so that he will always afford a clew to the construction, and will never mislead.

To accomplish all this, not only must you be thoroughly familiar with the language which you translate, but you should have deeply studied your own, and even known several besides.

It is an essential condition of producing a good translation, that you should be able to produce a literal one. Only this is far from being all. There are hundreds of good scholars who are able to do this, but who are not competent to write well. And on the other hand, clever men and practiced writers have failed in translations because they never took due pains to study the original language. Hence we have had so many bad translations from opposite causes. The literal translators necessarily fail, for want of a sufficiently high aim, a proper conception of their duty. The readable have been men who neglected or despised the niceties of scholastic learning. There are others also, from whose acquirements more might have been expected, who, carried away by the fervor of their imagination, or not liking the trouble of attending to words, have considered it sufficient to give the general meaning of an author, clothing it often in language which is purely their own.

To the class of loose translators belongs Leland. His version of Demosthenes is the best of the English, and has considerable merit. He appears also to have been a pretty good scholar, so that his faults are generally attributable rather to negligence than ignorance. I shall now proceed to show, by a few examples, what my views of proper translation are.

The following is from the Oration on the Crown; and I agree with Lord Brougham, that there is an unnecessary departure from the simplicity of the original:—

Τοῦτο τὸ ψήφισμα τὸν τότε τῇ πόλει περιστάντα κίνδυνον παρελθεῖν ἐποίησεν ὥσπερ νέφος.

Leland: *By this decree that danger, which hung lowering over our state, was in an instant dissipated like a cloud.*

So also this: *Οὐδ' ἂν εἷς ταῦτα φήσειεν.* Leland: *No! Let not the presumptuous assertion once be heard.*

In the Oration on the Chersonese, Demosthenes says that Philip has beaten the Athenians, *τῷ πρότερος πρὸς τοῖς πράγμασι γίγνεσθαι*, that is, *by being before us in his operations, first at his work, first in the field;* the last of which translations, though it might serve, as being a smart idiomatical phrase, wants comprehensiveness. Leland has: *his superior vigilance in improving all opportunities;* which is too vague. But here let me observe, I don't complain because his version does not show that the dative case is governed by the preposition, or on any ground of that kind. It was not his business to deal with a point of grammar, but to give a good translation. You might have it thus: *by commencing his operations earlier.*

I object to Leland's version; because the meaning is too vaguely expressed.

In the same oration we have: Δύο ἐν Εὐβοίᾳ κατέστησε τυράννους, τὸν μὲν ἀπαντικρὺ τῆς Ἀττικῆς ἐπιτειχίσας, τὸν δ' ἐπὶ Σκιάθῳ, ὑμεῖς δ' οὐδὲ ταῦτ' ἀπελύσασθε, εἰ μηδὲν ἄλλο ἐβούλεσθε, ἀλλ' εἰάκατε· ἀφέστατε δῆλον ὅτι αὐτῷ.

Leland: *Eubœa is commanded by his two tyrants; the one, just opposite to Attica, to keep you perpetually in awe; the other to Sciathus. Yet you have not attempted to oppose even this. No, you have submitted: you have been insensible to your wrongs.*

In this passage there are six instances in which the translator has needlessly departed from the original:

First,—the word *his* does not sufficiently express that Philip placed the tyrants in Eubœa. Observe, I don't complain of the change of construction. He was perfectly at liberty to invert it, and say, *two tyrants were placed by him in Eubœa,* had such inversion been required to make a neater sentence. The objection is, that the point of the matter is expressed too loosely.

Secondly,—ἐπιτειχίσας is not expressed fully enough.

Thirdly,—the word *perpetually* is not in Demosthenes.

Fourthly,—*oppose* is not a correct version of ἀπελύσασθε.

Fifthly,—the words εἰ μηδὲν ἄλλο ἐβούλεσθε are omitted.

Sixthly,—the last clause is an entire mistranslation.

Francis thus translates the passage:—

Philip had established two kings in Eubœa; one at Eretria, which he hath fortified, opposite to the coast of Attica; the other at Oreum, to awe your island of Sciathos. Nor have you asserted your own dignity by opposing these injuries, (since you seem unwilling to attempt any nobler design,) but even indolently suffered them; apparently remitted to him your own proper rights.

Francis has committed the same error as Leland in the ἀπελύσασθε, and has distinctly mistranslated the ἐπιτειχίσας which Leland has only shirked. Philip did not fortify Eretria, but established in it the sway of Clitarchus, his own partisan, and thus made him, and through him Eretria itself, a fortress against Attica; that is, a rallying point, a *point d'appui*, for the enemies of Athens, from which they might at any time sally forth, as the Lacedæmonians did from Decelea, to attack and ravage the country. And so Jacobs has it: *als feindlichen Hort.* Pabst: *in drohender fester Stellung.*

Francis has avoided some errors of Leland; but, besides a too great verbosity, which is his constant fault, I must notice another, which is too frequently committed, viz. the insertion of explanatory words, the proper place for which is a note, and not the text. Here we have the words, *Eretria, Oreum,* and *our island,* added to Demosthenes; and we might just as well have had the names of the tyrants, or any other historical fact introduced. The translation should be confined to the text.

A correct literal translation is:—

He established two tyrants in Eubœa, one opposite Attica, fixing him like a hostile fortress, the other against Sciathus; and you have not even got rid of these nuisances, if you would do nothing else: you have allowed them; you have manifestly given way to him.

Here the word *nuisances* is not wantonly added, for it is contained in the ταῦτα, and some such word is necessary to be introduced.

It may further be observed, that the literal translation of εἰ μηδὲν ἄλλο ἐβούλεσθε is hardly sufficient to convey to an English reader the exact meaning of the original, which, fully expressed, is: *these nuisances, at least, you should have got rid of, though you would do nothing else; yet you have never done so,* &c. But this expansion would weaken the translation too much. Therefore, I adopt a turn of expression which in English is equivalent to the Greek form, as those who are familiar with the Greek form will understand: and I translate thus:

He established two tyrants in Eubœa, one like a hostile fortress opposite Attica, one threatening Sciathus: and these nuisances you have never got rid of; not even this would you attempt: you have submitted; left the road open to him clearly.

In the four preceding examples I can not doubt that Leland

understood the text of his author. He has translated him loosely from carelessness. And, it may be observed, that, while he has mistranslated Demosthenes, he has not departed from the general sense and meaning. But this is not always so: and persons addicted to very loose translating frequently wander from the argument as well as from the words. Take the next example from the Oration on the Chersonese:

Ἡμεῖς οὔτε χρήματα εἰσφέρειν βουλόμεθα, οὔτε αὐτοὶ στρατεύεσθαι . . . . οὔτ', ἐπειδήπερ οὕτως ἔχομεν, τὰ ἡμέτερα αὐτῶν πράττειν ἐθέλομεν.

Which means:—

We are unwilling to pay contributions, or to perform military service, ... and yet, with such disposition, we are not content to mind our own business.

That is; the Athenians will neither take the proper means to carry on war, nor will they abstain from public business and Grecian politics. But Leland translates the last clause: *Thus we proceed quite regardless of our interests:* entirely mistaking the sense, which Auger puts clearly enough. *Ainsi disposés, nous ne pouvons nous résoudre à ne nous mêler que de ce qui nous regarde.*

Having thus noticed a few errors on the side of excessive freedom, let me turn to those which are equally injurious, on the side of excessive accuracy; whose tendency is, to degrade translation into a school-boy exercise. I must again have recourse to examples.

Take the famous oath:—

Μὰ τοὺς Μαραθῶνι προκινδυνεύσαντας τῶν προγόνων.

By your ancestors who met the peril at Marathon.

A person who reviewed Lord Brougham's translation in the *Times*, insists that it should be translated thus:—

By those of your forefathers, who at Marathon were the first to encounter the brunt of danger.

And I equally insist, that the critic's translation is detestable, as emasculating all the vigor of the clause. It is true that he expresses the genitive case more fully, and I would require the school-boy to do so in his lesson; but that is a totally different affair. Here it is essential to have the fewest possible words, to preserve the spirit of the appeal, and something may be sacrificed for this purpose. My translation, however, is not incorrect: it does not exclude the partitive signification, but only leaves a trifling ambiguity, which deceives no man. But here are eight words for προκινδυνεύσαντας, and the πρὸ virtually translated twice, by *first* and *brunt*. Over-accuracy always leads to verbiage.

Jacobs has:—

Bei den Ahnherrn schwör' ich, die zu Marathon kämpften.

Shortly before the last passage we have: Εἰ γὰρ ταῦτα προεῖτο ἀκονιτὶ, περὶ ὧν οὐδένα κίνδυνον ὅντιν' οὐχ ὑπέμειναν οἱ πρόγονοι, τίς οὐχὶ κατέπτυσεν ἂν σοῦ.

Lord Brougham has:—

For if she had given up without a struggle all that your forefathers encountered every danger to win, who but would have spurned you, Æschines?

His reviewer has:—

For if voluntarily and without an obstinate struggle, those honors had been abandoned, for which our ancestors braved every danger, where is the man who would not have spit on you with loathing?

Lord Brougham's is far the preferable version. In the other, the words *voluntarily*, *obstinate*, and *with loathing*, though intended to exhibit a wonderful accuracy, are utterly unwarranted. And as to κατέπτυσεν, which Lord Brougham is charged with frittering away, the critic needs to be informed, that metaphors can not always be transferred from one tongue to another. It happens sometimes, that a metaphorical expression, by frequent use, becomes familiar to the people of the country, but if literally translated into another language, it sounds harsh or strange to those who are not accustomed to it. I might call the critic a *goose* in English, but if I called him *anser* in Latin, the point would be lost. The phrase *classi immittit habenas* sounds ill, if literally rendered in English, though it has been so. We know that κατάπτυστος had become a common word of abuse at Athens, and, being such, is well enough represented by such a word as *despicable.* I do not, however, absolutely say, that the metaphor here may not be preserved; I only object to a criticism which assumes its positive necessity. But if perfect accuracy is insisted upon, why add the words *with loathing?* Jacobs has the simple *angespuckt.*

I should prefer, in Lord Brougham's version, the substitution of *what* for *all that;* and the omission of *you* before *Æschines.* The introduction of the last word, instead of *you*, may be good, to escape too many monosyllables.

In the Oration on the Crown, we have:—

Καὶ γὰρ ἄνδρα ἰδίᾳ καὶ πόλιν κοινῇ πρὸς τὰ κάλλιστα τῶν ὑπαρχόντων ἀεὶ δεῖ πειρᾶσθαι τὰ λοιπὰ πράττειν.

Lord Brougham and his critic both commit the error of attempting to translate ἰδίᾳ and κοινῇ literally; the one having, *individuals in their private concerns, and the state in public affairs;* and the other, *a man individually, and a state collectively.* The former of these is better in point of composition, the latter is closer to the original; but they are both faulty, by making prominent that which in Greek is a mere flourish, and can not be represented in our language. It is clear at once that the words *individually* and *collectively* add nothing to the sense in the above translation. It is a rhetorical antithesis not very unlike that of μὲν and δὲ, which is perpetually recurring, and has an elegance and a usefulness about it, which we can seldom express. Sometimes, indeed, it happens, that μὲν and δὲ may be represented by such expressions as, *on the one hand, and on the other;* but it is rare that they assume so much importance in the sentence.

Leland has avoided this puerility:—

By the most illustrious of their former actions it is, that private men or public bodies should model their succeeding conduct.

The only thing which I object to here is, *public bodies,* as being hardly dignified enough. Translate:—

For both individuals and communities should ever strive to model their future conduct by the noblest of their past.

Is there any thing here left unexpressed? That is the test of a faithful translation. Are not the words ἄνδρα ἰδίᾳ πράττειν fully enough represented by the words *individuals their conduct?* Or what further is wanted? It is no slight advantage, in my view, that the last translation is shorter than any other. Yet, brief as it is, it has one word more than the Greek, and this shows how important it is to struggle for brevity. The best versions in the world will exceed the Greek in number of words, if they are faithful; for obvious reasons. Ἀνὴρ is *a man;* πράττω, *I do,* or, *I am doing;* πραττέτω, *let him do;* ταῦτα, *these things;* Φιλίππου πολεμοῦντος, *Philip being at war,* or, *while Philip is at war.* These and the like expansions are inevitable; but they make it the more necessary to aim at brevity, wherever it can be had, consistently with good writing. The translator must seize upon every compensation which he can lay hold of, to attain this object; though it may cost him ten times the trouble of the ordinary method. Οὐδὲν ἄλλο ἢ χλευάζει ὑμᾶς, *he only mocks you.* Don't translate it, *he does nothing else but mock you,* though this be the literal translation; because, by so doing, you lose an advantage, which your own language here affords, as a set-off against many disadvantages. The literal version entails upon you the extra word *does,* from which you escape by using the idiomatical turn. This may seem very simple; but I find by experience, that from inattention to such simple matters hardly any translation in our language is what it ought to be.

Ἔστι γὰρ ἔχειν καὶ τἀλλότρια. (Orat. de Halonneso.)

Translate: *For it is possible to hold the property of others;* or, if you please, with Leland: *For a man may possess the property of others.*

The sentence expressed at full is: *For it is possible to hold the property of others, as well as your own.*

The last five words demonstrate the meaning of καί. Why do I omit them? Because that full demonstration is purchased at the price of too much verbiage; and the idea is sufficiently expressed without it, if you read the sentence properly, laying the emphasis where you ought. The translator, using that reserve which good taste requires, relies on the intelligence of the judicious reader. And with this reliance, I don't think it necessary to put any words in italics.

The German translators, Jacobs and Pabst, express the καὶ by *auch*. But in English neither *also* nor *even*, nor any thing short of a paraphrase can fairly represent it. Auger has, *Car on peut avoir le bien d'autrui.* If I am asked why I do not adopt the turn of Leland or Auger, who are both shorter than I am, my answer is, that I wish to avoid the ambiguity of their sentences, which might be construed as importing that it was lawful to have the property of others; and an emphatic word like *possible* is better than *may* or *can.*

Πότε ἃ χρὴ πράξετε; ἐπειδὰν τί γένηται; (First Philippic.)

Literally: *When will you do what is necessary! When what has happened?*

Better: *When will you perform your duty? In what event?*

Where Demosthenes urges the Athenians αὐτοὺς ἐξιέναι, I often translate it, *to serve in person;* because the literal expression is inadequate: and *to march out yourselves* gives but half the sense, as it refers to naval expeditions as well as land services.

Οὔτ' εἰμὶ μήτε γενοίμην, *I neither am, nor wish to be.*

Διατελῶ ἔχων. *I have ever had* is sufficient, without adding *and still continue to have*: for this makes too many words.

'Εκ μὲν πτωχῶν πλούσιοι γεγόνασιν, ἐκ δ' ἀδόξων ἔντιμοι.

From poor have become wealthy, from obscure honorable. But it is a little better to say: *Have risen from poverty to wealth, from obscurity to honor.*

Milton has imitated the Greek construction:—

How cam'st thou speakable of mute?

And in poetry I like it, but it does not suit so well in prose.

Τὰς εὐθύνας ἐπεσημαίνεσθε. *You passed my audit,* or *you approved my account.* But not, as more than one translator has it, *you passed and approved my accounts.*

I notice this once for all, in order to condemn the practice, common with some translators, of putting two words for one. This they do, either because they doubt which is the better word, and think, if they have both, they must be right; or because neither word seems sufficient of itself, and they are anxious to convey every tittle of the sense. But it is better to exercise a little reserve, than to indulge this rage for accuracy.

It frequently happens that a turn or paraphrase is not only allowable, but absolutely necessary; as in the following example from the Oration on the Crown:—

Οὐ γὰρ δήπου Κτησιφῶντα μὲν δύναται διώκειν δι' ἐμὲ, ἐμὲ δὲ, εἴπερ ἐξελέγξειν ἐνόμιζεν, αὐτὸν οὐκ ἂν ἐγράψατο.

In this passage, which all the English versions that I have seen mistranslate, it is only necessary to see that the first negative governs both clauses, and nothing is more simple. But if we translate the words without a little management, they make nonsense; as thus:—

For surely he can not prosecute Æschines on my account, and would not have indicted me myself, had he thought he should convict me.

That is wrong, because, though the Greek οὐ may apply to both clauses, the English *can not* is prevented from doing so by the change of tense. Otherwise it might have been literally rendered, as in the following:—

Οὐχ, ᾗ σὺ κνίζει, σὸν μὲν ἐχθαίρων λέχος,
καινῆς δὲ νύμφης ἱμέρῳ πεπληγμένος.

Not . . . . disliking your person and smitten with passion for the new bride.

Here I must give the sense by a turn:—

Surely it can not be, that he is able to prosecute Æschines on my account, and would not have indicted me myself, had he thought he would convict me.

But a little further deviation from the original form gives a more effective translation:—

Surely, if he can prosecute Ctesiphon on my account, he would not have forborne to indict me myself, had he thought he could convict me.

Auger saw the meaning:—

On ne dira pas sans doute qu'un homme, qui peu bien à cause de moi accuser Ctésiphon, ne m'eût pas accusé moi-même, s'il eût cru pouvoir me convaincre.

Jacobs is a little too wide:—

Denn kann er den Ctesiphon gerichtlich verfolgen um mienetwillen, so konnte er auch mich selbst anklagen, wenn er den Beweis gegen mich zu führen hoffte.

Pabst is better. But all the English translators whom I have seen are entirely wrong. They seem to have followed Taylor. Leland's and Spillan's I subjoin:—

Leland: *He can not pursue Ctesiphon on my account; and that he hath not directed his impeachment against me, can proceed but from a consciousness that such impeachment could not be supported.*

Spillan: *For he can not prosecute Ctesiphon through me, but if he thought he could convict me, he would not have impeached him.*

One more example, and I have done. We have at the beginning of the first Olynthiac:—

Ὅτε τοίνυν τούθ' οὕτως ἔχει, προσήκει προθύμως ἐθέλειν ἀκούειν τῶν βουλομένων συμβουλεύειν· οὐ γὰρ μόνον εἴ τι χρήσιμον ἐσκεμμένος ἥκει τις, τοῦτ' ἂν ἀκούσαντες λάβοιτε, ἀλλὰ καὶ τῆς ὑμετέρας τύχης ὑπολαμβάνω πολλὰ τῶν δεόντων ἐκ τοῦ παραχρῆμα ἐνίοις ἂν ἐπελθεῖν εἰπεῖν.

The literal translation is:—

Since therefore this is the case, you should be willing cheerfully to hear those who desire to advise you. For then, not only, when men have come prepared with useful counsel, will you hear and receive it, but I consider it also part of your good fortune, that it will occur to some persons to offer many fit suggestions at the moment.

In the last clause there is a change of construction, or a slight ellipse. The argument runs thus:—

Not only will you get useful counsel which men have prepared beforehand, but much more; for I consider, &c.

First, to improve the baldness of the literal translation,

ἀκούσαντες ἂν λάβοιτε may be thrown into an English form thus: *you will have the benefit of hearing.*

Secondly, *ἥκει* admits of a turn. It refers to the orator who has come to the assembly, a matter of common reference with Demosthenes. And the word is so placed in the sentence as to have no emphasis of importance. *Ἐσκεμμένος ἥκει τις* is little more than *ἔσκεπταί τις*, or *ἐσκεμμένοι εἰσιν οἱ λέγοντες*. Just as we often translate *ὁ παριὼν* *the orator*, without deeming it necessary to say *the person who comes forward on the hustings;* so we may deal with *ἥκει* in this place.

Thirdly, a turn may be found for the *ἐνίοις ἂν ἐπελθεῖν*, &c., and we may amend the translation thus:—

So shall you have the benefit of hearing not only such counsel as your orators have devised beforehand, but more than this; for I esteem it part of your good fortune, that many useful suggestions will occur to some speakers at the moment.

Or it may thus be shortened:—

So shall you have the benefit of all counsel, whether preconsidered or not; for, &c.

The best turn is given by Auger:—

Outre que vous pouvez profiter des réflexions sages qu'un orateur apporte à la Tribune, vous êtes encore assez heureux pour qu'il vienne sur le champ à quelques-uns des avis utiles.

And this I adopt. But it may be well to compare this with other translations.

Francis has:—

In this disposition therefore you ought to hear with a favorable attention whoever is willing to propose his advice. Not only should you hear the salutary scheme which hath been formed and matured by reflection, but I deem it an instance of your good fortune, that some of your orators are capable of conceiving upon the instant such expedients as may be useful to the public.

Here we see that Francis, by mistranslating *λάβοιτε ἂν*, departs from the logic of the orator, which is this—*You should be willing to hear all men, for thus you will not miss any good counsel.* Whereas Francis makes the second clause a repetition of the injunction, as if λάβοιτε ἂν signified *you ought to receive*.

And Leland is in this respect little better:—

It is your part therefore readily and cheerfully to attend to all who are disposed to offer their opinions. For your regards need not to be confined to those whose counsels are the effect of premeditation; it is your good fortune to have men among you who can at once suggest many points of moment.

Jacobs gives the argument correctly:—

Denn nicht blos, was Einer nach vorläufiger Ueberlegung hier Nützliches vorträgt, werdet Ihr anhören und zu Herzen nehmen.

I only object to *zu Herzen nehmen*, as being a little too strong for λάβοιτε. He passes over the ἥκει as I do.

An anonymous German version lying before me commits the error of Francis:—

Denn nicht blos das, was Einer nach vorhergegangener Ueberlegung Nützliches hier vorbringt, müsst Ihn anhören und erfassen.

So does Pabst:—

Ihr müsset nehmlich nicht blos es anhören und ergreifen wenn jemand vorbereitet auftritt, um etwas Nützliches vorzubringen.

I may seem to have been a long time in discussing a question upon a few words. But my object is to show how translation should be conducted, what are the difficulties attending it, and how they are to be overcome. The literal version is but the first stage of the process, though it is the stumbling-block with ill-taught scholars. Having analyzed your sentence, and made yourself perfect master of its construction and meaning, the next thing is to translate it. And this part of the affair is the principal difficulty, requiring a great command of your own language, and the exercise of much thought and discretion. Nor am I induced to say this only by observing the failures of others, but from the consciousness of my own deficiencies, and the conviction that I have fallen very far short of my own aims and endeavors.

I now come to another question, which is of some importance in translating Demosthenes, viz. how the translator is to deal with all the public and political nomenclature of the Athenians, the civil and military titles, names of offices and institutions, terms of law and jurisprudence. On this subject I am not disposed in the least to depart from the principle which I adopted many years ago, when I made my first essay on Demosthenes, and which I stated thus :—

"As a general rule, I think it better to translate into English than to Anglicize the Greek. Thus I say *jury*, *parish*, *indictment*, in preference to *dicast*, *deme*, *graphe*. It is true that in each of these cases the word but imperfectly describes the thing intended; for instance, the proceedings upon our indictment are very different from those of the Athenian prosecution so described. But, on the other hand, the vernacular term conveys the idea more pleasingly to the common reader; and be it remembered, a translation is more for the use of the unlearned than of the learned. I strive therefore to be as little as possible un-English; and while I always seek for the word which corresponds most nearly with the original, I am satisfied if it corresponds in some essential points."

I adhere to the above as the true principle of translation. Only with respect to the word *δῆμος*, I am now more inclined to adopt the version of *township*, which Mr. Whiston has used in the Archæological Dictionary.

The critic of Lord Brougham, whom I have before mentioned, and who may be taken to represent a certain class of scholars, strongly censures his lordship for attempting to convert the logistæ, liturgies, liturgi, &c., into English. And yet the same person insists that *γραφὴ* shall be an *indictment*, and *εἰσαγγελία* an *impeachment;* in which he is right, but that is inconsistent with his general condemnation of Lord Brougham's plan.

That indeed it is impossible fully to carry out the opposite system, is manifest. For how would you translate *ἐγράψατό με*? *He brought a graphe against me!* But who could tolerate this?

You must introduce into your text a heap of monstrosities, to please the ear of the pedant, and disgust every other. *Graphe, deme, psephism, dicast, agora, bema, liturgy, phyle, dice, ecclesia, symmory, chorege, logist, euthyne, stratege, hoplite, metic, cleruchian, hegemony, bule, cleter, lexiarchic, ecmartyry, anacrisis, hypomosy*, &c.

Nothing is easier than to do this. You have only to abdicate the functions of the translator, and save yourself some thought and trouble.

But as to the logic of the matter, it is true, that for many of these ancient terms it is not possible to find a perfectly apposite translation. But it does not follow that you are not to translate at all.

The *βουλὴ* of five hundred at Athens was very differently constituted from any English senate or council. But it may be translated by either of those words, because there is enough of similarity for that purpose.

Nor needs a court of justice to be called a *dicastery*, (or, as Mr. Grote will have it, a *dikastery*,) because there is a difference in the mode of legal procedure at Athens and in England. All this is sheer pedantry!

Judicial tribunals and deliberative bodies are things of universal existence. A court, a judge or juror, a council, a member or president of that council, may just as well be found at Athens as at Rome, or in London.

Shall I refuse to translate *ναῦς*, *a ship*, because Attic *triremes* and *pentecontors* are different from English steamboats and men-of-war? Or shall I insist on calling a Roman sword a *gladius*, because it was different from our own? Do we make no attempt to translate *buris, temo, dentale, stiva*, because Virgil's plow would not suit a modern agriculturist? The pedant would give his own pupil a sound whipping if he brought such an excuse.

Στρατηγὸς is commonly translated *general*. Yet the functions of the Athenian *Στρατηγὸς* are far from corresponding perfectly with those of a modern general. For, besides that he had various civil duties to perform, both as an administrative and judicial functionary, he was an admiral as well as general, there being no such distinction between the two services as we have in England. But I am content with the translation of *general* for all that.

In short, in the translation of many common words we are compelled by the difference of times and circumstances to be guilty of some inaccuracy. For example, *πλεῖν* is rendered *to sail*, in many cases where not sails but only oars impelled the ship; and it is commonly preferred to the word *navigate*, as being of more ordinary use. Ἱππεῖς is rendered *knights*, though our word conveys a somewhat different idea. *Charta* and *papyrus* are called *paper*, though the material was different from ours. The meals, the articles of dress of the Greeks and Romans, do not correspond with ours; but we make the best of it, and translate them. If I call the Roman *lectus, a couch*, I do not present an idea of its form, or of the mode in which Roman guests were placed at table. You must go to the dictionary of antiquities, or to some commentary, for an explanation of that. So, if I translate *λειτουργία, a public office, service, or duty*, I do not exhibit the peculiar nature of the service; yet I give a positive translation of the word, which is good as far as it goes.

But I grant there is some discretion to be observed. We must look also to the other side of the question. There are some terms entirely untranslatable. *Archon* can not be converted into English any more than *consul*. I do not reduce the Attic money to English, which would cause confusion; and for the same reason I do not imitate Leland in adopting the names of the Roman months. Further, I would eschew all fanciful similarities, all undignified expressions. I would not call any ancient vehicle a hackney-coach or a cabriolet, nor any ancient functionary a Lord Mayor. Nor do I approve of Francis converting *ταξίαρχοι* and *φύλαρχοι* into *colonels* and *aids-de-camp*. There is some truth in what Olivet says of the use of such terms, that to put them in the mouth of Demosthenes is like painting Alexander or Cæsar in a peruke or an embroidered coat.

I agree also with what Pope says with respect to a translation of Homer:—

"The use of modern terms of war and government, such as *platoon*, *campaign*, *junto*, or the like, into which some translators have fallen, can not be allowable; those only excepted, without which it is impossible to treat the subjects in any living language."

I have observed a similar rule in the translation of Virgil. But I must remark, that prose and poetry stand on a somewhat different footing. Archaisms are often allowable and good in poetry, to give it (as Pope says) a venerable cast; and, on the other hand, many modern words are fit for prose, which would not be suitable for poetry—as *campaign*.

In all these things taste and judgment are required. You must take care that your translations are as apposite as possible; and when you resort to words which can give but an imperfect idea of the original, select only such as are dignified, simple, significant, having rather a general and permanent, than a local or ephemeral character. I see, for example, no objection to words such as the following:—

Prince, general, captain, officer, commissioner, deputy, president, clerk, secretary, assessor, treasurer, paymaster, collector, board, rate, property-tax, register, audit, tribe, township, assembly, chairman, bill, decree, motion, resolution, statute, advocate, jury, summons, action, indictment, plea, verdict, damages, fine, information, arbitrator, award, mortgage, trespass.

But I will detain the reader no longer. I wish I were as sure that I had carried out my principles well, as I am that the principles themselves are sound.

CHRONOLOGICAL ABSTRACT

OF

EVENTS DURING THE LIFE OF DEMOSTHENES.

B.C.

385 Demosthenes is born.

This was just nineteen years after the termination of the Peloponnesian war. Greece was reposing under the peace of Antalcidas and the power of Sparta had reached its height.

383 Philip of Macedon is born.

His father, Amyntas II., has disputes with the Olynthians concerning their encroachment on his territories, and applies to Sparta for aid.

Apollonia and Acanthus, two of the Chalcidian cities, send an embassy to Sparta for the same purpose.

Sparta declares war against Olynthus, and sends a force under Eudamidas which takes possession of Potidæa.

382 Phœbidas, sent from Sparta to reinforce Eudamidas, stops on his road to Thebes, and seizes the Cadmea, in which he places a Lacedæmonian garrison. An oligarchical government is established at Thebes, at the head of which are Archias and Leontiades, devoted to Sparta. A multitude of Theban exiles fly to Athens; among them Pelopidas.

Teleutias, brother of Agesilaus, is sent with a larger force against Olynthus; is joined by a Theban contingent, by Amyntas, and Derdas prince of Elymia.

The Spartans require Athens to dismiss the Theban exiles. Athens refuses.

Teleutias defeats the Olynthians in a battle near the city, and shuts them in their walls.

381 Teleutias is defeated by the Olynthians, and slain.

380 Agesipolis, one of the kings, is sent with reinforcements from Sparta; takes Torone, and dies of a fever. Polybiades succeeds to the command, and besieges Olynthus.

379 The Olynthians sue for peace, and submit to join the Peloponnesian confederacy.

Pelopidas and his associates return to Thebes, where, having slain Archias and Leontiades, they are joined by their countrymen, and attack the Spartan garrison. A body of Athenian volunteers come to their assistance, and the garrison capitulates.

B.C.

378 Demosthenes loses his father, and is placed under the care of three guardians.

The Spartans send their king Cleombrotus into Bœotia.

Chabrias, with an Athenian force, occupies the pass at Eleutheræ; Cleombrotus enters by another road, and having dispersed a Theban force at Platæa, takes possession of Thespiæ, where he leaves Sphodrias, with a part of his army, and then returns to Peloponnesus.

The Athenians, alarmed at the Spartan invasion, condemn their generals who had aided in the recovery of the Cadmea.

Sphodrias marches against Athens, to surprise the Piræus; advances as far as the Thriasian plain, and retreats, after plundering the country.

The Athenians prepare for war with Sparta; strengthen the Piræus; increase their fleet, and make alliance with Thebes.

Chios, Byzantium, Rhodes, and Mitylene revolt from Sparta, and renew their confederacy with Athens.

Sphodrias is recalled, and Agesilaus sent with a large Peloponnesian army into Bœotia. He ravages the Theban territory, but having encountered an Athenian and Theban force, commanded by Chabrias and Gorgidas, is repulsed, and returns home, leaving Phœbidas in command at Thespiæ.

Phœbidas, after gaining partial success against Gorgidas, is defeated and slain.

377 Agesilaus again invades Bœotia; is joined by a force of Olynthian cavalry, gains some advantage over the Thebans, and, after strengthening the oligarchical party at Thespiæ, crosses over to Megara, where he falls ill.

The Sacred Band, consisting of three hundred men, is established at Thebes.

Acoris, king of Egypt, at war with Persia, engages the services of Chabrias, who, on complaint made by Artaxerxes, is recalled by the Athenians, and Iphicrates sent to assist the satrap Pharnabazus.

376 Cleombrotus is sent into Bœotia, where he is repulsed by the Athenians and Thebans, and returns home.

A Peloponnesian fleet is sent out under the command of Pollis, to intercept the corn-ships bound for Athens. Chabrias totally defeats this fleet at Naxos.

Athens regains her ascendency in the Ægean sea, and many of the islands return under her protection.

Timotheus sails with a fleet to Corcyra, which renews her alliance with Athens.

Jason of Pheræ establishes his power or influence over most of the towns of Thessaly.

375 Timotheus is successful against the Peloponnesians in the Ionian sea.

Pelopidas fails in an attempt to surprise Orchomenos, is attacked on his retreat by a superior force of Spartans at Tegyra. The Spartans are put to the rout, and their generals slain.

B.C.

374 The Thebans send an army into Phocis, which is in alliance with Sparta. Cleombrotus crosses the Gulf of Corinth, to the assistance of the Phocians, and forces the Thebans to retreat.

The Athenians attempt to make peace with Sparta, but this is interrupted by a dispute concerning some Zacynthian exiles restored by Timotheus. A Peloponnesian fleet under Mnasippus is sent to recover Corcyra. The Athenians determine to relieve it, and dispatch Timotheus with a fleet from Athens, who is forced for want of supplies to cruise about the Ægean isles and the coast of Macedonia and Thrace.

Pharnabazus and Iphicrates invade Egypt, which, after partial success, they are compelled to evacuate. Iphicrates quarrels with Pharnabazus, and returns to Athens.

373 Mnasippus lands in Corcyra, and blockades the city, but is routed in a sally, and slain. His fleet retires to Leucas.

Timotheus is recalled to Athens, and brought to trial, but acquitted. Iphicrates, Callistratus, and Chabrias, succeed to the command.

The Athenians sail to Corcyra, and capture a Syracusan fleet sent to the aid of Mnasippus. Cephallenia is brought over to the Athenian alliance.

The Thebans surprise Platæa, and raze the city to the ground. The inhabitants, allowed to depart, take refuge in Athens, and are admitted to the privileges of citizens.

Thespiæ is taken, and shares the same fate.

372 Iphicrates crosses to Acarnania, and carries on the war against the Peloponnesians with various success; is preparing to invade Laconia.

371 The Athenians send embassadors to Sparta, to conclude peace. The Thebans, invited to join in the embassy, send Epaminondas.

Peace is made between the Peloponnesians and the Athenian confederacy. Epaminondas refuses to concur in the treaty on behalf of Thebes, because she was required to acknowledge the independence of the Bœotian towns.

Cleombrotus is ordered to march from Phocis into Bœotia; encounters the Thebans under Epaminondas at Leuctra, is totally defeated and slain.

Jason of Pheræ arrives at Leuctra after the battle. By his mediation an armistice is effected, and the Lacedæmonian army retreats into Peloponnesus.

A congress is held at Athens, and attended by most of the Peloponnesian states, who resolve to maintain the independence declared by the peace of Antalcidas.

The Mantineans rebuild their city, which had been dismantled by the Lacedæmonians.

A democratical movement takes place in Peloponnesus.

The Arcadians, encouraged by Epaminondas, resolve to build a new city, to become the seat of a federal government, to be called Megalopolis. Pammenes is sent with a small Theban force into Arcadia.

B.C.

371 Tegea and Orchomenos, under the influence of Sparta and aristocratical institutions, oppose the Arcadian union. The Tegeans are defeated, and their city taken. Sparta declares war.

370 Amyntas II. dies, leaving three sons, Alexander, Perdiccas, and Philip. Alexander ascends the throne.

Jason of Pheræ announces his intention of marching to Delphi and presiding over the Pythian games. He collects a large army, and excites alarm; but is murdered a short time before the festival. His brothers Polydorus and Polyphron succeed him.

Agesilaus marches to Mantinea, ravages the country, and returns to Sparta.

The Thebans prepare to invade Peloponnesus; collect troops from Phocis, Locris, Thessaly, and various states of Northern Greece.

369 Pelopidas and Epaminondas lead the Theban army to Mantinea; are joined by the Arcadians, Eleans, and Argives, and invade Laconia. The Spartans are unable to oppose them in the field, but, reinforced by a small body of Peloponnesian auxiliaries, prepare to defend the capital. The Thebans, after ravaging the country, approach Sparta, are repulsed in a skirmish, and retire.

The Theban army enters Messenia, to accomplish the project of Epaminondas for the building of a new city, and the separation of that province from Laconia. The building is rapidly carried on under Theban protection. The city is called Messene, and peopled by the Messenian insurgents, with a multitude of exiles and revolted Helots. Epaminondas, leaving a garrison there, prepares for his return to Thebes.

The Lacedæmonians send an embassy to Athens, to implore her assistance, which is granted, and Iphicrates is sent with an army to Peloponnesus.

Polyphron of Pheræ, having survived Polydorus, is murdered by his nephew Alexander, who assumes the office of *Tagus*, and oppresses the Thessalian towns. The Aleuadæ of Larissa invoke the aid of Alexander, king of Macedon, who marches to their relief, and puts a garrison in Larissa and Cranon: but he is hastily recalled to Macedonia, in consequence of intrigues against him by his mother Eurydice and her paramour Ptolemy.

Iphicrates stations himself at the Isthmus of Corinth, to oppose Epaminondas, who passes by a different road, repulsing the Athenian cavalry.

368 The Thessalians apply to Thebes for aid against Alexander of Pheræ. Pelopidas is sent into Thessaly, while Epaminondas marches for the second time to invade Peloponnesus.

Dionysius of Syracuse sends a body of Celts and Iberians to the aid of Sparta.

The Spartans send an army to the Isthmus, and are joined by the Corinthians and Athenians under Chabrias. Epaminondas forces their lines, and effects a junction with his allies; after a short and unimportant campaign he makes an attempt on Corinth, is repulsed by Chabrias, and returns home.

B.C.

368 Alexander of Macedon is murdered, and Ptolemy assumes the regency.

The Arcadians carry on the war with success in the absence of Epaminondas.

Pelopidas, having marched to Larissa, and restored tranquillity, is invited into Macedonia, to compose the disputes in the royal family. He forces Ptolemy to give security for preserving the kingdom to the heirs of Amyntas; takes hostages from him, and receives the young Philip into his charge. Philip is taken to Thebes, where he resides for several years.

The satrap Ariobarzanes makes an ineffectual attempt for the pacification of Greece.

Alexander of Pheræ raises new disturbances. Pelopidas, sent on an embassy to Thessaly, is seized by him and thrown into prison. Alexander obtains the assistance of Athens, and defeats a body of Thebans who are sent against him, among whom Epaminondas, in temporary disgrace for the ill-success of his last campaign, was serving as a private soldier.

The Thebans destroy Orchomenos in Bœotia.

367 Iphicrates sails with an armament to the coast of Macedonia, for the purpose of recovering Amphipolis; is invited by Ptolemy and Eurydice to assist them against Pausanias, who aspired to the throne. He expels Pausanias, but is unable to reduce Amphipolis, which is supported by the Olynthians.

Epaminondas marches again into Thessaly, and effects the release of Pelopidas.

Archidamus, commanding the troops of Lacedæmon, Athens, and Corinth, with Syracusan auxiliaries, gains a great victory over the Arcadians and Argives on the borders of Laconia.

Pelopidas is sent on an embassy to Susa, and obtains the Persian king's sanction for the projects of the Thebans. On his return a congress is held at Thebes, and attended by the king's deputy, but the Greek states refuse to accept the dictation of Persia.

366 Demosthenes comes of age, and brings an action against his guardians for mal-administration of his estate, in which he obtains a verdict.

Iphicrates, with Charidemus of Oreus, sails to attack Amphipolis, but is opposed by Ptolemy and the Olynthians.

Epaminondas marches into Achaia, but without much success. Of the Achæan states Sicyon only is secured to the Theban alliance.

Themison of Eretria surprises Oropus. The Athenians send Chares to recover it, but the city is put in possession of the Thebans.

Athens makes a separate peace with the Arcadians.

365 Corinth and the Achæans make peace with Thebes.

Elis and Arcadia go to war, contending for the Triphylian towns.

Ptolemy is slain by Perdiccas III. who ascends the throne of Macedon.

The Amphipolitans negotiate with Iphicrates for the surrender of

B.C.
365 their town, and give him hostages; but he, being recalled to Athens, delivers the hostages to Charidemus, who goes off into the service of Cotys, king of Thrace, and sends back the hostages to Amphipolis.

364 Sparta assists Elis against the Arcadians, who defeat Archidamus.

The Arcadians invade Elis, and attempt to exclude the Eleans from the presidency of the Olympic games. The battle of Olympia is fought, in which the Arcadians and Argives are defeated by the troops of Elis and Achaia.

Callisthenes commands the Athenian fleet on the Macedonian coast, and makes war against Perdiccas, but agrees to an armistice. He is superseded by Timotheus, who takes Torone and Potidæa.

The Thebans are again invited into Thessaly, to give assistance against Alexander of Pheræ. Pelopidas goes with a small troop to Pharsalus, where he collects an army of Thessalians. Alexander is defeated in the battle of Cynoscephalæ, but Pelopidas is slain. Peace is made between Thebes and Alexander.

363 Dissensions arise between Mantinea and the other Arcadians. It is proposed to make peace with Elis and Sparta. The Thebans prepare for another invasion of Peloponnesus. The Matineans ally themselves to Sparta.

Timotheus takes Pydna and Methone.

The Thebans send a fleet to Byzantium, to detach it from the Athenian alliance. Laches is sent to oppose it, but without effect.

Alexander of Pheræ sends out a squadron to infest and plunder the small Ægean islands, and lays siege to Peparethus. The Athenians having sent Leosthenes against him, he sails to Attica, takes several Athenian ships, and plunders the Piræus.

362 Epaminondas leads his army into Peloponnesus, and, joined by his Arcadian allies, assaults Sparta, but is repulsed.

The Athenians send a force of six thousand men to the assistance of the Spartans. They march to Mantinea.

Epaminondas, retreating from Laconia, marches to attack Mantinea. His cavalry are defeated by the Athenians, who sally from the town.

Agesilaus marches with his army to join the Athenians and Mantineans. Epaminondas advances to attack them, and the battle of Matinea is fought, one of the most celebrated in Grecian history. On the one side are Bœotians, Thessalians, Eubœans, Locrians, and other northern allies, together with troops of Sicyon, Argos, Arcadia, and Messenia, to the number of thirty-three thousand. On the other, Lacedæmonians, Athenians, Mantineans, and troops of Elis and Achaia; considerably less in number. After an obstinate resistance, Epaminondas breaks the centre of the enemy, but is slain in the moment of victory.

A general peace follows, but the Spartans alone refuse to acknowledge the independence of Messenia.

Timotheus, assisted by the satrap Ariobarzanes, takes Sestus, Cri-

B.C.

362 thote, and Elæus, in the Thracian Chersonese; and afterward lays siege to Samos.

The satraps revolt from the king of Persia. They are promised assistance by Tachos, king of Egypt, Mausolus, king of Caria, and most of the maritime parts of the empire.

Miltocythes rebels against Cotys, king of Thrace, and engages the Athenians to assist him, by promising to cede to them the Chersonese. Cotys amuses the Athenians by negotiation, and overcomes Miltocythes.

361 Samos capitulates after a siege of eleven months.

Orontes betrays the conspirators to Artaxerxes. Datames, satrap of Cappadocia, is murdered. Tachos, preparing to make war against Persia, engages Agesilaus to command his army, and Chabrias for his admiral.

Agesilaus is sent with a thousand Spartans to Egypt, but quarrels with Tachos, and transfers his services to Nectanabis, to whom the Egyptian army revolts. Tachos flies to Persia, and Agesilaus establishes Nectanabis in the dominion of Egypt.

Artaxerxes Mnemon dies, and his son, Artaxerxes Ochus, ascends the throne of Persia.

360 Timotheus and Charidemus attack Amphipolis, which receives succor from Macedonia and Olynthus, and the Athenians are defeated.

Cotys marches into the Chersonese, and gets possession of Sestus.

Agesilaus dies on his return from Egypt.

Pammenes is sent with Theban troops to quell disturbances in Arcadia; establishes the preponderance of Megalopolis.

Artaxerxes makes an attempt to reconquer Egypt, which fails.

359 Perdiccas is slain in a battle with the Illyrians, leaving an infant son, Amyntas. Philip ascends the throne of Macedon.

At this time the Illyrians are preparing for a new invasion, the Pæonians make an irruption from the north, and there are two pretenders to the crown—Pausanias, assisted by Cotys, and Argæus, supported by the Athenians.

Philip accommodates matters with Cotys, and marches against Argæus, whom he defeats. He returns the Athenian prisoners without ransom, and makes peace with Athens. He then reduces the Pæonians to submission, and invades Illyria. Bardylis, the Illyrian prince, is defeated in a great battle, and a portion of his dominions is ceded to Macedonia.

358 Cotys, assisted by Charidemus, lays siege to Crithote and Elæus, but soon after is murdered, leaving three sons, Amadocus, Berisades, and Cersobleptes, among whom the dominions of Cotys are divided.

Charidemus takes Cersobleptes under his protection, and defeats the Athenian force.

Miltocythes again raising disturbances, is taken prisoner by Charidemus, who sends him to Cardia, where he is put to death.

Philip lays siege to Amphipolis.

The Olynthians send an embassy to Athens, to negotiate an alli-

B.C.

358 ance, which is prevented by the intrigues of Philip. He conciliates the Olynthians by the cession of Anthemus, and soon afterward obtains possession of Amphipolis. He then marches to Pydna, which is surrendered to him.

Alexander of Pheræ is murdered. Tisiphonus and his brother Lycophron get the command.

357 Berisades and Amadocus combine against Cersobleptes, and are assisted by Athenodorus, the Athenian general. Cersobleptes is forced to enter into a convention, by which the kingdom is equally divided, and the Chersonese ceded to Athens, with the exception of Cardia.

The Athenians quarrel with Philip about Amphipolis. He makes an alliance with the Olynthians.

The Thebans send an army into Eubœa, from which, after much fighting, they are expelled by the Athenians.

Chares is sent to take possession of the Chersonese, which, after some opposition from Charidemus, he effects.

The Social War breaks out, in which Byzantium, Chios, Cos, and Rhodes revolt from the Athenian league. The Athenians attack Chios, and are defeated; Chabrias is slain.

The Phocians send succor to some of the Bœotian towns, attempting to revolt from Thebes. The Thebans procure an Amphictyonic decree against the Phocians for having cultivated a portion of the consecrated plain near Delphi. This was the origin of the Sacred War.

356 Philip takes Potidæa, with the assistance of the Olynthians, and gives it up to them.

Alexander is born.

Parmenio, Philip's general, gains a victory over the Illyrians.

Philip takes the mine district of the Pangæus from the Thasians, and establishes a new colony at Crenides, which he names Philippi.

The Athenians besiege Byzantium, but the siege is raised by the fleet of the allies. Chares, Timotheus, and Iphicrates command the Athenian forces, but the two latter are recalled on the complaint of Chares.

The allies ravage Lemnos, Imbrus, and Samos, and levy contributions in the Ægean.

Chares, for want of supplies, lends assistance to Artabazus against the Persian satraps.

Philomelus, the Phocian general, takes possession of Delphi, and defeats the Locrians of Amphissa. He negotiates an alliance with Athens and Lacedæmon, while the Locrians obtain promises of assistance from Thebes and Thessaly.

Corcyra revolts from Athens.

355 The king of Persia threatens Athens with war on account of the aid furnished by Chares to Artabazus.

The Athenians terminate the Social War by acknowledging the independence of the revolted states.

Timotheus and Iphicrates are brought to trial for misconduct in

B.C.

355 the war. Timotheus is found guilty, and goes into exile. Shortly after, he dies at Chalcis.

The Athenians send an expedition against Olynthus, without success.

Chares takes Sestus.

Philomelus again defeats the Locrians, and being threatened with a general war, seizes the treasures of Delphi and collects a body of mercenaries. The Thessalians and Bœotians, having marched into Locris, are defeated by Philomelus, who is strongly reinforced from Peloponnesus.

Demosthenes makes the speeches against Leptines and Androtion.

354 The Thebans, largely reinforced, give battle to Philomelus in the defiles of Parnassus. He is defeated and slain. Onomarchus succeeds to the command, and the Thebans retire.

Philip sends Macedonian troops to assist Callias of Chalcis against Plutarch of Eretria. The latter applies to Athens for assistance, and is opposed by Demosthenes, who makes his first public speech on this occasion. The Athenians determine to assist Plutarch, and Phocion is sent with an army to Eubœa. He defeats Callias and the Macedonians at Tamynæ, and establishes popular government at Eretria.

The Athenians debate about making war with Persia. Demosthenes dissuades them in his speech *de Symmoriis.*

353 Onomarchus takes Thronium, and invades Bœotia. Here he takes Orchomenus, but is defeated by the Thebans at Chæronea.

Lycophron, now sovereign of Pheræ, enters into alliance with Onomarchus, and endeavors to oppress the independent Thessalians.

The Spartans declare war against Megalopolis, and apply for assistance to Athens. Demosthenes makes his speech *pro Megalopolitanis*, in which he urges the Athenians to espouse the other side. They remain neutral.

Demosthenes delivers the oration against Timocrates.

Philip takes Methone after a long siege, in which he lost an eye.

The Macedonian party prevail at Eretria, and dissolve the connection with Athens.

Mausolus, king of Caria, dies, and is succeeded by his widow Artemisia.

The Phœnicians revolt from Artaxerxes, and enter into alliance with Nectanabis. Cyprus soon after revolts.

352 Philip, invited by the Thessalians, marches against Lycophron, defeats Phayllus, brother of Onomarchus, and takes Pagasæ. Onomarchus marches with a large army into Thessaly, and defeats Philip in two battles, who retreats to Macedonia. Onomarchus then invades Bœotia, defeats the Thebans, and takes Coronea; but is recalled to Thessaly by intelligence that Philip had returned with large reinforcements. The decisive battle of Pagasæ is fought, in which Onomarchus is defeated and slain. Philip expels Lycophron from Pheræ, and takes the city of Magnesia. He then prepares to invade Phocis, and marches to

B.C.

352 Thermopylæ, but finds the pass guarded by an Athenian force, and retreats.

Phayllus, joined by a large force of auxiliaries from Sparta, Achaia, and Athens, invades Bœotia, but is defeated by the Thebans.

Philip sends out a fleet, plundering the Athenian coast, and ravages Lemnos, Imbrus, and Scyros. He himself marches into Thrace, where, after long being occupied in the interior extending his power over the different tribes, he turns toward the coast of the Propontis and attacks Heræum.

Demosthenes speaks the first Philippic.

The oration against Aristocrates is delivered.

Thebes, Argos, Sicyon, and Messene send assistance to Megalopolis. The Spartans, assisted by mercenaries from Phocis, after various indecisive battles, are compelled to make peace.

Artaxerxes makes great preparations to recover Phœnicia and Cyprus.

351 Phayllus overruns the country of the Epicnemidian Locrians, is defeated by the Bœotians at Abæ, afterward defeats them at Aryca, and dies; is succeeded by his nephew Phalæcus.

The democratical party at Rhodes solicit the aid of Athens, and are supported by Demosthenes in his speech *de Libertate Rhodiorum.*

Artemisia, queen of Caria, dies, and is succeeded by Idrieus, who, at the command of Artaxerxes, collects a large armament for the reduction of Cyprus. Phocion the Athenian is joined with Evagoras in the command of this expedition.

The Thessalians remonstrate with Philip for retaining Pagasæ and Magnesia.

350 Phalæcus invades Bœotia, and takes Chæronea, from which he is again driven by the Thebans, who invade and ravage Phocis.

Philip takes Apollonia, and threatens the Chalcidian towns. The Olynthians send to Athens to negotiate alliance.

Pitholaus, brother of Lycophron, recovers Pheræ, and Philip is invited to expel him. On his return from Thessaly he marches into the Chalcidian peninsula, and lays siege to Stagira.

Cyprus submits to Artaxerxes. Temnes, king of Sidon, assisted by Mentor at the head of Greek mercenaries, defeats the Persian satraps.

Demosthenes brings an action against Midias, which is afterward compromised.

349 The Thebans receive a large subsidy from Persia, to enable them to carry on the war against Phocis.

The Olynthians send an embassy to Athens to implore assistance. A warm debate takes place, in which Demosthenes speaks the first Olynthiac. The Athenians vote alliance, and dispatch Chares with a small force. The second and third Olynthiacs are delivered at short intervals after this.

Meanwhile Stagira capitulates; Torone is taken, and most of the Chalcidian towns hasten to make terms with Philip. The Olyn-

B.C.

349 thians send another embassy, pressing for more effectual assistance. A larger armament is sent from Athens, and put under the command of Charidemus.

The Olynthians, dissatisfied with Charidemus, send a third embassy, and entreat the aid of a native Athenian force. This is sent, but arrives too late.

Artaxerxes marches in person against the Phœnicians. Temnes betrays Sidon, and the Phœnicians submit. Mentor is taken into the service of Persia.

348 Philip takes Mecyberna, the port of Olynthus, and lays siege to the city. After various ineffectual sallies, Olynthus is betrayed to Philip, who razes it to the ground.

Phalæcus is deposed from his command by the Phocians. The Sacred War languishes.

Artaxerxes sends to the Greek states to collect mercenaries for the invasion of Egypt. Athens and Sparta refuse assistance. The Thebans send Lacrates with a thousand men; the Argives Nicostratus with three thousand. The Asiatic Greeks furnish a contingent, and the king marches in person into Egypt. The conquest of Egypt is ultimately effected, but the exact date is uncertain.

347 Philip celebrates his triumph over Olynthus by a festival at Dium in Pieria.

An assembly is held at Athens, to consider the expediency of rousing the Greeks against Philip. Æschines is sent for that purpose to Arcadia. The negotiations of Athens are unsuccessful.

Philip causes it to be intimated at Athens that he is desirous of peace. A decree passes at Athens to send embassadors to treat with him.

The Thebans, suffering by the depredations committed on their territories from the hostile garrisons in Bœotia, invite Philip to terminate the Sacred War. The Phocians pray for aid of the Athenians, and offer to put them in possession of Nicæa, Thronium, and Alponus. Meanwhile Phalæcus regains his power in Phocia, and refuses to admit the Athenian troops.

Parmenio besieges Halus in Thessaly.

Demosthenes, Æschines, and eight other embassadors, are sent to Pella to treat for peace. They return in the beginning of the following year.

346 Parmenio and Antipater are sent to Athens to negotiate the peace. A congress of the allies is held, and peace is concluded, on the terms of each party keeping his own possessions; but the Phocians and Cersobleptes are not named in the treaty.

The ten Athenian embassadors are sent to Macedonia to receive Philip's oath of ratification. On arriving at Pella, they find that Philip has marched into Thrace. There he had seized upon the Sacred Mount, and stripped Cersobleptes of a considerable part of his dominions. On his return to Pella he takes the embassadors with him to Pheræ, and there ratifies the peace. He then dismisses them, hastens to Thermopylæ, takes Nicæa, Thronium,

B.C.

346 and Alponus, and being joined by the Bœotians, marches into Phocis. Archidamus with the Spartan troops, and Phalæcus with his mercenaries, retire to Peloponnesus, while the Phocian towns are either taken by storm or capitulate.

The Athenians, alarmed at this intelligence, begin to prepare for their own defense, but are reassured by a letter of Philip.

A council of Amphictyons is held at Delphi, and sentence passed on the Phocians for their sacrilege. Philip becomes a member of the council, and is chosen to preside at the Pythian games.

The lost Bœotian towns are restored to Thebes by Philip, and Nicæa given to the Thessalians.

The Amphictyonic Council send an embassy to Athens, to notify their election of Philip, and demand her recognition of it. Demosthenes delivers his Oration on the Peace, in which he dissuades the Athenians from opposing the Amphictyonic league.

345 Philip promises to assist the Messenians and Arcadians against hostilities threatened by Lacedæmon.

The Athenians send Demosthenes at the head of an embassy to Messene and Argos, to counteract the influence of Philip.

Diopittes is sent with a body of Athenian settlers to the Thracian Chersonese, who become involved in disputes with the Cardians.

Philip ravages Illyria, and takes many of the towns in that district; after which he marches into Thessaly, where the regnant family had again made head, and expels them, leaving strong garrisons in Pheræ and Magnesia. Soon afterward he causes the whole country to be divided into tetrarchies, and governed by his own partisans.

344 Philip sends Python to Athens, to complain of the Athenian embassy to Peloponnesus. Demosthenes speaks the second Philippic.

Sostratus the pirate, having seized the island Halonnesus, is expelled by Philip. The Athenians demand its return.

Philip sends Python again to Athens, to adjust his disputes. The Athenians send Hegesippus and other envoys to make proposals for the amendment of the treaty.

The Cardians resist the attempt of Diopithes to take a portion of their territories, and apply to Philip for assistance.

343 Philip sends a letter to the Athenians, stating the terms which he is willing to consent to. Demosthenes and Hegesippus oppose them as unreasonable. The extant speech *de Halonneso* is supposed to be that of Hegesippus.

Phocion is sent to protect Megara against a conspiracy to betray it into the hands of the Macedonians. He secures it by fortifying Nicæa, and completing the long walls.

Philip invades Cassopia in Epirus, and annexes it to the dominions of his brother-in-law Alexander.

Demosthenes, Hegesippus, and Lycurgus are sent into Achaia and Acarnania, to form a league against Philip, to oppose his designs upon Ambracia and the western parts of Greece. They are successful, and an Athenian force is sent into Ambracia. Philip retreats from Epirus.

B.C.

343 Aristodemus with an Athenian force makes an unsuccessful attempt upon Magnesia.

Æschines is brought to trial by Demosthenes for misconduct in the embassy, and acquitted.

Philip sends assistance to the Cardians, and marches into the interior of Thrace to attack Teres. Diopithes, having collected a large body of mercenaries, endeavors to interrupt the conquests of Philip.

342 A Macedonian force is sent to Oreus in Eubœa, and establishes Philistides as governor. Clitarchus, a partisan of Philip, is secured in the government of Eretria.

Philip sends a letter to Athens, complaining of the proceedings of Diopithes as an infraction of the peace. Demosthenes makes the speech *de Chersoneso.*

Philip completes the conquest of Thrace, and drives Cersobleptes from his kingdom. He then marches toward the Propontine coast.

341 Demosthenes speaks the third Philippic. Early in the year Philip besieges Selymbria.

Twenty Athenian corn-ships, intended for the relief of Selymbria, are captured by Philip. The Athenians complain, and the ships are restored.

Phocion is sent with troops to Eubœa, and expels Clitarchus and Philistides. Demosthenes is crowned by the people for having advised this expedition.

Selymbria is taken, and Philip proceeds to besiege Perinthus.

The Athenians, under the advice of Demosthenes, apply for assistance to Persia.

340 Philip sends his letter to the Athenians (which is still extant), in which, after reproaching them for their conduct, he virtually declares war.

He sends an army into the Chersonese.

The Persians relieve Perinthus, and Philip, leaving troops to blockade it, lays siege to Byzantium.

Demosthenes goes to Byzantium, to offer Athenian succor, which is accepted, and Chares is sent with a fleet; but the Byzantines refuse to receive him, and Phocion is sent in his stead. At the same time assistance is sent from Chios, Cos, and Rhodes, and also from other parts of Greece.

Philip is compelled to raise the siege of Perinthus and Byzantium, and his troops are driven out of the Chersonese. He breaks up his camp, and marches into Scythia.

Artaxerxes is poisoned by the satrap Bagoas, and his son Arses succeeds him.

339 Æschines goes as one of the Athenian deputies to the Amphictyonic Council. He accuses the Locrians of Amphissa, for having cultivated the sacred plain. The Delphians having attacked Cirrha, are put to flight, and a resolution is passed to convoke an extraordinary meeting at Thermopylæ. At this meeting, unattended by Athens or Thebes, war is declared against the

B.C.

339 Locrians, and Cottyphus appointed to command an Amphictyonic army. He invades Locris, but without effect.

Philip, on his return from Scythia, is attacked by the Triballi, and is wounded in a hard-fought battle.

Phocion carries on successful operations against Philip in the north, but is severely wounded in an incursion into Macedonia.

Another Amphictyonic assembly is convened, at which Philip is elected general to carry into effect the decree against the Locrians.

338 Philip marches through Thessaly, and takes possession of Elatea, which he begins to fortify.

The Athenians in alarm hold an assembly of the people, at which Demosthenes proposes to send an embassy to Thebes. This is resolved upon, and Demosthenes himself heads the embassy. Meanwhile the Athenians muster all their troops, and collect a body of ten thousand mercenaries.

An assembly is convoked at Thebes, and attended by Python on Philip's behalf; but Demosthenes prevails on the Thebans to become allies of Athens.

Philip marches against Amphissa, and defeats Chares, who had been sent to succor the Locrians. After two indecisive battles, the hostile armies meet at Chæronea. Philip is at the head of thirty-two thousand men, chiefly Macedonians and Thessalians. On the other side are the forces of Athens and Thebes, with a few auxiliaries from Peloponnesus, somewhat inferior in number. Philip gains a decisive victory.

The Athenians take energetic measures for the defense of their city. Demosthenes pronounces the funeral orations in honor of the slain. Lysicles the general is condemned to death.

Ctesiphon proposes a decree, that Demosthenes be crowned at the Dionysian festival for his services in repairing the fortifications, and his general merits as a citizen. For this a prosecution is instituted against him by Æschines.

Philip grants peace to the Athenians, and puts a Macedonian garrison into Thebes. The Bœotian towns are emancipated, and Oropus given to Athens.

Philip holds a congress of the Greeks at Corinth, and declares war against Persia. He makes a triumphant march through Peloponnesus, and obtains universal submission.

337 Attalus and Parmenio are sent with a force into Asia Minor, to liberate the Greek cities.

Philip is engaged in a war with the Illyrians, after which he celebrates his marriage with Cleopatra, and is involved in domestic broils.

Arses is murdered, and Darius Codomanus raised to the throne of Persia.

336 A great festival is held at Ægæ in Macedonia, to solemnize the marriage of Philip's daughter with the king of Epirus; and attended from all parts of Greece. During the solemnity, Philip is murdered by Pausanias, one of his guards.

B.C.

336 Demosthenes receives speedy information of Philip's death, and takes instant measures to free the Greeks from Macedonia. Embassadors are sent to the Greek states, and a correspondence commenced with Attalus in Asia, and also with the Persian Court. A general rising is meditated in Greece, and also among the northern tribes.

Alexander hastens to Thermopylæ, joined by the Thessalians, and holds an Amphictyonic council, at which he is elected general of the Greeks. Thence he marches into Bœotia, and procures the submission of Thebes. The Athenians send embassadors to conciliate him, and among them Demosthenes, who, after going as far as Cithæron, returns. Alexander then proceeds to Corinth, where at a general congress he is chosen to conduct the war against Persia.

335 Alexander marches into Thrace, defeats the Triballi, crosses the Danube, and, after receiving the submission of some barbarous tribes, returns through Pæonia to attack the Illyrian prince Cleitus. While he is yet in Illyria, he hears of the revolt of Thebes.

The Thebans, having blockaded the Macedonian garrison in the Cadmea, send to divers Greek states for assistance. Demosthenes persuades the Athenians to vote alliance, and himself furnishes the Thebans with a supply of arms. Elis and other cities of Peloponnesus send troops to the aid of Thebes, but they march no farther than the Isthmus, hearing of the advance of Alexander.

Alexander besieges Thebes, which after a desperate resistance is taken by storm, and razed to the ground.

The Athenians send a deputation to appease Alexander, who requires them to deliver up the principal leaders of the war-party, among them, Demosthenes, Hyperides, and Lycurgus. But he is persuaded by Demades to waive this demand.

334 Alexander crosses the Hellespont into Asia Minor.

Battle of Granicus.

Memnon intrigues with the Greek states, especially Lacedæmon, to excite a rising against Macedonia. His death, which happens soon after, is fatal to the Persian cause.

333 Battle of Issus.

332 Siege of Tyre.

The Lacedæmonians send an embassy to Darius.

Agis, king of Sparta, sails to Crete, and reduces the island under the Persian dominion.

331 Alexandria in Egypt is founded.

Battle of Arbela.

Alexander enters the Persian capital.

Agis forms a confederacy in Peloponnesus.

330 Antipater marches to suppress an insurrection in Thrace. The Lacedæmonians, commanded by Agis, rise in arms, and, joined by the Eleans and Achaians, besiege Megalopolis. Antipater

B.C.

330 hastens to its relief, and an obstinate battle is fought, in which Agis is defeated and slain.

Æschines brings on the trial of Ctesiphon, and the two Orations for the Crown are delivered. Ctesiphon is acquitted, and Æschines retires in exile to Rhodes, where he opened a school of rhetoric, and died many years after.

Darius is murdered.

328 Alexander sets out on his march for India.

327 Porus is overcome.

326 The army embarks on the Indus.

325 Alexander returns to Persia.

324 An order sent by Alexander is read at the Olympic games, commanding the reception of exiles by the Greek states. Demosthenes goes to Olympia to remonstrate with the Macedonian envoy. The Athenians send an embassy to Alexander, to complain of this measure.

Messages are sent to the Greek cities, requiring them to pay divine honors to Alexander.

Harpalus, flying from Babylon with a large treasure, arrives in Athens. Antipater demands that he shall be given up by the Athenians, who throw him into prison, and pass a decree, on the motion of Demosthenes, to lodge his treasure in the Acropolis. A large portion of it is missing, and, on inquiry being instituted by the Areopagus, Demosthenes (among others) is charged with having received a bribe from Harpalus. He is found guilty, and sentenced to pay a fine of fifty talents.

Unable to pay this, he flies to Megara, and remains in exile.

323 Alexander dies at Babylon.

The Athenians resolve on war, and send embassadors to stir up the Greeks. A general rising takes place, and Leosthenes the Athenian is chosen commander. Sparta remains neutral, and the Bœotians adhere to Macedonia.

Leosthenes defeats the Bœotians at Platæa, and marches to meet Antipater in Thessaly. Antipater is totally defeated, and takes refuge in Lamia, where he is blockaded.

Macedonian envoys are sent to Peloponnesus, to counteract the efforts of the Athenians. Demosthenes opposes them successfully in Argos, Corinth, and Arcadia.

Demosthenes is recalled from exile by the Athenians, and a ship sent to bring him home.

Leosthenes is killed in a sally from Lamia. Antiphilus succeeds him as general.

The siege of Lamia is raised by the advance of Leonatus, who is himself defeated and slain; but Antipater effects a junction with his army, and receives large reinforcements from Macedonia.

322 The Athenian fleet is defeated by the Macedonian.

A Macedonian force lands at Marathon and ravages Attica, but is defeated by Phocion.

Antipater attacks the Greeks with a greatly superior army at Cran-

B.C.

322 non in Thessaly, and gains a doubtful victory, which becomes decisive by the general desertion of the allies.

Antipater advances against Athens, which submits, and receives a Macedonian garrison.

The Athenians are compelled to remodel their constitution, and adopt a property qualification, which disfranchises a large number of citizens.

Demosthenes and Hyperides, with other orators of the war-party, are demanded by Antipater. Demosthenes flies first to Ægina, and afterward to Calaurea, where he takes refuge in the temple of Neptune. Pursued by Archias, the Macedonian emissary, he puts an end to his life by poison.

THE

ORATIONS OF DEMOSTHENES.

THE FIRST OLYNTHIAC.

THE ARGUMENT.

Olynthus was a city in Macedonia, at the head of the Toronaic gulf, and north of the peninsula of Pallene. It was colonized by a people from Chalcis in Eubœa, and commanded a large district called Chalcidice, in which there were thirty-two cities. Over all this tract the sway of Olynthus was considerable, and she had waged wars anciently with Athens and Sparta, and been formidable to Philip's predecessors on the throne of Macedon. Soon after Philip's accession, the Olynthians had disputes with him, which were at first accommodated, and he gratified them by the cession of Anthemus. They then joined him in a war against Athens, and he gave up to them Potidæa, which had yielded to their united arms. After the lapse of some years, during which Philip had greatly increased his power, and acquired considerable influence in Thessaly and Thrace, the Olynthians became alarmed, and began to think him too dangerous a neighbor. The immediate cause of rupture was an attack which he made on one of the Chalcidian towns. An embassy was instantly sent to Athens, to negotiate an alliance. Philip, considering this as an infraction of their treaty with him, declared war against them, and invaded their territory. A second embassy was sent to Athens, pressing for assistance. The question was debated in the popular assembly. Demades, an orator of considerable ability, but profligate character, opposed the alliance. Many speakers were heard; and at length Demosthenes rose to support the prayer of the embassy, delivering one of those clear and forcible speeches, which seldom failed to make a strong impression on his audience. The alliance was accepted, and succors voted.

The orator here delicately touches on the law of Eubulus, which had made it capital to propose that the Theoric fund should be applied to military service. This fund was in fact the surplus revenue of the civil administration, which by the ancient law was appropriated to the defense of the commonwealth; but it had by various means been diverted from that purpose, and expended in largesses to the people, to enable them to attend the theatre, and other public shows and amusements. The law of Eubulus perpetuated this abuse. (See my article *Theorica* in the Archæological Dictionary.) Desmosthenes, seeing the necessity of a war supply, hints that this absurd law ought to be abolished, but does not openly propose it.

There has been much difference of opinion among the learned as to the order of the three Olynthiac orations; nor is it certain, whether they were spoken on the occasion of one embassy, or several embassies. The curious may consult Bishop Thirlwall's Appendix to the fifth volume of his Grecian History, and Jacobs' Introduction to his translation. I have followed the common order, as adopted by Bekker, whose edition of Demosthenes is the text of this translation; and indeed my opinion is, on the whole, in favor of preserving the common order, though the plan of this work prevents my entering into controversy on the question. To enable the reader more fully to understand the following orations, I have in an Appendix to this volume given a brief account of Olynthus, showing its position with reference to Macedonia, and the importance of its acquisition to Philip. The historical abstract prefixed to this volume is intended chiefly to assist the reader in reference to dates. Such occurrences only are noticed as may be useful to illustrate Demosthenes.

I BELIEVE, men of Athens, you would give much to know, what is the true policy to be adopted in the present matter of inquiry. This being the case, you should be willing to hear with attention those who offer you their counsel. Besides that you will have the benefit of all preconsidered advice, I esteem it part of your good fortune, that many fit suggestions will occur to some speakers at the moment, so that from them all you may easily choose what is profitable.

The present juncture, Athenians, all but proclaims aloud, that you must yourselves take these affairs in hand, if you care for their success. I know not how we seem disposed in the matter.[1] My own opinion is, vote succor immediately, and make the speediest preparations for sending it off from Athens, that you may not incur the same mishap as before; send also embassadors, to announce this, and watch the proceedings. For the danger is, that this man, being unscrupulous and clever at turning events to account, making concessions when it suits him, threatening at other times, (his threats may well be believed,) slandering us and urging our absence against us, may convert and wrest to his use some

[1] This is a cautious way of hinting at the general reluctance to adopt a vigorous policy. And the reader will observe the use of the first person, whereby the orator includes himself in the same insinuation.

of our main resources. Though, strange to say, Athenians, the very cause of Philip's strength is a circumstance favorable to you.[1] His having it in his sole power to publish or conceal his designs, his being at the same time general, sovereign, paymaster, and every where accompanying his army, is a great advantage for quick and timely operations in war; but, for a peace with the Olynthians, which he would gladly make, it has a contrary effect. For it is plain to the Olynthians, that now they are fighting, not for glory or a slice of territory, but to save their country from destruction and servitude. They know how he treated those Amphipolitans who surrendered to him their city, and those Pydneans who gave him admittance.[2] And generally, I believe, a despotic power is mistrusted by free states, especially if their dominions are adjoining. All this being known to you, Athenians, all else of importance considered, I say, you must take heart and spirit, and apply yourselves more than ever to the war, contributing promptly, serving personally, leaving nothing undone. No plea or pretense is left you for declining your duty. What you were all so clamorous about, that the Olynthians should be pressed into a war with Philip, has of itself come to pass,[3] and in a way most advantageous to you. For, had they undertaken the war at your instance, they

[1] After alarming the people by showing the strength of their adversary, he turns off skillfully to a topic of encouragement.

[2] Amphipolis was a city at the head of the Strymonic gulf, in that part of Macedonia which approaches western Thrace. It had been built formerly by an Athenian colony, and was taken by the Spartan general Brasidas in the Peloponnesian war. Ever since Athens regained her character of an imperial state, she had desired to recover Amphipolis, which was important for its maritime position, its exportation of iron, and especially from the vicinity of the forests near the Strymon, which afforded an inexhaustible supply of ship-timber. But she had never been able to accomplish that object. Philip, who at that time possessed no maritime town of importance, was for obvious reasons anxious to win Amphipolis for himself; and he got possession of it partly by force of arms, partly by the treachery of certain Amphipolitans who were attached to his interest. It seems the Athenians had been amused by a promise of Philip to give up the town to them. The non-performance of this compact led to their first long war with him. Immediately after the capture of Amphipolis, Philip marched against Pydna, and was admitted into the town.

[3] Compare Virgil, Æn. ix. 6.

Turne, quod optanti Divum promittere nemo
Auderet, volvenda dies en attulit ultro.

might have been slippery allies, with minds but half resolved perhaps: but since they hate him on a quarrel of their own, their enmity is like to endure on account of their fears and their wrongs. You must not then, Athenians, forego this lucky opportunity, nor commit the error which you have often done heretofore. For example, when we returned from succoring the Eubœans, and Hierax and Stratocles of Amphipolis came to this platform,[1] urging us to sail and receive possession of their city, if we had shown the same zeal for ourselves as for the safety of Eubœa, you would have held Amphipolis then and been rid of all the troubles that ensued. Again, when news came that Pydna,[2] Potidæa, Methone, Pagasæ, and the other places (not to waste time in enumerating them) were besieged, had we to any one of these in the first instance carried prompt and reasonable succor, we should have found Philip far more tractable and humble now. But, by always neglecting the present, and imagining the future would shift for itself, we, O men of Athens, have exalted Philip, and made him greater than any king of Macedon ever was. Here then is come a crisis, this of Olynthus, self-offered to the state, inferior to none of the former. And methinks, men of Athens, any man fairly estimating what the gods have done for us, notwithstanding many untoward circumstances, might with reason be grateful to them. Our numerous losses in war may justly be charged to our own negligence; but that they happened not long ago, and that an alliance, to counterbalance them, is open to our acceptance, I must regard as manifestations of divine favor. It is much the same as in money matters. If a man keep what he gets, he is thankful to fortune; if he lose it by im-

[1] The hustings from which the speakers addressed the people. It was cut to the height of ten feet out of the rock which formed the boundary wall of the assembly; and was ascended by a flight of steps.

[2] Potidæa was in the peninsula of Pallene, near Olynthus, and was therefore given by Philip to the Olynthians, as mentioned in the argument. Methone and Pydna are on the Macedonian coast approaching Thessaly. Pagasæ is a Thessalian town in the Magnesian district. It was the sea-port of Pheræ, capital of the tyrant Lycophron, against whom Philip was invited to assist the Thessalians. Philip overcame Lycophron, and restored republican government at Pheræ; but Pagasæ he garrisoned himself, and also Magnesia, a coast-town in the same district.

prudence, he loses withal his memory of the obligation. So in political affairs, they who misuse their opportunities forget even the good which the gods send them; for every prior event is judged commonly by the last result. Wherefore, Athenians, we must be exceedingly careful of our future measures, that by amendment therein we may efface the shame of the past. Should we abandon these men[1] too, and Philip reduce Olynthus, let any one tell me, what is to prevent him marching where he pleases? Does any one of you, Athenians, compute or consider the means, by which Philip, originally weak, has become great? Having first taken Amphipolis, then Pydna, Potidæa next, Methone afterward, he invaded Thessaly. Having ordered matters at Pheræ, Pagasæ, Magnesia, every where exactly as he pleased, he departed for Thrace; where, after displacing some kings and establishing others, he fell sick; again recovering, he lapsed not into indolence, but instantly attacked the Olynthians. I omit his expeditions to Illyria and Pæonia, that against Arymbas,[2] and some others.

Why, it may be said, do you mention all this now? That you, Athenians, may feel and understand both the folly of continually abandoning one thing after another, and the activity which forms part of Philip's habit and existence, which makes it impossible for him to rest content with his achievements. If it be his principle, ever to do more than he has done, and yours, to apply yourselves vigorously to nothing, see what the end promises to be. Heavens! which of you is so simple as not to know, that the war yonder will soon be here, if we are careless? And should this happen, I fear, O Athenians, that as men who thoughtlessly borrow on large interest, after a brief accommodation, lose their estate, so will it be with us; found to have paid dear for our idleness and self-indulgence, we shall be reduced to many hard and unpleasant shifts, and struggle for the salvation of our country.

To censure, I may be told, is easy for any man; to show what measures the case requires, is the part of a counselor. I am not ignorant, Athenians, that frequently, when any disappointment happens, you are angry, not with the parties in

[1] Here he points to the Olynthian embassadors.

[2] Arymbas was a king of the Molossians in Epirus, and uncle of Olympias, Philip's wife.

fault, but with the last speakers on the subject; yet never, with a view to self-protection, would I suppress what I deem for your interest. I say then, you must give a two-fold assistance here; first, save the Olynthians their towns,[1] and send out troops for that purpose; secondly, annoy the enemy's country with ships and other troops; omit either of these courses, and I doubt the expedition will be fruitless. For should he, suffering your incursion, reduce Olynthus, he will easily march to the defense of his kingdom; or, should you only throw succor into Olynthus, and he, seeing things out of danger at home, keep up a close and vigilant blockade, he must in time prevail over the besieged. Your assistance therefore must be effective, and two-fold.

Such are the operations I advise. As to a supply of money: you have money, Athenians; you have a larger military fund than any people; and you receive it just as you please. If ye will assign this to your troops, ye need no further supply; otherwise ye need a further, or rather ye have none at all. How then? some man may exclaim: do you move that this be a military fund? Verily, not I.[2] My opinion indeed is, that there should be soldiers raised, and a military fund, and one and the same regulation for receiving and performing what is due; only you just without trouble take your allowance for the festivals. It remains then, I imagine, that all must contribute, if much be wanted, much, if little, little. Money must be had; without it nothing proper can be done. Other persons propose other ways and means. Choose which ye think expedient; and put hands to the work, while it is yet time.

It may be well to consider and calculate how Philip's

[1] The Chalcidian towns. See the Argument. Philip commenced his aggressions upon the Olynthians by reducing several of these.

[2] There is some studied obscurity in this passage, owing to the necessity under which the speaker lay of avoiding the penalty of the law; and a little quiet satire on his countrymen, who seemed desirous of eating their pudding and having it too. The logic of the argument runs thus—My opinion is, that we ought to have a military fund, and that no man should receive public money, without performing public service. However, as you prefer taking the public money to pay for your places at the festivals, I will not break the law by moving to apply that money to another purpose. Only you gain nothing by it; for, as the troops must be paid, there must be an extraordinary contribution, or property tax, to meet the exigency of the case.

affairs now stand. They are not, as they appear, or as an inattentive observer might pronounce, in very good trim, or in the most favorable position. He would never have commenced this war, had he imagined he must fight. He expected to carry every thing on the first advance, and has been mistaken. This disappointment is one thing that troubles and dispirits him; another is, the state of Thessaly.[1] That people were always, you know, treacherous to all men; and just as they ever have been, they are to Philip. They have resolved to demand the restitution of Pagasæ, and have prevented his fortifying Magnesia; and I was told, they would no longer allow him to take the revenue of their harbors and markets, which they say should be applied to the public business of Thessaly, not received by Philip. Now, if he be deprived of this fund, his means will be much straitened for paying his mercenaries. And surely we must suppose, that Pæonians and Illyrians, and all such people, would rather be free and independent than under subjection; for they are unused to obedience, and the man is a tyrant. So report says, and I can well believe it; for undeserved success leads weak-minded men into folly; and thus it appears often, that to maintain prosperity is harder than to acquire it. Therefore must you, Athenians, looking on his difficulty as your opportunity, assist cheerfully in the war, sending embassies where required, taking arms yourselves, exciting all other

[1] Philip's influence in Thessaly was of material assistance to him in his ambitious projects. It was acquired in this way. The power established by Jason of Pheræ, who raised himself to a sort of royal authority under the title of Tagus, had devolved upon Lycophron. His sway extended more or less over the whole of Thessaly; but was, if not generally unpopular, at least unacceptable to the great families in the northern towns, among whom the Aleuadæ of Larissa held a prominent place. They invoked Philip's aid, while Lycophron was assisted by the Phocian Onomarchus. After various success, Onomarchus was defeated and slain, and Lycophron expelled from Pheræ. This established Philip's influence, and led to his being afterward called in to terminate the Sacred war. How far the assertions of Demosthenes, respecting the discontent of the Thessalians, are true, can not exactly be told. They are confirmed, however, in some degree by the fact, that at the close of the Sacred war Philip restored to them Magnesia. A new attempt by the regnant family caused Philip again to be invited, and Thessaly became virtually a province of Macedonia. Among other advantages therefrom was the aid of a numerous cavalry, for which Thessaly was famous.

people; for if Philip got such an opportunity against us, and there was a war on our frontier, how eagerly think ye he would attack you! Then are you not ashamed, that the very damage which you would suffer, if he had the power, you dare not seize the moment to inflict on him?

And let not this escape you, Athenians, that you have now the choice, whether you shall fight there, or he in your country. If Olynthus hold out, you will fight there and distress his dominions, enjoying your own home in peace. If Philip take that city, who shall then prevent his marching here? Thebans? I wish it be not too harsh to say, they will be ready to join in the invasion. Phocians? who can not defend their own country without your assistance. Or some other ally? But, good sir, he will not desire! Strange indeed, if, what he is thought fool-hardy for prating now, this he would not accomplish if he might. As to the vast difference between a war here or there, I fancy there needs no argument. If you were obliged to be out yourselves for thirty days only, and take the necessaries for camp-service from the land, (I mean, without an enemy therein,) your agricultural population would sustain, I believe, greater damage than what the whole expense of the late war[1] amounted to. But if a war should come, what damage must be expected? There is the insult too, and the disgrace of the thing, worse than any damage to right-thinking men.

On all these accounts, then, we must unite to lend our succor, and drive off the war yonder; the rich, that, spending a little for the abundance which they happily possess, they may enjoy the residue in security; the young,[2] that, gaining military experience in Philip's territory, they may become redoubtable champions to preserve their own; the

[1] The Amphipolitan war, said to have cost fifteen hundred talents.

[2] Strictly, *those of the military age,* which was from eighteen years to sixty. Youths between eighteen and twenty were liable only to serve in Attica, and were chiefly employed to garrison the walls. Afterward they were compellable to perform any military service, under the penalty of losing their privileges as citizens. The expression in the text, it will be seen, is not rendered with full accuracy; as those of the military age can only be called *young* by comparison. But a short and apt antithesis was needed. Sometimes I have "the serviceable," or "the able-bodied." Jacobs: *die waffenfähigen Jünglinge,* and elsewhere, *die Rüstige.*

orators, that they may pass a good account[1] of their statesmanship; for on the result of measures will depend your judgment of their conduct. May it for every cause be prosperous.

THE SECOND OLYNTHIAC.

THE ARGUMENT.

The Athenians had voted an alliance with the Olynthians, and resolved to send succors. But the sending of them was delayed, partly by the contrivance of the opposite faction, partly from the reluctance of the people themselves to engage in a war with Philip. Demosthenes stimulates them to exertion, and encourages them, by showing that Philip's power is not so great as it appears.

On many occasions, men of Athens, one may see the kindness of the gods to this country manifested, but most signally, I think, on the present. That here are men prepared for a war with Philip, possessed of a neighboring territory and some power, and (what is most important) so fixed in their hostility, as to regard any accommodation with him as insecure, and even ruinous to their country; this really appears like an extraordinary act of divine beneficence. It must then be our care, Athenians, that we are not more unkind to ourselves than circumstances have been; as it would be a foul, a most foul reproach, to have abandoned not only cities and places that once belonged to us, but also the allies and advantages provided by fortune.

To dilate, Athenians, on Philip's power, and by such discourse to incite you to your duty, I think improper: and why? Because all that may be said on that score involves matter of glory for him, and misconduct on our part. The more he has transcended his repute,[2] the more is he universally admired; you, as you have used your advantages

[1] Every man, who is required to justify the acts for which he is responsible, may be said to be "called to account." But Demosthenes speaks with peculiar reference to those accounts, which men in official situations at Athens were required to render at the close of their administration.

[2] Jacobs otherwise: *über sein Verdienst gelungen.*

unworthily, have incurred the greater disgrace. This topic, then, I shall pass over. Indeed, Athenians, a correct observer will find the source of his greatness here,[1] and not in himself. But of measures, for which Philip's partisans deserve his gratitude and your vengeance, I see no occasion to speak now. Other things are open to me, which it concerns you all to know, and which must, on a due examination, Athenians, reflect great disgrace on Philip. To these will I address myself.

To call him perjured and treacherous, without showing what he has done, might justly be termed idle abuse. But to go through all his actions and convict him in detail, will take, as it happens, but a short time, and is expedient, I think, for two reasons: first, that his baseness may appear in its true light; secondly, that they, whose terror imagines Philip to be invincible, may see he has run through all the artifices by which he rose to greatness, and his career is just come to an end. I myself, men of Athens, should most assuredly have regarded Philip as an object of fear and admiration, had I seen him exalted by honorable conduct; but observing and considering I find, that in the beginning, when certain persons drove away the Olynthians who desired a conference with us, he gained over our simplicity by engaging to surrender Amphipolis, and to execute the secret article[2] once so famous; afterward he got the friendship of the Olynthians, by taking Potidæa from you, wronging you his former allies, and delivering it to them; and lastly now the Thessalians, by promising to surrender Magnesia, and undertake the Phocian war on their behalf. In short, none who have dealt with him has he not deceived. He has risen by conciliating and cajoling the weakness of every people in turn who knew him not. As, therefore, by such means he

[1] In this assembly, by the contrivance of venal orators, or through the supineness of the people. In the first Philippic there is a more pointed allusion to the practices of Philip's adherents, who are charged with sending him secret intelligence of what passed at home. Such men as Aristodemus, Neoptolemus, perhaps Demades and others are referred to. Æschines had not yet begun to be a friend of Philip.

[2] A secret intrigue was carried on between Philip and the Athenians, by which he engaged to put Amphipolis in their hands, but on the understanding that they would deliver up Pydna to him. Demosthenes only mentions the former part of the arrangement, the latter not being honorable to his countrymen.

rose, when every people imagined he would advance their interest, so ought he by the same means to be pulled down again, when the selfish aim of his whole policy is exposed. To this crisis, O Athenians, are Philip's affairs come; or let any man stand forward and prove to me, or rather to you, that my assertions are false, or that men whom Philip has once overreached will trust him hereafter, or that the Thessalians who have been degraded into servitude would not gladly become free.

But if any among you, though agreeing in these statements, thinks that Philip will maintain his power by having occupied forts and havens and the like, this is a mistake. True, when a confederacy subsists by good-will, and all parties to the war have a common interest, men are willing to co-operate and bear hardships and persevere. But when one has grown strong, like Philip, by rapacity and artifice, on the first pretext, the slightest reverse, all is overturned and broken up.[1] Impossible is it,—impossible, Athenians,—to acquire a solid power by injustice and perjury and falsehood. Such things last for once, or for a short period; maybe, they blossom fairly with hope;[2] but in time they are discovered and drop away.[3] As a house, a ship, or the like, ought to have the lower parts firmest, so in human conduct, I ween, the principle and foundation should be just and true. But this is not so in Philip's conduct.

I say, then, we should at once aid the Olynthians, (the best and quickest way that can be suggested will please me

[1] The original ἀνεχαίτισε is "shakes off," or "throws off," as a horse does his rider, when he rears and tosses up his neck. It will be observed that Demosthenes is very high-flown in his language here, passing from one metaphor to another. Leland translates these words, "overthrows him, and all his greatness is dashed at once to the ground." Francis: "hath already shaken off the yoke and dissolved their alliance." Wilson: "turneth all things upside down and layeth it flat in the end." Auger, better: *suffisent pour l'ébranler et la dissoudre.* Jacobs: *reicht Alles umzustürzen und aufzulösen.* Pabst, very nearly the same.

[2] So in Henry VIII. Act iii. Sc. 2.

> Such is the state of man: to-day he puts forth
> The tender leaves of hope, to-morrow blossoms,
> And wears his blushing honors thick upon him.

[3] Like the leaves of a flower; pursuing the last metaphor. So says Moore, in *The Last Rose of Summer:* "the gems drop away." Jacobs: *fällt sie von selbst zusammen.* Pabst: *stürzt in sich selbst zusammen.*

most,) and send an embassy to the Thessalians, to inform some of our measures, and to stir up the rest; for they have now resolved to demand Pagasæ, and remonstrate about Magnesia. But look to this, Athenians, that our envoys shall not only make speeches, but have some real proof that we have gone forth as becomes our country, and are engaged in action. All speech without action appears vain and idle, but especially that of our commonwealth; as the more we are thought to excel therein, the more is our speaking distrusted by all. You must show yourselves greatly reformed, greatly changed, contributing, serving personally, acting promptly, before any one will pay attention to you. And if ye will perform these duties properly and becomingly, Athenians, not only will it appear that Philip's alliances are weak and precarious, but the poor state of his native empire and power will be revealed.

To speak roundly, the Macedonian power and empire is very well as a help, as it was for you in Timotheus' time against the Olynthians; likewise for them against Potidæa the conjunction was important; and lately it aided the Thessalians in their broils and troubles against the regnant house: and the accession of any power, however small, is undoubtedly useful. But the Macedonian is feeble of itself, and full of defects. The very operations which seem to constitute Philip's greatness, his wars and his expeditions, have made it more insecure than it was originally. Think not, Athenians, that Philip and his subjects have the same likings. He desires glory, makes that his passion, is ready for any consequence of adventure and peril, preferring to a life of safety the honor of achieving what no Macedonian king ever did before. They have no share in the glorious result; ever harassed by these excursions up and down, they suffer and toil incessantly, allowed no leisure for their employments or private concerns, unable even to dispose of their hard earnings, the markets of the country being closed on account of the war. By this then may easily be seen, how the Macedonians in general are disposed to Philip. His mercenaries and guards, indeed, have the reputation of admirable and well-trained soldiers, but, as I heard from one who had been in the country, a man incapable of falsehood, they are no better than others. For if there be any among them experienced in battles and campaigns, Philip is jealous of such men and drives them away, he says, wishing to keep the glory of all actions to himself; his jealousy (among other failings) being excessive. Or if any man be generally good and virtuous, unable to bear Philip's daily intemperances, drunkenness, and indecencies,[1] he is pushed aside and accounted as nobody. The rest about him are brigands and parasites, and men of that character, who will get drunk and perform dances which I scruple to name before you. My information is undoubtedly true; for persons whom all scouted here as worse rascals than mountebanks, Callias the town-slave and the like of him, antic-jesters,[2] and composers of ribald songs to lampoon their companions, such persons Philip caresses and keeps about him. Small matters these may be thought, Athenians, but to the wise they are strong indications of his character and wrong-headedness. Success perhaps throws a shade over them now; prosperity is a famous hider of such blemishes; but, on any miscarriage, they will be fully exposed. And this (trust me, Athenians) will appear in no long time, if the gods so will and you determine. For as in the human body, a man in health feels not partial ailments, but, when illness occurs, all are in motion, whether it be a rupture or a sprain or any thing else unsound; so with states and monarchs, while they wage eternal war, their weaknesses are

[1] The original signifies a certain lascivious dance, which formed a part of riotous festivities. We gather from history that the orator's description here is not wholly untrue, though exaggerated. Thirlwall thus writes of Philip: "There seem to have been two features in his character which, in another station, or under different circumstances, might have gone near to lower him to an ordinary person, but which were so controlled by his fortune as to contribute not a little to his success. He appears to have been by his temperament prone to almost every kind of sensual pleasure; but as his life was too busy to allow him often to indulge his bias, his occasional excesses wore the air of an amiable condescension. So his natural humor would perhaps have led him too often to forget his dignity in his intercourse with his inferiors; but to Philip, the great king, the conqueror, the restless politician, these intervals of relaxation occurred so rarely, that they might strengthen his influence with the vulgar, and could never expose *him* to contempt." It has been observed, that Philip's partiality for drinking and dancing, his drollery, and a dash of scurrility in his character, endeared him especially to the Thessalians. See Jacobs' note on this passage.

[2] *Μίμους γελοίων*, players of drolls, mimes, or farces. Our ancient word *droll* signifies, like *μῖμος*, both the actor and the thing acted.

undiscerned by most men, but the tug of a frontier war betrays all.

If any of you think Philip a formidable opponent, because they see he is fortunate, such reasoning is prudent, Athenians. Fortune has indeed a great preponderance—nay, is every thing, in human affairs. Not but that, if I had the choice, I should prefer our fortune to Philip's, would you but moderately perform your duty. For I see you have many more claims to the divine favor than he has. But we sit doing nothing; and a man idle himself can not require even his friends to act for him, much less the gods. No wonder then that he, marching and toiling in person, present on all occasions, neglecting no time or season, prevails over us delaying and voting and inquiring. I marvel not at that; the contrary would have been marvelous, if we doing none of the duties of war had beaten one doing all. But this surprises me, that formerly, Athenians, you resisted the Lacedæmonians for the rights of Greece, and rejecting many opportunities of selfish gain, to secure the rights of others, expended your property in contributions, and bore the brunt of the battle; yet now you are loth to serve, slow to contribute, in defense of your own possessions, and, though you have often saved the other nations of Greece collectively and individually, under your own losses you sit still. This surprises me, and one thing more, Athenians; that not one of you can reckon, how long your war with Philip has lasted, and what you have been doing while the time has passed. You surely know, that while you have been delaying, expecting others to act, accusing, trying one another, expecting again, doing much the same as ye do now, all the time has passed away. Then are ye so senseless, Athenians, as to imagine, that the same measures, which have brought the country from a prosperous to a poor condition, will bring it from a poor to a prosperous? Unreasonable were this and unnatural; for all things are easier kept than gotten. The war now has left us nothing to keep; we have all to get, and the work must be done by ourselves. I say then, you must contribute money, serve in person with alacrity, accuse no one, till you have gained your objects; then, judging from facts, honor the deserving, punish offenders; let there be no pretenses or defaults on your own part; for you can not harshly scrutinize the conduct of others, unless you have done what is right yourselves. Why, think you, do all the generals[1] whom you commission avoid this war, and seek wars of their own? (for of the generals too must a little truth be told.) Because here the prizes of the war are yours; for example, if Amphipolis be taken, you will immediately recover it; the commanders have all the risk and no reward. But in the other case the risks are less, and the gains belong to the commanders and soldiers; Lampsacus,[2] Sigeum, the vessels which they plunder. So they proceed to secure their several interests: you, when you look at the bad state of your affairs, bring the generals to trial; but when they get a hearing and plead these necessities, you dismiss them. The result is that, while you are quarreling and divided, some holding one opinion, some another, the commonwealth goes wrong. Formerly, Athenians, you had boards[3] for taxes; now you have boards for

[1] A system of employing mercenary troops sprang up at the close of the Peloponnesian war, when there were numerous Grecian bands accustomed to warfare and seeking employment. Such troops were eagerly sought for by the Persian satraps and their king, by such men as Jason of Pheræ, Dionysius of Syracuse, or Philomelus of Phocis. Athens, which had partially employed mercenaries before, began to make use of them on a large scale, while her citizens preferred staying at home, to attend to commerce, politics, and idle amusements. The ill effects however were soon apparent. Athenian generals, ill supplied with money, and having little control over their followers, were tempted or obliged to engage in enterprises unconnected with, and often adverse to, the interests of their country. Sometimes the general, as well as the troops, was an alien, and could be very little depended on. Such a person was Charidemus, a native of Oreus in Eubœa, who commenced his career as captain of a pirate vessel. He was often in the service of Athens, but did her more harm than good. See my article *Mercenarii*, Arch. Dict.

[2] Chares, the Athenian general, was said to have received these Asiatic cities from Artabazus, the Persian satrap, in return for the service he had performed. Probably it was some authority or privileges in those cities, not the actual dominion, that was conferred upon him. Sigeum, which is near the mouth of the Hellespont, and was a convenient situation for his adventures, was the ordinary residence of Chares.

[3] This refers to the institution of the *συμμορίαι*, or boards for management of the property-tax at Athens, as to which see Appendix IV. The argument of Demosthenes is as follows—The three hundred wealthier citizens, who were associated by law for purposes of taxation, had become a clique for political purposes, with an orator at their head, (he intentionally uses the term *ἡγεμών*, *chairman of the board,*) to conduct

politics. There is an orator presiding on either side, a general under him, and three hundred men to shout; the rest of you are attached to the one party or the other. This you must leave off; be yourselves again; establish a general liberty of speech, deliberation, and action. If some are appointed to command as with royal authority, some to be ship-captains, tax-payers, soldiers by compulsion, others only to vote against them, and help in nothing besides, no duty will be seasonably performed; the aggrieved parties will still fail you, and you will have to punish them instead of your enemies. I say, in short; you must all fairly contribute, according to each man's ability; take your turns of service till you have all been afield; give every speaker a hearing, and adopt the best counsel, not what this or that person advises. If ye act thus, not only will ye praise the speaker at the moment, but yourselves afterward, when the condition of the country is improved.

THE THIRD OLYNTHIAC.

THE ARGUMENT.

The Athenians had dispatched succors to Olynthus, and received, as Libanius says, some favorable intelligence; more probably, however, some vague rumors, which led them to imagine the danger was for the time averted. They began, very prematurely, as the result showed, to be confident of success, and talked of punishing Philip for his presumption. In this they were encouraged by certain foolish orators, who sought to flatter the national prejudices. Demosthenes in this oration strives to check the arrogance of the people; reminds them of the necessity of defensive rather than offensive measures, and especially of the importance of preserving their allies. He again adverts (and this time more boldly) to the law of Eubulus, which he intimates ought to be repealed; and he exhorts the Athenians generally to make strenuous exertions against Philip.

Not the same ideas, men of Athens, are presented to me, when I look at our condition, and when at the speeches which

the business of the assembly, while they stood to shout and applaud his speeches. The general, who held a judicial court to decide disputes about the property-tax, and who in matters of state ought to be independent, was subservient to the orator, who defended him in the popular assembly.

are delivered. The speeches, I find, are about punishing Philip; but our condition is come to this, that we must mind we are not first damaged ourselves. Therefore, it seems to me, these orators commit the simple error of not laying before you the true subject of debate. That once we might safely have held our own and punished Philip too, I know well enough; both have been possible in my own time, not very long ago. But now, I am persuaded, it is sufficient in the first instance to effect the preservation of our allies. When this has been secured, one may look out for revenge on Philip; but before we lay the foundation right, I deem it idle to talk about the end.

The present crisis, O Athenians, requires, if any ever did, much thought and counsel. Not that I am puzzled, what advice to give in the matter; I am only doubtful, in what way, Athenians, to address you thereupon. For I have been taught both by hearsay and experience, that most of your advantages have escaped you, from unwillingness to do your duty, not from ignorance. I request you, if I speak my mind, to be patient, and consider only, whether I speak the truth, and with a view to future amendment. You see to what wretched plight we are reduced by some men haranguing for popularity.

I think it necessary, however, first to recall to your memory a few past events. You remember, Athenians, when news came three or four years ago, that Philip was in Thrace besieging Heræum.[1] It was then the fifth month,[2] and after much discussion and tumult in the assembly you resolved to launch forty galleys, that every citizen under forty-five[3] should embark, and a tax be raised of sixty talents. That year passed; the first, second, third month arrived; in that

[1] A fortress on the Propontis, (now Sea of Marmora,) near Perinthus. This was a post of importance to the Athenians, who received large supplies of corn from that district.

[2] Corresponding nearly to our November. The Attic year began in July, and contained twelve lunar months, of alternately 29 and 30 days. The Greeks attempted to make the lunar and solar courses coincide by cycles of years, but fell into great confusion. See *Calendarium* in Arch. Dict.

[3] This large proportion of the serviceable citizens, τῶν ἐν ἡλικίᾳ, shows the alarm at Athens. Philip's illness seems to have put a stop to his progress in Thrace at this period. Immediately on his recovery he began his aggression against Olynthus. See the Chronological Abstract prefixed to this volume.

month, reluctantly, after the mysteries,[1] you dispatched Charidemus with ten empty ships and five talents in money; for as Philip was reported to be sick or dead, (both rumors came,) you thought there was no longer any occasion for succors, and discontinued the armament. But that was the very occasion; if we had then sent our succors quickly, as we resolved, Philip would not have been saved to trouble us now.

Those events can not be altered. But here is the crisis of another war, the cause why I mentioned the past, that you may not repeat your error. How shall we deal with it, men of Athens? If you lend not the utmost possible aid, see how you will have manœuvred every thing for Philip's benefit. There were the Olynthians, possessed of some power; and matters stood thus: Philip distrusted them, and they Philip. We negotiated for peace with them; this hampered (as it were) and annoyed Philip, that a great city, reconciled to us, should be watching opportunities against him. We thought it necessary by all means to make that people his enemies; and lo, what erewhile you clamored for, has somehow or other been accomplished. Then what remains, Athenians, but to assist them vigorously and promptly? I know not. For besides the disgrace that would fall upon us, if we sacrificed any of our interests, I am alarmed for the consequences, seeing how the Thebans are affected toward us, the Phocian treasury exhausted, nothing to prevent Philip, when he has subdued what lies before him, from turning to matters here. Whoever postpones until then the performance of his duty, wishes to see the peril at hand, when he may hear of it elsewhere, and to seek auxiliaries for himself, when he may be auxiliary to others; for that this will be the issue, if we throw away our present advantage, we all know pretty well.

But, it may be said, we have resolved that succors are necessary, and we will send them; tell us only how. Marvel not then, Athenians, if I say something to astonish the multitude. Appoint law-revisers:[2] at their session enact no

[1] The Eleusinian Mysteries, in honor of Ceres and Proserpine, called The Mysteries from their peculiar sanctity.

[2] A provision was made by Solon for a periodical revision of the Athenian laws by means of a legislative committee, called Νομοθέται. (See my article *Nomothetes*, Arch. Dict.) They were chosen by lot from

statutes, for you have enough, but repeal those which are at present injurious; I mean, just plainly, the laws concerning our theatrical fund, and some concerning the troops, whereof the former divide the military fund among stayers-at-home for theatrical amusement, the latter indemnify deserters, and so dishearten men well inclined to the service. When you have repealed these, and made the road to good counsel safe, then find a man to propose what you all know to be desirable. But before doing so, look not for one who will advise good measures and be destroyed by you for his pains. Such a person you will not find, especially as the only result would be, for the adviser and mover to suffer wrongfully, and, without forwarding matters, to render good counsel still more dangerous in future. Besides, Athenians, you should require the same men to repeal these laws, who have introduced them. It is unjust, that their authors should enjoy a popularity which has injured the commonwealth, while the adviser of salutary measures suffers by a displeasure that may lead to general improvement. Till this is set right, Athenians, look not that any one should be so powerful with you as to transgress these laws with impunity, or so senseless as to plunge into ruin right before him.

Another thing, too, you should observe, Athenians, that a decree is worth nothing, without a readiness on your part to do what you determine. Could decrees of themselves compel you to perform your duty, or execute what they prescribe, neither would you with many decrees have accomplished little or nothing, nor would Philip have insulted you so long. Had it depended on decrees, he would have been chastised long ago. But the course of things is otherwise. Action, posterior in order of time to speaking and voting, is in efficacy prior and superior. This requisite you want; the others you possess. There are among you, Athenians, men competent to advise what is needful, and you are exceedingly quick at understanding it; ay, and you will be able now to perform it,

the judicial body, on a reference to them by a vote of the popular assembly. Demosthenes says, "enact no statutes," instead of saying, "let the committee enact no statutes." This is because the committee would be taken from the people themselves, and the part are treated as the whole. So in speeches to juries we shall frequently observe that in mentioning the decision of some other jury he says, "you did this or that," as if they were the same persons.

if you act rightly. For what time or season would you have better than the present? When will you do your duty, if not now? Has not the man got possession of all our strongholds? And if he become master of this country, shall we not incur foul disgrace? Are not they, to whom we promised sure protection in case of war, at this moment in hostilities? Is he not an enemy, holding our possessions—a barbarian[1]—anything you like to call him? But, O heavens! after permitting, almost helping him to accomplish these things, shall we inquire who were to blame for them? I know we shall not take the blame to ourselves. For so in battles, no runaway accuses himself, but his general, his neighbor, any one rather; though, sure enough, the defeat is owing to all the runaways; for each one who accuses the rest might have stood his ground, and had each done so they would have conquered. Now then, does any man not give the best advice? Let another rise and give it, but not censure the last speaker. Does a second give better advice? Follow it, and success attend you! Perhaps it is not pleasant: but that is not the speaker's fault, unless he omits some needful prayer.[2] To pray is simple enough, Athenians, collecting all that one desires in a short petition: but to decide, when measures are the subject of consideration, is not quite so easy; for we must choose the profitable rather than the pleasant, where both are not compatible.

But if any one can let alone our theatrical fund, and suggest other supplies for the military, is he not cleverer? it may be asked. I grant it, if this were possible: but I wonder if any man ever was or will be able, after wasting his means in useless expenses, to find means for useful. The wishes of

[1] *Barbarians* (among the Greeks) designates persons who were not of Hellenic origin. Alexander, an ancestor of Philip, had obtained admission to the Olympic games by proving himself to be of Argive descent. But the Macedonian people were scarcely considered as Greeks till a much later period; and Demosthenes speaks rather with reference to the nation than to Philip personally.

[2] Demosthenes sneers at the custom of introducing into the debate sententious professions of good-will, and prayers for prosperity; a poor substitute (he would say) for good counsel. Compare Virg. Georg. III. 454.

Alitur vitium vivitque tegendo,
Dum medicas adhibere manus ad vulnera pastor
Abnegat, et meliora Deos sedet omina poscens.

men are indeed a great help to such arguments, and therefore the easiest thing in the world is self-deceit; for every man believes what he wishes, though the reality is often different. See then, Athenians, what the realities allow, and you will be able to serve and have pay. It becomes not a wise or magnanimous people, to neglect military operations for want of money, and bear disgraces like these; or, while you snatch up arms to march against Corinthians and Megarians, to let Philip enslave Greek cities for lack of provisions for your troops.

I have not spoken for the idle purpose of giving offense: I am not so foolish or perverse, as to provoke your displeasure without intending your good: but I think an upright citizen should prefer the advancement of the commonweal to the gratification of his audience. And I hear, as perhaps you do, that the speakers in our ancestors' time, whom all that address you praise, but not exactly imitate, were politicians after this form and fashion;—Aristides, Nicias, my namesake,[1] Pericles. But since these orators have appeared, who ask, What is your pleasure? what shall I move? how can I oblige you? the public welfare is complimented away for a moment's popularity, and these are the results; the orators thrive, you are disgraced. Mark, O Athenians, what a summary contrast may be drawn between the doings in our olden time and in yours. It is a tale brief and familiar to all; for the examples by which you may still be happy are found not abroad, men of Athens, but at home. Our forefathers, whom the speakers humored not nor caressed, as these men caress you, for five-and-forty years took the leadership of the Greeks by general consent, and brought above ten thousand talents into the citadel; and the king of this country was submissive to them, as a barbarian should be to Greeks; and many glorious trophies they erected for victories won by their own fighting on land and sea, and they are the sole people in the world who have bequeathed a renown superior to envy. Such were their merits in the affairs of Greece: see what they were at home, both as citizens and as men. Their public works are edifices and ornaments of such beauty and grandeur in temples and

[1] Demosthenes, the general so distinguished in the Peloponnesian war, who defeated the Spartans at Pylus, and afterward lost his life in Sicily.

consecrated furniture, that posterity have no power to surpass them. In private they were so modest and attached to the principle of our constitution, that whoever knows the style of house which Aristides had, or Miltiades, and the illustrious of that day, perceives it to be no grander than those of the neighbors. Their politics were not for money-making; each felt it his duty to exalt the commonwealth.[1] By a conduct honorable toward the Greeks, pious to the gods, brotherlike among themselves, they justly attained a high prosperity.

So fared matters with them under the statesmen I have mentioned. How fare they with you under the worthies of our time? Is there any likeness or resemblance? I pass over other topics, on which I could expatiate; but observe: in this utter absence of competitors, (Lacedæmonians depressed, Thebans employed, none of the rest capable of disputing the supremacy with us,) when we might hold our own securely and arbitrate the claims of others, we have been deprived of our rightful territory, and spent above fifteen hundred talents to no purpose; the allies, whom we gained in war, these persons have lost in peace, and we have trained up against ourselves an enemy thus formidable. Or let any one come forward and tell me, by whose contrivance but ours Philip has grown strong. Well, sir, this looks bad, but things at home are better. What proof can be adduced? The parapets that are whitewashed? The roads that are repaired? fountains, and fooleries?[2] Look at the men of whose statesmanship these are the fruits. They have risen from beggary to opulence, or from obscurity to honor; some have made their private houses more splendid than the public buildings; and in proportion as the state has declined, their fortunes have been exalted.

What has produced these results? How is it that all went prosperously then, and now goes wrong? Because anciently the people, having the courage to be soldiers, controlled the statesmen, and disposed of all emoluments; any of the

[1] As Horace says:—

> Privatus illis census erat brevis,
> Commune magnum.

[2] Jacobs: *und solches Geschwätz.* The proceedings of Eubulus are here more particularly referred to.

rest was happy to receive from the people his share of honor, office, or advantage. Now, contrariwise, the statesmen dispose of emoluments; through them every thing is done; you the people, enervated, stripped of treasure and allies, are become as underlings and hangers-on, happy if these persons dole you out show-money or send you paltry beeves;[1] and, the unmanliest part of all, you are grateful for receiving your own. They, cooping you in the city, lead you to your pleasures, and make you tame and submissive to their hands. It is impossible, I say, to have a high and noble spirit, while you are engaged in petty and mean employments: whatever be the pursuits of men, their characters must be similar. By Ceres, I should not wonder, if I, for mentioning these things, suffered more from your resentment than the men who have brought them to pass. For even liberty of speech you allow not on all subjects; I marvel indeed you have allowed it here.

Would you but even now, renouncing these practices, perform military service and act worthily of yourselves; would you employ these domestic superfluities as a means to gain advantage abroad; perhaps, Athenians, perhaps you might gain some solid and important advantage, and be rid of these perquisites, which are like the diet ordered by physicians for the sick. As that neither imparts strength, nor suffers the patient to die, so your allowances are not enough to be of substantial benefit, nor yet permit you to reject them and turn to something else. Thus do they increase the general apathy. What? I shall be asked: mean you stipendiary service? Yes, and forthwith the same arrangement for all, Athenians, that each, taking his dividend from the public, may be what the state requires. Is peace to be had? You

[1] Entertainments were frequently given to the people after sacrifices, at which a very small part of the victim was devoted to the gods, such as the legs and intestines, the rest being kept for more profane purposes. The Athenians were remarkably extravagant in sacrifices. Demades, ridiculing the donations of public meat, compared the republic to an old woman, sitting at home in slippers and supping her broth. Demosthenes, using the diminutive *βοΐδια*, charges the magistrates with supplying lean and poor oxen, whereas the victims ought to be healthy and large, *τέλεια*. See Virgil, Æn. xi. 739.

Hic amor, hoc studium; dum sacra secundus aruspex
Nuntiet, ac lucos vocet hostia pinguis in altos.

are better at home, under no compulsion to act dishonorably from indigence. Is there such an emergency as the present? Better to be a soldier, as you ought, in your country's cause, maintained by those very allowances. Is any one of you beyond the military age? What he now irregularly takes without doing service, let him take by just regulation, superintending and transacting needful business. Thus, without derogating from or adding to our political system, only removing some irregularity, I bring it into order, establishing a uniform rule for receiving money, for serving in war, for sitting on juries, for doing what each according to his age can do, and what occasion requires. I never advise we should give to idlers the wages of the diligent, or sit at leisure, passive and helpless, to hear that such a one's mercenaries are victorious; as we now do. Not that I blame any one who does you a service: I only call upon you, Athenians, to perform on your own account those duties for which you honor strangers, and not to surrender that post of dignity which, won through many glorious dangers, your ancestors have bequeathed.

I have said nearly all that I think necessary. I trust you will adopt that course which is best for the country and yourselves.

THE FIRST PHILIPPIC.

THE ARGUMENT.

Philip, after the defeat of Onomarchus, had marched toward the pass of Thermopylæ, which, however, he found occupied by the Athenians, who had sent a force for the purpose of preventing his advance. Being baffled there, he directed his march into Thrace, and alarmed the Athenians for the safety of their dominions in the Chersonese. At the same time he sent a fleet to attack the islands of Lemnos and Imbrus, infested the commerce of Athens with his cruisers, and even insulted her coast. In Thrace he became involved in the disputes between the rival kings Amadocus and Cersobleptes, espousing the cause of the former; and for some time he was engaged in the interior of that country, either at war with Cersobleptes, or extending his own influence over other parts of Thrace, where he established or expelled the rulers, as it suited him. It was just at that time that Demosthenes spoke the following oration, the first in which he called the attention of his countrymen to the dangerous increase of Philip's power. He had become convinced by the course of events, and by observing the restless activity of Philip, that Athens had more to fear from him than from Thebes, or from any new combination of the Grecian republics. The orator himself, perhaps, hardly appreciated the extent of Philip's resources, strengthened as he was now by the friendship of Thessaly, possessed of a navy and maritime towns, and relieved from the presence of any powerful neighbors. What were the precise views of Demosthenes as to the extent of the impending danger, we can not say. It was not for him to frighten the Athenians too much, but to awaken them from their lethargy. This he does in a speech, which, without idle declamation or useless ornament, is essentially practical. He alarms, but encourages, his countrymen; points out both their weakness and their strength; rouses them to a sense of danger, and shows the way to meet it; recommends not any extraordinary efforts, for which at the moment there was no urgent necessity, and to make which would have exceeded their power, but unfolds a scheme, simple and feasible, suiting the occasion, and calculated (if Athenians had not been too degenerate) to lay the foundation of better things.

Had the question for debate been any thing new, Athenians, I should have waited till most of the usual speakers[1] had been heard; if any of their counsels had been to my liking, I had remained silent, else proceeded to impart my own. But as the subjects of discussion is one upon which they have spoken oft before, I imagine, though I rise the first, I am entitled to indulgence. For if these men had advised properly in time past, there would be no necessity for deliberating now.

First I say, you must not despond, Athenians, under your present circumstances, wretched as they are; for that which is worst in them as regards the past, is best for the future. What do I mean? That your affairs are amiss, men of Athens, because you do nothing which is needful; if, notwithstanding you performed your duties, it were the same, there would be no hope of amendment.

Consider next, what you know by report, and men of experience remember; how vast a power the Lacedæmonians had not long ago, yet how nobly and becomingly you consulted

[1] By an ancient ordinance of Solon, those who were above fifty years of age were first called on to deliver their opinion. The law had ceased to be in force; but, as a decent custom, the older men usually commenced the debate. There would be frequent occasions for departing from such a custom, and Demosthenes, who was now thirty-three, assigns his reason for speaking first.

the dignity of Athens, and undertook the war[1] against them for the rights of Greece. Why do I mention this? To show and convince you, Athenians, that nothing, if you take precaution, is to be feared, nothing, if you are negligent, goes as you desire. Take for examples the strength of the Lacedæmonians then, which you overcame by attention to your duties, and the insolence of this man now, by which through neglect of our interests we are confounded. But if any among you, Athenians, deem Philip hard to be conquered, looking at the magnitude of his existing power, and the loss by us of all our strongholds, they reason rightly, but should reflect, that once we held Pydna and Potidæa and Methone and all the region round about as our own, and many of the nations now leagued with him were independent and free, and preferred our friendship to his. Had Philip then taken it into his head, that it was difficult to contend with Athens, when she had so many fortresses to infest his country, and he was destitute of allies, nothing that he has accomplished would he have undertaken, and never would he have acquired so large a dominion. But he saw well, Athenians, that all these places are the open prizes of war, that the possessions of the absent naturally belong to the present, those of the remiss to them that will venture and toil. Acting on such principle, he has won every thing and keeps it, either by way of conquest, or by friendly attachment and alliance; for all men will side with and respect those, whom they see prepared and willing to make proper exertion. If you, Athenians, will adopt this principle now, though you did not before, and every man, where he can and ought to give his service to the state, be ready to give it without excuse, the wealthy to contribute, the able-bodied to enlist; in a word, plainly, if you will become your own masters, and cease each expecting to do nothing himself, while his neighbor does every thing for him, you shall then with heaven's permission recover your own, and get back what has been frittered away, and chastise Philip. Do not imagine, that

[1] He refers to the war in which Athens assisted the Thebans against Lacedæmon, and in which Chabrias won the naval battle of Naxos. That war commenced twenty-six years before the speaking of the first Philippic, and would be well remembered by many of the hearers. See the Historical Abstract in this volume.

his empire is everlastingly secured to him as a god. There are who hate and fear and envy him, Athenians, even among those that seem most friendly; and all feelings that are in other men belong, we may assume, to his confederates. But now they are all cowed, having no refuge through your tardiness and indolence, which I say you must abandon forthwith. For you see, Athenians, the case, to what pitch of arrogance the man has advanced, who leaves you not even the choice of action or inaction, but threatens and uses (they say) outrageous language, and, unable to rest in possession of his conquests, continually widens their circle, and, while we dally and delay, throws his net all around us. When then, Athenians, when will ye act as becomes you? In what event? In that of necessity, I suppose. And how should we regard the events happening now? Methinks, to freemen the strongest necessity is the disgrace of their condition. Or tell me, do ye like walking about and asking one another:—is there any news? Why, could there be greater news than a man of Macedonia subduing Athenians, and directing the affairs of Greece? Is Philip dead? No, but he is sick. And what matters it to you? Should any thing befall this man, you will soon create another Philip, if you attend to business thus. For even he has been exalted not so much by his own strength, as by our negligence. And again; should any thing happen to him; should fortune, which still takes better care of us than we of ourselves, be good enough to accomplish this; observe that, being on the spot, you would step in while things were in confusion, and manage them as you pleased; but as you now are, though occasion offered Amphipolis, you would not be in a position to accept it, with neither forces nor counsels at hand.[1]

However, as to the importance of a general zeal in the discharge of duty, believing you are convinced and satisfied, I say no more.

As to the kind of force which I think may extricate you from your difficulties, the amount, the supplies of money, the best and speediest method (in my judgment) of providing all the necessaries, I shall endeavor to inform you forthwith,

[1] Important advice this, to men in all relations of life. Good luck is for those who are in a position to avail themselves of it.

Illi poma cadunt qui poma sub arbore quærit.

making only one request, men of Athens. When you have heard all, determine; prejudge not before. And let none think I delay our operations, because I recommend an entirely new force. Not those that cry, quickly! to-day! speak most to the purpose; (for what has already happened we shall not be able to prevent by our present armament;) but he that shows what and how great and whence procured must be the force capable of enduring, till either we have advisedly terminated the war, or overcome our enemies: for so shall we escape annoyance in future. This I think I am able to show, without offense to any other man who has a plan to offer. My promise indeed is large; it shall be tested by the performance; and you shall be my judges.

First, then, Athenians, I say we must provide fifty warships,[1] and hold ourselves prepared, in case of emergency, to embark and sail. I require also an equipment of transports for half the cavalry[2] and sufficient boats. This we must have ready against his sudden marches from his own country to Thermopylæ, the Chersonese, Olynthus, and any where he likes. For he should entertain the belief, that possibly you may rouse from this over-carelessness, and start off, as you did to Eubœa,[3] and formerly (they say) to Haliartus,[4] and very lately to Thermopylæ. And although you should not pursue just the course I would advise, it is no slight matter, that

[1] The Athenian ship of war at this time was the Trireme, or galley with three ranks of oars. It had at the prow a beak (ἔμβολον), with a sharp iron head, which, in a charge, (generally made at the broadside,) was able to shatter the planks of the enemy's vessel. An ordinary trireme carried two hundred men, including the crew and marines. These last (ἐπιβάται) were usually ten for each ship, but the number was often increased. The transports and vessels of burden, whether merchant vessels or boats for the carriage of military stores, were round-bottomed, more bulky in construction, and moved rather with sails than oars. Hence the fighting ship is called ταχεῖα, *swift*. It carried a sail, to be used upon occasion, though it was mainly worked with oars.

[2] The total number was one thousand, each tribe furnishing one hundred.

[3] The expedition about five years before, when the Thebans had sent an army to Eubœa, and Timotheus roused his countrymen to expel them from the island. Of this, Demosthenes gives an animated account at the close of the oration on the Chersonese.

[4] B.C. 395, when the war between Thebes and Sparta had begun, and Lysander besieged Haliartus. He was slain in a sally by the Thebans and Athenians.

Philip, knowing you to be in readiness—know it he will for certain; there are too many among our own people who report every thing to him—may either keep quiet from apprehension, or, not heeding your arrangements, be taken off his guard, there being nothing to prevent your sailing, if he give you a chance, to attack his territories. Such an armament, I say, ought instantly to be agreed upon and provided. But besides, men of Athens, you should keep in hand some force, that will incessantly make war and annoy him: none of your ten or twenty thousand mercenaries, not your forces on paper,[1] but one that shall belong to the state, and, whether you appoint one or more generals, or this or that man or any other, shall obey and follow him. Subsistence too I require for it. What the force shall be, how large, from what source maintained, how rendered efficient, I will show you, stating every particular. Mercenaries I recommend—and beware of doing what has often been injurious—thinking all measures below the occasion, adopting the strongest in your decrees, you fail to accomplish the least—rather, I say, perform and procure a little, add to it afterward, if it prove insufficient. I advise then two thousand soldiers in all, five hundred to be Athenians, of whatever age you think right, serving a limited time, not long, but such time as you think right, so as to relieve one another; the rest should be mercenaries. And with them two hundred horse, fifty at least Athenians, like the foot, on the same terms of service; and transports for them. Well; what besides? Ten swift galleys: for, as Philip has a navy, we must have swift galleys also, to convoy our power. How shall subsistence for these troops be provided? I will state and explain; but first let me tell you why I consider a force of this amount sufficient, and why I wish the men to be citizens.

Of that amount, Athenians, because it is impossible for us now to raise an army capable of meeting him in the field: we must plunder[2] and adopt such kind of warfare at first:

[1] Literally "written in letters," that is, promised to the generals or allies, but never sent. Jacobs: *eine Macht die auf dem Blatte steht.* Compare Shakspeare, Henry IV, Second Part, Act i.

We fortify in paper and in figures,
Using the names of men instead of men.

[2] Make predatory incursions, as Livy says, "populabundi magis quam justo more belli." Jacobs: *den Krieg als Freibeuter führen.* Another

our force, therefore, must not be over-large, (for there is not pay or subsistence,) nor altogether mean. Citizens I wish to attend and go on board, because I hear that formerly the state maintained mercenary troops at Corinth,[1] commanded by Polystratus and Iphicrates and Chabrias and some others, and that you served with them yourselves; and I am told, that these mercenaries fighting by your side and you by theirs defeated the Lacedæmonians. But ever since your hirelings have served by themselves, they have been vanquishing your friends and allies, while your enemies have become unduly great. Just glancing at the war of our state, they go off to Artabazus[2] or any where rather, and the general follows, naturally; for it is impossible to command without giving pay. What therefore ask I? To remove the excuses both of general and soldiers, by supplying pay, and attaching native soldiers, as inspectors of the general's conduct. The way we manage things now is a mockery. For if you were asked: Are you at peace, Athenians? No, indeed, you would say; we are at war with Philip. Did you not choose from yourselves ten captains and generals, and also captains and two generals[3] of horse? How are they em-

German: *Streifzüge zu machen* (guerilla warfare). Leland: "harass him with depredations." Wilson, an old English translator: "rob and spoil upon him."

[1] He alludes to the time when Corinth, Athens, Thebes, and Argos, were allied against Sparta, and held a congress at Corinth, B.C. 394. The allies were at first defeated, but Iphicrates gained some successes, and acquired considerable reputation by cutting off a small division (*mora*) of Spartan infantry.

[2] Diodorus relates that Chares, in the Social war, having no money to pay his troops, was forced to lend them to Artabazus, then in rebellion against the king of Persia. Chares gained a victory for the satrap, and received a supply of money. But this led to a complaint and menace of war by the king, which brought serious consequences. See the Historical Abstract.

[3] There were chosen at Athens every year

Ten generals (one for each tribe), *στρατηγοί*.
Ten captains (one for each tribe), *ταξίαρχοι*.
Two generals of cavalry, *ἵππαρχοι*.
Ten cavalry officers (one for each tribe), *φύλαρχοι*.

In a regular army of citizens, when each tribe formed its own division, both of horse and foot, all these generals and officers would be present. Thus, there were ten generals at Marathon. A change took place in later times, when the armies were more miscellaneous. Three

ployed? Except one man, whom you commission on service abroad, the rest conduct your processions with the sacrificers. Like puppet-makers, you elect your infantry and cavalry officers for the market-place, not for war. Consider, Athenians; should there not be native captains, a native general of horse, your own commanders, that the force might really be the state's? Or should your general of horse sail to Lemnos,[1] while Menelaus commands the cavalry fighting for your possessions? I speak not as objecting to the man, but he ought to be elected by you, whoever the person be.

Perhaps you admit the justice of these statements, but wish principally to hear about the supplies, what they must be and whence procured. I will satisfy you. Supplies, then, for maintenance, mere rations for these troops, come to ninety talents and a little more: for ten swift galleys forty talents, twenty minas a month to every ship; for two thousand soldiers forty more, that each soldier may receive for rations ten drachms a month; and for two hundred horsemen, each receiving thirty drachms a month, twelve talents.[2] Should any one think rations for the men a small provision, he judges erroneously. Furnish that, and I am sure the army itself will, without injuring any Greek or ally, procure every thing else from the war, so as to make out their full pay. I am ready to join the fleet as a volunteer, and submit to any thing, if this be not so. Now for the ways and means of the supply, which I demand from you.

[*Statement*[3] *of ways and means.*]

This, Athenians, is what we have been able to devise. When you vote upon the resolutions, pass what you[4] approve,

Athenian generals were frequently employed, and at a still later period only one. Demosthenes here touches on a very important matter, which we can well understand, viz. the necessity of officering the foreign mercenaries from home.

[1] To assist at a religious ceremony held annually at Lemnos, where many Athenians resided.

[2] As to Athenian money, see Appendix II.

[3] Here the clerk or secretary reads the scheme drawn up by Demosthenes, in the preparing of which he was probably assisted by the financial officers of the state. What follows was, according to Dionysius, spoken at a different time. The curious may consult Leland, and Jacobs' introduction to his translation.

[4] *I. e.* some measure, if not mine, whereby the war may be waged

that you may oppose Philip, not only by decrees and letters, but by action also.

I think it will assist your deliberations about the war and the whole arrangements, to regard the position, Athenians, of the hostile country, and consider, that Philip by the winds and seasons of the year gets the start in most of his operations, watching for the trade-winds[1] or the winter to commence them, when we are unable (he thinks) to reach the spot. On this account, we must carry on the war not with hasty levies, (or we shall be too late for every thing,) but with a permanent force and power. You may use as winter quarters for your troops Lemnos, and Thasus, and Sciathus, and the islands[2] in that neighborhood, which have harbors and corn and all necessaries for an army. In the season of the year, when it is easy to put ashore and there is no danger from the winds, they will easily take their station off the coast itself and at the entrances of the sea-ports.

How and when to employ the troops, the commander appointed by you will determine as occasion requires. What you must find, is stated in my bill. If, men of Athens, you will furnish the supplies which I mention, and then, after completing your preparations of soldiers, ships, cavalry, will oblige the entire force by law to remain in the service, and, while you become your own paymasters and commissaries, demand from your general an account of his conduct, you will cease to be always discussing the same questions without forwarding them in the least, and besides, Athenians, not only will you cut off his greatest revenue—What is this? He maintains war against you through the resources of your allies, by his piracies on their navigation—But what next? You will be out of the reach of injury yourselves: he will not do as in time past, when falling upon Lemnos and Imbrus he carried off your citizens captive, seizing the vessels at Geræstus he levied an incalculable sum, and lastly, made a descent at Marathon and carried off the sacred

effectually. The reading of ποιήσατε, adopted by Jacobs after Schaefer, is not in congruity with the sentence.

[1] The Etesian winds blowing from the northwest in July, which would impede a voyage from Athens to Macedonia and Thrace.

[2] As Scopelus, Halonnesus, Peparethus, which were then subject to Athens.

galley[1] from our coast, and you could neither prevent these things nor send succors by the appointed time. But how is it, think you, Athenians, that the Panathenaic and Dionysian festivals[2] take place always at the appointed time, whether expert or unqualified persons be chosen to conduct either of them, whereon you expend larger sums than upon any armament, and which are more numerously attended and magnificent than almost any thing in the world; while all your armaments are after the time, as that to Methone, to Pagasæ, to Potidæa? Because in the former case every thing is ordered by law, and each of you knows long beforehand, who is the choir-master[3] of his tribe, who the gymnastic[4] master, when, from whom, and what he is to receive, and what to do. Nothing there is left unascertained or undefined: whereas in the business of war and its preparations all is irregular, unsettled, indefinite. Therefore, no sooner have we heard any thing, than we appoint ship-captains, dispute with them on the exchanges,[5] and consider about ways

[1] A ship called Paralus, generally used on religious missions or to carry public dispatches.

[2] The Panathenaic festivals were in honor of Pallas or Athene, the protectress of Athens, and commemorated also the union of the old Attic towns under one government. There were two, the greater held every fourth year, the lesser annually. They were celebrated with sacrifices, races, gymnastic and musical contests, and various other amusements and solemnities, among which was the carrying the pictured robe of Pallas to her temple. The Dionysia, or festival of Bacchus, will be spoken of more fully hereafter.

[3] The choregus, or choir-master, of each tribe, had to defray the expense of the choruses, whether dramatic, lyric, or musical, which formed part of the entertainment on solemn occasions. This was one of the λειτουργίαι, or burdensome offices, to which men of property were liable at Athens; of which we shall see more in other parts of our author.

[4] The gymnasiarch, like the choregus, had a burden imposed on him by his tribe, to make certain provisions for the gymnasium, public place or school of exercise. Some of the contests at the festivals being of a gymnastic nature, such as the Torch-race, it was his duty to make arrangements for them, and more particularly to select the ablest youths of the school for performers.

[5] For every ship of war a captain, or trierarch, was appointed, whose duty it was, not merely to command, but take charge of the vessel, keep it in repair, and bear the expense (partly or wholly) of equipping it. In the Peloponnesian war we find the charge laid upon two joint captains, and afterward it was borne by an association formed like the Symmoriæ of the Property Tax. Demosthenes, when he came

and means; then it is resolved that resident aliens and householders[1] shall embark, then to put yourselves on board instead: but during these days the objects of our expedition are lost; for the time of action we waste in preparation, and favorable moments wait not our evasions and delays. The forces that we imagine we possess in the mean time, are found, when the crisis comes, utterly insufficient. And Philip has arrived at such a pitch of arrogance, as to send the following letter to the Eubœans:

[*The letter is read.*]

Of that which has been read, Athenians, most is true, unhappily true; perhaps not agreeable to hear. And if what one passes over in speaking, to avoid offense, one could pass over in reality, it is right to humor the audience: but if graciousness of speech, where it is out of place, does harm in action, shameful is it, Athenians, to delude ourselves, and by putting off every thing unpleasant to miss the time for all operations, and be unable even to understand, that skillful makers of war should not follow circumstances, but be in advance of them; that just as a general may be expected to lead his armies, so are men of prudent counsel to guide circumstances, in order that their resolutions may be accomplished, not their motions determined by the event. Yet you, Athenians, with larger means than any people—ships, infantry, cavalry, and revenue—have never up to this day made proper use of any of them; and your war with Philip differs in no respect from the boxing of barbarians. For among them the party struck feels always for the blow;[2] strike him somewhere else, there go his hands again; ward or look in the face he can not nor will. So you, if you hear of

to the head of affairs, introduced some useful reforms in the system of the Trierarchy.

The exchange, ἀντίδοσις, was a stringent but clumsy contrivance, to enforce the performance of these public duties by persons capable of bearing them. A party charged might call upon any other person to take the office, or exchange estates with him. If he refused, complaint was made to the magistrate who had cognizance of the business, and the dispute was judicially heard and decided.

[1] Freedmen, who had quitted their masters' house, and lived independently.

[2] Compare Virgil, Æn. ix. 577.

Ille manum projecto tegmine demens
Ad vulnus tulit.

Philip in the Chersonese, vote to send relief there, if at Thermopylæ, the same; if any where else, you run after his heels up and down, and are commanded by him; no plan have you devised for the war, no circumstance do you see beforehand, only[1] when you learn that something is done, or about to be done. Formerly perhaps this was allowable; now it is come to a crisis, to be tolerable no longer. And it seems, men of Athens, as if some god, ashamed for us at our proceedings, has put this activity into Philip. For had he been willing to remain quiet in possession of his conquests and prizes, and attempted nothing further, some of you, I think, would be satisfied with a state of things, which brands our nation with the shame of cowardice and the foulest disgrace. But by continually encroaching and grasping after more, he may possibly rouse you, if you have not altogether despaired. I marvel, indeed, that none of you, Athenians, notices with concern and anger, that the beginning of this war was to chastise Philip, the end is to protect ourselves against his attacks. One thing is clear: he will not stop, unless some one oppose him. And shall we wait for this? And if you dispatch empty galleys and hopes from this or that person, think ye all is well? Shall we not embark? Shall we not sail with at least a part of our national forces, now though not before? Shall we not make a descent upon his coast? Where, then, shall we land? some one asks. The war itself, men of Athens, will discover the rotten parts of his empire, if we make a trial; but if we sit at home, hearing the orators accuse and malign one another, no good can ever be achieved. Methinks, where a portion of our citizens, though not all, are commissioned with the rest, Heaven blesses, and Fortune aids the struggle: but where you send out a general and an empty decree and hopes from the hustings, nothing that you desire is done; your enemies scoff, and your allies die for fear of such an armament. For it is impossible—ay, impossible, for one man to execute all your wishes: to promise,[2] and assert, and accuse this or that person, is possible; but so your affairs are ruined.

[1] This loose mode of expression, which is found in the original, I designedly retain.

[2] Chares is particularly alluded to. The "promises of Chares" passed into a proverb.

The general commands wretched unpaid hirelings; here are persons easily found, who tell you lies of his conduct; you vote at random from what you hear: what then can be expected?

How is this to cease, Athenians? When you make the same persons soldiers, and witnesses of the general's conduct, and judges when they return home at his audit;[1] so that you may not only hear of your own affairs, but be present to see them. So disgraceful is our condition now, that every general is twice or thrice tried[2] before you for his life, though none dares even once to hazard his life against the enemy: they prefer the death of kidnappers and thieves to that which becomes them; for it is a malefactor's part to die by sentence of the law, a general's to die in battle. Among ourselves, some go about and say that Philip is concerting with the Lacedæmonians the destruction of Thebes and the dissolution of republics; some, that he has sent envoys to the king;[3] others, that he is fortifying cities in Illyria: so we wander about, each inventing stories. For my part, Athenians, by the gods I believe, that Philip is intoxicated with the magnitude of his exploits, and has many such dreams in his imagination, seeing the absence of opponents, and elated by success; but most certainly he has no such plan of action, as to let the silliest people among us know what his intentions are; for the silliest are these newsmongers. Let us dismiss such talk, and remember only that Philip is an enemy, who robs us of our own and has long insulted us; that wherever we have expected aid from any quarter, it has been found hostile, and that the future depends on ourselves, and unless we are willing to fight him there, we shall perhaps be compelled to fight here. This let us remember, and then we shall have

[1] The audit or scrutiny of his conduct which every officer of the republic had to undergo, before a jury, if necessary, at the end of his administration. In the case of a general, the scrutiny would be like a court-martial. The Athenian people, (says Demosthenes,) as represented by the citizen soldiers, would themselves be witnesses of the general's conduct. These same soldiers, when they came home, or at least a portion of them, might serve on the jury; and so the people would be both witnesses and judges.

[2] Chares was tried several times. Capital charges were preferred also against Autocles, Cephisodotus, Leosthenes, Callisthenes.

[3] The king of Persia, generally called *the king* by the Greeks.

determined wisely, and have done with idle conjectures. You need not pry into the future, but assure yourselves it will be disastrous, unless you attend to your duty, and are willing to act as becomes you.

As for me, never before have I courted favor, by speaking what I am not convinced is for your good, and now I have spoken my whole mind frankly and unreservedly. I could have wished, knowing the advantage of good counsel to you, I were equally certain of its advantage to the counselor: so should I have spoken with more satisfaction. Now, with an uncertainty of the consequence to myself, but with a conviction that you will benefit by adopting it, I proffer my advice. I trust only, that what is most for the common benefit will prevail.

THE ORATION ON THE PEACE.

THE ARGUMENT.

To understand as well the subject of this oration, as the motives of Demosthenes, who here recommends a course of action different from the vigorous measures counseled by him on other occasions, it is necessary to take a short review of the preceding events, and observe the position in which Athens stood at the time when the speech was delivered.

Philip, after taking Olynthus, turned his thoughts to new objects, of which the more immediate were, first, to get possession of the Greek towns on the Hellespont and the Chersonese; secondly, to get a footing in southern Greece. The first of these seemed comparatively easy since the reduction of Olynthus; the second was more difficult, and could only be accomplished by the aid or sufferance of certain Greek states. But the continuance of the Sacred war afforded Philip an opportunity of which he skillfully availed himself. Phalæcus, son of Onomarchus, had maintained his ground against the enemy, and both Thebans and Thessalians began to be desirous of Macedonian aid. But Athens was in alliance with Phocis, and Philip had seen some few years before, when the Athenians occupied the pass of Thermopylæ, that they were still capable of vigorous efforts, if under able direction or any strong excitement. It became therefore his policy to conciliate Athens for the present. He caused it to be announced by means of his agents and partisans, that he was desirous of peace, and reports of various acts of kindness done by him to Athenian citizens in Macedonia were studiously disseminated. This seems to have been the period at which Philip gained over to his interest, or even retained in his service, divers active members of the Athenian assembly.

Among them was Philocrates, who first made a formal motion, that Philip should have leave to open a negotiation. Soon after he carried a decree to send embassadors to Philip, and ten were dispatched, among them Philocrates himself, Æschines, and Demosthenes. They returned with a letter from Philip, and were soon followed by three Macedonian envoys of high distinction, Antipater, Parmenio, and Eurylochus. The Athenians met in assembly; peace was determined on, and the embassadors were again ordered to sail to Macedonia to receive the oath of Philip. In the mean time Philip had marched into Thrace, where he defeated Cersobleptes, the king of that country, and took possession of a part of his dominions. From this expedition he had not returned when the Athenian embassadors arrived at Pella, the Macedonian capital. Here they waited a month, and, on Philip's return, were induced by that monarch, who had secretly prepared for his invasion of Phocis, to accompany him as far as Pheræ in Thessaly. From Pheræ they departed for Athens, and Philip marched straight to Thermopylæ. The Athenians, deceived by his promises, were lulled into security; Phalæcus, seeing no hope of assistance, withdrew from Phocis, while Philip, strengthened by the forces of Thessaly and Thebes, overran the country, and took possession of Delphi. An Amphictyonic council was convened to sit in judgment on the sacrilegious Phocians. Sentence was passed on them, which (besides other penalties) deprived them of their seat in the council of Amphictyons, and transferred their privileges to the king of Macedonia.

The first intelligence of these transactions was received at Athens with consternation. Measures were taken to put the city in a state of defense, as if an invasion were threatened. Philip sent a calm letter of remonstrance, which allayed the fears of the people, but did not abate their anger and ill-humor A feeling of disappointment was mingled with shame for their own credulity, and alarm at the increase of Macedonian influence. They saw too, with deep vexation, that Philip, instead of conferring any benefit upon Athens, as they had fondly hoped he would, had exerted himself to promote the advantage of Thebes, which, by his assistance, recovered her subject Bœotian towns, and even obtained some of the Phocian territory for herself. Nothing more strongly marked the state of public feeling at Athens, than her refusal at this time to attend the Pythian games, at which Philip had been chosen to preside by the Amphictyonic decree. The Athenians by absenting themselves made a sort of protest against his election.

It was in this state of things that Macedonian embassadors, accompanied by Thessalian and Bœotian, arrived at Athens, to demand from her a formal sanction of the decree by which Philip had become a member of the Amphictyonic council. An assembly was held to consider the question. The people were exceedingly clamorous, and applauded those orators who opposed the claim of Philip. Æschines, who supported it, could scarcely obtain a hearing. Demosthenes at length addressed the assembly, and, without advising any dishonorable submission, or even direct concession to what the envoys required, strongly dissuaded his countrymen from taking any course which might draw Athens into a war. It was not that Philip was less to be dreaded now than he was before; on the contrary, his power had greatly increased; but this was not the time to provoke his hostility, backed as he was by Thessaly and Thebes; and even if Athens could stand alone against such a combination, a mere Amphictyonic title was not a proper subject of quarrel.

It appears that the Athenians came to no formal vote on this matter, but their anger was so far calmed by the arguments of Demosthenes, that the envoys departed with full confidence that the peace would not be broken.

I SEE, men of Athens, our affairs are in great perplexity and confusion, not only because many interests have been sacrificed, and it is useless to make fine speeches about them, but because, for preserving what remains, you can not agree upon any single expedient, some holding one opinion, and some another. And besides, perplexing and difficult as deliberation of itself is, you, Athenians, have rendered it far more so. For other men usually hold counsel before action, you hold it after: the result of which during all the time of my remembrance has been, that the censurer of your errors gets repute and credit as a good speaker, while your interests and objects of deliberation are lost. Yet, even under these circumstances, I believe, and I have risen with the persuasion, that if you will desist from wrangling and tumult, and listen as becomes men on a political consultation of such importance, I shall be able to suggest and advise measures by which our affairs may be improved and our losses retrieved.

Well as I know, Athenians, that to talk before you of one's self and one's own counsels is a successful artifice with unscrupulous men, I think it so vulgar and offensive, that I shrink from it even in a case of necessity. However, I think you will better appreciate what I shall say now, by calling to mind a little that I said on former occasions. For example, Athenians, when they were advising you in the troubles of Eubœa to assist Plutarch,[1] and undertake a dis-

[1] Callias, sovereign of Chalcis, had invited Philip into Eubœa, to assist him against Plutarch, sovereign of Eretria; Plutarch applied to Athens for assistance, and Phocion was sent with an army into Eubœa, where, by the carelessness or treachery of Plutarch, he was exposed in a defile at Tamynæ, and attacked by Callias with a superior force of Chalcidians and Macedonians. He gained the victory, but to punish Plutarch expelled him from Eretria. This happened B.C. 354. After Phocion quitted the island, a Macedonian party began to prevail at Eretria, and Philip got possession of the city, defeating and taking prisoner Molossus, the Athenian commander.

creditable and expensive war, I, and I alone, stood forward to oppose it, and was nearly torn to pieces by the men who for petty lucre have seduced you into many grievous errors. A short time later, when you incurred disgrace, and suffered what no mortals ever did from parties whom they assisted, you all acknowledged the worthlessness of their counsels who misled you, and the soundness of mine. Again, Athenians, when I saw that Neoptolemus[1] the actor, privileged under color of his profession, was doing serious mischief to the state, managing and directing things at Athens on Philip's behalf, I came and informed you, not from any private enmity or malice, as subsequent occurrences have shown. And herein I shall not blame the advocates of Neoptolemus, (for there were none,) but you yourselves; for had you been seeing a tragedy in the temple of Bacchus, instead of it being a debate on the public weal and safety, you could not have heard him with more partiality, or me with more intolerance. But I suppose you all now understand, that he made his journey to the enemy, in order (as he said) to get the debts there owing to him, and defray thereout his public charges at home; and, after urging this argument, that it was hard to reproach men who brought over their effects from abroad, as soon as he obtained security through the peace, he converted into money all the real estate which he possessed here, and has gone off with it to Philip. Thus two of my warnings, justly and rightfully pronounced, in accordance with the truth, testify in my favor as a counselor. A third, men of Athens, I will mention, this one only, and straight proceed to the subject of my address. When we embassadors, after receiving the oaths on the peace, had returned, and certain men were promising that Thespiæ and Platæa[2] would be repeopled; that Philip, if he got the mastery, would save the Phocians, and disperse the population of Thebes;[3] that Oropus[4]

[1] Neoptolemus on some professional engagement at Pella had probably been bribed by Philip. He was active in promoting the peace, and afterward abandoned his country for Macedonia.

[2] Thespiæ and Platæa were taken and razed to the ground by the Thebans under Epaminondas, B.C. 373.

[3] That is, dismantle the city, and disperse the inhabitants into villages in order to destroy their power. An example of such a διοίκισις was the dismemberment of Mantinea by the Spartans in the year B.C. 385.

[4] Oropus was a border town, for the possession of which Thebes and

would be yours, and Eubœa given as compensation for Amphipolis, with more of the like hopes and delusions, which led you on, against policy, equity and honor, to abandon the Phocians; you will find, I neither aided in any of these deceits, nor held my tongue. I warned you, as you surely remember, that I knew not of these things nor expected them, and deemed it all idle gossip.

These instances, wherein I have shown greater foresight than others, I mention not by way of boast, nor ascribe, Athenians, to any sagacity of my own, nor will I pretend to discover or discern the future from any but two causes, which I will state: first, men of Athens, through good fortune, which I observe beats all the craft and cleverness of man; secondly, because I judge and estimate things disinterestedly, and no one can show that any lucre is attached to my politics or my speeches. Therefore, whatever be your true policy, as indicated by the circumstances, I have a correct view of it; but when you put money on one side as in a balance, it carries away and pulls down the judgment with it, and he that does so can no longer reason upon any thing justly or soundly.

The first thing which I maintain to be necessary is this. Whether you seek to obtain allies, or contribution,[1] or aught else for the state, do it without disturbing the present peace; not that it is very glorious or worthy of you, but, whatever be its character, it had better suited our interests never to have made peace, than to break it ourselves: for we have thrown away many advantages, which would have rendered the war then safer and easier for us than it can be now. Secondly, Athenians, we must take care that these people assembled and calling themselves Amphictyons[2] are not by

Athens had long contended. Themison of Eretria had taken it from Athens, and put it in the hands of the Thebans.

[1] *I. e.* money contributed by allies. When the Athenians re-established their confederacy, which had been dissolved by the Peloponnesian war, the payments received from the allies received the name of *contributions*, *σύνταξις*, as less obnoxious than *tribute*, *φόρος*.

[2] The Amphictyonic league, at the head of which Philip was now placed, was a federal union of Hellenic (or Greek) tribes, having for its object the maintenance of a common religion and nationality. The various deputies met twice a year, in the spring at Delphi, in the autumn at Anthela near Thermopylæ. They met, not only to celebrate games and festivals, but to transact the business of the league, to determine

us necessitated, or furnished with a plea, to make a common war against us. I grant, if we renewed the war with Philip on account of Amphipolis, or any such private quarrel, in which Thessalians, Argives and Thebans are not concerned, none of them would join in it, and least of all—hear me before you cry out—the Thebans: not that they are kindly disposed to us, or would not gratify Philip, but they see clearly, stupid as one may think them,[1] that, if they had a war with you, the hardships would all be theirs, while another sat waiting for the advantages. Therefore they would not throw themselves into it, unless the ground and origin of the war were common. So if we again went to war with the Thebans for Oropus or any private cause, I should fear no disaster, because our respective auxiliaries would assist us or them, if either country were invaded, but would join with neither in aggression. Such is the spirit of alliances that are worth regard, and so the thing naturally is. People are not friendly either to us or the Thebans, to the extent of equally desiring our safety and our predominance. Safe they would all have us for their own sakes; dominant, so as to become their masters, they would not have either of us. What then, say I, is the danger? what to be guarded against? Lest in the coming war there be found a common plea, a common grievance for all. If Argives, and Messenians, and Megalopolitans, and some of the other Peloponnesians, who are in league with them, are hostile to us on account of our negotiating with the Lacedæmonians and seeming to take up some of their enterprises; if the Thebans are (as they say) our enemies, and will be more so, because we harbor their

questions of international law and religion. The oracular sanctity of Delphi gave a dignity to these meetings, but the rivalry and jealousies of the more powerful Greek states did not permit them (in general) to be controlled by Amphictyonic decrees. The three Sacred wars are instances in which their decrees were enforced by combination; but in the two last, for which Philip's aid was invited, there was but little enthusiasm in the cause from any motive of religion or patriotism. The meeting at which Philip had been chosen president was so tumultuous and irregular, that the Athenians would not allow it to be a legal convocation of the Amphictyonic body. Philip greatly resented this, because his election was considered to establish the title of his countrymen to rank among the Greek nations.

[1] Bœotian stupidity was proverbial. So Horace, Epist. II. i. 224.

Bœotûm in crasso jurares aere natum.

exiles and in every way manifest our aversion to them; Thessalians again, because we harbor the Phocian exiles, and Philip, because we oppose his admission to the Amphictyonic body; I fear that, each incensed on a private quarrel, they will combine to bring war upon you, setting up the decrees of the Amphictyons, and be drawn on (beyond what their single interests require) to battle it with us, as they did with the Phocians. For you are surely aware, that now the Thebans and Philip and the Thessalians have co-operated, without having each exactly the same views. For example, the Thebans could not hinder Philip from advancing and occupying the passes, nor yet from coming last and having the credit of their labors. True, in respect of territorial acquisition, something has been done for them; but in regard to honor and reputation, they have fared wretchedly; since, had Philip not stepped in, they would (it seems) have got nothing. This was not agreeable to them, but having the wish without the power to obtain Orchomenos and Coronea, they submitted to it all. Of Philip, you know, some persons venture to say, that he would not have given Orchomenos and Coronea to the Thebans, but was compelled to do so. I wish them joy of their opinion,[1] but thus far I believe, that he cared not so much about that business, as he desired to occupy the passes, and have the glory of the war, as being determined by his agency, and the direction of the Pythian games. Such were the objects of his ambition. The Thessalians wished not either Philip or Thebes to be aggrandized, since in both they saw danger to themselves; but sought to obtain these two advant-

[1] Demosthenes did not entirely scout the suggestion made with regard to Philip's views; but perhaps he thought that Philip could not venture to offend his Theban allies then; and one of the means of humbling Athens was, to increase the power of her neighbor. If it be asked why Philip might not have seized upon Elatea at this time, as well as eight years later, I should say, not on account of the peace with Athens, but because he desired to rest upon his Amphictyonic honors, and have the full benefit of the moral ascendency which he had acquired. It was not clear that his grand object, which was rather to lead than to conquer Greece, might not be obtained without a war against any of her principal states. Afterward, when the Athenians, under the active administration of Demosthenes, baffled his efforts in the north, and showed a determination to counteract all his projects, it became necessary for him to strike a decisive blow, even at the risk of irritating Thebes. He ran this risk, and succeeded, but not without danger.

ages, the synod at Thermopylæ, and the privileges at Delphi;[1] for which objects they aided the confederacy. Thus you will find that each party has been led into many acts unwillingly: and against this danger, being such as I describe, you must take precautions.

Must we then do as we are bidden, for fear of the consequences? and do you recommend this? Far from it. I advise you so to act, as not to compromise your dignity, to avoid war, to prove yourselves right-thinking, just-speaking men. With those who think we should boldly suffer any thing, and do not foresee the war, I would reason thus. We permit the Thebans to have Oropus; and if one asked us why, and required a true answer, we should say, To avoid war. And to Philip now we have ceded Amphipolis by treaty, and allow the Cardians[2] to be excepted from the other people of the Chersonese; and the Carian[3] to seize the islands Chios, Cos, and Rhodes, and the Byzantines to detain[4] our vessels; evidently because we think the tranquillity of peace more beneficial than strife and contest about such questions. It were folly then and utter absurdity, after dealing thus with each party singly on matters of vital moment to ourselves, to battle now with them all for a shadow at Delphi.

[1] The Thessalians were peculiarly aggrieved by their exclusion (during the Sacred war) from the national synod, and from the oracle and festivities of Delphi. Their country had been the cradle of the Hellenic race, their deputies were the most numerous in the council, and their vicinity to the places of meeting gave them a greater interest in the proceedings. Hence they most eagerly pressed for punishment of the Phocians. The tribes of Mount Œta proposed, that the male population of Phocis should be precipitated from the Delphian rock; which cruelty was not permitted by Philip. To gratify the Thessalians, Philip put them in possession of Nicæa, one of the towns near the pass of Thermopylæ, but even there he kept a Macedonian garrison. The Thebans had expected to have that town themselves, and were disappointed.

[2] Cardia was a city at the northwestern extremity of the Chersonese, and from its position on the isthmus was considered the key of the peninsula. Among the towns ceded to Athens by Cersobleptes, Cardia had not been included; but the Athenians afterward laid claim to it, and Philip supported the Cardians in resisting that claim.

[3] Idrieus, king of Caria, who was now in possession of these islands, which had revolted from Athens in the Social war.

[4] Compel them to go into their port to pay harbor duties.

THE SECOND PHILIPPIC.

THE ARGUMENT.

Soon after the close of the Phocian war, the attention of Philip was called to Peloponnesus, where the dissensions between Sparta and her old enemies afforded him an occasion of interference. The Spartans had never abandoned their right to the province of Messenia, which had been wrested from them by Epaminondas; and since Thebes was no longer to be feared, they seem to have conceived hopes of regaining their lost power. The Argives and the Arcadians of Megalopolis were in league with Messenia, but Sparta had her allies in the Peloponnesus, and even Athens was suspected of favoring her cause. It does not appear that any open hostilities had taken place; but about this time the fears of the Messenians induced them to solicit the alliance of Philip. He willingly promised them his protection, and sent a body of troops into the Peninsula. The progress which Macedonian influence was making there having alarmed the Athenians, they sent Demosthenes with an embassy to counteract it. He went to Messene and to Argos, addressed the people, and pointed out the dangers to which all Greece was exposed by Philip's ambition. It seems that he failed in rousing their suspicions, or they were too much occupied by an immediate peril to heed one that appeared remote. Philip however resented this proceeding on the part of the Athenians, and sent an embassy to expostulate with them, especially on the charge of bad faith and treachery which had been preferred against him by Demosthenes. Embassadors from Argos and Messene accompanied those of Macedon, and complained of the connection that appeared to subsist between Athens and Lacedæmon, hostile (they thought) to the liberties of Peloponnesus. In answer to these complaints, Demosthenes addressed his second Philippic to the Popular Assembly; repeating the substance of what he had said to the Peloponnesians, vindicating his own conduct, and denouncing the Macedonian party at Athens. The embassy led to no immediate result; but the influence of Demosthenes at home was increased.

In all the speeches, men of Athens, about Philip's measures and infringements of the peace, I observe that statements made on our behalf are thought just and generous,[1] and all

[1] *Generous*, as regards the Greek states, whose independence the Athenians stand up for. This praise Demosthenes frequently claims for his countrymen, and, compared with the rest of the Greeks, they deserved it. Leland understood the word φιλανθρώπους in the same

who accuse Philip are heard with approbation; yet nothing (I may say) that is proper, or for the sake of which the speeches are worth hearing, is done. To this point are the affairs of Athens brought, that the more fully and clearly one convicts Philip of violating the peace with you, and plotting against the whole of Greece, the more difficult it becomes to advise you how to act. The cause lies in all of us, Athenians, that, when we ought to oppose an ambitious power by deeds and actions, not by words, we men of the hustings[1] shrink from our duty of moving and advising, for fear of your displeasure, and only declaim on the heinousness and atrocity of Philip's conduct; you of the assembly, though better instructed than Philip to argue justly, or comprehend the argument of another, to check him in the execution of his designs are totally unprepared. The result is inevitable, I imagine, and perhaps just. You each succeed better in what you are busy and earnest about; Philip in actions, you in words. If you are still satisfied with using the better arguments, it is an easy matter, and there is no trouble: but if we are to take measures for the correction of these evils, to prevent their insensible progress, and the rising up of a mighty power, against which we could have no defense, then our course of deliberation is not the same as formerly; the orators, and you that hear them, must prefer good and salutary counsels to those which are easy and agreeable.

First, men of Athens, if any one regards without uneasiness the might and dominion of Philip, and imagines that it threatens no danger to the state, or that all his preparations are not against you, I marvel, and would entreat you every one to hear briefly from me the reasons, why I am led to form a contrary expectation, and wherefore I deem Philip an enemy; that, if I appear to have the clearer foresight, you

sense, though he translates it *humane*. We use the term *philanthropic* in a sense not unlike that of the orator; but, as Leland truly observes, "the distinction of Greek and barbarian precluded the rest of mankind from a just share in Grecian philanthropy;" and he might have added, that their notions of slavery were not in accordance with an enlarged humanity. Therefore, I prefer a word of a less arrogant meaning. Jacobs: *billig*. Francis: "filled with sentiments of exceeding moderation."

[1] Auger has: "nous qui montons à la tribune."

may hearken to me; if they, who have such confidence and trust in Philip, you may give your adherence to them.

Thus then I reason, Athenians. What did Philip first make himself master of after the peace? Thermopylæ and the Phocian state. Well, and how used he his power? He chose to act for the benefit of Thebes, not of Athens. Why so? Because, I conceive, measuring his calculations by ambition, by his desire of universal empire, without regard to peace, quiet, or justice, he saw plainly, that to a people of our character and principles nothing could he offer or give, that would induce you for self-interest to sacrifice any of the Greeks to him. He sees that you, having respect for justice, dreading the infamy of the thing, and exercising proper forethought, would oppose him in any such attempt as much as if you were at war: but the Thebans he expected (and events prove him right) would, in return for the services done them, allow him in every thing else to have his way, and, so far from thwarting or impeding him, would fight on his side if he required it. From the same persuasion he befriended lately the Messenians and Argives, which is the highest panegyric upon you, Athenians; for you are adjudged by these proceedings to be the only people incapable of betraying for lucre the national rights of Greece, or bartering your attachment to her for any obligation or benefit. And this opinion of you, that (so different) of the Argives and Thebans, he has naturally formed, not only from a view of present times, but by reflection on the past. For assuredly he finds and hears that your ancestors, who might have governed the rest of Greece on terms of submitting to Persia, not only spurned the proposal, when Alexander,[1] this man's ancestor, came as herald to negotiate, but preferred to abandon their country and endure any suffering, and thereafter

[1] Alexander of Macedon, son of Amyntas, was sent by Mardonius, the Persian commander, to offer the most favorable terms to the Athenians, if they would desert the cause of the Greeks. The Spartans at the same time sent an embassy, to remind them of their duty. The spirited reply which the Athenians made to both embassies is related by Herodotus. The Thebans submitted to Xerxes, and fought against the Greeks at the battle of Platæa. The Argives were neutral, chiefly from jealousy of Sparta. They demanded half the command of the allied army, as a condition of their assistance, but this could not be complied with.

achieved such exploits as all the world loves to mention, though none could ever speak them worthily, and therefore I must be silent; for their deeds are too mighty to be uttered[1] in words. But the forefathers of the Argives and Thebans, they either joined the barbarian's army, or did not oppose it; and therefore he knows that both will selfishly embrace their advantage, without considering the common interest of the Greeks. He thought then, if he chose your friendship, it must be on just principles; if he attached himself to them, he should find auxiliaries of his ambition. This is the reason of his preferring them to you both then and now. For certainly he does not see them with a larger navy than you, nor has he acquired an inland empire and renounced that of the sea and the ports, nor does he forget the professions and promises on which he obtained the peace.

Well, it may be said, he knew all this, yet he so acted, not from ambition or the motives which I charge, but because the demands of the Thebans were more equitable than yours. Of all pleas, this now is the least open to him. He that bids the Lacedæmonians resign Messene, how can he pretend, when he delivered Orchomenos and Coronea to the Thebans, to have acted on a conviction of justice?

But, forsooth, he was compelled,—this plea remains—he made concessions against his will, being surrounded by Thessalian horse and Theban infantry. Excellent! So of his intentions they talk; he will mistrust the Thebans; and some carry news about, that he will fortify Elatea. All this he intends and will intend, I dare say; but to attack the Lacedæmonians on behalf of Messene and Argos he does not intend; he actually sends mercenaries and money into the country, and is expected himself with a great force. The Lacedæmonians, who are enemies of Thebes, he overthrows; the Phocians, whom he himself before destroyed, will he now preserve?

And who can believe this? I can not think that Philip,

[1] The simple εἰπεῖν in the original is more forcible than if it had been ἐπαινεῖν, or the like. Compare Shakspeare, Coriolanus, Act ii. sc. 2.

I shall lack voice: the deeds of Coriolanus
Should not be uttered feebly——
For this last,
Before and in Corioli, let me say,
I can not speak him home,

either if he was forced into his former measures, or if he were now giving up the Thebans, would pertinaciously oppose their enemies; his present conduct rather shows that he adopted those measures by choice. All things prove to a correct observer, that his whole plan of action is against our state. And this has now become to him a sort of necessity. Consider. He desires empire: he conceives you to be his only opponents. He has been for some time wronging you, as his own conscience best informs him, since, by retaining what belongs to you, he secures the rest of his dominion: had he given up Amphipolis and Potidæa, he deemed himself unsafe at home. He knows therefore, both that he is plotting against you, and that you are aware of it; and, supposing you to have intelligence, he thinks you must hate him; he is alarmed, expecting some disaster, if you get the chance, unless he hastes to prevent you. Therefore he is awake, and on the watch against us; he courts certain people, Thebans, and people in Peloponnesus of the like views, who from cupidity, he thinks, will be satisfied with the present, and from dullness of understanding will foresee none of the consequences. And yet men of even moderate sense might notice striking facts, which I had occasion to quote to the Messenians and Argives, and perhaps it is better they should be repeated to you.

Ye men of Messene, said I, how do ye think the Olynthians would have brooked to hear any thing against Philip at those times, when he surrendered to them Anthemus, which all former kings of Macedonia claimed, when he cast out the Athenian colonists and gave them Potidæa, taking on himself your enmity, and giving them the land to enjoy? Think ye they expected such treatment as they got, or would have believed it if they had been told? Nevertheless, said I, they, after enjoying for a short time the land of others, are for a long time deprived by him of their own, shamefully expelled, not only vanquished, but betrayed by one another and sold. In truth, these too close connections with despots are not safe for republics. The Thessalians, again, think ye, said I, when he ejected their tyrants, and gave back Nicæa and Magnesia, they expected to have the decemvirate[1] which is now estab-

[1] Thessaly was anciently divided into four districts, each called a *tetras*, and this, as we learn from the third Philippic, was restored soon

lished? or that he who restored the meeting at Pylæ[1] would take away their revenues? Surely not. And yet these things have occurred, as all mankind may know. You behold Philip, I said, a dispenser of gifts and promises: pray, if you are wise, that you may never know him for a cheat and a deceiver. By Jupiter, I said, there are manifold contrivances for the guarding and defending of cities, as ramparts, walls, trenches, and the like: these are all made with hands, and require expense; but there is one common safeguard in the nature of prudent men, which is a good security for all, but especially for democracies against despots. What do I mean? Mistrust. Keep this, hold to this; preserve this only, and you can never be injured. What do ye desire? Freedom. Then see ye not that Philip's very titles are at variance therewith? Every king and despot is a foe to freedom, an antagonist to laws. Will ye not beware, I said, lest, seeking deliverance from war, you find a master?

They heard me with a tumult of approbation; and many other speeches they heard from the embassadors, both in my presence and afterward; yet none the more, as it appears, will they keep aloof from Philip's friendship and promises. And no wonder, that Messenians and certain Peloponnesians should act contrary to what their reason approves; but you,

after the termination of the Sacred war. The object of Philip in effecting this arrangement was, no doubt, to weaken the influence of the great Thessalian families by a division of power; otherwise the Pheræan tyranny might have been exchanged for an oligarchy powerful enough to be independent of Macedonia. The decemvirate here spoken of (if the text be correct) was a further contrivance to forward Philip's views; whether we adopt Leland's opinion, that each tetrarchy was governed by a council of ten, or Schaefer's, that each city was placed under ten governors. Jacobs understands the word *decemvirate* not to refer to any positive form of government, but generally to designate a *tyranny*, such as that which the Lacedæmonians used to introduce into conquered cities. So, for example, the Romans might have spoken of a decemvirate after the time of Appius. However this be, Philip seems to have contrived that the ruling body, whether in the tetrarchy or the decadarchy, should be his own creatures. Two of them, Eudicus and Simus, are particularly mentioned by Demosthenes as traitors.

[1] *Pylæ*, which signifies *gates*, was a name applied by the Greeks to divers passes, or defiles, but especially to the pass of *Thermopylæ*, which opened through the ridges of Mount Œta into the country of the Epicnemidian Locrians, and was so called from the hot sulphureous springs that gushed from the foot of the mountain.

who understand yourselves, and by us orators are told, how you are plotted against, how you are inclosed! you, I fear, to escape present exertion, will come to ruin ere you are aware. So doth the moment's ease and indulgence prevail over distant advantage.

As to your measures, you will in prudence, I presume, consult hereafter by yourselves. I will furnish you with such an answer as it becomes the assembly to decide upon.

[*Here the proposed answer was read.*]

It were just, men of Athens, to call the persons who brought those promises, on the faith whereof you concluded peace. For I should never have submitted to go as embassador, and you would certainly not have discontinued the war, had you supposed that Philip, on obtaining peace, would act thus; but the statements then made were very different. Ay, and others you should call. Whom? The men who declared—after the peace, when I had returned from my second mission, that for the oaths, when, perceiving your delusion, I gave warning, and protested, and opposed the abandonment of Thermopylæ and the Phocians—that I, being a water-drinker,[2] was naturally a churlish and morose fellow, that Philip, if he passed the straits, would do just as you desired, fortify Thespiæ and Platæa, humble the Thebans, cut through the Chersonese[3] at his own expense, and give you Oropus and Eubœa in exchange for Amphipolis. All these declarations on the hustings I am sure you remember, though you are not famous for remembering injuries. And, the most disgraceful thing of all, you voted in your confidence, that this same peace should descend to your posterity; so completely were you misled. Why mention I this now, and desire these men to be called? By the gods, I will tell you the truth frankly and without reserve. Not that I may fall a-wrangling, to provoke recrimination before you,[4]

[1] Whether this was moved by the orator himself, or formally read as his motion by the officer of the assembly, does not appear.

[2] It was Philocrates who said this. There were many jokes against Demosthenes as a water-drinker.

[3] This peninsula being exposed to incursions from Thrace, a plan was conceived of cutting through the isthmus from Pteleon to Leuce-Acte, to protect the Athenian settlements. See the Appendix to this volume, on the Thracian Chersonese.

[4] Similarly Auger: "Ce n'est pas pour m'attirer les invectives de mes anciens adversaires en les invectivant moi-même." Jacobs otherwise: *Nicht um durch Schmähungen mir auf gleiche Weise Gehör bei*

and afford my old adversaries a fresh pretext for getting more from Philip, nor for the purpose of idle garrulity. But I imagine that what Philip is doing will grieve you hereafter more than it does now. I see the thing progressing, and would that my surmises were false; but I doubt it is too near already. So when you are able no longer to disregard events, when, instead of hearing from me or others that these measures are against Athens, you all see it yourselves, and know it for certain, I expect you will be wrathful and exasperated. I fear then, as your embassadors have concealed the purpose for which they know they were corrupted, those who endeavor to repair what the others have lost may chance to encounter your resentment; for I see it is a practice with many to vent their anger, not upon the guilty, but on persons most in their power. While therefore the mischief is only coming and preparing, while we hear one another speak, I wish every man, though he knows it well, to be reminded, who it was[1] persuaded you to abandon Phocis and Thermopylæ, by the command of which Philip commands the road to Attica and Peloponnesus, and has brought it to this, that your deliberation must be, not about claims and interests abroad, but concerning the defense of your home and a war in Attica, which will grieve every citizen when it comes, and indeed it has commenced from that day. Had you not been then deceived, there would be nothing to distress the state. Philip would certainly never have prevailed at sea and come to Attica with a fleet, nor would he have marched with a land-force by Phocis and Thermopylæ: he must either have acted honorably, observing the peace and keeping quiet, or been immediately in a war similar to that which made him desire the peace. Enough has been said to awaken recollection. Grant, O ye gods, it be not all fully confirmed! I would have no man punished, though death he may deserve, to the damage and danger of the country.

Euch zu verschaffen. But I do not think that *ἐμαυτῷ λόγον ποιήσω* can bear the sense of *λόγου τύχοιμι*, "get a hearing for myself." And the orator's object is, not so much to sneer at the people by hinting that they are ready to hear abuse, as to deter his opponents from retaliation, or weaken its effect, by denouncing their opposition as corrupt. Leland saw the meaning: "Not that, by breaking out into invectives, I may expose myself to the like treatment."

[1] He means Æschines.

THE ORATION ON HALONNESUS.

THE ARGUMENT.

The occasion from which this Oration has received its title, was a dispute between Philip and the Athenians concerning the small island of Halonnesus, which lies off the coast of Thessaly, below the entrance to the Thermaic gulf. A group of small islands here, among which were also Sciathus, Scopelus, and Peparethus, belonged to Athens. Halonnesus, not long after the termination of the Phocian war, was taken by a pirate named Sostratus. He, having given annoyance to Philip, was expelled by that king from the island; but Philip, instead of restoring it to the Athenians, kept it in his own hands. At this the Athenians took umbrage, and probably thought that Halonnesus being so near to Eubœa, as well as to the other islands, it might be dangerous to leave it in Philip's possession. An embassy was sent to Macedonia, B.C. 343, to negotiate about this, and also various other subjects of dispute which at that time existed, such as Amphipolis, Potidæa, and the affairs of the Chersonese. At the head of the embassy was Hegesippus, a friend of Demosthenes. The claims made by the Athenians were deemed by Philip so preposterous, that he rejected them at once, and dismissed the envoys. Soon after, he sent an embassy to Athens, with a letter written by himself, in which he pointed out the extravagance of their demands, but expressed his willingness to make certain concessions. With respect to Halonnesus, he contended that it had become his by conquest, the Athenians having lost it, but offered to make them a present of the island. The letter was read in the assembly. All that we know of it is from the following speech, in which the orator comments on its various statements, and endeavors to show that Philip was in the wrong. The whole of the speech has not come down to us; for it appears to have contained a resolution, moved by the orator, by way of reply to Philip.

Most modern critics, following Libanius, have come to the opinion, that not Demosthenes, but Hegesippus, was the author of this Oration. The argument rests, not only upon the style of the Oration itself, which is beneath the general character of Demosthenes, but also on collateral circumstances, some of which will be noticed in the course of the notes. There is, indeed, good evidence that Demosthenes made a speech on the same question, and also that he took the same views upon it as Hegesippus, with whom he generally agreed in politics. This may account for the fact, that the only extant speech on the subject has been attributed to Demosthenes, when his own is lost.

Men of Athens, never can we who maintain your rights in this assembly be deterred by the complaints of Philip from advising you for the best. It would be monstrous, if our privilege on the hustings could be destroyed by his epistles. I will first, men of Athens, go through the articles of Philip's letter; and then I will answer the statements of the embassadors.

Philip begins about Halonnesus, saying, it belongs to him, but he gives it you. He denies your claim to restitution, as he neither took it from Athens, nor detains it from her. He addressed the like argument to us on our embassy to Macedon;[1] that he had won the island from pirates, and it was properly his own. It is not difficult to deprive him of this argument, by showing its fallacy. All pirates seizing places wrongfully, and fortifying themselves therein, make excursions to annoy other people. One who has chastised and vanquished the pirates surely can not urge with reason, that what they robbed the owners of becomes his property. If you grant this, then, supposing that pirates seized a place in Attica,[2] or Lemnos, or Imbrus, or Scyrus, and some persons dislodged the pirates, what is to prevent that place where the pirates were, and which belonged to us, from instantly becoming their property who chastised the pirates? Philip is not ignorant of the injustice of this plea; he knows it better than any one; but he expects you will be cajoled by a set of men, who, having undertaken to manage things here as he desires, are performing that service now. Moreover, he can not fail to see, that under either title, whichever you adopt, you will have the island, whether it be given, or given back.[3] Why then is it material to him, not to use

[1] This tends to prove that Hegesippus was the speaker. For he conducted the embassy referred to, and Demosthenes did not accompany him.

[2] The example put by the orator carries the argument no further, looking on it as a question of international law. The right of the new conqueror might depend on the length of time since the first conquest, or any other circumstances, showing an acquiescence therein by the original owner. If France now were to take Gibraltar from England, this would afford no *casus belli* for Spain against France. No doubt the general argument here rests on the piratical character of the first seizure. And yet a successful robber becomes a conqueror after a certain lapse of time.

[3] This passage is relied on by Weiske as a proof that Demosthenes made the speech; because it is an undoubted fact, that Demosthenes was ridiculed by Æschines and others for the distinction which he drew

the just phrase and restore it to you, but to use the unjust, and make it a present? His object is, not to charge it to you as an obligation, (for such an obligation would be ridiculous,) but to display to all Greece, that the Athenians are glad to receive their maritime dependencies from the Macedonian. This you must not allow, men of Athens.

When he says that he wishes to submit to arbitration on these questions, he only mocks you, in asking Athenians to refer a dispute with a man of Pella concerning their title to the islands. And besides, if your power, which delivered Greece, is unable to preserve your maritime dominion, and the judges to whom you refer, and with whom the award rests, preserve it for you, supposing Philip does not corrupt them; do you not confessedly, by taking such course, renounce all possessions on the continent, and demonstrate to the world that you will not contend with him for any, when even for possessions on the sea, where you consider your strength lies, you contend not by arms, but litigation?

Further, he says he has sent commissioners here to settle a judicial treaty,[1] to be in force not after ratification in your

between the *giving* and the *giving back* of the island. It proves very little, in my opinion. The argument here used must have occurred to any orator who spoke on the same side of the question, and was doubtless urged both by Hegesippus and Demosthenes. It is far from being a captious quibble. Daily it happens that men refuse to take as a gift what they claim as a right. But with nations this is a more important matter than with individuals: what is pride in the one case, is policy in the other. The point was first made by Philip himself. If he was so anxious about the distinction, the question naturally arose, why was he so? and the reason was not difficult to see.

[1] Arrangements (called σύμβολα) were sometimes made between different countries, for the administration of justice between their respective people. These arrangements would embrace certain general principles of jurisprudence, according to which any dispute between a native and an alien should be determined by the tribunal of either country; the complainant always seeking justice in the court of his adversary's domicile. Thus, supposing such a legal tariff to be agreed upon between Athens and Philip, an Athenian having a complaint against one of his subjects would prefer his suit in Macedonia, but the judge must decide the cause not entirely by Macedonian law, but in accordance with the articles of the compact; and conversely if a Macedonian were the plaintiff. For further information see title *Symbolon* in the Archæological Dictionary. The argument of the orator here is somewhat captious. How the proposed arrangement could affect the claim of Athens to Potidæa, does not appear. Philip's letter indeed might

court, as the law commands, but after reference to him; giving an appeal to himself from your judgment. He wishes to get this advantage of you, and procure an admission in the treaty, that you made no complaint for his aggression on Potidæa, but confirm the lawfulness both of his taking and holding it. Yet the Athenians who dwelt in Potidæa, while they were not at war, but in alliance with Philip, and notwithstanding the oath which Philip swore to the inhabitants of Potidæa, were deprived by him of their property. I say, he wishes to get your absolute acknowledgment, that you complain not of these wrongful acts, nor deem yourselves injured. That there is no need of a judicial treaty between Athens and Macedonia, past times may suffice to show. Neither Amyntas, Philip's father, nor any other kings of Macedon, ever had such a contract with our state; although the intercourse between us was formerly greater than it is now: for Macedonia was dependent on us, and paid us tribute,[1] and we then resorted to their ports, and they to ours, more frequently than now, and there were not the monthly sittings punctually held, as at present, for mercantile causes,[2] dispensing with the necessity of a law-treaty between such distant countries. Though nothing of the sort then existed, it was not requisite to make a treaty, so that people should sail from Macedonia to Athens for justice, or Athenians to Macedonia: we obtained redress by their laws and they by ours. Be assured, therefore, these articles are drawn for an admission that you have no further pretense for claiming Potidæa.

have thrown some light on the question. It is not improbable that Potidæa may have been named for the seat of Macedonian jurisdiction, as being more convenient for the trial of international causes than Pella, or any inland town. Athens then, agreeing to the arrangement, might be said to have acknowledged Philip's right.

[1] We have seen a similar boast in the third Olynthiac. But neither of the statements is to be understood as strictly true. While the kings of Macedonia possessed no towns on the coast, they (no doubt) submitted to the maritime supremacy of Athens, and paid harbor dues and tolls, which might be called tribute in loose language. Or it may be a mere oratorical flourish, for which the dependency of the maritime towns and the friendly relations between Athens and Macedonia afforded some color.

[2] The sittings here alluded to had not very long been established. They were held in the six winter months for the speedy trial of mercantile suits.

As to pirates, you ought jointly, he says, you and himself, to guard the sea against these depredators: but he really asks to be introduced by us to maritime power, for you to confess that you are unable even to keep guard of the sea without Philip, and further for the privilege to be granted him of sailing about and touching at the islands, under the pretense of watching pirates, so that he may corrupt the islanders and seduce them from you; and besides restoring to Thasus[1] by means of your commanders the exiles whom he harbored, he designs to gain over the other islands, by sending his agents to sail with your commanders on the joint protective service. And yet some persons deny that he wants the sea. But, without any want, he is equipping galleys, building docks, seeking to send out armaments and incur no trifling expense for maritime enterprises on which he sets no value.[2]

Do you think, then, Athenians, that Philip would ask you to make these concessions, if he did not despise you, and rely on the men whom he has chosen to be his friends here? men who are not ashamed to live for Philip and not for their country, and think they carry home his presents, when all at home they sell!

Concerning the peace, which the embassadors sent by him[3] permitted us to amend, because we made an amendment, which all mankind allow to be just, that each party should hold his own, he denies that he gave the permission, or that his embassadors so stated to you; doubtless, having been instructed by his friends here, that you remember not what is said before the people. This, however, of all things it is impossible for you to forget; since it was in the same assembly

[1] Thasus is an island off the coast of Thrace opposite the mouth of the Nestus. It was celebrated for its wine, and also for its marble quarries and mines. The gold mines on the adjacent continent belonged to the Thasians, when they were seized by Philip. The island, having been wrested from the Athenians in the Peloponnesian war, was afterward recovered, and at this time they kept a garrison in it.

[2] So Jacobs: *das ihm so gleichgültig ist.* And Reiske so explains it in his index. The irony is of course continued. Pabst, however, contends that this is wrong, and takes the more ordinary construction of the words: *worauf er den grossten Werth legt.*

[3] This Macedonian embassy preceded the one from Athens, which Hegesippus conducted, and which conveyed the Athenian proposals for the amendment of the treaty.

that his embassadors addressed you, and that the decree was drawn; and so it is not possible, as the words had just been spoken and the decree was instantly read, that you could have passed a resolution which misrepresented the embassadors. Wherefore, this charge in his letter is not against me, but against you, that you sent a decree in answer to something which you never heard. And the embassadors themselves, whom the decree misrepresented, when you read them your answer and invited them to partake your hospitality, ventured not to come forward and say, "You misrepresent us, Athenians, and make us to have stated what we never did," but went their way in silence.

I wish, men of Athens, (as Python,[1] who was then embassador, obtained credit with you for his address,) to remind you of the very words which he spoke. I am sure you will remember them; they were exactly like what Philip has now written. While he complained of us who decry Philip, he found fault with you also, that notwithstanding his intentions to serve you, his preference of your friendship to that of any of the Greeks, you oppose him yourselves, and listen to slanderers who ask him for money and abuse him: that by such language—when people report that he was calumniated, and you listened to it—his feelings are altered, finding himself mistrusted by those whom he had purposed to befriend. He therefore advised the public speakers not to disparage the peace, for it were better not to break peace; but if there were aught amiss in the articles, to rectify it, as Philip would concur in any resolution of yours. Should they persist in slander, without proposing any thing themselves, by which the peace might stand and Philip cease to be suspected, you ought not (he said) to attend to such persons.

You heard and approved these statements, and said that Python's argument was just. And just it was. But he made

[1] Python of Byzantium, who was an able speaker and diplomatist, and employed with great advantage by Philip in his negotiations with other states. Demosthenes seems to have been the only man who could cope with him, and boasts in his speech on the Crown, that on one occasion he reduced him to silence in the presence of a multitude of embassadors. Perhaps it was on the embassy here referred to; or it might be on that which gave occasion to the second Philippic. It is probable, but not certain, that this was the same Python who murdered Cotys, king of Thrace.

those statements, not that any articles might be canceled, which were advantageous to Philip, and for the insertion of which he had spent large sums of money, but at the suggestion of his instructors here, who thought no man would move any thing counter to the decree of Philocrates, which lost Amphipolis. I, men of Athens, have never dared to make an unlawful motion, but I made one contravening the decree of Philocrates, which was unlawful, as I will show. The decree of Philocrates, according to which you lost Amphipolis, ran counter to the former decrees, through which you acquired that territory. Therefore that decree of Philocrates was unlawful, and it was impossible for the author of a legal motion to move in accordance with an unlawful decree. But moving in accordance with those former decrees, which were lawful and preserved your territory, I moved a lawful resolution, and convicted Philip of deceiving you, and desiring, not to amend the peace, but to bring your honest counselors into discredit.

That he then allowed the amendment and now denies it, you all know. But he says Amphipolis belongs to him, because you declared it to be his, when you resolved he should keep what he held.[1] You did indeed pass that resolution, but not that Amphipolis should be his: for it is possible to hold the property of another, and all holders hold not their own. Many possess what belongs to others; therefore this sophistry of his is absurd. And he remembers the decree of Philocrates, but has forgotten the letter which he sent you when he was besieging Amphipolis, in which he acknowledged that Amphipolis was yours; for he promised after its reduction to restore it to Athens, as it belonged to her, and not to the holders. So they, it seems, who occupied Amphipolis before Philip's conquest, held the domain of Athenians, but, since Philip has conquered it, he holds not the domain of Athenians, but his own. Olynthus too, Apollonia and Pallene, belong to him, not by usurpation, but in his own right. Think you he studies in all his dispatches to you, to show himself by word and deed an observer of what

[1] The treaty had for its basis the principle of the *uti possidetis*, to adopt the expression of modern diplomacy. According to the true construction of this, Amphipolis would belong to Philip, and the reasoning of the orator is unsound. But no doubt, in the whole affair of Amphipolis, and the peace also, Philip overreached the Athenians.

the world calls justice, or rather has he set it at defiance, when a land, which the Greeks and the Persian monarch have voted and acknowledged to be yours, he asserts to be not yours, but his own?

As to the other amendment which you made in the articles, that the Greeks not included in the peace should be free and independent, and, if any one attacked them, should be succored by all parties to the treaty, you deeming it equitable and righteous, that not only we and our allies, and Philip and his allies, should enjoy the peace, while those who were neither our allies nor Philip's were exposed, and might be oppressed by the powerful, but that they also should have security by your peace, and we should lay down our arms and enjoy peace in reality; although he confesses in the letter, as you hear, that this amendment is just, and that he allows it, he has taken their town from the Pheræans and put a garrison in the citadel, doubtless to make them independent; he marches against Ambracia,[1] bursts into three Cassopian[2] cities, Pandosia, Bucheta, and Elatea, colonies of Elis, after ravaging their territories, and gives them in vassalage to his kinsman Alexander. Proofs how much he desires the freedom and independence of Greece!

Respecting his continual promises of doing you important service, he says that I misrepresent and slander him to the Greeks; for he never promised you any thing. So impudent is this man, who has written in a letter, which is now in the senate-house, (when he declared he would silence us his opponents if the peace were made,) that he would confer on you such an obligation as, were he sure of the peace, he would instantly communicate; implying that these favors, intended for us in the event of peace, were ready and pro-

[1] Philip's expedition against Ambracia followed the campaign in Epirus, which took place in B.C. 343. His designs against Ambracia were defeated by the exertions of the Athenians, who formed a league against him, and sent troops to assist the Ambracians. Demosthenes in the third Philippic speaks of an embassy, in which both himself and Hegesippus were engaged, which had the effect of stopping Philip's invasion of Ambracia and Peloponnesus.

[2] Cassopia is a district of Epirus, which Philip invaded B.C. 343, and added to the kingdom of Alexander his brother-in-law, between whom and Philip's uncle, Arymbas, the province of Epirus was divided. The Cassopian Elatea must not be confounded with the Phocian.

vided. After the peace was made, the good things intended for us all vanished, and among the Greeks has been wrought such ruin as you have seen. In his present letter he promises you, that if you will trust his friends and advocates, and punish us who slander him to the people, he will greatly serve you. Such, however, will be the character of his service; he will not return you your own, for he claims it himself; nor will his grants be in this part of the world, for fear of offending the Greeks: but I suppose some other land and locality will be found, where his gifts may take effect.

As to the places which he has taken during the peace, taken from you in contempt of the treaty and violation of its terms, since he has nothing to urge, but stands convicted of injustice, he offers to submit to a fair and impartial tribunal, on a question which, of all others, requires no arbitration, for the number of days determines it. We all know the month and the day when the peace was concluded. As surely do we know in what month and on what day Serrium, Ergisce, and the Sacred Mount[1] were taken. These transactions are not so obscure; they need no trial; it is notorious to all, which month was the earlier, that in which the peace was signed, or that in which the places were captured.

He says also that he has returned all our prisoners who were taken in war. Yet in the case of that Carystian,[2] the friend of our state, for whom you sent three embassies to demand his liberty, Philip was so anxious to oblige you that he killed the man, and would not even suffer him to be taken up for burial.

It is worth while to examine what he writes to you about

[1] These were places in Thrace, taken by Philip from Cersobleptes.

[2] Carystus is a town of Eubœa. The Proxenus, or public friend of a foreign state, was one who protected its interests in his own country, performing duties not unlike that of a modern consul. A relation of mutual hospitality subsisted (as the word imports) between him and the citizens of the friendly state; and he was expected to entertain the embassadors, or any persons who came on public business. (See title *Hospitium*, Arch. Dict.) We have no word by which Proxenus can be translated; nor any indeed which expresses the double relation of *host* and *guest*, as ξένος and *hospes* do. In German we have *Staatsgastfreund*.

the Chersonese, and likewise to ascertain what his conduct is. All the district beyond Agora,[1] as if it were his own, and belonged not to you, he has given into the possession of Apollonides the Cardian. Yet the boundary of the Chersonese is not Agora, but the altar of Terminal Jupiter, which is between Pteleum and Leuce-Acte, where the canal was to be cut through the Chersonese, as the inscription on the altar of Terminal Jupiter shows. Mark the words:—

> This holy altar built by native hands,
> 'Twixt Pteleum and Chalky Beach it stands,
> Stands for the limit of their just domains,
> The guardian He who in Olympus reigns.

This territory, large as most of you know it to be, he claims: part he enjoys himself, part he has given to others, and so he reduces all your property into his possession. And not only does he appropriate the country beyond Agora, but also with reference to the Cardians, who dwell on this side Agora, he writes in his present letter, that if you have any difference with the Cardians, (who dwell in your dominions,) you must refer it to arbitration. They have a difference with you; see if it is about a small matter. They say, the land they inhabit belongs to them, not to you; that yours are mere occupations in a foreign country, theirs are possessions in their own; and that your fellow-citizen, Callippus of Pæania,[2] alleged this in a decree. And here they are right; he did so allege, and, on my indicting him for an unlawful measure, you acquitted him; and thus he has caused your title to the land to be contested. But if you could bring yourselves to refer this dispute with the Cardians, whether the land be yours or theirs, why should not the other people of the Chersonese be

[1] This was a place in the Chersonese, the whole of which, except Cardia, belonged to Athens. The orator contends, that the boundary of the Chersonese was a line drawn across the isthmus from Pteleum to Leuce-Acte, the latter of which places was probably named from the white cliffs on the beach. In the centre of this line was erected the altar, which anciently separated the boundaries of those towns. Agora was within the line. For further information concerning the Chersonese, see the following oration, and Appendix III.

[2] Pæania is one of the townships, δῆμοι, into which Attica was divided. Libanius says, it was Hegesippus who preferred this indictment against Callippus.

dealt with on the same principle? His treatment of you is so insolent, that he says, if the Cardians will not submit to arbitration, he will compel them, as if you were unable even to compel Cardians to do you justice. As you are unable, he says he will himself compel them. Don't you really find him a great benefactor? And some men have declared this epistle to be well written; men who are far more deserving of your detestation than Philip. He, by constant opposition to you, acquires honor and signal advantage for himself: Athenians who exhibit zeal, not for their country, but for Philip, are wretches that ought to be exterminated by you, if you carry your brains in your temples, and not trodden down in your heels.[1]

It now remains, that to this well-drawn epistle and the speeches of the embassadors I propose an answer, which in my opinion is just and expedient for Athens.

[1] Libanius censures the coarseness of this expression, and contends that Demosthenes never could have used it. Weiske thinks differently, and quotes the examples of coarse language adduced against his rival by Æschines. (Or. cont. Ctes.) Libanius, however, thinks that the whole style of this oration is beneath the Demosthenic character. The reader must form his own opinion. It has been remarked, both by Photius and Dr. Johnson, that there may be much difference between the best and the worst productions of an author. Yet there is in most good authors a general character, by which those who are familiar with them may form a judgment of what is genuine.

THE ORATION ON THE CHERSONESE.

THE ARGUMENT.

The Athenians had sent a body of citizens, commanded by Diopithes, to receive allotments of land in the Chersonese, and at the same time to protect the interests of Athens by acting as an army of observation. They soon fell into disputes with the Cardians about the limits of their territory. Philip, who at this time was engaged in a Thracian war, sent assistance to the Cardians; but Diopithes, having collected a troop of mercenaries, kept the field successfully, and, not content with acting on the defensive, carried the war into Thrace, assisted the enemies of Philip, and wrested from him some of his conquests. Philip, who, as we have seen in the last oration, had written before to the Athenians on the subject of Cardia, now wrote them a letter complaining of the conduct of Diopithes, charging them with an infringement of the peace. This letter arrived early in the summer of the year B.C. 342, and an assembly was immediately called to consider what measures should be taken. The Macedonian party were vehement in denouncing Diopithes, and urging his recall. Demosthenes, seeing that Athens, though nominally at peace with Philip, was really defending herself against his aggressions, rose to justify Diopithes, insisted on the necessity, which he had so strongly urged in the first Philippic, of keeping a permanent force on the northern coast, and contended that the army of Diopithes should rather be reinforced, than recalled at a time when its presence was peculiarly necessary. He again warns his countrymen of impending danger, and points out the measures which, as men of spirit and prudence, they ought to pursue.

This oration is full of good sense and manly eloquence. It had the success which it deserved. Diopithes was continued in his command; and the exertions of Athens in the next few years had the effect of preserving the Chersonese and the Bosphorus.

Diopithes was father to Menander, the celebrated comic poet, whose plays have been copied by Terence.

For further information on the subject of the Chersonese, see Appendix III. to this volume.

It were just, men of Athens, that the orators in your assembly should make no speeches to gratify either friendship or malice, but every one declare what he considers for the best, especially when you are deliberating on public measures of importance. However, since there are persons who are impelled to address you from factious motives, or others which

I can not name, it becomes you, Athenians, the majority, laying all else aside, to determine and to do what you find beneficial to the state. The serious question here is, the position of the Chersonese, and the campaign in Thrace, which Philip has now for upward of ten months been carrying on; yet most of the speeches have been about Diopithes, his conduct and designs. It seems to me, that on a charge against any of these men, whom according to the laws you may punish when you please, it is in your option either to proceed immediately or at a later time, and needless for me, or for any one, to argue the point strongly: but for the defense of our dominions, which Philip, our standing enemy, and now in great force about the Hellespont, is making haste to conquer, and, if we are once too late, we shall never recover, our duty is to consult and prepare with the utmost speed, and not for clamors and charges about other matters to run off from this.

I wonder at many things which are commonly said here, but I have been particularly surprised, Athenians, at what I lately heard a man declare in the Council,[1] that a statesman's advice should be, either to make war decidedly, or to observe the peace. True; if Philip keeps quiet, neither holding any of our territories contrary to the treaty, nor packing a world of enemies against us, there is nothing to say: peace we must absolutely observe, and I see every readiness on your part. But if the conditions of the peace, which we swore to, are recorded and open to inspection; if it appears that from the beginning, (before Diopithes and the settlers,[2] who are accused as authors of the war, ever sailed from Athens,) Philip has robbed us of divers territories, of which you still complain in these unrepealed resolutions, and has been all along incessantly gathering the spoil of other nations, Greek and barbarian, for the materials of an attack upon you, what mean they by saying we must have war or

[1] The Council or Senate of Five Hundred, of which Demosthenes became a member when he was thirty-six years of age.

[2] The settlers called κληροῦχοι were citizens sent out to receive parcels of land in some country dependent on Athens, but who still retained rights of Athenian citizenship, whether or not they permanently resided abroad. The word signifies "allotment-holders," or "allottees of lands." Jacobs: *die Ansiedler.*

peace? We have no choice in the matter: there remains but one most just and necessary course, which these men purposely overlook. What is it? To defend ourselves against an aggressor. Unless indeed they mean, that, so long as Philip keeps aloof from Attica and Piræus, he neither wrongs you nor commits hostility.[1] But if they put our rights on this principle, and so define the peace, besides that the argument is iniquitous, monstrous, and perilous for Athens, as I imagine is evident to all, it happens also to be inconsistent with their complaint against Diopithes. For why, I wonder, should we give Philip license to do what he pleases, provided he abstain from Attica, while Diopithes is not suffered even to assist the Thracians, without our saying that he makes war? Here, it will be granted, they are shown in the wrong: but the mercenaries make sad work ravaging the Hellespontine coast, and Diopithes has no right to detain vessels, and we must not allow him! Well; be it so! I am content. Yet I think, if they really give this counsel in good faith, as their object is to disband a force in your service, while they denounce the general who maintains it, they ought likewise to show that Philip's army will be disbanded if you follow their advice. Otherwise, observe, they just bring the country into the same way, through which all our past measures have miscarried.[2] For you surely know, that by nothing in the world has Philip beaten us so much, as by being earlier in his operations. He with an army always attending him, knowing his own designs, pounces on whom he pleases in a moment:[3] we, when we hear that something

[1] Philip sought to conquer Athens in Thrace, as Napoleon to conquer England in Egypt or Portugal. And we shall find that precisely the same arguments were used in our Parliament, to show the necessity of continuing the French war, which Demosthenes here urges to alarm the Athenians against Philip.

[2] I follow the common reading ἀπόλωλεν. The explanation which Schaefer gives of his own reading does not satisfy me.

[3] More closely, "is upon the enemy, whom he pleases to attack, in a moment." Francis: "surprises upon the instant whom he thinks proper to destroy;" which is not bad, except for the last two words. Leland is too wide: "can in a moment strike the blow where he pleases." Jacobs is good: "*steht augenblicklich Jedem gegenüber, den er angreifen will.* Compare Virgil, Georgic III.

Hosti
Ante expectatem positis stat in agmine castris.

is going on, begin to bustle and prepare. Methinks the result is, that he very quietly secures what he goes for; we arrive too late, and have incurred all the expense for nothing. Our enmity and our hostile intention we manifest, and get the disgrace of missing the time for action.

Then be sure, Athenians, now, that all the rest is talk and pretense, the real aim and contrivance is, that while you remain at home, and the country has no force abroad, Philip may accomplish what he pleases without interruption. First, consider what is actually going on. Philip is staying with a large army in Thrace, and sending for reinforcements, as eyewitnesses report, from Macedonia and Thessaly. Now, should he wait for the trade-winds, and then march to the siege of Byzantium,[1] think ye the Byzantines would persist in their present folly, and would not invite you and implore your assistance? I don't believe it. No; they will receive any people, even those they distrust more than us, sooner than surrender their city to Philip; unless indeed he is beforehand with them and captures it. If then we are unable to sail northward, and there be no help at hand, nothing can prevent their destruction. Well! the men are infatuated and besotted. Very likely; yet they must be rescued for all that, because it is good for Athens. And this also is not clear to us, that he will not attack the Chersonese: nay, if we may judge from the letter which he sent us, he says he will chastise the people in the Chersonese. Then if the present army be kept on foot, it will be able to defend that country, and attack some of Philip's dominions; but if it be once disbanded, what shall we do, if he march against the Chersonese? Try Diopithes, I suppose. And how will our affairs be bettered? But we shall send succor from Athens. And suppose the winds prevent us? Oh, but he won't come! And who will insure that? Do you mark and consider, men of Athens, the approaching season of the year, against which certain persons desire to get the Hellespont clear of you, and deliver it up to Philip? Suppose he should leave Thrace,

[1] Athens and Byzantium had not been on good terms since the Social war. Even at this period the Byzantines looked with more suspicion upon the Athenians than on Philip. Yet less than a year elapsed before the predictions of Demosthenes were fulfilled. Athens was in alliance with Byzantium, and defending her successfully against Philip.

and without going near Chersonesus or Byzantium, (I beg you also to consider this,) he should invade Chalcis or Megara, as he lately did Oreus,[1] think you it is better to resist him here and suffer the war to approach Attica, or to find employment for him yonder? I think the last.

With such facts and arguments before you, so far from disparaging and seeking to disband this army, which Diopithes is endeavoring to organize for Athens, you ought yourselves to provide an additional one, to support him with money and other friendly co-operation. For if Philip were asked, "Which would you prefer, that these soldiers of Diopithes, whatever be their character, (I dispute not about that,) should thrive and have credit at Athens, and be reinforced with the assistance of the state, or that they should be dispersed and destroyed at the instance of calumniators and accusers?"—I think he would say, the latter. And what Philip would pray to the gods for, certain persons among us are bringing about; and after this you ask how the state is ruined!

I wish, therefore, to examine with freedom our present affairs, to consider how we are dealing with them, and what we are ourselves about. We like not to contribute money, we dare not take the field, we can not abstain from the public funds, we neither give supplies to Diopithes nor approve what he finds for himself, but grumble and inquire how he got them, and what he intends to do, and the like; and yet, though thus disposed, we are not willing to mind our own business, but with our mouths applaud those who speak worthily of the state, while in action we co-operate with their adversaries. You like always to ask the speaker—What must we do? I will ask you this—What must I say? For if you will neither contribute, nor take the field, nor abstain from the public funds, nor give supplies to Diopithes, nor let alone what he finds for himself, nor be content to mind your own business, I have nothing to say. If to these men, so prompt to accuse and calumniate, you already give such a license, as to hear them complain by anticipation of projects which they impute to Diopithes, what can one say?

[1] Oreus of Eubœa was betrayed to Philip not long before this time, as explained in the third Philippic. The designs of Philip on Megara were baffled.

But the probable effect of such conduct some of you should hear. I will speak frankly; indeed, I could not speak otherwise. All the generals who have ever sailed from Athens, (or let me suffer any penalty,) take money from Chians, from Erythræans[1], from whom they severally can, I mean from the people who dwell in Asia. Those who have one or two galleys take less, those who have a greater fleet, more. And the givers give not, either the small or the larger sums, for nothing, (they are not so mad,) but by way of bargain, that the merchants who leave their harbors may not be wronged or plundered, that their vessels may be convoyed, or the like. They say they give benevolences:[2] that is the name of the presents. And so Diopithes, having an army, is well aware that all these people will give money: for how else do you suppose, that a man who has received nothing from you, and has nothing of his own to pay withal, can maintain his troops? From the skies? Impossible. He goes on with what he collects, begs, or borrows. Therefore they, who accuse him before you, in effect warn all people to give him nothing, as being sure to be punished for his intentions, much more for his acts, either as principal or auxiliary. Hence their clamors—he is preparing a siege! he is giving up the Greeks! So concerned are many of these persons for the Asiatic Greeks: perhaps quicker to feel for strangers than for their country. And this is the meaning of our sending another general to the Hellespont.[3] Why, if Diopithes commits outrage and detains vessels, a small, very small summons, men of Athens, can stop it all; and the laws prescribe this, to impeach the guilty parties, but not to watch them ourselves at a great expense and with a large navy, for that were the extreme of madness. Against our enemies, whom we can not bring under the laws, it is right

[1] Erythræ is a city of Asia Minor.

[2] It is singular that the same name should be given so many centuries after to the illegal contributions which were extorted by some of our English kings from their subjects, under the pretense of their being voluntary gifts. Edward the Fourth and Henry the Seventh were most oppressive in this way.

[3] The argument is—This is what my opponents mean by recommending, that another general should be sent to supersede and send back Diopithes. Such a course is wholly unnecessary, for you can summon him home by an order of state.

and needful to maintain troops, and dispatch a fleet, and contribute money; but against ourselves a decree, an impeachment, the state-galley,[1] are sufficient. Thus would men of discretion act; malignant and mischievous politicians would proceed as these do. And that certain of these men are thus disposed, bad though it be, is not the worst. For you of the assembly are so minded now, that if any one comes forward and says, that Diopithes is the author of all your misfortunes, or Chares, or Aristophon, or what citizen he likes to name, you instantly assent and shout approbation; but if one rises to speak the truth—Athenians, you are trifling; of all these misfortunes and troubles Philip is the cause; had he only kept quiet, the state would have had no trouble—you are unable to contradict these statements, yet, methinks, you are annoyed, and feel as if something were lost. The reason is—and pray allow me, when I speak for the best, to speak freely—certain statesmen have long since got you to be severe and terrible in the assemblies, in warlike preparations feeble and contemptible. If the party blamed be one whom you are certain to find within your reach, you say ay, and are content: but if one be accused, whom you can not punish without vanquishing him by arms, you appear confounded and pained at the exposure. It ought, Athenians, to have been the reverse; your statesmen should have accustomed you to be mild and merciful in the assembly, since there your dealings are with citizens and allies; in warlike preparations they should have shown you to be terrible and severe, since in them the contest is with adversaries and foes. But by excessive coaxing and humoring they have brought you to such a condition, that in the assembly you give yourselves airs and are flattered at hearing nothing but compliments, while in your measures and proceedings you are putting every thing to hazard.

By Jupiter! suppose the Greeks called you to account for the opportunities which you have indolently lost, and asked you, saying, "Men of Athens, you send us embassadors on every occasion, and assert that Philip is plotting against us

[1] The Paralus, or the Salaminia, which were employed for state purposes, and sometimes to fetch home criminals to be tried or punished. Thus the Salaminia was dispatched to bring Alcibiades back from Sicily.

and all the Greeks, and that we should take precautions against the man, and more to the same effect:" (we must admit and acknowledge it; for so we do:) "and yet, O ye wretchedest of mankind, though Philip has been ten months away, and by illness and winter and wars prevented from returning home, you have neither liberated Eubœa, nor recovered any of your dominions. He, on the contrary, while you were staying at home, at leisure, in health, (if men so acting may be called in health,) established two rulers in Eubœa, one like a hostile fortress opposite Attica, one threatening Sciathus;[1] and these nuisances you have never got rid of; not even this would ye attempt; you have submitted, left the road open to him clearly, and made it manifest that, if he died a hundred times, you would stir never a step the more. Then wherefore send embassies and make accusations and give us trouble?" If they asked this, what could we answer or say, men of Athens? I really can not tell.

There are some persons indeed, who imagine they confute the speaker by asking, What must we do? I can give them a perfectly just and true answer—Do not what you are now doing: however, I will enter into more full detail; and I trust they will be as ready to act as to interrogate. First, men of Athens, you must be satisfied in your minds that Philip is at war with the republic, and has broken the peace; (pray cease reproaching one another about this;) that he is ill-disposed and hostile to all Athens, to her very ground, and (I may say) to all her inhabitants, even those who think they oblige him most. Or let them look at Euthycrates and Lasthenes the Olynthians,[2] who fancied themselves on the most friendly footing with him, but, since they betrayed their country, are sunk to the most abject state. But there is nothing that his wars and his schemes are directed against so

[1] Clitarchus was established in Eretria, which is opposite the coast of Athens; Philistides in Oreus, which is in the north of Eubœa. The island of Sciathus is a little above Eubœa, and off the Magnesian coast of Thessaly. As the group of islands, of which Sciathus was one, belonged to Athens, Oreus was a dangerous position to be occupied by an enemy.

[2] They betrayed Olynthus to Philip, and went to reside afterward at his court. But they were universally scouted as traitors, and on their complaining to Philip, he said, the Macedonians were a plain-spoken people, who called a spade a spade.

much, as our constitution; nothing in the world is he so earnest to destroy. And this policy is in some sort natural for him. He knows perfectly, that even if he conquer every thing else, he can hold nothing secure, while your democracy subsists; but on the occurrence of any reverse, (and many may happen to a man,) all who are now under constraint will come and seek refuge with you. For you are not inclined yourselves to encroach and usurp dominion; you are famous for checking the usurper or depriving him of his conquest; ever ready to molest the aspirants for empire, and vindicate the liberties of all people. He likes not that a free spirit should proceed from Athens, to watch the moments of his peril: far otherwise; nor is his reasoning weak or idle. First then, you must assume him for this reason to be an irreconcilable enemy of our constitution and democracy: without such conviction upon your minds, you will have no zeal for public duty. Secondly, you must be assured that all his operations and contrivances are planned against our country, and, wherever he is resisted, the resistance will be for our benefit. None of you surely is so foolish, as to suppose that Philip covets those miseries[1] in Thrace, (for what else can one call Drongilus, and Cabyle, and Mastira, and the places which he is taking and conquering now?) and to get them endures toils and winters and the extreme of danger, but covets not the Athenian harbors, and docks, and galleys, and silver mines,[2] and revenues of such value; and that he will suffer you to keep them, while for the sake of the barley and millet in Thracian caverns he winters in the midst of horrors.[3] Impossible. The object of that and every other enterprise is to become master here. What then is the duty of wise men? With these assurances and convictions, to lay aside an indolence which is becoming outrageous and incurable, to pay contributions and to call upon your allies,

[1] I thought it better to adhere to the original, which explains itself, than to use any such expression as "paltry villages," or "bicoques," or *elenden Besitzthümern.* Jacobs has the simple *Armseligkeiten.*

[2] The mines of Laurium in Attica. See Appendix II.

[3] The original βαράθρῳ signifies a pit, into which condemned criminals were thrown at Athens. It is pretty much the same as if we were to speak of the black hole: and the horrors of Thrace would convey to an Athenian the same sort of idea as the horrors of Siberia to an Englishman.

see to and provide for the continuance of the present force, that, as Philip has a power ready to injure and enslave all the Greeks, so you may have one ready to save and to succor all. It is not possible with hasty levies to perform any effective service. You must have an army on foot, provide maintenance for it, and paymasters and commissaries, so ordering it that the strictest care shall be taken of your funds, and demand from those officers an account of the expenditure, from your general an account of the campaign. If ye so act and so resolve in earnest, you will compel Philip to observe a just peace and abide in his own country, (the greatest of all blessings,) or you will fight him on equal terms.

It may be thought, and truly enough, that these are affairs of great expense and toil and trouble: yet only consider what the consequences to us must be, if we decline these measures, and you will find it is our interest to perform our duties cheerfully. Suppose some god would be your surety—for certainly no mortal could guarantee such an event—that, notwithstanding you kept quiet and abandoned every thing, Philip would not attack you at last, yet, by Jupiter and all the gods, it were disgraceful, unworthy of yourselves, of the character of Athens and the deeds of your ancestors, for the sake of selfish ease to abandon the rest of Greece to servitude. For my own part, I would rather die than have given such counsel; though, if another man advises it, and you are satisfied, well and good; make no resistance, abandon all. If however no man holds this opinion, if, on the contrary, we all foresee, that the more we let Philip conquer the more ruthless and powerful an enemy we shall find him, what subterfuge remains? what excuse for delay? Or when, O Athenians, shall we be willing to perform our duty? Peradventure, when there is some necessity. But what may be called the necessity of freemen, is not only come, but past long ago: and surely you must deprecate that of slaves. What is the difference? To a freeman, the greatest necessity is shame for his proceedings; I know not what greater you can suggest: to a slave, stripes and bodily chastisement; abominable things! too shocking to mention!

I would gladly enter into every particular, and show how certain politicians abuse you; but I confine myself to one.

When any question about Philip arises, people start up and cry, What a blessing it is to be at peace! what a burden to maintain a large army! certain persons wish to plunder our treasury!—and more to the same effect; by which they amuse you, and leave him at leisure to do what he pleases. The result is, to you, Athenians, ease and idleness for the present, which, I fear, you may hereafter think dearly purchased; to these men, popularity and payment for their speeches. Methinks it is not you that need persuading to peace, who sit here pacifically disposed; but the person who commits hostilities: let him be persuaded, and all is ready on your part. Burdensome we should deem, not what we expend for our deliverance, but what we shall suffer in case of our refusal to do so. Plunder of the treasury should be prevented by a plan for its safe keeping, not by abandonment of our interests. But this very thing makes me indignant, that some of you, Athenians, are grieved at the thought of your treasury being robbed, though it depends on yourselves to keep it safe and to chastise the peculator, yet are not grieved at Philip's conduct, seizing thus successively on every country in Greece, and seizing them for his designs upon you.

What then is the reason, men of Athens, that while Philip is thus openly in arms, committing aggressions, capturing cities, none of these persons ever say that he is making war; but they denounce as authors of the war, whoever advises you to oppose him and prevent these losses? I will explain. Their desire is, that any anger, which may be naturally excited by your sufferings in the war, may be turned upon your honest counselors, so that you may try them instead of resisting Philip, and they themselves be accusers instead of paying the penalty of their conduct. Such is the meaning of their assertion, that there is a war-party among you; and such is the object of this present debate. I am indeed sure, that, before any Athenian moved a declaration of war, Philip had taken many of our possessions, and recently sent succor to Cardia. If however we choose to assume that he is not at war with us, it were extreme folly in him to convince us of our mistake. But when he marches to attack us, what shall we say? He will assure us that he is not making war, as he assured the people of Oreus when his troops were in their country, as he assured the Pheræans before he assaulted their walls, and the Olynthians at first, until he was actually in their territories with his army. Shall we then declare, that men who bid us defend ourselves make war? If so, we must be slaves: nothing else remains, if we neither resist nor are suffered to be at peace. And remember, you have more at stake than other people: Philip seeks not to subdue, but to extirpate our city. He knows for certain, you will not submit to servitude; you could not if you would, being accustomed to empire; and if you get the opportunity, you will be able to give him more annoyance than all the rest of the world.

You must therefore be convinced that this is a struggle for existence: these men who have sold themselves to Philip you must execrate and cudgel to death; for it is impossible, impossible to overcome your enemies abroad, until you have punished your enemies (his ministers) at home. They will be the stumbling-blocks that prevent your reaching the others.[1] Why do you suppose Philip now insults you, (for to this, in my opinion, his conduct amounts,) and while to other people, though he deceives them, he at least renders services, he is already threatening you? For example, the Thessalians by many benefits he seduced into their present servitude: how he cheated the wretched Olynthians, first giving them Potidæa and divers other things, no man can describe: now he is enticing the Thebans by giving up to them Bœotia, and delivering them from a toilsome and vexatious war. Thus did each of these people grasp a certain advantage, but some of them have suffered what all the world know, others will suffer what may hereafter befall them. From you—all that has been taken I recount not: but in the very making of the peace, how have you been abused! how despoiled! Of Phocis, Thermopylæ, places in Thrace, Doriscus, Serrium, Cersobleptes himself! Does he not now possess the city of Cardia and avow it? Wherefore, I say, deals he thus with

[1] The word πρόβολος is explained by Wolf: "impedimentum, sive sit scopulus in mari, sive vallum in terrâ." Leland translates the sentence: "else, while we strike on these, as so many obstacles, our enemies must necessarily prove superior to us." This is both vague and weak. Auger avoids the simile. Francis introduces "quicksands," Pabst: *es ist unvermeidlich, dass Ihr an sie wie an Klippen anstosst und dadurch aufgehalten werdet.* Jacobs: *immer wird durch sie, wie durch Felsen des Anstosses, Euer Fortgang gehemmt werden.*

other people, and not in the same manner with you? Because yours is the only state in which a privilege is allowed of speaking for the enemy, and an individual taking a bribe may safely address the assembly, though you have been robbed of your dominions. It was not safe at Olynthus to be Philip's advocate unless the Olynthian commonalty had shared the advantage by possession of Potidæa: it was not safe in Thessaly to be Philip's advocate, unless the people of Thessaly had shared the advantage, by Philip's expelling their tyrants and restoring the Pylæan synod: it was not safe in Thebes, until he gave up Bœotia to them and destroyed the Phocians. Yet at Athens, though Philip has deprived you of Amphipolis and the Cardian territory, nay, is even making Eubœa a fortress to curb us, and advancing to attack Byzantium,[1] it is safe to speak on Philip's behalf. Therefore of these men, some, from being poor, have become rapidly rich, from nameless and obscure, have become honored and distinguished; you have done the reverse, fallen from honor to obscurity, from wealth to poverty; for I deem the riches of a state, allies, confidence, attachment, of all which you are destitute. And from your neglecting these matters and suffering them to be lost, Philip has grown prosperous and mighty, formidable to all the Greeks and barbarians, while you are abject and forlorn, magnificent in the abundance of your market, but in provision for actual need ridiculous. I observe however, that some of our orators take different thought for you and for themselves. You, they say, should be quiet even under injustice; they can not live in quiet among you themselves, though no man injures them.

Then some one steps forward and says, "Why, you won't move any resolution, or run any risk;[2] you are cowardly and faint-hearted." Let me say this: bold, brutal, and impudent I neither am nor wish to be; yet, methinks, I possess far more courage than your headstrong politicians. For a man who, neglecting the interest of the state, tries, confiscates,

[1] Not that Philip had commenced any operations against Byzantium, but from his march in that direction Demosthenes rightly conjectured that he had designs thereupon.

[2] By subjecting yourself to a γραφὴ παρανόμων, "indictment for having proposed an illegal decree;" and also to the general responsibility which a statesman incurred by advising important measures.

bribes, accuses, does not act from any courage, Athenians; the popularity of his speeches and his measures serves for a pledge of security, and he is bold without danger. But one who acting for the best frequently opposes your wishes, who never speaks to flatter but always to benefit you, and adopts a line of policy in which more depends on fortune than on calculations, while he makes himself responsible to you for both, this is a courageous man, ay, and a useful citizen is he; not they who for ephemeral pleasure have thrown away the main resources of the country; whom I am so far from emulating or esteeming as worthy citizens of Athens, that if I were asked to declare, what service I had done the state, although, ye men of Athens, I could mention services as ship-captain and choir-master, payment of contributions, ransom of prisoners, and similar acts of liberality, I would mention none of them; I would say, that I espouse a different course of politics from these, that although I might perhaps, like others, accuse and bribe and confiscate and do every thing which these men do, I have never engaged myself in such a task, never been induced either by avarice or ambition; I continue to offer counsel, by which I sink below others in your regard; but you, if you followed it, would be exalted. So perhaps might one speak without offense. I consider it not the part of an honest citizen, to devise measures by which I shall speedily become the first among you, and you the last among nations: with the measures of good citizens the advancement of their country should keep pace: their counsel should still be the salutary, rather than the agreeable; to the latter will nature herself incline; to the former a good citizen must direct by argument and instruction.

I have ere now heard an objection of this kind, that true it is I always advise for the best, yet my services are only words, and you want deeds and something practical. Upon which I will tell you my sentiments without reserve. I do not think a counselor has any other business but to give the best advice: and that this is so, I can easily demonstrate. You are aware doubtless, that the brave Timotheus once harangued the people, urging them to send troops and save the Eubœans, when the Thebans were attempting their conquest; and to this effect he spake:—"What? do you deliberate," said he, "when you have Thebans in the island, how to deal with them, how to proceed? Will you not cover the sea, Athenians, with your galleys? Will you not start up and march to Piræus? will you not launch your vessels?" Thus Timotheus spake and you acted,[1] and through both together success was obtained. But had his advice been ever so good, as it was, and you shrunk from exertion and disregarded it, would any of those results have accrued to Athens? Impossible. Then do likewise in regard to my counsels or any other man's; for action look to yourselves, to the orator for the best instruction in his power.

I will sum up my advice, and quit the platform. I say, you must contribute money, maintain the existing troops, rectifying what abuses you may discover, but not on the first accusation disbanding the force. Send out embassadors every where, to instruct, to warn, to effect what they can for Athens. Yet further I say, punish your corrupt statesmen, execrate them at all times and places, to prove that men of virtue and honorable conduct have consulted wisely both for others and themselves. If you thus attend to your affairs, and cease entirely neglecting them, perhaps, perhaps even yet they may improve. But while ye sit here, zealous as far as clamor and applause, laggards when any action is required, I see not how any talking, unaided by your needful exertions, can possibly save the country.

[1] Diocles and Chares conducted this expedition, which took place B.C. 357, and which, after various combats in the island of Eubœa, ended in the expulsion of the Thebans. Just at that time the finances of the Athenians were exceedingly low, and the generosity of the wealthier citizens was largely taxed to provide necessaries for the armament. Demosthenes himself came forward as a liberal contributor. The language of Timotheus on this occasion may be compared with Virgil's Æneid, IV. 592.

Non arma expedient totaque ex urbe sequentur,
Deripientque rates alii navalibus? Ite,
Ferte citi flammas, date vela, impellite remos.

THE THIRD PHILIPPIC.

THE ARGUMENT.

This speech was delivered about three months after the last, while Philip was advancing into Thrace, and threatening both the Chersonese and the Propontine coast. No new event had happened, which called for any special consultation; but Demosthenes, alarmed by the formidable character of Philip's enterprises and vast military preparations, felt the necessity of rousing the Athenians to exertion. He repeats in substance the arguments which he had used in the Oration on the Chersonese; points out the danger to be apprehended from the disunion among the Greek states, from their general apathy and lack of patriotism, which he contrasts with the high and noble spirit of ancient times. From the past conduct of Philip he shows what is to be expected in future; explains the difference between Philip's new method of warfare and that adopted in the Peloponnesian war, and urges the necessity of corresponding measures for defense. The peaceful professions of Philip were not to be trusted; he was never more dangerous than when he made overtures of peace and friendship. The most powerful instruments that he employed for gaining ascendency were the venal orators, who were to be found in every Grecian city, and on whom it was necessary to inflict signal punishment, before they had a chance of opposing foreign enemies. The advice of Demosthenes now is, to dispatch reinforcements to the Chersonese, to stir up the people of Greece, and even to solicit the assistance of the Persian king, who had no less reason than themselves to dread the ambition of Philip.

The events of the following year, when Philip attacked the Propontine cities, fully justified the warning of Demosthenes. And the extraordinary activity, which the Athenians displayed in resisting him, shows that the exertions of the orator had their due effect. Even Mitford confesses, with reference to the operations of that period, that Athens found in Demosthenes an able and effective minister.

MANY speeches, men of Athens, are made in almost every assembly about the hostilities of Philip, hostilities which ever since the treaty of peace he has been committing as well against you as against the rest of the Greeks; and all (I am sure) are ready to avow, though they forbear to do so, that our counsels and our measures should be directed to his humiliation and chastisement: nevertheless, so low have our affairs been brought by inattention and negligence, I fear it is a harsh truth to say, that if all the orators had sought to suggest, and you to pass resolutions for the utter ruining of the commonwealth, we could not methinks be worse off than we are. A variety of circumstances may have brought us to this state; our affairs have not declined from one or two causes only: but, if you rightly examine, you will find it chiefly owing to the orators, who study to please you rather than advise for the best. Some of whom, Athenians, seeking to maintain the basis of their own power and repute, have no forethought for the future, and therefore think you also ought to have none; others, accusing and calumniating practical statesmen, labor only to make Athens punish Athens, and in such occupations to engage her, that Philip may have liberty to say and do what he pleases. Politics of this kind are common here, but are the causes of your failures and embarrassment. I beg, Athenians, that you will not resent my plain speaking of the truth. Only consider. You hold liberty of speech in other matters to be the general right of all residents in Athens, insomuch that you allow a measure of it even to foreigners and slaves, and many servants may be seen among you speaking their thoughts more freely than citizens in some other states; and yet you have altogether banished it from your councils. The result has been, that in the assembly you give yourselves airs and are flattered at hearing nothing but compliments, in your measures and proceedings you are brought to the utmost peril. If such be your disposition now, I must be silent: if you will listen to good advice without flattery, I am ready to speak. For though our affairs are in a deplorable condition, though many sacrifices have been made, still, if you will choose to perform your duty, it is possible to repair it all. A paradox, and yet a truth, am I about to state. That which is the most lamentable in the past is best for the future. How is this? Because you performed no part of your duty, great or small, and therefore you fared ill: had you done all that became you, and your situation were the same, there would be no hope of amendment. Philip has indeed prevailed over your sloth and negligence, but not over the country: you have not been worsted; you have not even bestirred yourselves.

If now we were all agreed that Philip is at war with Athens and infringing the peace, nothing would a speaker need to urge or advise but the safest and easiest way of resisting him. But since, at the very time when Philip is capturing cities and retaining divers of our dominions and assailing all people, there are men so unreasonable as to listen to repeated declarations in the assembly, that some of us are kindling war, one must be cautious and set this matter right: for whoever moves or advises a measure of defense, is in danger of being accused afterward as author of the war.

I will first then examine and determine this point, whether it be in our power to deliberate on peace or war. If the country may be at peace, if it depends on us, (to begin with this,) I say we ought to maintain peace, and I call upon the affirmant to move a resolution, to take some measure, and not to palter with us. But if another, having arms in his hand and a large force around him, amuses you with the name of peace, while he carries on the operations of war, what is left but to defend yourselves? You may profess to be at peace, if you like, as he does; I quarrel not with that. But if any man supposes this to be a peace, which will enable Philip to master all else and attack you last, he is a madman, or he talks of a peace observed toward him by you, not toward you by him. This it is that Philip purchases by all his expenditure, the privilege of assailing you without being assailed in turn.

If we really wait until he avows that he is at war with us, we are the simplest of mortals, for he would not declare that, though he marched even against Attica and Piræus, at least if we may judge from his conduct to others. For example, to the Olynthians he declared, when he was forty furlongs from their city, that there was no alternative, but either they must quit Olynthus or he Macedonia; though before that time, whenever he was accused of such an intent, he took it ill and sent embassadors to justify himself. Again, he marched towards the Phocions as if they were allies, and there were Phocian envoys who accompanied his march, and many among you contended that his advance would not benefit the Thebans. And he came into Thessaly of late as a friend and ally, yet he has taken possession of Pheræ: and lastly he told these wretched people of Oreus,[1] that he

[1] When he established his creature Philistides in the government of Oreus, as mentioned in the last oration and at the end of this.

had sent his soldiers out of good-will to visit them, as he heard they were in trouble and dissension, and it was the part of allies and true friends to lend assistance on such occasions. People who would never have harmed him, though they might have adopted measures of defense, he chose to deceive rather than warn them of his attack; and think ye he would declare war against you before he began it, and that while you are willing to be deceived? Impossible. He would be the silliest of mankind, if, while you the injured parties make no complaint against him, but are accusing your own countrymen, he should terminate your intestine strife and jealousies, warn you to turn against him, and remove the pretexts of his hirelings for asserting, to amuse you, that he makes no war upon Athens. O heavens! would any rational being judge by words rather than by actions, who is at peace with him and who at war? Surely none. Well then; Philip immediately after the peace, before Diopithes was in command or the settlers in the Chersonese had been sent out, took Serrium and Doriscus, and expelled from Serrium and the Sacred Mount the troops whom your general had stationed there.[1] What do you call such conduct? He had sworn the peace. Don't say—what does it signify? how is the state concerned?—Whether it be a trifling matter, or of no concernment to you, is a different question: religion and justice have the same obligation, be the subject of the offense great or small. Tell me now; when he sends mercenaries into Chersonesus, which the king and all the Greeks have acknowledged to be yours, when he avows himself an auxiliary and writes us word so, what are such proceedings? He says he is not at war; I can not however admit such conduct to be an observance of the peace; far

[1] This general was Chares, to whom Cersobleptes had intrusted the defense of those places. The Sacred Mount was a fortified position on the northern coast of the Hellespont. It was here that Miltocythes intrenched himself, when he rebelled against Cotys; and Philip took possession of it just before the peace with Athens was concluded, as being important to his operations against Cersobleptes. The statement of Demosthenes, that the oaths had then been taken, is, as Jacobs observes, incorrect; for they were sworn afterward in Thessaly. But the argument is substantially the same; for the peace had been agreed to, and the ratification was purposely delayed by Philip, to gain time for the completion of his designs.

otherwise: I say, by his attempt on Megara,[1] by his setting up despotism in Eubœa, by his present advance into Thrace, by his intrigues in Peloponnesus, by the whole course of operations with his army, he has been breaking the peace and making war upon you; unless indeed you will say, that those who establish batteries are not at war, until they apply them to the walls. But that you will not say: for whoever contrives and prepares the means for my conquest, is at war with me, before he darts or draws the bow. What, if any thing should happen, is the risk you run? The alienation of the Hellespont, the subjection of Megara and Eubœa to your enemy, the siding of the Peloponnesians with him. Then can I allow, that one who sets such an engine at work against Athens is at peace with her? Quite the contrary. From the day that he destroyed the Phocians I date his commencement of hostilities. Defend yourselves instantly, and I say you will be wise: delay it, and you may wish in vain to do so hereafter. So much do I dissent from your other counselors, men of Athens, that I deem any discussion about Chersonesus or Byzantium out of place. Succor them—I advise that—watch that no harm befalls them, send all necessary supplies to your troops in that quarter; but let your deliberations be for the safety of all Greece, as being in the utmost peril. I must tell you why I am so alarmed at the state of our affairs: that, if my reasonings are correct, you may share them, and make some provision at least for yourselves, however disinclined to do so for others: but if, in your judgment, I talk nonsense and absurdity, you may treat me as crazed, and not listen to me, either now or in future.

That Philip from a mean and humble origin has grown mighty, that the Greeks are jealous and quarreling among

[1] Not long before this oration was delivered, Philip was suspected of a design to seize Megara. Demosthenes gives an account, in his speech on the Embassy, of a conspiracy between two Megarians, Ptæodorus and Perilaus, to introduce Macedonian troops into the city. Phocion was sent by the Athenians to Megara, with the consent of the Megarian people, to protect them against foreign attack. He fortified the city and port, connecting them by long walls, and put them in security. The occupation of Megara by Philip must have been most perilous to Athens, especially while Eubœa and Thebes were in his interest; he would thus have inclosed her as it were in a net.

themselves, that it was far more wonderful for him to rise from that insignificance, than it would now be, after so many acquisitions, to conquer what is left; these and similar matters, which I might dwell upon, I pass over. But I observe that all people, beginning with you, have conceded to him a right, which in former times has been the subject of contest in every Grecian war. And what is this? The right of doing what he pleases, openly fleecing and pillaging the Greeks, one after another, attacking and enslaving their cities. You were at the head of the Greeks for seventy-three years,[1] the Lacedæmonians for twenty-nine;[2] and the Thebans had some power in these latter times after the battle of Leuctra. Yet neither you, my countrymen, nor Thebans nor Lacedæmonians, were ever licensed by the Greeks to act as you pleased; far otherwise. When you, or rather the Athenians at that time, appeared to be dealing harshly with certain people, all the rest, even such as had no complaint against Athens, thought proper to side with the injured parties in a war against her. So, when the Lacedæmonians became masters and succeeded to your empire, on their attempting to encroach and make oppressive innovations,[3] a general war was declared against them, even

[1] This would be from about the end of the Persian war to the end of the Peloponnesian, B.C. 405. Isocrates speaks of the Athenian sway as having lasted sixty-five or seventy years. But statements of this kind are hardly intended to be made with perfect accuracy. In the third Olynthiac, as we have seen, (page 57,) Demosthenes says, the Athenians had the leadership by *consent of the Greeks* for forty-five years. This would exclude the Peloponnesian war.

[2] From the end of the Peloponnesian war to the battle of Naxos, B.C. 376.

[3] The Spartans, whose severe military discipline rendered them far the best soldiers in Greece, were totally unfit to manage the empire, at the head of which they found themselves after the humiliation of Athens. Their attempt to force an oligarchy upon every dependent state was an unwise policy, which made them generally odious. The decemvirates of Lysander, and the governors (ἁρμοσταὶ) established in various Greek cities to maintain Lacedæmonian influence, were regarded as instruments of tyranny. It was found that Spartan governors and generals, when away from home, gave loose to their vicious inclinations, as if to indemnify themselves for the strictness of domestic discipline. It became a maxim in their politics, that the end justified the means. The most flagrant proof was given by the seizure of the Cadmea at Thebes; a measure, which led to a formidable confederacy against Sparta, and brought her to the verge of destruction.

by such as had no cause of complaint. But wherefore mention other people? We ourselves and the Lacedæmonians, although at the outset we could not allege any natural injuries, thought proper to make war for the injustice that we saw done to our neighbors. Yet all the faults committed by the Spartans in those thirty years, and by our ancestors in the seventy, are less, men of Athens, than the wrongs which, in thirteen incomplete years that Philip has been uppermost,[1] he has inflicted on the Greeks: nay they are scarcely a fraction of these, as may easily be shown in a few words. Olynthus and Methone and Apollonia, and thirty-two cities[2] on the borders of Thrace, I pass over; all which he has so cruelly destroyed, that a visitor could hardly tell if they were ever inhabited: and of the Phocians, so considerable a people exterminated, I say nothing. But what is the condition of Thessaly? Has he not taken away her constitutions and her cities, and established tetrarchies, to parcel her out,[3] not only by cities, but also by provinces, for subjection? Are not the Eubœan states governed now by despots, and that in an island near to Thebes and Athens? Does he not expressly write in his epistles, "I am at peace with those who are willing to obey me?" Nor does he write so and not act accordingly. He is gone to the Hellespont; he marched formerly against Ambracia; Elis, such an important city in Peloponnesus, he possesses;[4] he plotted lately

[1] *I. e.* in power; but, as Smead, an American editor, truly observes, *ἐπιπολάζει* has a contemptuous signification. Jacobs: *oben schwimmt.* The thirteen years are reckoned from the time when Philip's interference in Thessaly began; before which he had not assumed an important character in southern Greece.

[2] The Chalcidian cities.

[3] This statement does not disagree with the mention of the *δεκαδαρχία* in the second Philippic. Supposing that Thessaly was not only divided into tetrarchies, four provinces or cantons, but also governed by decemvirates of Philip's appointment, placed in divers of her cities, then by the former contrivance she might be said *δουλεύειν κατ ἔθνη*, by the latter *κατὰ πόλεις*. It is not clear indeed whether several decemvirates, or one for the whole country, is to be understood. The singular number is equally capable of either interpretation.

[4] That is to say; a Macedonian faction prevailed in Elis. The democratical party had some time before endeavored to regain the ascendency, by aid of the Phocian mercenaries of Phalæcus; but they had been defeated by the troops of Arcadia and Elis.

to get Megara: neither Hellenic nor Barbaric land contains the man's ambition.[1] And we the Greek community, seeing and hearing this, instead of sending embassies to one another about it and expressing indignation, are in such a miserable state, so intrenched in our miserable towns, that to this day we can attempt nothing that interest or necessity requires; we can not combine, or form any association for succor and alliance; we look unconcernedly on the man's growing power, each resolving (methinks) to enjoy the interval that another is destroyed in, not caring or striving for the salvation of Greece: for none can be ignorant, that Philip, like some course or attack of fever or other disease, is coming even on those that yet seem very far removed. And you must be sensible, that whatever wrong the Greeks sustained from Lacedæmonians or from us, was at least inflicted by genuine people of Greece; and it might be felt in the same manner as if a lawful son, born to a large fortune, committed some fault or error in the management of it; on that ground one would consider him open to censure and reproach, yet it could not be said that he was an alien, and not heir to the property which he so dealt with. But if a slave or a spurious child wasted and spoiled what he had no interest in—Heavens! how much more heinous and hateful would all have pronounced it! And yet in regard to Philip and his conduct they feel not this, although he is not only no Greek and noway akin to Greeks, but not even a barbarian of a place honorable to mention; in fact, a vile fellow of Macedon, from which a respectable slave could not be purchased formerly.

What is wanting to make his insolence complete? Besides his destruction of Grecian cities, does he not hold the Pythian games, the common festival of Greece, and, if he comes not himself, send his vassals to preside? Is he not master of Thermopylæ and the passes into Greece, and holds he not those places by garrisons and mercenaries? Has he not thrust aside Thessalians, ourselves, Dorians, the whole

[1] So Juvenal, Sat. X. 169:

Æstuat infelix angusto limite mundi,
Ut Gyaræ clausus scopulis parvâque Seripho.

And Virgil, Æn. IX. 644:

Nec te Troja capit.

Amphictyonic body, and got preaudience of the oracle,[1] to which even the Greeks do not all pretend? Does he not write to the Thessalians, what form of government to adopt? send mercenaries to Porthmus,[2] to expel the Eretrian commonalty; others to Oreus, to set up Philistides as ruler? Yet the Greeks endure to see all this; methinks they view it as they would a hailstorm, each praying that it may not fall on himself, none trying to prevent it. And not only are the outrages which he does to Greece submitted to, but even the private wrongs of every people: nothing can go beyond this! Has he not wronged the Corinthians by attacking Ambracia[3] and Leucas? the Achaians, by swearing to give Naupactus[4] to the Ætolians? from the Thebans taken Echinus?[5] Is he not marching against the Byzantines his allies? From us—I omit the rest—but keeps he not Cardia, the greatest city of the Chersonese? Still under these indignities we are all

[1] This privilege, which had belonged to the Phocians, was transferred to Philip. It was considered an advantage as well as an honor in ancient times; for there were only certain days appointed in every month, when the oracle could be consulted, and the order of consultation was determined by lot in common cases. The Delphians used to confer the right of pre-consultation on particular states or persons as a reward for some service or act of piety. Thus the Spartans received it; and Crœsus, king of Lydia, for the magnificent presents which he sent to the temple.

[2] Porthmus was the port of Eretria, on the strait, opposite Athens. The circumstances are stated by Demosthenes at the latter end of the speech. By expelling the δῆμος of Eretria, he means of course the popular party, *die Volkspartei*, as Pabst has it; but they would by their own partisans be called the people.

[3] Divers colonies were planted on the northwestern coast of Greece by the Corinthians, and also by the Corcyræans, who were themselves colonists from Corinth. Among them were Leucas, Ambracia, Anactorium, Epidamnus, and Apollonia. Leucas afterward became insular, by cutting through the isthmus. Philip's meditated attack was in 343 B.C. after the conquest of Cassopia. Leucas, by its insular position, would have been convenient for a descent on Peloponnesus. We have seen that this design of Philip was baffled by the exertions of Demosthenes.

[4] Naupactus, now *Lepanto*, lay on the northern coast of the Corinthian gulf. At the close of the Peloponnesian war it came into the hands of the Achaians, from whom it was taken by Epaminondas, but after his death they regained it. The Ætolians got possession of the town some time after, perhaps by Macedonian assistance.

[5] The Echinus here mentioned was a city on the northern coast of the Maliac gulf in Thessaly.

slack and disheartened, and look toward our neighbors, distrusting one another, instead of the common enemy. And how think ye a man, who behaves so insolently to all, how will he act, when he gets each separately under his control?

But what has caused the mischief? There must be some cause, some good reason, why the Greeks were so eager for liberty then, and now are eager for servitude. There was something, men of Athens, something in the hearts of the multitude then, which there is not now, which overcame the wealth of Persia and maintained the freedom of Greece, and quailed not under any battle by land or sea; the loss whereof has ruined all, and thrown the affairs of Greece into confusion. What was this? Nothing subtle or clever: simply that whoever took money from the aspirants for power or the corruptors of Greece were universally detested: it was dreadful to be convicted of bribery; the severest punishment was inflicted on the guilty, and there was no intercession or pardon. The favorable moments for enterprise, which fortune frequently offers to the careless against the vigilant, to them that will do nothing against those that discharge all their duty, could not be bought from orators or generals; no more could mutual concord, nor distrust of tyrants and barbarians, nor any thing of the kind. But now all such principles have been sold as in open market, and those imported in exchange, by which Greece is ruined and diseased.[1] What are they? Envy where a man gets a bribe; laughter if he confesses it; mercy to the convicted; hatred of those that denounce the crime: all the usual attendants upon corruption.[2] For as to ships and men and revenues and abundance of other materials, all that may be reckoned as constituting national strength—assuredly the Greeks of our day are more fully and perfectly supplied with such advantages than Greeks of the olden time. But they are all rendered useless, unavailable, unprofitable, by the agency of these traffickers.

[1] *'Απόλωλε* in reference to foreign affairs; *νενόσηκεν* in regard to internal broils and commotions. Compare Shakspeare, Macbeth IV. 3.

O nation miserable,
When shalt thou see thy wholesome days again?

[2] He glances more particularly at Philocrates, Demades, and Æschines.

That such is the present state of things, you must see, without requiring my testimony: that it was different in former times, I will demonstrate, not by speaking my own words, but by showing an inscription of your ancestors, which they graved on a brazen column and deposited in the citadel, not for their own benefit, (they were right-minded enough without such records,) but for a memorial and example to instruct you, how seriously such conduct should be taken up. What says the inscription then? It says: "Let Arthmius, son of Pythonax the Zelite,[1] be declared an outlaw,[2] and an enemy of the Athenian people and their allies, him and his family." Then the cause is written why this was done: because he brought the Median gold into Peloponnesus. That is the inscription. By the gods! only consider and reflect among yourselves, what must have been the spirit, what the dignity of those Athenians who acted so! One Arthmius a Zelite, subject of the king, (for Zelea is in Asia,) because in his master's service he brought gold into Peloponnesus, not to Athens, they proclaimed an enemy of the Athenians and their allies, him and his family, and outlawed. That is, not the outlawry commonly spoken of: for what would a Zelite care, to be excluded from Athenian franchises? It means not that; but in the statutes of homicide it is written, in cases where a prosecution for murder is not allowed, but killing is sanctioned, "and let him die an outlaw," says the legislator: by which he means, that whoever kills such a person shall be unpolluted.[3] Therefore they considered that the preservation of all Greece was their own concern: (but for such opinion, they would not have cared, whether people in Peloponnesus were bought and corrupted:) and whomsoever they discovered taking bribes, they chastised

[1] Zelea is a town in Mysia. Arthmius was sent by Artaxerxes into Peloponnesus, to stir up a war against the Athenians, who had irritated him by the assistance which they lent to Egypt. Æschines says that Arthmius was the *πρόξενος* of Athens, which may partly account for the decree passed against him.

[2] Of the various degrees of *ἀτιμία* at Athens I shall speak hereafter. I translate the word here, so as to meet the case of a foreigner, who had nothing to do with the franchises of the Athenians, but who by their decree was excommunicated from the benefit of all international law.

[3] That is, his act being justifiable homicide, he shall not be deemed (in a religious point of view) impure. As to the Athenian law of homicide, see my article *Phonos* in the Archæological Dictionary.

and punished so severely as to record their names in brass. The natural result was, that Greece was formidable to the Barbarian, not the Barbarian to Greece. 'Tis not so now: since neither in this nor in other respects are your sentiments the same. But what are they? You know yourselves: why am I to upbraid you with every thing? The Greeks in general are alike and no better than you. Therefore I say, our present affairs demand earnest attention and wholesome counsel. Shall I say what? Do you bid me, and won't you be angry?

[*Here is read the public document which Demosthenes produces, after which he resumes his address.*[1]]

There is a foolish saying of persons who wish to make us easy, that Philip is not yet as powerful as the Lacedæmonians were formerly, who ruled every where by land and sea, and had the king for their ally, and nothing withstood them; yet Athens resisted even that nation, and was not destroyed. I myself believe, that, while every thing has received great improvement, and the present bears no resemblance to the past, nothing has been so changed and improved as the practice of war. For anciently, as I am informed, the Lacedæmonians and all Grecian people would for four or five months, during the season[2] only, invade and ravage the land of their enemies with heavy-armed and national troops, and return home again: and their ideas were so old-fashioned, or rather national, they never purchased[3] an advantage from any; theirs was a legitimate and open warfare. But now you doubtless perceive, that the majority of disasters have been

[1] The Secretary of the Assembly stood by the side of the orator, and read any public documents, such as statutes, decrees, bills and the like, which the orator desired to refer to or to verify. It does not appear what the document was, which Demosthenes caused to be read here. If we may judge from the argument, it was some energetic resolution of the people, such as he would propose for an example on the present occasion.

[2] The campaigning season, during the summer and fine time of the year. The Peloponnesians generally invaded Attica when the corn was ripe, burning and plundering all in their route. Thucydides in his history divides the year into two parts, summer and winter.

[3] Compare the old lines of Ennius:

Non cauponantes bellum sed belligerantes
Ferro, non auro, vitam cernamus utrique.

effected by treason; nothing is done in fair field or combat. You hear of Philip marching where he pleases, not because he commands troops of the line, but because he has attached to him a host of skirmishers, cavalry, archers, mercenaries, and the like. When with these he falls upon a people in civil dissension, and none (for mistrust) will march out to defend the country, he applies engines and besieges them. I need not mention, that he makes no difference between winter and summer, that he has no stated season of repose. You, knowing these things, reflecting on them, must not let the war approach your territories, nor get your necks broken, relying on the simplicity of the old war with the Lacedæmonians, but take the longest time beforehand for defensive measures and preparations, see that he stirs not from home, avoid any decisive engagement. For a war, if we choose, men of Athens, to pursue a right course, we have many natural advantages; such as the position of his kingdom, which we may extensively plunder and ravage, and a thousand more; but for a battle he is better trained than we are.[1]

Nor is it enough to adopt these resolutions and oppose him by warlike measures: you must on calculation and on principle abhor his advocates here, remembering that it is impossible to overcome your enemies abroad, until you have chastised those who are his ministers within the city. Which, by Jupiter and all the gods, you can not and will not do! You have arrived at such a pitch of folly or madness or—I know not what to call it: I am tempted often to think, that some evil genius is driving you to ruin—for the sake of scandal or envy or jest or any other cause, you command hirelings to speak, (some of whom would not deny themselves to be hirelings,) and laugh when they abuse people. And this, bad as it is, is not the worst: you have allowed these persons more liberty for their political conduct than your faithful counselors: and see what evils are caused by listening to such men with indulgence. I will mention facts that you will all remember:

In Olynthus some of the statesmen were in Philip's inter-

[1] Chæronea proved the wisdom of this advice. Similar counsel was given by Pericles in the Peloponnesian war. Had the Athenians attempted to meet the invading army in the field, they must inevitably have been defeated in the early period of the war.

est, doing every thing for him; some were on the honest side, aiming to preserve their fellow-citizens from slavery. Which party now destroyed their country? or which betrayed the cavalry,[1] by whose betrayal Olynthus fell? The creatures of Philip; they that, while the city stood, slandered and calumniated the honest counselors so effectually, that the Olynthian people were induced to banish Apollonides.

Nor is it there only, and nowhere else, that such practice has been ruinous. In Eretria, when, after riddance of Plutarch[2] and his mercenaries, the people got possession of their city and of Porthmus, some were for bringing the government over to you, others to Philip. His partisans were generally, rather exclusively, attended to by the wretched and unfortunate Eretrians, who at length were persuaded to expel their faithful advisers. Philip, their ally and friend, sent Hipponicus and a thousand mercenaries, demolished the walls of Porthmus, and established three rulers, Hipparchus, Automedon, Clitarchus. Since that he has driven them out of the country, twice attempting their deliverance: once he sent the troops with Eurylochus, afterward those of Parmenio.

What need of many words? In Oreus Philip's agents were Philistides, Menippus, Socrates, Thoas, and Agapæus, who now hold the government: that was quite notorious: one Euphræus, a man that formerly dwelt here among you, was laboring for freedom and independence. How this man was in other respects insulted and trampled on by the people of Oreus, were long to tell: but a year before the capture, discovering what Philistides and his accomplices were about, he laid an information against them for treason. A multitude then combining, having Philip for their paymaster, and acting under his direction, take Euphræus off to prison as a disturber of the public peace. Seeing which, the people of Oreus, instead of assisting the one and beating the others to death, with them were not angry, but said his punishment

[1] After Olynthus was besieged by Philip, various sallies were made from the city, some of which were successful. But the treachery of Lasthenes and his accomplices ruined all. A body of five hundred horse were led by him into an ambuscade, and captured by the besiegers. See Appendix I.

[2] When he was expelled by Phocion after the battle of Tamynæ, B.C. 354.

was just, and rejoiced at it. So the conspirators, having full liberty of action, laid their schemes and took their measures for the surrender of the city; if any of the people observed it, they were silent and intimidated, remembering the treatment of Euphræus; and so wretched was their condition, that on the approach of such a calamity none dared to utter a word, until the enemy drew up before the walls: then some were for defense, others for betrayal. Since the city was thus basely and wickedly taken, the traitors have held despotic rule; people who formerly rescued them, and were ready for any maltreatment of Euphræus, they have either banished or put to death; Euphræus killed himself, proving by deed, that he had resisted Philip honestly and purely for the good of his countrymen.

What can be the reason—perhaps you wonder—why the Olynthians and Eretrians and Orites were more indulgent to Philip's advocates than to their own? The same which operates with you. They who advise for the best can not always gratify their audience, though they would; for the safety of the state must be attended to: their opponents by the very counsel which is agreeable advance Philip's interest. One party required contribution; the other said there was no necessity: one were for war and mistrust; the other for peace, until they were ensnared. And so on for every thing else; (not to dwell on particulars;) the one made speeches to please for the moment, and gave no annoyance; the other offered salutary counsel, that was offensive. Many rights did the people surrender at last, not from any such motive of indulgence or ignorance, but submitting in the belief that all was lost. Which, by Jupiter and Apollo, I fear will be your case, when on calculation you see that nothing can be done. I pray, men of Athens, it may never come to this! Better die a thousand deaths than render homage to Philip, or sacrifice any of your faithful counselors. A fine recompense have the people of Oreus got, for trusting themselves to Philip's friends and spurning Euphræus! Finely are the Eretrian commons rewarded, for having driven away your embassadors and yielded to Clitarchus! Yes; they are slaves, exposed to the lash and the torture. Finally he spared the Olynthians, who appointed Lasthenes to command their horse, and expelled Apollonides! It is folly and cowardice to cherish such hopes, and, while you take evil counsel and shirk every duty, and even listen to those who plead for your enemies, to think you inhabit a city of such magnitude, that you can not suffer any serious misfortune. Yea, and it is disgraceful to exclaim on any occurrence, when it is too late, "Who would have expected it? However—this or that should have been done, the other left undone." Many things could the Olynthians mention now, which, if foreseen at the time, would have prevented their destruction. Many could the Orites mention, many the Phocians, and each of the ruined states. But what would it avail them? As long as the vessel is safe, whether it be great or small, the mariner, the pilot, every man in turn should exert himself, and prevent its being overturned either by accident or design: but when the sea hath rolled over it, their efforts are vain. And we, likewise, O Athenians, while we are safe, with a magnificent city, plentiful resources, lofty reputation — what[1] must we do? Many of you,[2] I dare say, have been longing to ask. Well then, I will tell you; I will move a resolution: pass it, if you please.

First, let us prepare for our own defense; provide ourselves, I mean, with ships, money, and troops — for surely, though all other people consented to be slaves, we at least ought to struggle for freedom. When we have completed our own preparations and made them apparent to the Greeks, then let us invite the rest, and send our embassadors every where with the intelligence, to Peloponnesus, to Rhodes, to Chios, to the king, I say; (for it concerns his interests, not to let Philip make universal conquest;) that, if you prevail, you may have partners of your dangers and expenses, in case of necessity, or at all events that you may delay the operations. For,

[1] Smead remarks here on the adroitness of the orator, who, instead of applying the simile of the ship to the administration of the state, which he felt that his quick-minded hearers had already done, suddenly interrupts himself with a question, which would naturally occur to the audience.

[2] *You*, οἱ καθήμενοι. See my observations in the preface. I can not forbear noticing the manner in which Francis translates the following νὴ Δί ἐρῶ. "Let Jupiter be witness, with what integrity I shall declare my opinion." The original means nothing of the kind. It is rare that νὴ Δία can be translated literally with effect. Jacobs here has *wohlan*.

since the war is against an individual,[1] not against the collected power of a state, even this may be useful; as were the embassies last year to Peloponnesus, and the remonstrances with which I and Polyeuctus, that excellent man, and Hegesippus, and Clitomachus, and Lycurgus, and the other envoys went round, and arrested Philip's progress, so that he neither attacked Ambracia nor started for Peloponnesus. I say not, however, that you should invite the rest without adopting measures to protect yourselves: it would be folly, while you sacrifice your own interest, to profess a regard for that of strangers, or to alarm others about the future, while for the present you are unconcerned. I advise not this: I bid you send supplies to the troops in Chersonesus, and do what else they require; prepare yourselves and make every effort first, then summon, gather, instruct the rest of the Greeks. That is the duty of a state possessing a dignity such as yours. If you imagine that Chalcidians or Megarians will save Greece, while you run away from the contest, you imagine wrong. Well for any of those people, if they are safe themselves. This work belongs to you: this privilege your ancestors bequeathed to you, the prize of many perilous exertions. But if every one will sit seeking his pleasure, and studying to be idle himself, never will he find others to do his work, and more than this, I fear we shall be under the necessity of doing all that we like not at one time. Were proxies to be had, our inactivity would have found them long ago; but they are not.

Such are the measures which I advise, which I propose: adopt them, and even yet, I believe, our prosperity may be re-established. If any man has better advice to offer, let him communicate it openly. Whatever you determine, I pray to all the gods for a happy result.

[1] Because a state is a permanent power; a single man is liable to a variety of accidents, and his power terminates with his life.

THE FOURTH PHILIPPIC.

THE ARGUMENT.

The subject of this Oration is the same as the last, viz., the necessity of resistance to Philip. The time of its delivery would appear to have been a little later, while Philip was yet in Thrace, and before he commenced the siege of the Propontine towns. No new event is alluded to, except the seizure of Hermias by the satrap Mentor, the exact date of which is uncertain. The orator urges here, still more strongly than he had done in the third Philippic, the necessity of applying to Persia for assistance. His advice was followed, and a negotiation was opened with that monarchy, which led to the effective relief of Perinthus. There is a remarkable passage in this speech, on the importance of general unanimity, which seems to imply that disputes had arisen between the richer and poorer classes, chiefly in regard to the application of the public revenue. The view which is here taken on the subject of the Theoric distributions is so different from the argument in the Olynthiacs, that modern critics have generally considered this Oration to be spurious. Another ground for such opinion is, that it contains various passages borrowed from other speeches, and not very skillfully put together. Yet the genuineness seems not to have been doubted by any of the ancient grammarians.

Believing, men of Athens, that the subject of your consultation is serious and momentous to the state, I will endeavor to advise what I think important. Many have been the faults, accumulated for some time past, which have brought us to this wretched condition; but none is under the circumstances so distressing as this, men of Athens; that your minds are alienated from public business; you are attentive just while you sit listening to some news, afterward you all go away, and, so far from caring for what you heard, you forget it altogether.

Well; of the extent of Philip's arrogance and ambition, as evinced in his dealings with every people, you have been informed. That it is not possible to restrain him in such course by speeches and harangues, no man can be ignorant: or, if other reasons fail to convince you, reflect on this. Whenever we have had to discuss our claims, on no occasion have we been worsted or judged in the wrong; we have still beaten and got the better of all in argument. But do his affairs go badly on this account, or ours well? By no means. For as Philip immediately proceeds, with arms in his hand, to put all he possesses boldly at stake, while we with our equities, the speakers as well as the hearers, are sitting still, actions (naturally enough) outstrip words, and people attend not to what we have argued or may argue, but to what we do. And our doings are not likely to protect any of our injured neighbors: I need not say more upon the subject. Therefore, as the states are divided into two parties, one that would neither hold arbitrary government nor submit to it, but live under free and equal laws; another desiring to govern their fellow-citizens, and be subject to some third power, by whose assistance they hope to accomplish that object; the partisans of Philip,[1] who desire tyranny and despotism, have every where prevailed, and I know not whether there is any state left, besides our own, with a popular constitution firmly established. And those, that hold the government through him, have prevailed by all the means efficacious in worldly affairs; principally and mainly, by having a person to bribe the corruptible; secondly, a point no less important, by having at their command, at whatever season they required, an army to put down their opponents. We, men of Athens, are not only in these respects behindhand; we can not even be awaked; like men that have drunk mandrake[2] or some other sleeping potion; and methinks—for I judge the truth must be spoken—we are by reason thereof held in such disrepute and contempt, that, among the states in imminent danger, some dispute with us for the lead, some for the place of congress; others have resolved to defend themselves separately rather than in union with us.

Why am I so particular in mentioning these things? I

[1] I agree with Pabst and Auger that *ἐκείνου* signifies Philip. Schaefer takes it neutrally.

[2] Used for a powerful opiate by the ancients. It is called Mandragora also in English. See Othello, Act III. Sc. 3.

> Not poppy, nor mandragora,
> Nor all the drowsy sirups of the world,
> Shall ever medicine thee to that sweet sleep
> Which thou ow'dst yesterday.

seek not to give offense; so help me all the powers of heaven! I wish, men of Athens, to make it clear and manifest to you all, that habitual sloth and indolence, the same in public matters as in private life, is not immediately felt on every occasion of neglect, but shows itself in the general result.[1] Look at Serrium and Doriscus; which were first disregarded after the peace. Their names perhaps are unknown to many of you: yet your careless abandonment of these lost Thrace and Cersobleptes your ally. Again, seeing these places neglected and unsupported by you, he demolished Porthmus, and raised a tyrant in Eubœa like a fortress against Attica. This being disregarded, Megara was very nearly taken. You were insensible, indifferent to all his aggressions; gave no intimation that you would not permit their continuance. He purchased Antrones,[2] and not long after had got Oreus into his power. Many transactions I omit; Pheræ, the march against Ambracia, the massacres at Elis,[3] and numberless others: for I have not entered upon these details, to enumerate the people whom Philip has oppressed and wronged, but to show you that Philip will not desist from wronging all people and pursuing his conquests, until an effort is made to prevent him.

There are persons whose custom it is, before they hear any speech in the debate, to ask immediately—"What must we do?"—not with the intention of doing what they are told, (or they would be the most serviceable of men,) but in order to get rid of the speaker. Nevertheless you should be advised what to do. First, O my countrymen, you must be firmly convinced in your minds, that Philip is at war with our

[1] Auger: "présentent à la fin un total effrayant."

[2] A town in Thessaly. We do not know all the details of Philip's proceedings in that country, but we have seen enough to show, that under the guise of a protector he was not far short of being the master of the Thessalian people. Some of their towns were actually in his possession, as Pheræ and Pagasæ. But that the Thessalians were never entirely subjugated to Macedonia, and still retained a hankering after independence, was proved at a later period by their desertion of Antipater.

[3] The Elean exiles, having engaged in their service a body of the Phocian mercenaries, made an irruption into Elis, but were defeated. A large number of prisoners were taken and put to death. This happened B.C. 343. The government of Elis was at that time in the hands of a Macedonian party.

state, and has broken the peace; that, while he is inimical and hostile to the whole of Athens, to the ground of Athens, and I may add, to the gods in Athens, (may they exterminate him!) there is nothing which he strives and plots against so much as our constitution, nothing in the world that he is so anxious about, as its destruction. And thereunto he is driven in some sort by necessity. Consider. He wishes for empire: he believes you to be his only opponents. He has been a long time injuring you, as his own conscience best informs him; for by means of your possessions, which he is able to enjoy, he secures all the rest of his kingdom: had he given up Amphipolis and Potidæa, he would not have deemed himself safe even in Macedonia. He knows therefore, both that he is plotting against you, and that you are aware of it; and, supposing you to have common sense, he judges that you detest him as you ought. Besides these important considerations, he is assured that, though he became master of every thing else, nothing can be safe for him while you are under popular government: should any reverse ever befall him, (and many may happen to a man,) all who are now under constraint will come for refuge to you. For you are not inclined yourselves to encroach and usurp dominion; but famous rather for checking the usurper or depriving him of his conquests, ever ready to molest the aspirants for empire, and vindicate the liberty of all nations. He would not like that a free spirit should proceed from Athens, to watch the occasions of his weakness; nor is such reasoning foolish or idle. First then you must assume, that he is an irreconcilable enemy of our constitution and democracy; secondly, you must be convinced, that all his operations and contrivances are designed for the injury of our state. None of you can be so silly as to suppose, that Philip covets those miseries in Thrace, (for what else can one call Drongilus and Cabyle and Mastira and the places which he is said now to occupy?) and that to get possession of them he endures hardships and winters and the utmost peril, but covets not the harbors of Athens, the docks, the galleys, the silver mines, the revenues of such value, the place and the glory—never may he or any other man obtain these by the conquest of our city!—or that he will suffer you to keep these things, while for the sake of the barley and millet in Thracian caverns he winters in the midst of horrors.[1] Impossible. The object of that and every other enterprise of Philip is, to become master here.

So should every man be persuaded and convinced; and therefore, I say, should not call upon your faithful and upright counselor to move a resolution for war:[2] such were the part of men seeking an enemy to fight with, not men forwarding the interests of the state. Only see. Suppose for the first breach of the treaty by Philip, or for the second or third, (for there is a series of breaches,) any one had made a motion for war with him, and Philip, just as he has now without such motion, had aided the Cardians, would not the mover have been sacrificed?[3] would not all have imputed Philip's aid of the Cardians to that cause? Don't then look for a person to vent your anger on for Philip's trespasses, to throw to Philip's hirelings to be torn in pieces. Do not, after yourselves voting for war, dispute with each other, whether you ought or ought not to have done so. As Philip conducts the war, so resist him: furnish those who are resisting him now[4] with money and what else they demand; pay your contributions, men of Athens, provide an army, swift-sailing galleys, horses, transports, all the materials of war. Our present mode of operation is ridiculous; and by the gods I believe, that Philip could not wish our republic to take any other course than what ye now pursue. You miss your time, waste your money, look for a person to manage your affairs, are discontented, accuse one another. How all this comes about, I will explain, and how it may cease I will inform you.

Nothing, O men of Athens, have you ever set on foot or contrived rightly in the beginning: you always follow the event, stop when you are too late, on any new occurrence prepare and bustle again. But that is not the way of proceeding. It is never possible with sudden levies to perform

[1] See the note in the Oration on the Chersonese, page 108, where the same words nearly are repeated.

[2] He deprecates here, as elsewhere, the factious proceedings of certain opponents, who sought to fasten the responsibility of a war on the orator, by forcing him to propose a decree. This (argues Demosthenes) was unnecessary, as they were at war already.

[3] Pabst, following Wolf, takes this in the more limited sense of being carried off to prison: *ins Gefängniss geworfen*. The English translators, who have "torn to pieces," understand the word in the same sense that I do, as meaning generally "destroyed, exterminated."

[4] Referring to Diopithes and his troops in the Chersonese.

any essential service. You must establish an army, provide maintenance for it, and paymasters, and commissaries, so ordering it that the strictest care be taken of your funds; demand from those officers an account of the expenditure, from your general an account of the campaign; and leave not the general any excuse for sailing elsewhere or prosecuting another enterprise. If ye so act and so resolve in earnest, you will compel Philip to observe a just peace and remain in his own country, or will contend with him on equal terms; and perhaps, Athenians, perhaps, as you now inquire what Philip is doing, and whither marching, so he may be anxious to learn, whither the troops of Athens are bound, and where they will make their appearance.

Should any man think that these are affairs of great expense and toil and difficulty, he thinks rightly enough: but let him consider what the consequences to Athens must be, if she refuse so to act, and he will find it is our interest to perform our duties cheerfully. Suppose you had some god for your surety—for certainly no mortal could guarantee a thing so fortunate—that, although you kept quiet and sacrificed every thing, Philip would not attack you at last, yet, by Jupiter and all the gods, it would be disgraceful, unworthy of yourselves, of the dignity of your state, and the deeds of your ancestors, for the sake of selfish indolence to abandon the rest of Greece to servitude. For my part, I would rather die than have advised such a course: however, if any other man advises it, and can prevail on you, be it so; make no defense, abandon all. But if no man holds such an opinion, if on the contrary we all foresee, that, the more we permit Philip to conquer, the more fierce and formidable an enemy we shall find him, what subterfuge remains? what excuse for delay? Or when, O Athenians, shall we be willing to act as becomes us? Peradventure, when there is some necessity. But what may be called the necessity of freemen is not only come, but past long ago; and that of slaves you must surely deprecate. What is the difference? To a freeman shame for what is occurring is the strongest necessity; I know of none stronger that can be mentioned: to a slave, stripes and bodily chastisement; abominable things! too shocking to name!

To be backward, men of Athens, in performing those services to which the person and property of every one are liable, is wrong, very wrong, and yet it admits of some excuse: but refusing even to hear what is necessary to be heard, and fit to be considered, this calls for the severest censure. Your practice however is, neither to attend until the business actually presses, as it does now, nor to deliberate about any thing at leisure. When Philip is preparing, you, instead of doing the like and making counter-preparation, remain listless, and, if any one speaks a word, clamor him down: when you receive news that any place is lost or besieged, then you listen and prepare. But the time to have heard and consulted was then when you declined; the time to act and employ your preparations is now that you are hearing. Such being your habits, you are the only people who adopt this singular course: others deliberate usually before action, you deliberate after action.

One thing[1] remains, which should have been done long ago, but even yet is not too late: I will mention it. Nothing in the world does Athens need so much, as money for approaching exigencies. Lucky events have occurred, and, if we rightly improve them, perhaps good service may be done. In the first place, those,[2] whom the king trusts and regards as his benefactors, are at enmity and war with Philip. Secondly, the agent and confidant[3] of all Philip's preparations against the king has been snatched off, and the king will hear all the proceedings, not from Athenian accusers, whom he might consider to be speaking for their own interests, but from the acting minister himself; the charges therefore will be credible, and the only remaining argument for our embassadors will be, one which the Persian monarch will rejoice to hear, that we should take common vengeance on the injurer of both, and that Philip is much more formidable to the king, if he attack us first; for, should we be left in the lurch and suffer any mishap, he will march against the king without

[1] He means negotiation with Persia, to obtain pecuniary assistance.

[2] The Thracians, who had always been regarded as benefactors of the Persian king, since they assisted Darius on his invasion of Scythia. Philip was making war in Thrace at this time, and had subjected a considerable part of the country.

[3] Hermias, governor of Atarneus in Mysia, who for his treasonable practices against Artaxerxes was seized by Mentor and sent in chains to Susa, where he was put to death. He was a friend of Aristotle, who was at his court, when he was taken prisoner. The philosopher afterward married his sister.

fear. On all these matters then I advise that you dispatch an embassy to confer with the king, and put aside that nonsense which has so often damaged you—"the barbarian," forsooth, "the common enemy"—and the like. I confess, when I see a man alarmed at a prince in Susa and Ecbatana, and declaring him to be an enemy of Athens, him that formerly[1] assisted in re-establishing her power, and lately made overtures[2]—if you did not accept them, but voted refusal, the fault is not his—while the same man speaks a different language of one who is close at our doors, and growing up in the centre of Greece to be the plunderer of her people; I marvel, I dread this man, whoever he is, because he dreads not Philip.

There is another thing too, the attacking of which by unjust reproach and improper language hurts the state, and affords an excuse to men who are unwilling to perform any public duty: indeed you will find that every failure to discharge the obligation of a citizen is attributable to this. I am really afraid to discuss the matter; however, I will speak out.

I believe I can suggest, for the advantage of the state, a plea for the poor against the rich, and for men of property against the indigent; could we remove the clamor which some persons unfairly raise about the theatric fund,[3] and the

[1] In the confederate war, when the Persian fleet enabled Conon to defeat the Lacedæmonians at Cnidus, B.C. 394.

[2] Artaxerxes had applied both to Athens and Lacedæmon to aid him in the recovery of Egypt, which for many years had been held in a state of revolt. Both these states refused to assist him. He then applied to Thebes and Argos, each of which sent an auxiliary force.

[3] Boeckh, Schaefer, and others, regard it as conclusive against the genuineness of this Oration, that a different view is here taken on the subject of the Theoric fund from that which Demosthenes had expressed in the Olynthiacs. And certainly it is a strong argument. It is possible, however, that circumstances may have induced him to modify his opinion, or he may have thought it dangerous to meddle with the law of Eubulus at the present crisis, which called for the greatest unanimity among all classes. We may partly gather from this speech, that there had been some agitation among the lower classes, occasioned by the complaints of the wealthy against this law. Any agitation tending to a spirit of communism must have been extremely dangerous at Athens, where the people had such power of mulcting the higher classes by their votes in the popular assembly and courts of justice. It might therefore be better to let the people alone with their theatrical

fear that it can not stand without some signal mischief. No greater help to our affairs could we introduce;[1] none that would more strengthen the whole community. Look at it thus. I will commence on behalf of those who are considered the needy class. There was a time with us, not long ago, when only a hundred and thirty talents came into the state;[2] and among the persons qualified to command ships or pay property-tax, there was not one who claimed exemption from his duty because no surplus existed:[3] galleys sailed, money was forthcoming, every thing needful was done. Since that time fortune happily has increased the revenue, and four hundred talents come in instead of one, without loss to any men of property, but with gain to them; for all the wealthy come for their share of the fund, and they are welcome to it.[4] Why then do we reproach one another on this account, and make it an excuse for declining our duties, unless we grudge the relief given by fortune to the poor? I would be sorry to blame them myself, and I think it not right. In private families I never see a young man behaving

treats, their fees and largesses, than to provoke retaliation by abridging such enjoyments. Leland observes on the subject as follows—"All that the orator here says in defense of the theatrical appointments is expressed with a caution and reserve quite opposite to his usual openness and freedom; and which plainly betray a consciousness of his being inconsistent with his former sentiments. How far he may be excused by the supposed necessity of yielding to the violent prepossessions of the people, and giving up a favorite point, I can not pretend to determine. But it is certainly not very honorable to Demosthenes, to suppose with Ulpian, that his former opposition was merely personal, and that the death of Eubulus now put an end to it."

[1] Viz., than the removal of this clamor and alarm about the theatric fund.

[2] This must be understood (according to Boeckh) of the tribute only, which came in from the allies. The total revenue of Athens must have greatly exceeded this.

[3] There was as much ground for legal exemption then as there is now; and yet it was never claimed. Why should the rich seek to be relieved from their burdens because of an abundance of revenue? That abundance is for the general benefit of the state, not for theirs in particular. Such appears to be the argument, perhaps not quite satisfactory; but such it is. Pabst, apparently reading ἀφ' ἑαυτοῦ, has: *der nicht aus eigenem Antrieb seine Schuldigkeit zu thun bereit war, weil kein Geldüberschuss vorhanden war.*

[4] *I. e.* the Theoric fund, in which every member of the commonwealth had a right to share.

so to his elders, so unfeeling or so unreasonable, as to refuse to do any thing himself, unless all the rest will do what he does. Such a person would certainly be amenable to the laws against undutiful conduct:[1] for I ween there is a tribute assigned to parents both by nature and by law, which ought to be cheerfully offered and amply paid. Accordingly, as each individual among us hath a parent, so should we regard the whole people as parents of the state, and, so far from depriving them of what the state bestows, we ought, in the absence of such bounty, to find other means to keep them from destitution. If the rich will adopt this principle, I think they will act both justly and wisely; for to deprive any class of a necessary provision, is to unite them in disaffection to the commonwealth.

To the poor I would recommend, that they remove the cause, which makes men of property discontented with the present system, and excites their just complaints. I shall take the same course on behalf of the wealthy as I did just now, and not hesitate to speak the truth. There can not, I believe, be found a wretch so hard-hearted—I will not say among Athenians, but among any other people—who would be sorry to see poor men, men without the necessaries of life, receiving these bounties. Where then is the pinch[2] of the matter? where the difficulty? When they see certain persons transferring the usage established for the public revenue to private property, and the orator becoming immediately powerful with you, yea, (so far as privilege can make him,) immortal, and your secret vote contradicting your public clam-

[1] Pabst: *die Gesetze wegen ungebührlicher Behandlung der Eltern.* Κάκωσις, "maltreatment," was a technical term in the Attic law, denoting a failure of duty on the part of husbands, children, or guardians, toward their wives, parents, or wards, for which they were liable to be tried and punished in a suit called *κακώσεως δίκη*. The jurisdiction over this offense belonged to the Archon, who was the protector of all family rights.

[2] The expression "Where is the rub?" would be still nearer to the original, and the expression reminds one of the line in Hamlet:

To sleep! perchance to dream! ay, there's the rub.

Reiske says the simile is taken from the collision of chariots in the race; but this is confining it too much. His vernacular explanation is: *woran stösst es sich? wo ist der Haken?* Pabst has: ***woran stösst*** *sich die Sache, und was erzeugt den Verdruss?*

or.[1] Hence arises mistrust, hence indignation. We ought, O ye men of Athens, to have a just communion of political rights; the opulent holding themselves secure in their fortunes, and without fear of losing them, yet in time of danger imparting their substance freely for the defense of their country; while the rest consider the public revenue as public, and receive their share, but look on private property as belonging to the individual owner. Thus it is that a small commonwealth becomes great, and a great one is preserved. To speak generally then, such are the obligations of each class; to insure their performance according to law, some regulation should be made.

The causes of our present troubles and embarrassment are many and of ancient date: if you are willing to hear, I will declare them. You have quitted, O Athenians, the position in which your ancestors left you; you have been persuaded by these politicians, that to stand foremost of the Greeks, to keep a permanent force and redress injured nations, is all vanity and idle expense; you imagine that to live in quiet, to perform no duty, to abandon one thing after another and let strangers seize on all, brings with it marvelous welfare and abundant security. By such means a stranger has advanced

[1] Having admonished the higher classes to pay their property-tax and perform their public services cheerfully, and without seeking to be relieved at the expense of the public revenue, he proceeds to remind the lower classes of their duty. He warns them, that, while they receive a benefit from the funds of the state, they must not endeavor to increase those funds unduly by an invasion of the rights of property. His language is not open, but would easily be understood by his audience. The Athenians ought not to promote lawsuits to increase court-fees; not to encourage prosecutions against wealthy citizens, in order to obtain fines and confiscations. He insinuates that there was too much cause for complaint already. Τὸν λέγοντα is, not as Schaefer contends, the rich man pleading his cause before the people, but, as Wolf explains it, the popular orator or informer, who speedily rose to favor and influence, of which it was not easy to deprive him. His opponent, speaking in a just cause, might be applauded at the time, but the votes showed what was the real bias of the people. In courts of justice at Athens the voting was usually by a secret ballot; (see my article *Psephus* in the Archæological Dictionary;) and there being a large number of jurors, it would be difficult to discover by whose votes the verdict was obtained. It is impossible to read the frequent appeals made by Athenian speakers to the passions and prejudices of the jury, without seeing that there was some ground for the insinuations of the orator in this passage.

to the post which you ought to have occupied, has become prosperous and great, and made large conquests; naturally enough. A prize there was, noble, great, and glorious, one for which the mightiest states were contending all along; but as the Lacedæmonians were humbled, the Thebans had their hands full through the Phocian war, and we took no regard, he carried it off without competition. The result has been, to others terror, to him a vast alliance and extended power; while difficulties so many and so distressing surround the Greeks, that even advice is not easy to be found.

Yet, perilous as I conceive the present crisis to be for all, no people are in such danger as you, men of Athens; not only because Philip's designs are especially aimed at you, but because of all people you are the most remiss. If, seeing the abundance of commodities and cheapness in your market, you are beguiled into a belief that the state is in no danger, your judgment is neither becoming nor correct. A market or a fair one may, from such appearances, judge to be well or ill supplied: but for a state, which every aspirant for the empire of Greece has deemed to be alone capable of opposing him, and defending the liberty of all — for such a state! verily her marketable commodities are not the test of prosperity, but this—whether she can depend on the good-will of her allies; whether she is puissant in arms. On behalf of such a state these are the things to be considered; and in these respects your condition is wretched and deplorable. You will understand it by a simple reflection. When have the affairs of Greece been in the greatest confusion? No other time could any man point out but the present. In former times Greece was divided into two parties, that of the Lacedæmonians and ours: some of the Greeks were subject to us, some to them. The Persian, on his own account, was mistrusted equally by all, but he used to make friends of the vanquished parties, and retain their confidence, until he put them on an equality with the other side; after which those that he succored would hate him as much as his original enemies. Now however the king is on friendly terms with all the Greeks, though least friendly with us, unless we put matters right. Now too there are protectors[1] springing up

[1] This is said with some irony: many states offer to come forward as protectors, but only on condition of taking the lead: they will not join

in every quarter, and all claim the precedency, though some indeed have abandoned the cause, or envy and distrust each other—more shame for them—and every state is isolated, Argives, Thebans, Lacedæmonians, Corinthians, Arcadians, and ourselves. But, divided as Greece is among so many parties and so many leaderships, if I must speak the truth freely, there is no state whose offices and halls of council appear more deserted by Grecian politics than ours. And no wonder; when neither friendship, nor confidence, nor fear leads any to negotiate with us.

This, ye men of Athens, has come not from any single cause, (or you might easily mend it,) but from a great variety and long series of errors. I will not stop to recount them, but will mention one, to which all may be referred, beseeching you not to be offended, if I boldly speak the truth.

Your interests are sold on every favorable opportunity: you partake of the idleness and ease, under the charm whereof you resent not your wrongs; while other persons get the reward.[1] Into all these cases I could not enter now: but when any question about Philip arises, some one starts up directly and says—"We must have no trifling, no proposal of war"—and then goes on to say—"What a blessing it is to be at peace! what a grievance to maintain a large army!"—and again—"Certain persons wish to plunder the treasury"—and other arguments they urge, no doubt, in the full conviction of their truth.[2] But surely there is no need of persuading you to observe peace, you that sit here persuaded already. It is Philip (who is making war) that needs persuasion: prevail on him, and all is ready on your part. We should consider as grievous, not what we expend for our

the common cause on fair terms. Many of the translations miss the sense here. Leland understands it rightly: "there are several cities which affect the character of guardians and protectors." Auger confounds this sentence with the next: "il s' élève de tous côtés plusieurs puissances qui aspirent toutes à la primauté."

[1] Schaefer rightly explains τιμὰς to mean the price received for treason. But most of the translators, following Wolf, understand it to mean the honors won by Philip. Τοῖς ἀδικοῦσιν is rendered by Auger, Leland, and Francis, "the traitors." I think it rather refers to, or at least includes, the enemies who profited by the treason, and made conquests from Athens: of course meaning Philip in particular.

[2] There is no difficulty in this, if we understand it to be ironical; and no need of any amendment.

deliverance, but what we shall suffer in case of refusal. Plunder of the treasury should be prevented by devising a plan for its safe custody, not by abandoning our interests. Yet this very thing makes me indignant, that some of you are pained at the thought of your treasury being robbed, though it depends on yourselves to guard it and to punish the criminal, but are not pained to see Philip plundering Greece, plundering as he does one people after another, to forward his designs upon you.

How comes it, ye men of Athens, that of this flagrant aggressor, this capturer of cities, no one has ever declared that he commits hostility or injustice, while those who counsel against submission and sacrifice are charged as the authors of war? The reason is, that people wish to cast upon your faithful counselors the blame of any untoward events in the war; for war must necessarily be attended with many misfortunes. They believe that, if you resist Philip with one heart and mind, you will prevail against him, and they can be hirelings no longer; but that if on the first outcry[1] you arraign certain persons and bring them to trial, they by accusing such persons will gain a double advantage, repute among the Athenians and recompense from Philip; and that you will punish your friendly advisers for a cause for which you ought to punish the traitors. Such are the hopes, such the contrivance of these charges, "that certain persons wish to kindle a war." I am sure, however, that, without any Athenian moving a declaration of war, Philip has taken many of our possessions, and has recently sent succor to Cardia. If we choose to assume that he is not making war against us, he would be the simplest of mankind to convince us of our mistake: for when the sufferers disclaim the injury, what should the offenders do? But when he marches to attack us, what shall we say then? He will assure us that he is not making war, as he assured the Orites, when his troops were in their country, as he assured the Pheræans before he assaulted their walls, and the Olynthians in the first instance, until he was in their territories with his army. Shall we then say, that persons who bid us defend our-

[1] Leland: "the first unhappy accident." Francis gives the right meaning, but with too many words; "the first tumults occasioned by any unfortunate success." Spillan: "the first alarm."

selves kindle a war? If so, we must be slaves; for nothing else remains.

But remember: you have more at stake than some other people. Philip desires not to subjugate your city, but to destroy it utterly. He is convinced, you will not submit to be slaves; if you were inclined, you would not know how, having been accustomed to command: you will be able, should occasion offer, to give him more trouble than any people in the world. For this reason he will show us no mercy, if he get us into his power: and therefore you must make up your minds, that the struggle will be one for life and death. These persons, who have openly sold themselves to Philip, you must execrate, you must beat their brains out: for it is impossible, I say impossible, to vanquish your foreign enemies, until you have punished your enemies within the city: these are the stumbling-blocks that must cripple your efforts against the foreigner.

From what cause, do ye think, Philip insults you now; (for his conduct, in my judgment, amounts to nothing less;) and while he deceives other people by doing them services—this at least is something—you he threatens already? For example, the Thessalians by many benefits he seduced into their present servitude: no man can tell how he cheated the poor Olynthians, giving them first Potidæa and many other places: now he is luring the Thebans, having delivered up Bœotia to them, and freed them from a tedious and harassing war. Of these people, who each got a certain advantage, some have suffered what is notorious to all, others have yet to suffer what may befall them. As to yourselves; the amount of your losses I do not mention: but in the very making of the peace how have you been deceived! how plundered! Lost you not the Phocians, Thermopylæ, country toward Thrace, Doriscus, Serrium, Cersobleptes himself? Holds he not Cardia now, and avows it? Why then does he behave thus to other people, and in a different way to you? Because our city is the only one where liberty is allowed to speak for the enemy, where a man taking a bribe may safely address the people, though they have been deprived of their possessions. It was not safe at Olynthus to advocate Philip's cause, without the Olynthian people sharing the benefit by possession of Potidæa. It was not safe to advocate Philip's cause in Thessaly, without the people of Thessaly sharing the benefit, by Philip's expelling their tyrants and restoring the Pylæan Synod. It was not safe at Thebes, until he restored Bœotia to them, and destroyed the Phocians. But at Athens, though Philip has taken from you Amphipolis and the Cardian territory, and is even turning Eubœa into a hostile post, and advancing to attack Byzantium, it is safe to speak on Philip's behalf. Yea, among these men, some have risen rapidly from poverty to wealth, from meanness and obscurity to repute and honor, while you, on the contrary, have fallen from honor to obscurity, from wealth to indigence. For the riches of a state I consider to be allies, confidence, good-will; of all which you are destitute. And by your neglecting these things and suffering your interests thus to be swept away, Philip has grown prosperous and mighty, formidable to all the Greeks and barbarians, while you are forlorn and abject, in the abundance of your market magnificent, but in your national defenses ridiculous.[1]

Some of our orators, I observe, take not the same thought for you as for themselves. They say that you should keep quiet, though you are injured; but they can not themselves keep quiet among you, though no one injures them. Come, raillery apart, suppose you were thus questioned, Aristodemus,[2]—" Tell me, as you know perfectly well, what every one else knows, that the life of private men is secure and free from trouble and danger, while that of statesmen is exposed to scandal[3] and misfortune, full of trials and hardships every

[1] The whole of the foregoing passage is taken, with some little variation, from the speech on the Chersonese. It certainly would seem strange, if this Oration had been forged by any grammarian, that he should have borrowed thus by wholesale from Demosthenes. There is perhaps less difficulty in the supposition that Demosthenes repeated his own words.

[2] This man was a tragic actor, and charged by Demosthenes with being a partisan of Philip. He was the first person who proposed peace with Macedonia, shortly before the embassy of ten. See the Argument to the Oration on the Peace.

[3] I have taken φιλαίτιον in the passive sense, as it is explained by Reiske and Schaefer, though it scarcely suits the character of the word. Compare Shakspeare, Henry V. Act IV. Sc. 1.

O hard condition, twin-born with greatness,
Subjected to the breath of every fool!
What infinite heart's ease must kings neglect,
That private men enjoy!

day, how comes it that you prefer, not the quiet and easy life, but the one surrounded with peril?"—what should you say? If we admitted the truth of what would be your best possible answer, namely, that all you do is for honor and renown, I wonder what puts it into your head, that you ought from such motives to exert yourself and undergo toil and danger, while you advise the state to give up exertion and remain idle. You can not surely allege, that Aristodemus ought to be of importance at Athens, and Athens to be of no account among the Greeks. Nor again do I see, that for the commonwealth it is safe to mind her own affairs only, and hazardous for you, not to be a superlative busy-body.[1] On the contrary, to you I see the utmost peril from your meddling and over-meddling, to the commonwealth peril from her inactivity. But I suppose, you inherit a reputation from your father and grandfather, which it were disgraceful in your own person to extinguish, whereas the ancestry of the state was ignoble and mean. This again is not so. Your father was a thief,[2] if he resembled you, whereas by the ancestors of the commonwealth, as all men know, the Greeks have twice been rescued from the brink of destruction. Truly the behaviour of some persons, in private and in public, is neither equitable nor constitutional. How is it equitable, that certain of these men, returned from prison, should not know themselves, while the state, that once protected all Greece and held the foremost place, is sunk in ignominy and humiliation?

Much could I add on many points, but I will forbear. It is not, I believe, to lack of words that our distresses have been owing either now or heretofore. The mischief is when you, after listening to sound arguments, and all agreeing in their justice, sit to hear with equal favor those who try to defeat and pervert them; not that you are ignorant of the men; (you are certain at the first glance, who speak for hire and are Philip's political agents, and who speak sincerely for

[1] All the translators have mistaken τῶν ἄλλων πλέον, which is simply "more than others," as Wolf explains it.

[2] This seems to shock Leland, who spoils the pungency of the expression by rendering it: "Your father was like you, and therefore base and infamous." Auger remarks: "L'invective de Démosthène est fort éloquente, mais bien violente. L'amour de la patrie, contre laquelle sans doute agissait Aristodème, peut seul en excuser la vivacité."

your good;) your object is to find fault with these, turn the thing into laughter and raillery, and escape the performance of your duty.

Such is the truth, spoken with perfect freedom, purely from good-will and for the best: not a speech fraught with flattery and mischief and deceit, to earn money for the speaker, and to put the commonwealth into the hands of our enemies. I say, you must either desist from these practices, or blame none but yourselves for the wretched condition of your affairs.

THE ORATION OF THE LETTER.

THE ARGUMENT.

The Athenians had been persuaded by the advice of Demosthenes to solicit the aid of Persia. This was accorded, and events had happened on the Propontine coast, which made it peculiarly needful. Toward the close of the year B.C. 342 Philip commenced the siege of Selymbria, and early in the following year, that city having been taken, laid siege to Perinthus. But here he met with an obstinate resistance: Perinthus was strong by nature and well fortified. The satraps of Western Asia had supplied it with a stock of provisions and ammunition, and a large body of Greek mercenaries. Byzantium also had sent assistance. Philip, after making great efforts to take Perinthus by storm, turned the siege into a blockade, and marched northward against Byzantium. Here he was no more successful than he had been at Perinthus. The Byzantines had well prepared themselves to resist his attack, and received powerful aid not only from their old allies of Cos, Chios, and Rhodes, but also from other parts of Greece, and especially from Athens. In order to reconcile the Byzantines to his countrymen, with whom they had been at variance ever since the Social war, Demosthenes himself undertook a voyage to the Bosphorus. By his exertions an alliance was concluded, and an Athenian fleet was sent under the command of Chares; but Chares being feared and disliked by the Byzantines, they refused to admit him into the town; and afterward Phocion was dispatched with a hundred and twenty ships and a considerable body of troops. The result of these effective measures was, that Philip was baffled in his attempts on both cities, and compelled to raise the siege.

In the mean time important operations had taken place elsewhere. An expedition had been sent under the command of Phocion to Eubœa, of which we have no detailed account, but the result was, that the Macedonian party was overpowered, and Clitarchus and Philistides, the partisans of Philip, were expelled from the island. A fleet was then sent by the Athenians into the Pagasæan bay, which took some Thessalian towns, and seized Macedonian merchant-men on the coast. The island of Halonnesus was recovered from Philip by a sudden incursion of the Peparethians. This was revenged by Philip, who ravaged Peparethus, and compelled the islanders to restore their conquest.

Philip saw that peace with Athens could no longer be preserved even in name. Under this conviction, and not, as Mitford says, in alarm at the fourth Philippic, he wrote a letter to the Athenians, (the letter which follows this Oration,) in which he reproaches them with the various acts of hostility which they had committed, and concludes with a virtual declaration of war. An assembly was held, at which this letter was read, and Demosthenes is supposed to have delivered the following speech in reply to it. The exact time when the letter was received is uncertain; but it would appear from the internal evidence, to have been after the siege of Perinthus had commenced, and before that of Byzantium. The arguments of Philip produced no effect; things had gone too far for reconciliation; and it was not difficult for Demosthenes to obtain a decree for the vigorous prosecution of the war.

It will be seen on a perusal of the letter and answer, that the orator does not attempt to meet the specific charges and complaints of Philip. We have nothing but the old arguments, showing the necessity of succoring Perinthus and Byzantium, as formerly of succoring Olynthus; the real weakness of Philip's empire, and the good chance that by vigorous measures it might be overturned. Mitford considers that it was impossible to confute the reasoning of Philip, and therefore that bold invective was the only thing that remained for the orator. And even Leland says, it would have been difficult to answer the letter particularly, because, though Athens had the better cause, she had committed many irregularities. I can not agree with this view of the question. If Philip had been the good-natured, easy person that Mitford represents, who was raised to the surface of Greek affairs by the merest accidents, and rather had greatness thrust upon him by the opposition of the Athenians, than either sought or desired it himself, then indeed the acts of hostility which Philip complains of might justly be regarded as breaches of good faith, and violations by Athens of the law of nations. But I read the history of the times very differently. Philip had been for many years pursuing his career of conquest steadily and successfully. The Chersonese, Eubœa, all the possessions of the Athenians, their commerce and their corn-trade, were at this time in imminent danger. War between Athens and Macedonia, if not open, was understood: argument was out of the question.

But why should Philip address a letter of complaint to a people so bent on hostilities? Why did the wolf complain of the lamb? An aggressive power has never lacked a pretext for making war in either ancient times or modern. It was a part of Philip's system, not only in his dealings with Athens, but with other states, to make friendly overtures and pacific professions, when he meditated some decisive blow. By this means he gained credit for moderation with neutral states, and he created a party for himself within the state which he had designs upon. He put colorable arguments into the mouths of his adherents, distracted the efforts of the people, and at all events gained time for the prosecution of his schemes. It is argued with much force and justice in the exordium of the Oration on Halonnesus, that the tendency of such correspondence was, to deter the adversaries of Philip from expressing their opinions freely.

But for motives of this kind, Philip would hardly have adopted the strain of remonstrance which we read in the Letter. He could never seriously believe, that the Athenians would resign their claims on Amphipolis, because it belonged to Macedonia in very early times, or would give up the Persian alliance because it was a disgraceful connection. It should be observed, however, that the Athenians afforded him a handle for using such arguments, by declaiming in the same style themselves when it suited them; and Philip perhaps was pleased at the idea of beating them with their own weapons. The language of the epistle is simple and dignified, and may be regarded as a good specimen of a diplomatic paper. The pith lies in the last clause, which contains a threat of war.

For these reasons it could scarcely have been worth while for the orator, to answer every particular charge contained in the Letter. Nor can such omission be deemed an argument against the genuineness of the Oration. This, however, has been doubted by many critics; and it may be allowed, that a good part of the speech is not very suitable to the occasion upon which it purports to have been spoken.

ATHENIANS! that Philip, instead of concluding peace with us, only deferred the war, has now become manifest to you all. Ever since he gave Halus to the Pharsalians,[1] and settled the Phocian business, and subdued all Thrace, making fictitious charges and inventing unjust pretexts, he has been actually carrying on war against Athens; and now in the letter which he has sent he avowedly declares it. That it becomes you, neither to fear his power nor to withstand him ignobly, but with men and money and ships, in short, with all you have unsparingly to prosecute the war, I will endeavor to show.

In the first place, O Athenians, you may expect that the gods are your greatest allies and defenders, when Philip, violating his faith and disregarding his oaths to them, has

[1] Parmenio was besieging Halus in Thessaly during the first embassy of the Athenians for peace. Philip told the embassadors, he desired their mediation between the people of Halus and Pharsalus. He afterward took the former city, and gave it up to the Pharsalians, who were his devoted allies.

perfidiously broken the peace. In the second place, he has exhausted all the tricks by which he once rose to greatness, continually deceiving some people and promising them signal benefits. It is understood by the Perinthians and Byzantines and their allies, that he wishes to deal with them in the same manner that he dealt with the Olynthians formerly: it escapes not the Thessalians, that he designs to be the master of his allies and not their chief: he is suspected by the Thebans, for holding Nicæa[1] with a garrison, for having crept into the Amphictyonic council, for drawing to himself the embassies from Peloponnesus,[2] and stealing their confederacy from them: so that of his former friends some are at war with him irreconcilably, some are no longer hearty auxiliaries, all are jealous and complaining of him. Besides—what is of no small moment—the satraps of Asia have just thrown in mercenary troops for the relief of Perinthus, and now that hostility has begun between them, and the peril is imminent if Byzantium should be reduced, not only will they assist us with alacrity themselves, but they will urge the Persian king to supply us with money; and he possesses greater wealth than all nations put together; he has such influence over proceedings here, that in our former wars with Lacedæmon, whichsoever side he joined, he caused them to vanquish their opponents, and now siding with us he will easily beat down the power of Philip.

With these advantages, I will not deny, that Philip has by favor of the peace snatched from us many fortresses and harbors and other like conveniences for war; yet I observe, that if an alliance is consolidated by good-will, and all who take part in the wars have a common interest, the union is firm and lasting; whereas, if it be kept up by deceit and violence, with insidious and ambitious views, (as this of

[1] On account of its neighborhood to the pass of Thermopylæ.

[2] The Messenians and Arcadians. See the Argument to the second Philippic. Those people had been the allies of the Thebans since the time of Epaminondas, but were now more inclined to Philip, as being better able to protect them. Jacobs renders the following words: *und ein Bündniss mit Jenen beabsichtigt hat*, reading προαιρούμενος. Mitford, who in his history of Greece has given a full translation of Philip's letter and the speech in answer, renders this passage vaguely: "The Peloponnesians he requires to attend him by their embassies, and to make their alliance with him exclusive."

Philip is,) any slight pretense, any accidental failure, shakes to pieces and destroys it all in a moment.[1] And by much consideration, men of Athens, I find, not only that the allies of Philip have come to distrust and dislike him, but that even his own subjects are not well-disposed or loyal, or what people imagine. Generally speaking, the Macedonian power, as an auxiliary,[2] is important and useful, but by itself it is feeble, and ridiculously disproportioned to these gigantic enterprises. Moreover this very man by his wars, his expeditions, and all the proceedings which may seem to establish his greatness, has rendered it more precarious for himself. Don't suppose, men of Athens, that Philip and his subjects delight in the same things. Bear in mind, that he desires glory, they security; he cannot gain his object without hazard; they want not to leave parents, wives, and children at home, to wear themselves out and risk their lives for him every day.[3]

Hence one may judge, what the feelings of the Macedonian people toward Philip are. As to his guards and the leaders of his mercenaries, you will find they have a reputation for courage, yet live in greater terror than men of no repute. For those are in danger only from the enemy; these fear flatterers and calumniators more than battles: those together with the whole army fight their opponents in the field; these have their full share in the hardships of war, and it is also their peculiar lot to dread the humors of the king. Besides, if any common soldier does wrong, he is punished according to his desert; but with these men, it is when they have achieved the most signal success that they are most outrageously vilified and abused. No reasonable man can disbelieve this statement; for he is reported by those who have

[1] Compare the second Olynthiac, p. 47, where this same passage occurs with some variation.

[2] The following is Mitford's translation of this passage—"The Macedonian power is become considerable by accretion. Of itself it is weak, and utterly unproportioned to support the authority which must ultimately rest on it." This is a strange mistake. Jacobs' version is:—*Kann zwar die makedonische Macht als Zugabe einen Ausschlag geben, an sich uber ist sie schwach, und in Kücksicht auf die Grösse der Sache verachtlich.*

[3] Many of these observations are applicable to France, harassed and worn out by conscriptions in the latter part of Napoleon's reign.

lived with him to be so covetous of honor,[1] that, wishing all the noblest exploits to be considered his own, he is more offended with the generals and officers who have achieved any thing praiseworthy, than with those who have altogether miscarried.

How then, under such circumstances, have they for a long time faithfully adhered to him? Because for the present, men of Athens, success throws a shade over all this: good fortune covers the faults of men, screens them wonderfully: but let him fail in something, and all will be fully revealed. It is the same as in the human body. When a man is healthy, he has no feeling of local disorders; but when he falls ill, every sore is felt, whether he has a rupture, or a sprain, or any member not perfectly sound. Just so with monarchies or other states: while they are successful in war, their weaknesses are imperceptible to most men; but when they have suffered a reverse, (which Philip very likely will, having taken on him a burden beyond his strength,) all their difficulties become manifest to the world.

Yet if any Athenian, seeing that Philip has been fortunate, therefore thinks it hard and terrible to contend with him, such person, I grant, exercises a prudent forethought. For indeed fortune is the prime—nay, the sole mover in all the business of mankind. Nevertheless in many respects might our good fortune be preferred to Philip's. The leadership that we have received from our ancestors takes its date, not before Philip only, but (let me say roundly) before all the kings that ever reigned in Macedonia. They have paid tribute to the Athenians, but Athens has never paid tribute to any nation. We have more title than Philip to the favor of the gods, inasmuch as we have invariably shown more regard to religion and justice.

[1] In the similar passage, in the second Olynthiac, p. 49, I have translated φιλοτιμία *jealousy*, not, with the majority of translators, *ambition*. My reason was, that the Greek word appears to be used in a bad sense, which would not be suitably expressed by *ambition*. I concede, however, that *jealousy* does not comprehend the whole meaning. Nor would any single word. Shakspeare's "jealous in honor" has a somewhat different application. The expression in the text here is Shakspearian. See Henry V. Act IV. Sc. 3.

But if it be a sin to covet honor,
I am the most offending soul alive.

How comes it then, that Philip has obtained more successes than you in the former war? Because, O men of Athens, (I will tell you candidly,) he takes the field himself, he toils, he faces the danger, letting slip no opportunity, omitting no season of the year: while we—the truth must be spoken—sit idling here, delaying always and voting, and asking in the market-place if there is any news. But what greater news could there be, than a man of Macedonia contemning Athenians, and daring to send such an epistle as you have just heard? Again; he keeps soldiers in his pay, ay, and some of our orators besides, who, imagining they carry his presents home, are not ashamed to live for Philip, and perceive not, that they are selling for petty lucre all that belongs to their country and themselves. We neither attempt to disturb any of his proceedings, nor like to maintain mercenaries, nor dare to take the field in person. It is no wonder then, that he has gained advantages over us in the former war: it is rather strange that we, doing nothing that becomes a people at war, expect to vanquish one who pursues all the measures necessary to conquest.

You must reflect on all this, men of Athens, consider that we have not even the power of saying we are at peace—since Philip has now declared war and commenced it in earnest—spare not any treasures, public or private; march eagerly all to battle, wherever occasion calls; and employ better generals than before. Let none of you suppose, that by the same proceedings[1] which have damaged the commonwealth it can again recover and improve. Imagine not, that while you are as remiss as you have been, others will strive zealously for your welfare. Bear in mind how disgraceful it is, that your fathers underwent numerous hardships and fearful dangers warring with the Lacedæmonians, while you will not courageously defend even the well-earned honors which they bequeathed you; and that a man springing from Macedonia is so enamored of danger, that, to enlarge his empire, he has

[1] Auger and the English translators take *δι' ὧν—διὰ τούτων* to mean persons, supposing *γὰρ* to refer only to the last clause of the preceding sentence. I understand *γὰρ* as referring to the whole of the orator's advice, not to the last point only. The reader will find that in the similar passage in the second Olynthiac (26, Bekker's edition) the words *τῶν αὐτῶν πράξεων* are introduced: which makes it more probable that *τούτων* here is neuter. Jacobs and Pabst take it as I do.

been wounded all over his body fighting with the enemy, while Athenians, whose birthright it is to submit to none but to conquer all in war, through slackness or effeminacy desert the conduct of their ancestors and the interests of their country.

Not to be tedious, I say we must all prepare ourselves for war; the Greeks we must invite, not by words but by deeds, to espouse our alliance. All speech is idle, unattended by action; and Athenian speech the more so on this account, that we are reputed more dexterous in the use of it than any of the Greeks.

THE LETTER OF PHILIP.

THE ARGUMENT.

This is the Letter to which the preceding Oration purports to be a reply. For the circumstances which gave rise to it, see the Argument of the Oration.

PHILIP to the senate and people of Athens greeting:—

Whereas I have frequently sent embassadors, that we may abide by our oaths and agreements, and you paid them no regard, I thought proper to write to you concerning the matters in which I consider myself aggrieved. Marvel not at the length of this epistle; for, there being many articles of complaint, it is necessary to explain myself clearly upon all.

First then; after Nicias the herald was snatched from my dominions, you chastised not the culprits, but imprisoned the injured party for ten months; and my letters, of which he was the bearer, you read on the hustings.[1]

Secondly, when the Thasians were receiving in their port the Byzantine galleys and all pirates that chose to enter, you took no notice, although the treaty expressly declares, that whoever act thus shall be enemies.

Again, about the same time Diopithes made an irruption

[1] It is mentioned by Plutarch that a letter from Philip to his Queen Olympias, which fell into the hands of the Athenians, was returned unopened. But whether it was on this or another occasion, does not appear.

into my territory, carried off the inhabitants of Crobyle and Tiristasis[1] for slaves, and ravaged the adjacent parts of Thrace; proceeding to such lawless extremities, that he seized Amphilochus who came to negotiate about the prisoners, and, after putting on him the hardest durance, took from him a ransom of nine talents. And this he did with the approbation of the people. Howbeit, to offer violence to a herald and embassadors is considered impious by all nations, and especially by you. Certain it is, when the Megarians killed Anthemocritus,[2] your people went so far as to exclude them from the mysteries, and erect a statue before their gates for a monument of the crime. Then is it not shameful that you are seen committing the same offense, for which, when you were the sufferers, you so detested the authors?

Further, Callias[3] your general took all the towns situate

[1] Crobyle must have been in Thrace. Tiristasis is mentioned by Pliny as a place in the Chersonese. Probably then it was near Cardia, not far from the isthmus.

[2] The Athenians, having charged the people of Megara with profaning a piece of consecrated ground, sent Anthemocritus to admonish them to desist from the sacrilege. The Megarians put him to death, and drew upon themselves the wrath of their powerful neighbors, who passed the decree of excommunication here referred to. The monument which recorded their impiety was to be seen in the time of Pausanias, on the sacred road leading from Athens to Eleusis.

[3] This is the same Callias, ruler of Chalcis, whom we have seen opposing the Athenians at the time when Phocion was sent to assist Plutarch of Eretria. (See the Oration on the Peace, p. 75, note.) At the battle of Tamynæ Callias had been aided by Macedonian troops; but after the departure of Phocion, and the decline of the Athenian interest in Eubœa, he formed the scheme of bringing the whole island under his own sway, or at least of making it independent. This did not suit the views of Philip, and Callias, having lost his favor, tried to form a connection with the Thebans. Failing in this attempt, he determined to unite himself to Athens, and accordingly came over and concerted with Demosthenes and his party a plan for a revolution in Eubœa. It was not possible to accomplish this by negotiation, owing to the strength of Macedonian influence, which was confirmed by the occurrences at Oreus and Eretria. (See the Oration on the Chersonese, p. 107, note 1.) At length, by the exertions of Demosthenes, a decree was passed to send troops into Eubœa; and Phocion, to whom the command was intrusted, overpowered the Macedonian garrisons, and expelled Clitarchus and Philistides from the island. This was B.C. 341. Afterward, it seems, an Athenian force, under the command of Callias, crossed the narrow strait that separates the north of Eubœa from Thessaly, and made the attack, which Philip here speaks of, on the towns in the bay of Pagasæ.

in the Pagasæan bay, towns under treaty with you and in alliance with me; and sold all people bound for Macedonia, adjudging them enemies; and on this account you praised him in your decrees. So that I am puzzled to think, what worse could happen, if you were confessedly at war with me: for when we were in open hostility, you used to send out privateers and sell people sailing to our coast, you assisted my enemies, infested my country.

Yet more; you have carried your animosity and violence so far, that you have even sent embassadors to the Persian, to persuade him to make war against me: a thing which is most surprising: for before he gained Egypt and Phœnicia, you resolved,[1] in case of any aggression on his part, to invite me as well as the other Greeks to oppose him; but now you have such an overflow of malice against me, as to negotiate with him for an offensive alliance. Anciently, as I am informed, your ancestors condemned the Pisistratids for bringing the Persian to invade Greece: yet you are not ashamed of doing the same thing, for which you continue to reproach the tyrants.[2]

In addition to other matters, you write in your decrees, commanding me to let Teres[3] and Cersobleptes rule in Thrace, because they are Athenians. I know nothing of them as being included in the treaty of peace with you, or as inscribed on the pillars, or as being Athenians; I know however, that Teres took arms with me against you, and that Cersobleptes was anxious to take the oaths separately to my embassadors,

[1] The time referred to is B.C. 354, when there was a rumor of a Persian invasion, and a proposal at Athens to declare war against Artaxerxes, upon which Demosthenes made the speech *de Symmoriis.* Phœnicia and Egypt were recovered some years after that. The argument of Philip is, that since the recovery of those provinces Persia was more dangerous than before, and therefore it was more disgraceful for a Greek state to be connected with that monarchy.

[2] If the Emperor of Russia at the present day was to reproach England with the alliance of Turkey, designating the Sultan as the common enemy of Europe, we should scarcely think it worth a serious reply. His relation to us is not unlike that of Philip to the Athenians; nor would it be very surprising, if some years hence an English garrison occupied Constantinople.

[3] Of Teres nothing is known, but from this passage: he must have been a prince in the interior of Thrace. As to Cersobleptes, so frequently mentioned in the orations of Demosthenes, see Appendix III. on the Thracian Chersonese.

but was prevented by your generals pronouncing him an enemy of Athens. How can it be equitable or just, when it suits your purpose, to call him an enemy of the state, and when you desire to calumniate me, to declare the same person your citizen—and on the death of Sitalces,[1] to whom you imparted the freedom of your city, to make friendship immediately with his murderer, but on behalf of Cersobleptes to espouse a war with me?—knowing too as you must, that, of the persons who receive such gifts, none have the least regard for your laws or decrees? However—to omit all else and be concise—you bestowed citizenship on Evagoras of Cyprus,[2]

[1] It is impossible, for the reasons stated in Jacobs' note, that this can refer to the Sitalces, King of the Odrysæ, and ally of the Athenians, whose wars and death are related by Thucydides. He fell in a battle with the Triballi, and was succeeded by his nephew Seuthes. It was his son Sadocus, and not he, that was made a citizen of Athens. Tourneil tries to get over the difficulty by suggesting that Seuthes was suspected of murdering him; but there is no evidence that the Athenians entered into treaty with Seuthes till long afterward. However, the circumstances here mentioned exactly apply to Cotys, father of Cersobleptes, who had the honor of Athenian citizenship conferred on him, for which he showed very little gratitude in his subsequent conduct, and accordingly, when he was murdered by Python and Heraclides of Ænus, the Athenians rewarded them with citizenship and a golden crown. Sitalces therefore may have been a mistake, or a slip of the pen, for Cotys. Mitford had come to the same conclusion before Jacobs.

[2] Evagoras, the friend of Conon, who assisted the Athenians in the re-establishment of their independence, was made a citizen of Athens, and statues of him and of Conon were placed side by side in the Ceramicus. He aimed at becoming absolute master of Cyprus, and was engaged in a long war against the Persian king, in which he was ultimately overpowered, but, on submission to Artaxerxes, was permitted to rule in Salamis. On his death, B.C. 374, he was succeeded by his son Nicocles, who was father of the Evagoras here referred to. Nicocles did not reign long, and the young Evagoras was afterward driven from Salamis by a successful usurper. Cyprus was at this period divided among several princes, who afterward joined the great rebellion of Phœnicia and Egypt against Artaxerxes. Meanwhile Evagoras had passed into the service of the Persian king, and was perhaps dwelling in Caria, when Idrieus the prince of Caria appointed him, together with Phocion the Athenian, to command the armament collected for the reduction of Cyprus. This was B.C. 351. Cyprus was reduced in the following year; but Evagoras, instead of being rewarded, as he expected, with the principality of his native town, was appointed to a government in Asia. In this he misconducted himself, and fled to Cyprus, where he was arrested and put to death. The honor which it appears he received, of Athenian citizenship, may have been owing to respect to his

and Dionysius of Syracuse,[1] and their descendants. If you can persuade the people who expelled each of those princes to reinstate them in their government, then recover Thrace from me, all that Teres and Cersobleptes reigned over. But if against the parties, who mastered Evagoras and Dionysius, you will not utter a word of complaint, and yet continue to annoy me, how can I be wrong in resisting you?

On this head I have many arguments yet remaining, which I purposely omit. But as to the Cardians, I avow myself their auxiliary; for I was allied to them before the peace, and you refused to come to an arbitration, although I made many offers, and they not a few. Surely I should be the basest of men, if, deserting my allies, I paid more regard to you, who have harassed me all along, than to those who have always been my steadfast friends.

Another thing I must not leave unnoticed. You have arrived at such a pitch of arrogance, that, while formerly you did but remonstrate with me on the matters aforesaid, in the recent case, where the Peparethians complained of harsh treatment, you ordered your general to obtain satisfaction from me on their account.[2] Yet I punished them less severely than they deserved. For they in time of peace seized Halonnesus, and would restore neither the place nor the garrison, though I sent many times about them. You objected[3] not to the injury which the Peparethians had done me, but only

grandfather's memory and his connection with Phocion. Or perhaps the honor inherited from his grandfather may be referred to, or possibly Philip may be confounding the elder and younger Evagoras. At all events, the comparison is not a happy one.

[1] This refers to the younger Dionysius, twice expelled from Syracuse, first by Dion, B.C. 356, afterward by Timoleon, B.C. 343. He was in alliance with Sparta, and sent troops to her assistance against Epaminondas. His connection with Athens began, after she had made common cause with Sparta: from that time many Athenians resorted to his court, and (among others) Plato is said to have visited him.

[2] Peparethus is in the same group of islands with Halonnesus. Philip's ravaging of Peparethus is spoken of in the Oration for the Crown. As to these circumstances, see the Argument to the Oration on Halonnesus.

[3] The critics find a difficulty here, because ἐπισκήπτω commonly governs a dative case; and it has been proposed to read ἐπεσκέψασθε, which Auger, Jacobs, and Schaefer prefer. But it might well be, that Philip's Greek was not the very best Attic; of which there is more than one example to be found in this letter.

to their punishment, well knowing that I took the island neither from them nor from you, but from the pirate Sostratus. If now you declare, that you gave it up to Sostratus, you acknowledge to having commissioned pirates; but if he got possession against your will, what hardship have you suffered by my taking it and rendering the coast safe for navigators? I had such regard for your state, that I offered you the island; yet your orators would not let you accept it, but counseled you to obtain restitution, in order that, if I submitted to your command, I might confess my occupation to be unlawful, if I refused to abandon the place, your commonalty might suspect me. Perceiving which, I challenged you to a reference of the question, so that, if it were decided to be mine, the place should be given by me to you, if it were adjudged yours, then I should restore it to the people. This I frequently urged; you would not listen; and the Peparethians seized the island. What then became it me to do? Not to punish the violators of their oaths? not to avenge myself on the perpetrators of these gross outrages? If the island belonged to the Peparethians, what business had Athenians to demand it? If it was yours, why resent you not their unlawful seizure?

To such a degree of enmity have we advanced, that, wishing to pass with my ships into the Hellespont, I was compelled to escort them along the coast through the Chersonese with my army, as your colonists according to the resolution of Polycrates were making war against me, and you were sanctioning it by your decrees, and your general was inviting the Byzantines to join him, and proclaiming every where, that he had your instructions to commence war on the first opportunity. Notwithstanding these injuries, I refrained from attacking either your fleet or your territory,[1] though I was in a

[1] I take *τῆς πόλεως* to be the genitive governed by *τῶν τριήρων* and *τῆς χώρας*, while all other translators take it to be dependent on *ἀπεσχόμην*. Leland and Spillan render it "your city," meaning the city of Athens, I suppose. Jacobs and Pabst are to the same effect. It appears to me, that there is no reference here to any measures against Attica or the city of Athens, nor to any other hostilities against her but such as might have been taken in the neighborhood of the Hellespont. Philip says: "I did not attack either the ships or the territory of your state;" that is; "I neither attacked your fleet which was watching in the Hellespont to prevent the passage of mine into the Propontis, nor

condition to take the greater part, if not all; and I have persisted in offering to submit our mutual complaints to arbitration. Consider now, whether it is fairer to decide by arms or by argument, to pronounce the award yourselves or persuade others to do so: reflect also, how unreasonable it is, that Athens should compel Thasians and Maronites to a judicial settlement of their claims to Stryme,[1] yet refuse to determine her disputes with me in the same manner, especially when you know, that, if beaten, you will lose nothing, if successful, you will get what is in my possession.

The most unaccountable thing of all, in my opinion, is this —when I sent embassadors from the whole confederacy,[2] that they might be witnesses, and desired to make a just arrangement with you on behalf of the Greeks, you would not even hear what the deputies had to propose on the subject, though it was in your power, either to secure against all danger the parties mistrustful of me, or plainly to prove me the basest of mankind. That was the interest of the people, but it suited not the orators. To them—as persons acquainted with your government say—peace is war, and war is peace: for they always get something from the generals, either by supporting or calumniating them, and also, by railing on your hustings at the most eminent citizens and most illustrious

did I commit any hostilities in the Chersonese, but only marched through it, as a measure of necessity, passing along the coast to protect my fleet."—The presence of a land force on the coast, to protect a fleet, was not uncommon in Greek warfare.—Francis saw the difficulty of supposing an allusion to the city of Athens, and has rendered it: "We restrained ourselves from attempting aught against your republic, your galleys, and your territories." And Auger too, whose translation is: "Je vous épargnai; je ne touchai ni à nos vaisseaux ni à vos domaines." Next to the construction which I adopt, I should prefer taking the two last genitives as an epexegesis of τῆς πόλεως. By the τὰ πλεῖστα ἢ πάντα, I understand both the ships and the towns in the Chersonese. Philip's boast would be an extraordinary one, according to the majority of the translators. Mitford avoided the difficulty by rendering τῆς πόλεως, "your towns."

[1] Maronea and Stryme were neighboring towns, on the coast of Thrace, northeast of the island of Thasos. Stryme was founded by the Thasians, whom the Maronites endeavored to deprive of their colony.

[2] This seems to have been the embassy that led to the second Philippic. See the argument to that Oration. By "the whole confederacy," he means the Amphictyonic union, and affects to treat the Athenians as belonging to it.

foreigners, they acquire credit with the multitude for being friends of the constitution.

Easy were it for me, at a very small expense, to silence their invectives, and make them pronounce my panegyric.[1] But I should be ashamed to purchase your good-will from these men, who—besides other things—have reached such a point of assurance, as to contest Amphipolis with me, to which I conceive I have a far juster title than the claimants. For if it belongs to the earliest conquerors, how can my right be questioned, when Alexander my ancestor first occupied the place, from which, as the first fruits of the captive Medes, he brought the offering of a golden statue to Delphi?[2] Or, should this be disputed, and the argument be, that it belongs to the last possessors, so likewise I have the best title; for I besieged and took the place from a people, who expelled you and were planted by the Lacedæmonians.[3] But we all hold cities either by inheritance from our ancestors, or by conquest in war. You claim this city, not being either the first occupants or the present possessors, having abode for a very short period in the district, and after having yourselves given the strongest testimony in my favor. For I have

[1] This observation laid Philip open to a severe retort. What experience had he of the facility of bribing orators at Athens or elsewhere? If he had none, it was a gratuitous piece of slander, and an insult to the Athenians, to suppose their leading statesmen so corruptible. If he spoke from experience, he proved the justice of what Demosthenes asserted of him, and the danger to be apprehended from his intrigues.

[2] Auger has justly remarked, that Philip's assertion here is contrary to the historical evidence which has been handed down to us. The city of Amphipolis did not exist in the time of this Alexander, but was founded many years after by Hagnon the Athenian. Nor is there any account of his having gained a victory over the Persians, though Herodotus speaks of the golden statue which he erected at Delphi. He was at first compelled to follow in the train of Xerxes, though he afterward came over to the Greeks, and his desertion was considered by them as highly meritorious. It is not unlikely, that there were traditions concerning him in Macedonia, unknown to the southern Greeks, and Philip himself might well put faith in them. Supposing the facts here asserted to be true, the argument, as against the Athenians, who set up a prior title in point of time, was conclusive. But, except as an *argumentum ad hominem*, it could be worth little or nothing.

[3] After the death of Brasidas, the Amphipolitans paid divine honors to his memory, and treated him as their founder, destroying every vestige of Hagnon the Athenian. Therefore they are spoken of as being a Lacedæmonian colony.

frequently written in letters concerning it, and you have acknowledged the justice of my tenure, first by making the peace while I held the city, and next by concluding alliance on the same terms. How can any property stand on a firmer title then this, which was left to me originally by my forefathers, has again become mine in war, and thirdly has been conceded by you, who are accustomed to claim what you have not the least pretensions to?

Such are the complaints which I prefer. As you are the aggressors, as by reason of my forbearance you are making new encroachments, and doing me all the mischief you can, I will in a just cause defend myself, and, calling the gods to witness, bring the quarrel between us to an issue.

THE ORATION ON THE DUTIES OF THE STATE.

THE ARGUMENT.

The object of this Oration is, to show the necessity of making a proper application of the public revenue, and compelling every citizen to perform service to the state. With respect to the first point, the advice given in the first and third Olynthiacs is in substance repeated, viz., that the Theoric distributions should be put on a different footing; that the fund should either not be distributed at all, or that every man should accept his share as a remuneration for service in the army and navy, or the discharge of some other duty. This was but a circuitous way of proposing (as before observed) that the law of Eubulus should be repealed. (See the argument to the first Olynthiac.) It is here further recommended, that the duties required by the state should be systematically divided among all classes, and performed with regularity. No specific plan however is pointed out.

At what time or on what occasion this speech was delivered, we can not determine. It is mentioned in the exordium, that an assembly of the people was held to consider how certain public moneys should be disposed of. But this gives us no clew to the circumstances. There is no mention of Philip, or of any historical event in connection with the subject. It is stated by the orator, that he had discussed the same question before; and perhaps it may be inferred from hence, that the present speech was later than the Olynthiacs. Again, it may be presumed to have been earlier than the fourth Philippic, in which Demosthenes appears to have changed or modified his views on the subject of the Theoric fund. If however the fourth Philippic be not genuine, as some persons contend, the last argument can have no weight.

In consequence of this uncertainty, commentators are not agreed as to the date of the Oration before us. Pabst and some others think it was spoken soon after the Olynthiacs. Mitford, following Ulpian, places it before all the Philippics. Leland and Francis place it after the Philippics; but there is very little ground for their opinion.

Dionysius makes no mention of this speech in his letter to Ammæus; and some critics have thought it spurious.

WITH respect to the present money and the purpose for which you hold the assembly, men of Athens, it appears to me that two courses are equally easy; either to condemn those who distribute and give away the public funds, to gain their esteem who think the commonwealth is injured by such means, or to advocate and recommend the system of allowances, to gratify those who are pressingly in need of them. Both parties praise or blame the practice, not out of regard to the public interest, but according to their several conditions of indigence or affluence. For my part, I would neither propose that the allowances be discontinued, nor speak against them; yet I advise you to consider and reflect in your minds, that this money about which you are deliberating is a trifle, but the usage that grows up with it is important. If you will ordain it so, that your allowances be associated with the performance of duty, so far from injuring, you will signally benefit the commonwealth and yourselves. But if for your allowances a festival or any excuse be sufficient, while about your further obligations you will not even hear a word, beware lest, what you now consider a right practice, you may hereafter deem a grievous error.

My opinion is—don't clamor at what I am going to say, but hear and judge—that, as we appointed an assembly for the receiving of money, so should we appoint an assembly for the regulation of duties[1] and the making provision for war;

[1] Σύνταξις, which often signifies an assessment of taxes or tribute, is here used in a more enlarged sense, importing a general arrangement of political duties, under which every citizen is obliged to perform some service befitting his age and condition; for example, to pay taxes, or serve in the army, or hold some civil office. Thus the word bears a meaning similar to Shakspeare's *Act of Order:* Henry V. Act I. Sc. 2. I have adopted a title to the Oration, which seemed nearer to the sense than any of the old. Leland calls it, *The Oration on the Regulation of the State.* Francis, *On the State of the Republic.* Pabst, *Ueber*

and every man should exhibit not only a willingness to hear the discussion, but a readiness to act, that you may derive your hopes of advantage from yourselves, Athenians, and not be inquiring what this or that person is about. All the revenue of the state, what you now expend out of your private fortunes to no purpose, and what is obtained from your allies, I say you ought to receive, every man his share, those of the military age as pay, those exempt from the roll[1] as inspection-money,[2] or what you please to call it; but you must take the field yourselves, yield that privilege to none; the force of the state must be native, and provided from these resources; that you may want for nothing while you perform your obligations. And the general should command[3] that force, so that you, Athenians, may experience not the same results as at present—you try the generals, and the issue of your affairs is, "Such a one, the son of such a one, impeached such a one;" nothing else—but what results?—first, that your allies may be attached to you not by garrisons, but by community of interest; secondly, that your generals may not have mercenaries to plunder the allies, without even seeing the enemy, (a course from which the emoluments are theirs in private, while the odium and reproach fall upon the whole country,) but have citizens to follow them, and do unto the enemy what they now do unto your friends. Besides, many operations require your presence, and (not to mention the advantage of employing our own army for our own wars) it is necessary also for other purposes. If indeed you were content to be quiet, and not to meddle with the politics of

die Einrichtung des Staats. Auger, *Sur le Gouvernement de la République.* Wolf, *De Ordinandâ Republica.* From some of these expressions it might be inferred, that the speech was about constitutional reform.

[1] The roll in which were inscribed the names of all citizens qualified to serve in the cavalry or heavy-armed infantry. Men past the military age were exempt.

[2] Pabst: *Aufsehergebühren.* It would be the duty of these persons who received such fees, to inspect the militia roll, see that it was complete, that all the qualified citizens took their turns of service, were properly armed and equipped, &c.

[3] *I. e.* really and effectually command it; not be reduced by their necessities to relax the discipline of the troops, or to employ them on a service foreign to the interests of Athens. See the second Olynthiac, p. 51, note 1.

Greece, it would be a different matter: but you assume to take the lead and determine the rights of others, and yet have not provided, nor endeavor to provide for yourselves, a force to guard and maintain that superiority. While you never stirred, while you kept entirely aloof, the people of Mitylene[1] have lost their constitution; while you never stirred, the Rhodians[2] have lost theirs—our enemies, it may be said—true, men of Athens; but a strife with oligarchies for the principle of government should be considered more deadly than a strife with popular states on any account whatsoever.

But let me return to the point—I say, your duties must be marshaled; there must be the same rule for receiving money and performing what service is required. I have discussed this question with you before, and shown the method of arranging you all, you of the heavy-armed, you of the cavalry, and you that are neither, and how to make a common provision for all. But what has caused me the greatest despondency, I will tell you without reserve. Amidst such a number of important and noble objects, no man remembers any of the rest, but all remember the two obols.[3] Yet two obols can never be worth more than two obols; while, what I proposed in connection therewith, is worth the treasures of the Persian king—that a state possessing such a force of infantry, such a navy, cavalry, and revenue, should be put in order and preparation.

Why, it may be asked, do I mention these things now? For this reason. There are men shocked at the idea of enlisting all the citizens on hire, while the advantage of order and preparation is universally acknowledged. Here then, I say, you should begin, and permit any person that pleases to deliver his opinion upon the subject. For thus it is. If you can be persuaded to believe that now is the time for making arrangements, when you come to want them, they will be ready: but if you neglect the present time as unseasonable, you will be compelled to make preparations when you have occasion for their use.

[1] The establishment of oligarchy at Mitylene is again alluded to in the speech on the Liberty of the Rhodians.

[2] For further particulars with respect to the Rhodians, see the argument to the speech above referred to.

[3] The sum distributed as the price of admittance to the theatres.

It has been said before now, I believe, Athenians, not by you the multitude, but by persons who would burst if these measures were carried into effect—"What benefit have we got from the harangues of Demosthenes? He comes forward when he likes, he stuffs[1] our ears with declamation, he abuses the present state of things, he praises our forefathers, he excites and puffs up our imaginations, and then sits down." I can only say, could I persuade you to follow some of my counsels, I should confer upon the state such important benefits, as, if I now attempted to describe them, would appear incredible to many, as exceeding possibility. Yet even this I conceive to be no small advantage, if I accustom you to hear the best advice. For it is necessary, O men of Athens, that whosoever desires to render your commonwealth a service should begin by curing your ears. They are corrupted: so many falsehoods have you been accustomed to hear, any thing indeed rather than what is salutary. For instance—let me not be interrupted by clamor, before I have finished—certain persons lately, you know, broke open the treasury:[2] and all the orators cried out, that the democracy was overthrown, the laws were annihilated; or to that effect. Now, ye men of Athens—only see whether I speak truly—the guilty parties committed a crime worthy of death; but the democracy is not overthrown by such means. Again, some oars were stolen:[3] and people clamored for stripes and torture, saying

[1] Compare Shakspeare, Henry IV. Second Part, Prologue:
Stuffing the ears of men with false reports.

[2] The ὀπισθόδομος was a chamber at the back of the Parthenon, used for a treasury,

[3] If this circumstance in any way related to the story of Antiphon, mentioned in the Oration on the Crown, it might help to determine the date of this Oration. But the connection is not sufficiently apparent. Leland has the following note on this passage: "We can not well suppose, that the depredations made in their naval stores were really so slight and inconsiderable as they are represented in these extenuating terms. A design had lately been concerted of a very momentous and alarming nature, and an attempt made on the naval stores at Athens, which Demosthenes himself labored with the utmost zeal to detect and punish. A man named Antiphon had been for some time considered an Athenian citizen, till by examination of the registers he was found to be really a foreigner, was accordingly deprived of all the privileges of a native, and driven with ignominy from the city. Enraged at this disgrace, he went to Philip, and proposed to him to steal privately into Athens and set fire to the arsenal. The Macedonian

the democracy was in danger. But what do I say? I agree with them, that the thief merits death; but I deny that the constitution is by such means overturned. How indeed it is in danger of subversion, no man is bold enough to tell you; but I will declare. It is when you, men of Athens, are under bad leading,[1] a helpless multitude, without arms, without order, without unanimity; when neither general nor any other person pays regard to your resolutions, no one will inform you of your errors, or correct them, or endeavor to effect a change. This it is that happens now.

And by Jupiter, O Athenians, another sort of language is current among you, false and most injurious to the constitution; such as this, that your safety lies in the courts of justice, and you must guard the constitution by your votes. It is true, these courts are public tribunals for the decision of your mutual rights; but by arms must your enemies be vanquished, by arms the safety of the constitution must be maintained. Voting will not make your soldiers victorious, but they who by soldiership have overcome the enemy provide you with liberty and security for voting and doing what you please. In arms you should be terrible, in courts of justice humane.

If any one thinks I talk a language above my position, this very quality of the speech is laudable. An oration to be

listened readily to the proposal, and by bribes and promises encouraged him to make the attempt. Antiphon repaired to Athens, and was lodged in the port, ready to put the enterprise into execution, when Demosthenes, who received intimation of the design, flew to the Piræus, seized and dragged the delinquent before an assembly of the people. Here the clamors of the Macedonian party were so violent, that the accusation was slighted, and Antiphon dismissed without the formality of a trial. He departed, triumphing in his escape, to pursue his designs with greater confidence. But the court of Areopagus, whose province it was to take cognizance of all matters of treason against the state, caused him to be again seized and examined. Torture forced from him a full confession of his guilt, and sentence of death was passed and executed upon him. The detection of so dangerous a design might have quickened the vigilance of the people, and exasperated their resentment against the least attempts made on their military stores." This seems to have happened some time after the peace.

[1] So Pabst: *schlecht geleitet.* Auger: "mal gouverné." Leland: "without conduct." Wolf takes it in a different sense: "malè educati." Francis: "held in contempt." I take *ἠγμένοι* to be used as in Thucydides, II. 65, *οὐκ ἤγετο μᾶλλον ὑπ' αὐτοῦ ἢ αὐτὸς ἦγε.*

spoken for a state so illustrious, and on affairs so important, should transcend the character of the speaker, whoever he be; it should approximate to your dignity rather than his. Why none of your favorites speak in such a style, I will explain to you. The candidates for office and employment go about and cringe to the voting interest,[1] each ambitious to be created[2] general, not to perform any man-like deed. Or if there be a man capable of noble enterprise, he thinks now, that starting with the name and reputation of the state, profiting by the absence of opponents, holding out hopes to you, and nothing else, he shall himself inherit your advantages—which really happens—whereas, if you did every thing by yourselves, you would share with the rest, not in the actions only, but also in their results. Your politicians and that class of men, neglecting to give you honest advice, ally themselves to the former class: and as you once had boards for taxes, so now you have boards for politics; an orator presiding, a general under him, and three hundred men to shout on either side; while the rest of you are attached some to one party, some to the other.[3] Accordingly—this is what you get by the system—such and such a person has a brazen statue; here and there is an individual more thriving than the commonwealth: you, the people, sit as witnesses of their good fortune, abandoning to them for an ephemeral indolence your great and glorious heritage of prosperity.

But see how it was in the time of your ancestors; for by domestic (not foreign) examples you may learn your lesson of

[1] Pabst: *Gehen mit sklavischer Demuth herum, um sich die Begünstigung durch Stimmen zu verschaffen.* Auger: "Vous font bassement la cour, et briguent vos suffrages." Τῆς ἐπὶ τῷ χειροτονεῖσθαι χάριτος, I understand to mean, "favor or interest for being elected," χάρις being "the favor of the voters toward the candidate." But Reiske takes χάρις to signify "the courting of the voters by the candidate," and thus explains it: "Ea gratia activa, ea contentio alii gratificandi, studium placendi alii, penes quem sit potestas tibi honorem, quem ambis, suffragio tuo addicendi."

[2] I have followed Reiske in giving a simple meaning to τελεσθῆναι. But Schaefer thinks, and perhaps with reason, that it means something more. He says: "Videtur locutio esse oratoris stomachantis: singuli operam dantes ut strategiæ initientur mysteriis: *Jeder sich abmühend zum Strategos geweiht zu werden.* Pabst translates it: *Sich zu Strategen weihen zu lassen:* thinking it refers to the solemnity of an election by votes, as contradistinguished from an appointment by lot.

[3] See the second Olynthiac, p. 51, note 3.

duty. Themistocles who commanded in the sea-fight at Salamis, and Miltiades who led at Marathon, and many others, who performed services unlike the generals of the present day—assuredly they were not set up in brass nor overvalued by your forefathers, who honored them, but only as persons on a level with themselves. Your forefathers, O my countrymen, surrendered not their part in any of those glories. There is no man who will attribute the victory of Salamis to Themistocles, but to the Athenians; nor the battle of Marathon to Miltiades, but to the republic. But now people say, that Timotheus took Corcyra,[1] and Iphicrates cut off the Spartan division,[2] and Chabrias won the naval victory at Naxos:[3] for you seem to resign the merit of these actions, by the extravagance of the honors which you have bestowed on their account upon each of the commanders.

So wisely did the Athenians of that day confer political rewards; so improperly do you. But how the rewards of foreigners? To Menon the Pharsalian, who gave twelve talents in money for the war at Eion[4] by Amphipolis, and

[1] Timotheus brought back Corcyra to the Athenian alliance, B.C. 376. The Lacedæmonians attempted to recover it three years after, but were defeated.

[2] At Lechæum near Corinth. See the first Philippic, p. 66, note 1. The division of the Lacedæmonian army called *μόρα*, which Iphicrates defeated, was little more than four hundred men. The fame of the exploit, so disproportioned to the numbers engaged, was owing, partly to the great renown of the Spartan infantry, which had not been defeated in a pitched battle for a long period before, and partly to the new kind of troops employed by the Athenian general. These were the *peltastæ* or *targeteers*, who were something between heavy-armed and light-armed soldiers, combining in some degree the advantages of both. Their shield (*pelta*) was lighter, their spear and sword were longer. Until this occasion they had never been fairly tried against the heavy troops of the line. Afterward they came into more general use.

[3] Which annihilated the Spartan navy, B.C. 376. In this battle Phocion first distinguished himself.

[4] Eion is a city on the Strymon below Amphipolis. In the eighth year of the Peloponnesian war, when Brasidas had taken Amphipolis, he sailed down the Strymon to attack Eion, but the town had been put in a posture of defense by Thucydides the historian, who came to its relief with some ships from Thasos. There is no mention in Thucydides of Menon the Pharsalian. Brasidas had partisans in Pharsalus, and marched through Thessaly on his expedition to Chalcidice, aided by some of the nobles of that country. But the Thessalian people in general sided with the Athenians, and an endeavor was made to prevent his march. Afterward they stopped the passage of the Spartan

assisted them with two hundred horsemen of his own retainers,[1] the Athenians then voted not the freedom of their city, but only granted immunity from imposts.[2] And in earlier times to Perdiccas,[3] who reigned in Macedonia during the invasion of the Barbarian—when he had destroyed the Persians who retreated from Platæa after their defeat, and completed the disaster of the king—they voted not the freedom of their city, but only granted immunity from imposts; doubtless, esteeming their country to be of high value, honor, and dignity, surpassing all possible obligation. But now, ye men of Athens, ye adopt the vilest of mankind, menials and the sons of menials, to be your citizens, receiving a price as for any other saleable commodity. And you have fallen into such a practice, not because your natures are inferior to your ancestors, but because they were in a condition to think highly of themselves, while from you, men of Athens, this power is taken away. It can never be, methinks, that your spirit is generous and noble, while you are engaged in petty and mean employments; no more than you can be abject and mean-spirited, while your actions are honorable and glorious. Whatever be the pursuits of men, their sentiments must necessarily be similar.

Mark what a summary view may be taken of the deeds performed by your ancestors and by you. Possibly from such comparison you may rise superior to yourselves. They for a period of five-and-forty years took the lead of the Greeks by general consent, and carried up more than ten thousand

re-enforcements. We can have no difficulty therefore in believing this story of Menon. There was little regular government in Thessaly; and the great families, among whom it was parceled, would not always agree in their policy and alliances.

[1] The *Penestæ* of Thessaly were serfs or vassals, whose condition was somewhat like, though superior to, that of the Laconian Helots. They were in fact the ancient inhabitants, reduced to a state of dependence by the Thessalian conquerors.

[2] Such an immunity, when granted to a foreigner, would exempt him from customs and harbor dues. In the case of a person like Menon, it would be little more than an honorary distinction. But to a citizen or a foreigner residing at Athens an exemption from duties and taxes would be more important, as we shall see hereafter.

[3] It was Alexander who reigned in Macedonia at this time. This then is either a mistake of the orator, or we may suppose with Lucchesini, that Perdiccas, the son of Alexander, was governor of a principality, and therefore dignified with the kingly title.

talents into the citadel; and many glorious trophies they erected for victories by land and sea, wherein even yet we take a pride. And remember, they erected these, not merely that we may survey them with admiration, but also that we may emulate the virtues of the dedicators.[1] Such was their conduct: but for ours—fallen as we have on a solitude[2] manifest to you all—look if it bears any resemblance. Have not more than fifteen hundred talents been lavished ineffectually on the distressed people of Greece?[3] Have not all private fortunes, the revenues of the state, the contributions from our allies, been squandered? Have not the allies, whom we gained in the war, been lost recently in the peace?[4] But forsooth, in these respects only was it better anciently than now, in other respects worse. Very far from that! Let us examine what instances you please. The edifices which they left, the ornaments of the city in temples, harbors, and the like, were so magnificent and beautiful, that room is not left

[1] The trophy, which consisted of armor and spoils taken from the enemy, was hung up, usually on a tree, near the field of battle, and consecrated to some god, with an inscription showing the names of the conquerors and the conquered. See Juvenal, Sat. X. 133.

> Bellorum exuviæ, truncis affixa tropæis
> Lorica, et fractâ de casside buccula pendens,
> Et curtum temone jugum, victæque triremis
> Aplustre.

And Virgil, Æn. XI. 5.

> Ingentem quercum decisis undique ramis
> Constituit tumulo, fulgentiaque induit arma,
> Mezentî ducis exuvias; tibi, magne, tropæum,
> Bellipotens.

But sometimes pillars of brass and stone were erected, as lasting memorials of important victories.

[2] *I. e.* an absence of competitors.

[3] What this refers to is unknown. It has been suggested, that Athens may have sent supplies of corn for the relief of certain Greek cities. Schaefer, justly considering this an unsatisfactory explanation, prefers the reading of *ἀποστόλους*, which Pabst follows, and translates, *für die Seemacht der Hellenen.* There is still however a difficulty in understanding what *τῶν Ἑλλήνων* means. The passage is suspicious, as being a clumsy adaptation of a similar passage in the third Olynthiac. See p. 58 of this volume.

[4] What this particularly refers to, can not be understood without determining the date of the Oration.

for any succeeding generation to surpass them: yonder gateway,[1] the Parthenon, docks, porticoes, and other structures, which they adorned the city withal and bequeathed to us. The private houses of the men in power were so modest and in accordance with the name of the constitution, that if any one knows the style of house which Themistocles occupied, or Cimon, or Aristides, or Miltiades, and the illustrious of that day, he perceives it to be no grander than that of the neighbors. But now, ye men of Athens—as regards public measures—our government is content to furnish roads, fountains, white-washing, and trumpery; not that I blame the authors of these works; far otherwise; I blame you, if you suppose that such measures are all you have to execute. As regards individual conduct—your men in office have (some of them) made their private houses, not only more ostentatious than the multitude, but more splendid than the public buildings; others are farming land which they have purchased of such an extent, as once they never hoped for in a dream.

The cause of this difference is, that formerly the people were lords and masters of all; any individual citizen was glad to receive from them his share of honor, office, or profit. Now, on the contrary, these persons are the disposers of emoluments; every thing is done by their agency; the people are treated as underlings and dependents, and you are happy to take what these men allow you for your portion.

Accordingly the affairs of the republic are in such a state, that, if any one read your decrees and recounted your actions directly afterward, no man would believe that both came from the same persons. Take for example the decrees that you passed against the accursed Megarians,[2] when they were cultivating the sacred ground; that you would sally forth and prevent and not allow it: your decrees in

[1] The Propylæa, which could be seen from the Pnyx, where the people assembled, and were pointed to by the orator. This was an ornamental fortification in front of the Acropolis, considered the most beautiful structure in Athens. It was constructed of white marble, at an immense expense, in the time of Pericles, and took five years in building. Particular descriptions of it may be found in Thirlwall's and Grote's Histories of Greece, and various works on the Antiquities of Athens.

[2] See the Letter of Philip, p. 157, note 2.

regard to the Phliasians,[1] when they were driven lately into exile; that you would assist, and not abandon them to the murderers, and invite the Peloponnesians who were inclined to join you. All these were honorable, men of Athens, and just and worthy of the country: but the deeds that followed them, utterly worthless.[2] Thus by decrees you manifest your hostility, yet can not execute a single undertaking: for your decrees are proportioned to the dignity of the state, while your power corresponds not with them. I would advise you—and let no man be angry with me—to lower your pride and be content with minding your own business, or to provide yourselves with a greater force. If I knew you to be Siphnians or Cythnians[3] or any other people of that sort, I would have advised you to lower your pride; but, as you are Athenians, I recommend the providing a force. It were disgraceful, men of Athens, disgraceful, to desert that post of magnanimity, which your ancestors bequeathed to you. Besides, even should you desire to withdraw from Grecian affairs, it is not in your power. For many feats have been performed by you from the earliest time; and your established friends it were disgraceful to abandon, your enemies you can not trust and suffer to become great. In short, the position which your statesmen hold relative to you—they can not retire when they choose—is precisely that which you have arrived at: for you have interfered in the politics of Greece.

I can sum up all that has been spoken, men of Athens.

[1] The Phliasians had for some time been at enmity with their neighbors the Argives, partly in consequence of their attachment to Sparta. When the Thebans invaded Peloponnesus, B.C. 366, Chares was sent from Athens to assist the Phliasians, whose city was threatened by the confederates. The events here referred to must have been of a much later date, though we can not exactly determine it. We learn from Diodorus, that as early as B.C. 374 some Phliasian exiles made an ineffectual attempt to betray their city to the Argives. It seems, this attempt was afterward repeated with more success. Whether Philip had any thing to do with it, as Lucchesini supposes; or whether the Argives alone, or in conjunction with their Peloponnesian allies, effected the reduction of Phlius, we can not ascertain. The exiled party implored the assistance of Athens, and obtained the promises which the orator refers to.

[2] I agree with Schaefer's interpretation. Others take the words differently, as Auger: "Les actions qui devoient suivre, où sont-elles?"

[3] Siphnos and Cythnos are small islands in the Ægean Sea.

Your orators never make you either vicious or good, but you make them whichever you please: for you aim not at what they desire, but they at what they suppose to be your objects. You therefore must begin by having noble purposes, and all will be well. Either men will abstain from unworthy counsels, or will gain nothing by them, having none to follow their advice.

THE ORATION ON THE NAVY BOARDS.

THE ARGUMENT.

This was (according to Dionysius) the first speech delivered by Demosthenes before the popular assembly. The date of it was B.C. 354; the occasion as follows.

In the second year of the Social war Chares, who commanded the Athenian fleet, either from inability to maintain his troops, or from motives of selfish avarice, or both causes combined, went into the service of Artabazus, the Ionian satrap, then in revolt against Artaxerxes. To him Chares rendered important assistance, and received a rich recompense in money. At first this measure was approved of at Athens; but in the beginning of the next year an embassy was sent by Artaxerxes, to prefer a formal complaint against Chares, for his violation of the peace between Athens and Persia. Chares was immediately ordered to quit the service of Artabazus; but the Athenians soon received intelligence, that the Persian king was making vast naval preparations, and they conjectured, not without reason, that these were intended to support their revolted allies. Accordingly they hastened to put an end to the Social war, in which they had met with nothing but disasters, and the same year a negotiation was opened with the allies, and a peace concluded, by which their independence was acknowledged.

Meanwhile the Persian armament was still talked of at Athens, and there were rumors of a threatened invasion, which excited alarm in some, and stirred up the patriotism of others. Statesmen of the old school recalled to mind the glorious days of their ancestors, and imagined the time was come for taking vengeance on the common enemy of Greece. Isocrates was a patriot of that class, as we learn from his extant orations. Others, less honest than Isocrates, took advantage of the general agitation, and would, for selfish purposes, have precipitated their country into a useless and unseasonable war. An assembly was held to consider what measures should be adopted. A proposal was actually made, to declare war against Persia, and invite the other states of Greece to join in the common cause. Orators who supported this motion declaimed about the older times, boasted of Marathon and Salamis, flattered the vanity of their countrymen, and appealed to the national prejudices. What the temper of the assembly was, may partly be gathered from the following Oration. Demosthenes rose, (then in his thirty-first year of age, according to others, in his twenty-eighth,) and in a calm and temperate speech dissuaded the Athenians from adopting any such absurd resolution. He pointed out the folly of commencing hostilities, which they had not sufficient means to carry on: that the project of uniting the Greeks for such a purpose was chimerical: they were too jealous of one another and especially of Athens, to join in any aggressive war, though they might possibly combine to resist a Persian invasion, if it were really attempted. At present there was no cause for alarm: if Athens would keep quiet, the Persian king would leave her alone; but if she attacked him without provocation, he would in all probability get some of the Greek people on his own side. The true way of averting the supposed danger was, not to begin the attack, but to put the country in a posture of defense, so that, whether menaced with war from Persia or from any other quarter, they might not be taken unprepared. How to make their defensive preparations, was the chief thing to be considered; and to this question Demosthenes addressed himself in so masterly and practical a style, that in the youthful orator might already be discerned the future statesman.

In this speech there is no effort to make a display of eloquence: it is confined to the giving of useful and simple advice. A definite plan is proposed for the regulation of the Athenian navy, by which the number of ships might be increased to three hundred, and a provision made for their speedy and punctual equipment. To effect this object, Demosthenes proposes a reform, from which the Oration takes its title, in the system of *Symmoriæ*, or *Boards for the Management of the Trierarchy:* for a full explanation whereof I must refer to Appendix V. at the end of this volume. The details of the proposed scheme are plainly set forth in the Oration itself, and will easily be understood by the reader, when he has made himself acquainted with the general features of the existing law.

It is pleasing to see Demosthenes, at the outset of his political career, coming forward to moderate the intemperate zeal of the people, to allay the ferment excited by factious demagogues and foolish dreamers—showing himself at the same time attached to the government of his country, and even to the form of her institutions, while he is desirous of adapting them to circumstances, and correcting the abuses by which their proper working was impeded. Here indeed is struck the key-note of that which for many years continued to be the policy of this great man: viz., to uphold the dignity of Athens on the basis of wise laws, to maintain her independence by the spirit and exertions of her own people, to rally round her, for empire and for safety, a host of willing confederates, united by the bonds of common interest, mutual confidence, and esteem.

It appears to me, O Athenians, that the men who praise your ancestors adopt a flattering language, not a course beneficial to the people whom they eulogize. For attempting to speak on subjects, which no man can fully reach by words, they carry away the reputation of clever speakers themselves, but cause the glory of those ancients to fall below its estimation in the minds of the hearers. For my part, I consider the highest praise of our ancestors to be the length of time which has elapsed, during which no other men have been able to excel the pattern of their deeds. I will myself endeavor to show, in what way, according to my judgment, your preparations may most conveniently be made. For thus it is. Though all of us who[1] intend to speak should prove ourselves capital orators, your affairs, I am certain, would prosper none the more: but if any person whomsoever[2] came forward, and could show and convince you what kind and what amount of force will be serviceable to the state, and from what resources it should be provided, all our present apprehensions would be removed. This will I endeavor to do, as far as I am able, first briefly informing you, what my opinion is concerning our relations with the king.

I hold the king to be the common enemy of all the Greeks; yet not on this account would I advise you, without the rest, to undertake a war against him. For I do not observe that the Greeks themselves are common friends to one another; on the contrary, some have more confidence in him than in certain of their own people. Such being the case, I deem it expedient for you, to look that the cause of war be equitable and just, that all necessary preparations should be made, and that this should be the groundwork of your resolution. For I think, men of Athens, if there were any clear and manifest proof that the Persian king was about to attack the Greeks, they would join alliance and be exceedingly grateful to those, who sided with and defended them against him: but if we rush into a quarrel before his intentions are declared, I fear, men of Athens, we shall be driven to a war with both, the king and the people whom we are anxious to protect. He will suspend his designs—if he really has resolved to attack the Greeks—will give money to some of them and promise friendship: they, desiring to carry on their private wars with better

[1] Reiske makes a difficulty about the *οἱ μέλλοντες λέγειν*. I understand it thus. Demosthenes guessed that many other orators would follow him on the opposite side of the question. He endeavors by a gentle sarcasm to weaken the effect of their arguments.

[2] This is a modest allusion to himself.

success, and intent on projects of that kind, will disregard the common safety of all.

I beseech you, not to betray our country into such embarrassment and folly. For you, I see, can not adopt the same principles of action in reference to the king as the other Greeks can. It is open, I conceive, to many of them, to prosecute their selfish interests and neglect the body of the nation: it would be dishonorable in you, though you had suffered wrong, to punish the offenders in such a way, as to let any of them fall under the power of the barbarian.

Under these circumstances, we must take care, that we ourselves engage not in the war upon unequal terms, and that he, whom we suppose to entertain designs upon the Greeks, do not gain the credit of appearing their friend. How can it be managed? By giving proof to the world, that the forces of our state are mustered and prepared, and that possessing such forces we espouse sentiments of justice. To the over-daring, who are vehement in urging you to war, I have this to say:—It is not difficult, in the season for deliberation to earn the repute of courage, or, when danger is nigh, to be exceeding eloquent: it is however both difficult and becoming, in the hour of danger to exhibit courage, in counsel to find better advice than other men.

It is my opinion, men of Athens, that a war with the king would distress our republic, though any action in the course of the war would be an easy affair. Why so? Because, methinks, every war necessarily requires a fleet and money and posts; and of all these things I perceive that he has a greater abundance than ourselves: but for action, I observe, nothing is so much needed as brave soldiers, and of these, I imagine, we and our confederates have the greater number. My advice therefore is, that we should by no means begin the war, though for action we ought to be fully prepared. If indeed there were one description of force wherewith barbarians could be resisted, and another wherewith Greeks, we might reasonably perhaps be regarded as arraying ourselves against Persia: but since all arming is of the same character; and your force must amount to the same thing,[1] namely, the means of resisting your enemies, of succouring your allies, of

[1] Jacobs: *es immer dabei auf dieselben Hauptsachen ankommt.* Pabst: *es bei einer Kriegsmacht auf dieselben Hauptpunkte ankommt.*

preserving your valuable possessions; why, when we have professed enemies,[1] do we look out for others? why do we not rather prepare ourselves against the former, and be ready to resist the king also, if he attempt to injure us?

And now you invite the Greeks to join you. But if you will not act as they desire, some of them having no good-will toward you, how can you expect they will obey your call? Because, forsooth, they will hear from you that the Persian has designs against them. And pray, do you imagine they don't foresee it themselves? I believe they do: but at present this fear outweighs not the enmity, which some of them bear toward you and toward each other. Your embassadors then will only travel round and rhapsodize.[2] But when the time

[1] This refers principally to the Thebans, between whom and the Athenians an enmity had subsisted ever since the severance of their alliance, when the Athenians, jealous of the growing power of Thebes under Epaminondas, went over to the side of Sparta. This enmity was increased by the events of the Sacred war, which had now been raging for two years, and in which the Thebans were engaged as principals on one side, while the Phocians received assistance from Athens and Lacedæmon. The Locrians and most of the tribes of Thessaly, then in alliance with Thebes, are to be reckoned among the enemies, whom Demosthenes refers to: perhaps also the Olynthians and the revolted subjects of Athens.

[2] I have chosen to preserve the original word, which has come into use familiar enough in our own language. Francis has done the same. Leland has: "the remonstrances of your embassadors will but appear like the tales of idle wanderers." Jacobs: *werden eure Gesandten nichts ausrichten, sondern mit irhem Spruche wie Bänkelsänger umher ziehn.* The meaning is, that they will go about from city to city, and repeat the same idle tale or sing-song, which no one will listen to: as Pabst expresses it: *vergeblich dasselbe Lied wiederholen.* The rhapsodists were a class of persons who in the early times of Greece went about reciting pieces of poetry, and in particular the Homeric. By the constant practice of reciting, they could retain an immense number of verses in their memory; and, before the art of writing was much known, this talent was a source of amusement and instruction, and made the rhapsodist welcome wherever he came. In the time of Demosthenes this class of men had fallen into disrepute, and indeed their occupation was nearly gone. Afterward *ῥαψωδεῖν* came to be synonymous with *φλυαρεῖν*, "to talk nonsense, to string words together without meaning;" and in this sense the word has been appropriated to our own language. Compare Shakspeare, Hamlet, Act III. Sc. 4.

Oh, such a deed,
As from the body of contraction plucks
The very soul, and sweet religion makes
A rhapsody of words.

comes, if what we now expect be really brought to pass, I fancy none of the Greek community rate themselves so high, that, when they see you possessed of a thousand horse, as many infantry soldiers as one could desire, and three hundred ships, they would not come with entreaties, and regard such aid as their surest means of deliverance. The consequences then are—by inviting them now, you are suppliants, and, if your petition be not granted, you fail: whereas, by waiting your time and completing your preparations, you save men at their own request, and are sure they will all come over to you.

Swayed by these and the like considerations, men of Athens, I sought not to compose a bold harangue of tedious length: but have taken exceeding pains in devising a plan, the best and the speediest, for getting your forces ready. It will be for you to hear it, and, if it meet your approval, to vote for its adoption.

The first and most essential part of preparation, men of Athens, is to be so disposed in your minds, that every citizen is willing and earnest to perform his duty. For you see, O Athenians: whenever you have had a common wish, and every man has thought afterward, that the accomplishment belonged to himself, nothing has ever escaped you; but when you have wished only, and then looked to one another, each expecting to be idle while his neighbor did the work, none of your designs have been executed.

You being so animated and determined, I advise that we fill up the twelve hundred and make two thousand, adding eight hundred to them: for if you appoint that number, I reckon that, after deducting the heiresses and wards, and holders of allotments and partnership property,[1] and persons

[1] The persons here enumerated were exempt from service of the *Trierarchia*. Heiresses and wards were exempt, because, although they might have property enough to defray the contingent expense, yet the service was connected with a personal trust, which by reason of sex and age they were incapable of performing. The colonial allottees (*κληροῦχοι*) were exempt, by reason of their absence., (See p. 101, note 2.) *Κοινωνοὶ* are any partners or joint owners, who would fairly be exempt, when the share of each was not sufficient to qualify him; as in the case suggested by Harpocration, of brothers having an undivided inheritance. The operation of the law would be as follows. The state in the first instance looks to the visible property of the citizens, such as land, houses, stock in trade or agriculture. A register is formed of the twelve hundred owners of property most competent to serve the office

in reduced circumstances, you will still have your twelve hundred members. Of them I think you should make twenty boards, as at present, each having sixty members. Each of these boards I would have you divide into five sections of twelve men, putting always with the wealthiest person some of the least wealth, to preserve equality. And thus I say the members ought to be arranged: the reason you will understand, when you have heard the whole scheme of arrangement. But how about the ships? I recommend you to fix the whole number at three hundred, and form twenty divisions of fifteen vessels each, giving five of the first hundred and five of the second hundred and five of the third hundred to each division; then allot one division of fifteen ships to every board of men, and let the board assign three ships to each of their own sections.

When these regulations have been made, I propose—as the

of *trierarch*. This register continues the same, until circumstances have happened which call for an alteration; and, practically speaking, the same families continue for a long period in the register. But (says Demosthenes) the thing worked so, that at any given time, when there was a call for service, the register could not be depended on for the whole number. Thus, the name of Timon is found in the register; but Timon is dead, and the estate has descended to his three sons, or his three brothers, who are not liable, because the share of each is inadequate. Or Timon has sold his property, and it is in the hands of three or four partners. Or Timon has mortgaged it, and become himself too poor to undertake the office. There would not be time always to investigate the excuses alleged by the registered party, or the condition of his heirs or successors. That false excuses and evasions were sometimes resorted to, we learn from the orators. On the other hand, the presumption against a man, from his name being in the register, would sometimes operate unjustly to a man in reduced circumstances. The law of the *exchange* was indeed a mode of relief, but attended with difficulty. (See Appendix V.)

We may suppose, that when a registered estate was found to have devolved upon several joint proprietors, the excuse would at once be admitted in the first instance; though, if a man's separate estate, together with his joint estate, were of the requisite amount, one can hardly suppose he would escape ultimate liability. Thus, if Callias be one of Timon's heirs, his share of that inheritance not being sufficient to serve the *trierarchy*, and his other property not being sufficient, but both together being sufficient, he would not have his name immediately substituted for Timon's, but the fact afterward appearing, either in a judicial contest, or on a general revision of the register, his name would be entered.

With respect to the adjectives *ὀρφανικῶν*, &c., I understand *σωμάτων*, "persons of the class of orphans," &c.

ratable capital of the country is six thousand talents[1]—in order that your supplies may be apportioned, you should divide this capital and make a hundred parts of sixty talents each; then allot five of these hundredth parts to each of the twenty larger boards, and let the board assign one hundredth part to each of their own sections; so that, if you have need of a hundred ships, sixty talents may be applied[2] to the expense, and there may be twelve to serve as commanders;[3] if of two hundred, there may be thirty talents applied to the expense, and six persons to serve; if of three hundred, there may be twenty talents defraying the expense, and four persons to serve.

In the same manner, O Athenians, I advise that all the furniture of the ships, which is out on loan,[4] should be valued according to the register, and divided into twenty parts; that you then allot one good[5] portion to every large board; that every board distribute equal shares among their own sections; that the twelve in each section call their implements in, and get the ships which are severally allotted to them in readiness. Thus do I think the supplies, the vessels, the commanders, and the collection of implements, may be most effectually provided and arranged. How the manning may be made sure and easy, I proceed to explain.

I say the generals should divide the dock-yards into ten departments, taking care that there be thirty docks in each as near as possible to one another; and when they have done this, let them attach two boards and thirty ships to each of these departments, then allot the tribes and the several commanders to each dock-yard, so that there may be two boards, thirty ships, one tribe. And whichever department be allotted to a tribe, let them divide it in three and the ships likewise, and

[1] See Appendix IV.

[2] *I. e.* that shall be the proportion of the whole ratable capital, upon which a tax shall be levied to meet the expense. It is a short way of expressing this. See Appendix IV. and V.

[3] *Trierarchs.* The name was kept up, when it had become a matter of contribution and civil trust, rather than of naval service. So, the Lord High Admiral of our own government might never have seen the sea.

[4] It was customary for individuals to borrow the naval implements and stores from the public arsenal, when the state had no occasion for them.

[5] Al. *χρηστῶν*, *debtors.*

then allot the third of a tribe to each, so that of the whole dock-yards there may be one division belonging to every tribe, and the third of a tribe may have the third part of every division, and you may know, in case of necessity, first, where the tribe is stationed, next, where the third of the tribe next, who are the commanders and how many ships there are; and the tribe may have thirty ships, and every third of a tribe have ten. Let the system be only put in train, and though we should forget something now—for it is difficult to make all the details perfect—it will be ascertained in the working; and there will be one arrangement for all the ships and every division.

In regard to money and real supplies, I know that I am about to make an extraordinary statement, yet still it shall be made; for I am persuaded that, on a correct view, I alone shall be found to have declared and predicted the truth. I say, we ought not at present to speak of money: a supply there is, if occasion require it, ample, honorable, and just: if we look for it immediately, we shall not think we have it even in reserve; so far shall we be from providing it now; but if we leave it alone, we shall have it. What then is this supply, which hath no being now, but will exist hereafter?—for certainly it is like a riddle. I will explain.

You see the extent of this city, men of Athens. It contains treasures equal, I may almost say, to the rest of the states put together. But the owners are so minded, that—if all your orators alarmed them with intelligence that the king was coming, that he was at hand, that the danger was inevitable—if, besides the orators, an equal number of persons gave oracular warning—so far from contributing, they would not even discover their wealth or acknowledge the possession. Yet if they knew that these proceedings, so terrible in report, were actually begun, there is not a man so foolish, who would not be ready to give and foremost to contribute. For who would rather perish with all his possessions, than contribute a part of his possessions to preserve himself and the remainder? Thus, I say, we have money against the time of actual need, but not before. And therefore I advise you not to search for it now. Indeed what you would raise, if you determined to raise it, would be more ridiculous than nothing at all. For example:—Let a tax be proposed of one per cent

—there are sixty talents. Let twice as much, namely two per cent, be proposed—there are a hundred and twenty. But what is this to the twelve hundred camels, which, these men say, carry the king's gold? Let me suppose however, that we contributed the twelfth of our property, five hundred talents. This you would not submit to; but if you did pay it, the sum would be insufficient for the war. Your proper course then is, to complete your other preparations; let the owners retain their money for the present; (it can not be in better keeping[1] for the state;) and should the occasion ever arrive, then take it from them in voluntary contributions.

These, O my countrymen, are practicable measures, these are honorable and advantageous, fit to be reported as your proceedings to the king; and by them no little terror would be excited in him. He knows right well, that by three hundred galleys, whereof we furnished a hundred, his ancestors lost a thousand ships; and he will hear that we ourselves have now equipped three hundred; so that, were he ever so mad, he could hardly deem it a light matter to provoke the hostility of our republic. Should he however entertain an overweening confidence in his wealth, even this he will find to be a weaker support than yours. He is coming, they say, with gold. But if he give it away he will lack supplies: for even wells and fountains are apt to fail, if you draw from them constantly and by wholesale. He will hear that the valuation of our land is a capital of six thousand talents. That we shall defend it against invaders from that quarter, his ancestors who were at Marathon would know best: and certainly, as long as we are victorious, money can never fail us.

Nor is there, as it appears to me, any ground for what some persons fear, that having money he will collect a large body of mercenaries. I do indeed believe, that against Egypt[2]

[1] Direct taxation in time of peace, when there is no urgent necessity, is like killing the goose for the golden eggs.

[2] Egypt had been in a state of revolt from Persia ever since the reign of Darius Nothus. An attempt was made to recover it by his successor Artaxerxes Mnemon, who engaged the services of the Athenian Iphicrates, and sent him with a powerful fleet and army under the satrap Pharnabazus B.C. 374. This expedition failed, owing to the misconduct of Pharnabazus. After the accession of Artaxerxes Ochus, repeated efforts were made to reconquer this valuable province. At length

and Orontes,[1] and any other barbarians, many of the Greeks would be willing to serve in his pay, not that he may subdue any of those adversaries, but in order to obtain supplies for themselves to relieve their several necessities. Against Greece however I do not believe that any Grecian would march. For whither could he betake himself afterward? Go to Phrygia and be a slave?—Remember, a war with the barbarian can be for no other stake, than for country and life and customs and freedom and every thing of the kind. Who then is so wretched, that he would sacrifice himself, parents, sepulchres, fatherland, for the sake of a paltry pittance? I believe, no man. But further—it is not even the king's interest, that mercenaries should conquer the Greeks. For they that conquer us must have been his masters already: and he desires, not to subdue us and then be dependent on others, but to rule, if possible, over all; if that be not possible, at least over his present subjects.

Should any one think the Thebans will be on his side—I know it is difficult to speak to you about that people: you hate them so, you will not like to hear even the truth or any thing favorable of them—however men who are considering important questions must not omit any useful argument on any pretext. My opinion then is, the Thebans, so far from being likely to join him in any attack upon Greece, would

about the year B.C. 348 or later the king collected a considerable force of Greek mercenaries, and marched against Egypt in person. Mentor of Rhodes, and the Theban Lacrates greatly distinguished themselves in the king's service on this occasion, and Egypt was again brought under the dominion of Persia; in which it remained until the overthrow of that empire by Alexander.

[1] Orontes was satrap of Mysia in the reign of Artaxerxes Mnemon. He joined the great conspiracy of the satraps and the king of Egypt in the year B.C. 362. He was chosen to command their forces, and intrusted with a large fund which had been collected to carry on the war. He was induced however to change sides; and the trust which had been reposed in him enabled him to betray his party to the king most effectually. Other rebels followed his example; and this confederacy which at one time had threatened the very existence of the Persian monarchy, was suddenly dissolved. What became of Orontes afterward, is unknown. The other satraps who joined this coalition were Ariobarzanes of Phrygia, Autophradates of Lydia, Datames of Cappadocia, and Mausolus king of Caria. Datames was a man of great ability. The treacherous manner in which his destruction was accomplished is recorded by Cornelius Nepos, who wrote his life.

give a large sum of money, if they had it, for the opportunity of repairing their former offenses against her.[1] But supposing the Thebans to be so utterly wrong-headed, of this at least you are all aware, that, if the Thebans are in his interest, their enemies must necessarily be in the interest of the Greeks.

I believe then, that our cause (the cause of justice) and its adherents will be better armed against all adversaries than the traitors and the barbarian can be. And therefore my advice is—be not over-alarmed at the war; neither be led on to commence it. I do not see indeed, that any other people of Greece have reason to fear this war. For which of them is ignorant, that while, looking on the Persian as a common enemy, they were in concord among themselves, they enjoyed many advantages; but since they have regarded him as a friend and quarreled about private disputes with each other, they have suffered greater calamities than could have been wished in pronouncing a curse upon them? Then should we fear a man, whom fortune and heaven declare to be unprof-

[1] The Thebans had always been reproached for siding with Xerxes against the Greeks. (See the second Philippic, p. 83.) After the capture of Thebes by Alexander, this old charge was (not very fairly) revived against them by their enemies: "studia in Persas non præsentia tantum, verum et vetera adversus Græciæ libertatem increpantes; quamobrem odium eos omnium populorum esse:" as Justin says. The penalty which had been denounced against them ever since the Persian war was then inflicted, and Thebes was razed to the ground.

Here we find Demosthenes speaking more liberally of the Thebans than his countrymen were wont to do. The Athenians, besides their recent grounds of quarrel, had a long standing enmity with that people, arising out of various causes. The Thebans had been their most bitter opponents in the Peloponnesian war, and at its termination had proposed to destroy Athens altogether. Their merciless treatment of the Platæans, both in that war, and afterward B.C. 373, when they destroyed the city, could never be forgotten by the Athenians, between whom and the Platæans the closest friendship had subsisted ever since the battle of Marathon. Neighborhood had brought the two people into frequent contest about their frontiers; and their estrangement was increased by dissimilarity of character, customs, and institutions. Athenians sneered at Bœotian stupidity, while they had reason to dread Theban arms: and Thebans were jealous of a city, which by its external splendor and attractions of every kind so greatly eclipsed their own. Sixteen years after this speech was delivered, Thebes and Athens were united in a mortal struggle against a common enemy; yet owing to their long dissension, the utmost difficulty was found in bringing them together; and this was only effected by the powerful exertions of Demosthenes.

itable as a friend, and useful as an enemy? Let us do no such thing! Yet do him no injustice either; having regard to ourselves, and to the disturbances and jealousies among the other people of Greece. If it were possible with one heart and with combined forces to attack him alone, such an injury I would not have pronounced an injustice. But since this can not be, I say we must be cautious, and not afford the king a pretense for vindicating the rights of the other Greeks. As long as we remain quiet, any such attempt on his part would awaken suspicion; but if we are the first to commence hostilities, it will naturally be thought, that he courts their friendship because of his enmity with us.

Do not expose the melancholy condition of Greece, by convoking her people when you can not persuade them, and making war when you can not carry it on. Only keep quiet, fear nothing, and prepare yourselves. Let it be reported of you to the king—not (for heaven's sake) that all the Greeks and the Athenians are in distress and alarm and confusion; which is very far from the truth—but that, if falsehood and perjury were not considered as disgraceful by the Greeks, as by him they are considered honorable, you would have marched against him long ago; that you will forbear to do this for your own sakes, but you pray unto all the gods, that he may be inspired with the same madness that his ancestors were formerly. Should he come to reflect on these matters, he will find that your resolutions are taken with prudence. He knows assuredly, that Athens by her wars with his ancestors became prosperous and great, while by the repose, which she enjoyed before, she was not raised above any Grecian state so much as she is at present. And as to the Greeks, he perceives that they stand in need of some mediator, either a voluntary or an involuntary one; and he knows that he should himself step in as such a mediator, if he stirred up war. Therefore the accounts that he will receive from his informants will be intelligible and credible.

Not to trouble you, men of Athens, with over-many words, I will give a summary of my advice and retire. I bid you prepare yourselves against existing enemies, and I declare that with this same force you should resist the king and all other people, if they attempt to injure you; but never commence an injustice either in word or deed. Let us look that our actions, and not our speeches on the platform, be worthy of our ancestors. If you pursue this course, you will do service, not only to yourselves, but also to them who give the opposite counsel; since you will not be angry with them afterward for your errors committed now.[1]

THE ORATION ON THE LIBERTY OF THE RHODIANS.

THE ARGUMENT.

This Oration was delivered B.C. 351 on the following occasion.

In the island of Rhodes, as in divers other of the Grecian states, there had been many contests between the democratical party and the oligarchical. At the close of the Peloponnesian war it was in the hands of an oligarchy, under the protection of Lacedæmon. About the year 396 Conon, being at the head of a considerable fleet in that part of the Ægean, drove the Peloponnesians from the port of Rhodes, and compelled the islanders to renew their connection with Athens. Democracy was then re-established; but four years afterward the opposite faction again prevailed, a Spartan fleet made its appearance, the popular leaders and the friends of Athens were banished or put to death. For the next thirty years or more following that event little is known of Rhodian history. After the destruction of the Spartan navy, Rhodes with most of the Ægean isles returned to the Athenian confederacy, and we may fairly presume that a new democratical revolution was effected in the island during that period. But in the year 358 a rupture of a most serious kind took place between Rhodes and Athens, pregnant with disastrous consequences to both. This was the breaking out of the Social war, the immediate causes of which are obscurely reported to us, though there is sufficient evidence to show, that the provocation to revolt proceeded from the misconduct, or at least the imprudence of the Athenians themselves.

We learn from various parts of Demosthenes, especially from the Oration on the Chersonese, (p. 105,) how the Athenian commanders at this period, sent out with inadequate forces and supplies, were tempted or driven to commit irregularities, amounting often to acts of plunder and violence, in order to maintain their armaments or carry on their wars. Not confining their aggressions to the enemies

---

[1] The speech of Demosthenes was so far successful, that it calmed the excitement of the Athenians; and they were content to make a show of preparation, without adopting any actual measures of war. In the following Oration he refers with some satisfaction to this result.

of Athens, or even to neutrals, they harassed the allies, by extorting from them loans and contributions, and thus brought the name of their country into general odium and discredit. It seems that Chares, having the command of a fleet destined to act against Amphipolis, and conceiving himself to hold large discretionary powers, sailed to Rhodes, and by his vexatious and arbitrary proceedings so irritated the people, that they were ready on the first opportunity to throw off their connection with Athens. The islands of Cos and Chios had been alienated from the Athenians by similar causes, and desired to recover their independence. These three states entered into a league with Byzantium, which in fact had been meditated some years before, and raising a fleet powerful enough set the Athenians at defiance, commenced the Social war, which, after a three years' continuance, was terminated (as we have seen) by a peace humiliating to Athens B.C. 355.

In the course of this war the allies received assistance from Mausolus, king of Caria. He had formed the design of annexing Rhodes to his own dominions, to which it was so conveniently adjacent; but there was little hope of accomplishing this purpose, unless he could sever it from the Athenian alliance. The oligarchical party in Rhodes, still watching for a new revolution, were easily brought over to his views; and at the close of the war a Carian garrison was introduced into the island, which established the oligarchy, and in effect brought the island in subjection to a foreign yoke. The Rhodians had no hopes of recovering their liberty; they had lost the protection of a powerful state; while Mausolus could obtain effectual aid from the Persian king, whose vassal he was, and to whom it was important to acquire any of the islands near Asia Minor. Mausolus died in the year B.C. 353, and was succeeded by his queen Artemisia. In her reign the government of Rhodes became oppressive to the people; who at length resolving to throw off their yoke, sent a deputation to Athens, to implore her assistance. These petitioners, who were not very favorably received at Athens, found an advocate in Demosthenes.

It was natural to expect, that there would be a strong feeling at Athens against a people who had deeply injured her. A very few years had elapsed since the Social war, and the events were fresh in the memory of all. To overcome this feeling of resentment was the principal difficulty which an advocate of the Rhodian people had to encounter. Demosthenes appeals to the higher and nobler feelings of his countrymen. Motives of honor, generosity and compassion should influence Athenians: it was not worth while to remember the wrongs done them by so insignificant a people as the Rhodian; they should consider only what was due from them to Athens and to Greece. It was their duty as well as their interest, to vindicate the liberties of a Greek people under oppression, and more especially to defend the cause of popular government against oligarchs and tyrants. Unless they did so, their own constitution might soon be in danger; for there was a perpetual strife going on between oligarchy and democracy, and, if all other democracies were put down, the Athenian must be assailed at last. It was urged on the other side, that interference with Rhodes might provoke the hostility of the Persian king. Demosthenes contends, that the loss of Rhodes, which did not properly belong to him, was not likely to provoke the king; that in the present state of the Persian empire both he and Artemisia would probably remain neutral; but that at all events the Athenians ought to espouse the cause of the Rhodian people, even at the risk of Persian hostility.

I THINK, men of Athens, that on a consultation of such moment you ought to grant liberty of speech to every one of your advisers. For my own part, I have never thought it difficult to make you understand right counsel—for to speak plainly, you seem all to possess the knowledge yourselves—but to persuade you to follow it I have found difficult; for when any measure has been voted and resolved, you are then as far from the performance as you were from the resolution before.

One of the events, for which I consider you should be thankful to the gods, is that a people, who to gratify their own insolence went to war with you not long ago, now place their hopes of safety in you alone. Well may we be rejoiced at the present crisis: for if your measures thereupon be wisely taken, the result will be, that the calumnies of those who traduce our country you will practically and with credit and honor refute. The Chians, Byzantines, and Rhodians, accused us of a design to oppress them, and therefore combined to make the last war against us. It will turn out, that Mausolus, who contrived and instigated these proceedings, pretending to be a friend of the Rhodians, has deprived them of their liberty; the Chians and Byzantines, who called them allies, have not aided them in misfortune; while you, whom they dreaded, are the only people who have wrought their deliverance. And, this being seen by all the world, you will cause the people in every state to regard your friendship as the token of their security: nor can there be a greater blessing for you, than thus to obtain from all men a voluntary attachment and confidence.

I marvel to see the same persons advising you to oppose the king on behalf of the Egyptians,[1] and afraid of him in the

[1] This can have no reference to the expedition, conducted by the king in person, when by aid of the Greek mercenaries he finally conquered Egypt. For that expedition certainly took place at a later period, though the exact date is a matter of controversy. See Thirlwall's History of Greece, vol. vi. p. 142, note 2. It appears from

matter of the Rhodian people. All men know, that the latter are Greeks, the former a portion of his subjects. And I think some of you remember, that, when you were debating about the king's business, I first came forward and advised—nay, I was the only one, or one of two, that gave such counsel—that your prudent course in my opinion was, not to allege your quarrel with the king as the excuse for your arming, but to arm against your existing enemies, and defend yourselves against him also, if he attempted to injure you. Nor did I offer this advice without obtaining your approval; for you agreed with me. Well then: my reasoning of to-day is consistent with the argument on that occasion.[1] For, would the

Diodorus, that there had been various attempts made by Artaxerxes to recover Egypt, and it is likely enough that the Egyptian king applied to Athens for succor, and that the question of granting succor was discussed at Athens. The Athenians however appear to have abstained from all interference, not wishing to violate their treaty of peace with Persia. Chabrias indeed was appointed to command the fleet of Tachos in 361 B.C., but Diodorus expressly states that he was not sent out by his country, but went as a volunteer at the solicitation of Tachos. On the last occasion, when Artaxerxes applied to Athens for assistance against Egypt, the Athenians refused it, but promised neutrality. The passage of Diodorus above referred to is in lib. xvi. s. 40, and the words are as follows:—"The Egyptians having revolted from Persia at a former period, Artaxerxes Ochus, not liking war, remained himself inactive, but dispatched troops and generals, and incurred numerous failures by the cowardice and ignorance of his commanders. Wherefore he was despised by the Egyptians, but forced to submit, by reason of his indolence and love of peace. At this crisis however, as the Phœnicians and princes of Cyprus had followed the example of the Egyptians, and broken into rebellion out of contempt for his authority, he was roused to anger and resolved on war with his revolted subjects. He decided not to commission generals, but to contend in person for the preservation of his empire." It appears from another circumstance in the narrative of Diodorus, that the king had not commenced his final invasion of Egypt when this speech was delivered. It did not take place, according to the historian, till after he had given orders for the expedition against Cyprus; but those orders were given to Idrieus, after he had succeeded to the kingdom of Caria, which was at the close of the year 351; and at the time of the speech Artemisia was alive. There is a great difficulty attending the inference that we must draw from Diodorus, that the king only once invaded Egypt in person; for it is not only inconsistent with the express statement of Isocrates, quoted by Thirlwall in the passage above-mentioned, but it is not easily reconcilable with the language of Demosthenes in this Oration (below, page 194).

[1] The argument runs thus—I advised you then [in the last Oration]

king take me to his counsels, I should advise him as I advise you, in defense of his own possessions to make war upon any Greeks that opposed him, but not to think of claiming dominions to which he had no manner of title. If now it be your general determination, Athenians, to surrender to the king all places that he gets possession of, whether by surprise, or by deluding certain of the inhabitants, you have determined, in my judgment, unwisely: but if in the cause of justice you esteem it your duty, either to make war, if needful, or to suffer any extremity; in the first place, there will be the less necessity for such trials, in proportion as you are resolved to meet them; and secondly, you will manifest a spirit that becomes you.

That I suggest nothing new, in urging you to liberate the Rhodians—that you will do nothing new, in following my counsel—will appear, if I remind you of certain measures that succeeded. Once, O Athenians, you sent Timotheus out to assist Ariobarzanes,[1] annexing to the decree, "that he was

not to declare war against Persia, because such war would have been aggressive, and attended with serious difficulties. At the same time I recommended you to make defensive preparations, as the surest means of averting hostilities on the side of Persia, or defeating them if undertaken. I now advise you to assist the Rhodians, on the same principle that I counseled measures of defense; because they are a Greek people, with whom the Persian king has no right to interfere. It is not his interest to interfere with them, if he sees you in earnest (as you ought to be) for their defense: so I should tell him myself, if I were his adviser: and therefore I calculate he will be neutral.

The state of the Persian empire at this time fully justified the calculation of Demosthenes. See the last note.

[1] Ariobarzanes, satrap of Phrygia, was concerned in the rebellion of B.C. 362. See p. 186, note. It seems that, in soliciting Athenian aid, which he obtained the more easily on account of his connection with the state—he having received the honor of citizenship—Ariobarzanes had concealed the object of his preparations; and therefore the Athenians, in sending Timotheus, took the precaution of restricting his powers in the way mentioned by the orator. Timotheus, in return for some service which he had done, was helped by the satrap to get possession of Sestus and Crithote in the Chersonese. Cornelius Nepos praises the Athenian general, because, instead of getting any private recompense from Ariobarzanes, he had looked only to the advantage of his country; while Agesilaus, who had gone out on the same service, took a pecuniary reward for himself. Timotheus then proceeded to besiege Samos, which was occupied by a Persian garrison, and took it in the course of the following year. Isocrates the orator, who acted as the secretary of

not to infringe your treaty with the king." Timotheus, seeing that Ariobarzanes had openly revolted from the king, and that Samos was garrisoned by Cyprothemis, under the appointment of Tigranes, the king's deputy, renounced the intention of assisting Ariobarzanes, but invested the island with his forces and delivered it. And to this day there has been no war against you on that account. Men will not fight for aggressive purposes so readily as for defensive. To resist spoliation they strive with all their might; not so to gratify ambition: this they will attempt, if there be none to hinder them; but, if prevented, they regard not their opponents as having done them an injury.

My belief is, that Artemisia would not even oppose this enterprise now,[1] if our state were embarked in the measure. Attend a moment and see, whether my calculation be right or wrong. I consider—were the king succeeding in all his designs in Egypt, Artemisia would make a strenuous effort to get Rhodes into his power, not from affection to the king, but from a desire, while he tarried in her neighborhood,[2] to confer an important obligation upon him, so that he might give her the most friendly reception: but since he

Timotheus, was at the siege of Samos, and praises the general for having taken it with little or no cost to Athens.

The occupation of Samos by the Persians was an infringement of the peace of Antalcidas, by the terms of which the Greek islands were to be independent. Therefore the conduct of Timotheus, in wresting Samos from Persia, afforded an apt illustration for the argument of Demosthenes.

[1] Leland erroneously translates this as follows: "Nor do I think that Artemisia will act contrary to these principles." The position of the word *οὐδὲ* shows this to be wrong. Jacobs renders it: *Glaube ich nun aber, dass Artemisia der Stadt, wenn sie sich auf dieses Unternehmen einliesse, keinen Widerstand thun würde.*

[2] These words, *πλήσιον αὐτῆς διατρίβοντος ἐκείνου*, which are loosely rendered by most translators, suppose the case of Artaxerxes having conquered Egypt in person. In that event he would be brought nearer to Caria, than if he had remained at Susa. Then would Demosthenes put this case here, if he had not heard of an expedition conducted by the king in person? One can hardly think he would. Leland and other critics, assuming that Demosthenes speaks of the final invasion which led to the conquest of Egypt, explain the words, *πράττοντος ὡς λέγεται καὶ διημαρτηκότος*, by suggesting that false rumors may have come to Athens. This however does not solve the whole difficulty; and it seems more probable, that there were two occasions on which Artaxerxes marched in person against Egypt. See p. 191, note.

fares as they report, having miscarried in his attempts, she judges that this island—and so the fact is—would be of no further use to the king at present, but only a fortress to overawe her kingdom and prevent disturbances. Therefore it seems to me, she would rather you had the island, without her appearing to have surrendered it, than that he should obtain possession. I think indeed, she will send no succors at all,[1] but, if she do, they will be scanty and feeble. As to the king —what he will do, I can not pretend to know; but this I will maintain, that it is expedient for Athens to have it immediately understood, whether he means to claim the Rhodian city or not; for, if he should, you will have to deliberate not on the concerns of Rhodes only, but on those of Athens and all Greece.

Even[2] if the Rhodians, who are now in the government, had held it by themselves, I would not have advised you to espouse their cause; not though they promised to do every thing for you. But I see, that in the beginning, in order to put down the democracy, they gained over a certain number of citizens, and afterward banished those very men, when they had accomplished their purpose. I think therefore, that people who have been false to two parties,[3] would be no steadier allies to you. And never would I have proffered this counsel, had I thought it would benefit the Rhodian people only; for I am not their state-friend,[4] nor is any one of them connected with me by ties of private hospitality. And even if both these causes had existed, I would not have spoken, unless I had considered it for your advantage. Indeed, as far as the Rhodians are concerned, if the advocate for their deliver-

[1] To the Rhodian government, in case of Athenian interference: as Schaefer rightly explains it.

[2] Leland mistranslates this: "Yet, were these Rhodians who now possess the city strong enough to maintain their possession, I should not have advised you to grant them aid:" as if Demosthenes actually did advise the Athenians to aid the Rhodian government. And then he has a long note, which is transcribed by Jacobs, to explain this mistranslation. The meaning of Demosthenes is as follows:—If this had been a question not between Rhodes and a foreign power, but only between the Rhodian government and the popular party, still I would have advised you to side with the latter against the former.

[3] *I. e.* to the people at large, and to the select few whom they associated with themselves in the first instance.

[4] See p. 97, note 2.

ance may be allowed to say so, I am rejoiced at what has happened—that, after grudging to you the recovery of your rights, they have lost their own liberty; and, when they might have had an alliance on equal terms with Greeks and their betters, they are under subjection to barbarians and slaves, whom they have admitted into their fortresses.[1] I would almost say, that, if you determine to assist them, these events have turned out for their good. For, during prosperity, I doubt whether they would have learned discretion, being Rhodians;[2] but since they are taught by experience, that folly is mightily injurious to men, they may possibly perhaps become wiser for the future; and this I think would be no small advantage to them. I say therefore, you should endeavor to rescue these people, and not harbor resentment, considering that you too have often been deceived by miscreants, but for no such deceit would you allow that you merited punishment yourselves.

Observe also, men of Athens, that you have waged many wars both against democracies and against oligarchies—this indeed you know without my telling—but for what cause you have been at war with either, perhaps not one of you considers. What are the causes? Against democratical states your wars have been either for private grievances, when you could not make public satisfaction, or for territory, or bound-

[1] Vitruvius relates a strategem, by which Artemisia got complete dominion of Rhodes. The Rhodians had plotted with a party in Halicarnassus to overthrow the Carian government, and sent a fleet with troops to assist in the execution of their design. The troops landed and advanced to the city, where the inhabitants were ranged under the walls as if to give them a friendly reception. But this was done by order of Artemisia, who had discovered the plot and laid an ambush for the Rhodians. They were surrounded and slain. Artemisia took their ships, and put a Carian force on board, which sailing to Rhodes, and being mistaken by the people for their own armament returning, got possession of the Rhodian capital. If the story be well founded, the occurrence was probably later than this Oration, which refers to no act of hostility between the Rhodians and the ruler of Caria. It should be noticed, that besides the capital city of Rhodes, there were other considerable and much more ancient towns in the island, Lindus, Ialysus, and Camirus.

[2] Homer calls the Rhodians ἀγερῶχοι, which is translated *magnanimi* or *superbi*, and seems to be a term of praise. Though the orator speaks slightingly of them, they became celebrated for their commerce and their laws.

aries, or a point of honor, or the leadership: against oligarchies, for none of these matters, but for your constitution and freedom. Therefore I would not hesitate to say, I think it better that all the Greeks should be your enemies with a popular government, than your friends under oligarchal. For with freemen I consider you would have no difficulty in making peace when you chose; but with people under an oligarchy even friendship I hold to be insecure. It is impossible that the few can be attached to the many, the seekers of power to the lovers of constitutional equality.

I marvel none of you conceive—when the Chians and Mitylenæans are governed by oligarchies, when the Rhodians and nearly all people are about being drawn into this slavery—that our constitution is in the same peril: and none consider, it is impossible, if all establishments are on the principle of oligarchy, that they will let your democracy alone. They know too well, that no other people will bring things back to the state of liberty: therefore they will wish to destroy a government, from which they apprehend mischief to themselves. Ordinary doers of wrong you may regard as enemies to the sufferers only; they that subvert constitutions and transform them into oligarchies must be looked upon, I say, as the common enemies to all lovers of freedom. And besides, men of Athens, it is right that you, living under self-government, should show the same feeling for a free people in misfortune, that you would expect others to have for you in case of a similar calamity; which I trust may never befall! Though indeed it may be said that the Rhodians have had their deserts, the occasion is not a fit one for triumph: the fortunate should always be seen to interest themselves for the benefit of the unfortunate, since the future is uncertain to all men.[1]

I often hear it said before this assembly, that, when our commonwealth was in misfortune, certain people were solicitous for its preservation; among whom—I will here men-

[1] The Melian orator, in the debate written by Thucydides, warns the Athenians not to be cruel and oppressive to others, for fear of retaliation at some future time; lest, rendering no mercy, they should find none. Demosthenes recommends a still higher policy, to succor the unfortunate; to win golden opinions in the hour of prosperity, and secure friends against the day of misfortune.

tion a little circumstance of the Argives alone.[1] I would not have you, famous as you have ever been for succoring the distressed, appear in a matter of this kind inferior to the Argives: who, inhabiting a country adjacent to the Lacedæmonians, seeing them to have dominion over land and sea, did not fear or hesitate to show their attachment to you, but even passed a vote—when embassadors had come from Lacedæmon (as we are told) to demand certain Athenian refugees—that, unless they departed before sunset, they should be adjudged enemies. Would it not be disgraceful, my countrymen, if, when the commons of Argos dreaded not the power and empire of the Lacedæmonians in those times, you, who are Athenians, should be frightened at a person of barbarian origin, and a woman too? They indeed might allege, that they have often been defeated by the Lacedæmonians: whereas you have often vanquished the king, and not once been defeated either by the king himself or by his subjects; for, if ever the king has obtained an advantage over our state, he has obtained it in this way—and in no other—by bribing the betrayers of Greece and the basest of her people. And even such advantage has not benefited him. At the very time, when he had enfeebled Athens by aid of the Lacedæmonians, you will find him struggling for his kingdom with Clearchus and Cyrus.[2] Thus he has neither beaten us openly, nor done himself any good by his intrigues. There are some, I observe, who are used to slight Philip[3] as a person of no account, but

[1] This occurred soon after the Peloponnesian war, when Athens was under the dominion of the thirty tyrants, and a large number of Athenian citizens were compelled to seek safety in exile.

[2] It was to the pecuniary assistance of Persia, obtained by the management of Lysander, that the Spartans were mainly indebted for their success in the Peloponnesian war. A few years afterward Cyrus, who had been most active in the Spartan cause, marched from his province in Asia Minor to contend for the crown with his brother Artaxerxes. Clearchus commanded the Greek mercenaries in his service. The death of Cyrus, who was slain charging at the head of his troops in the battle of Cunaxa, delivered Artaxerxes and his kingdom from further danger. This expedition is the subject of Xenophon's Anabasis. The retreat of the ten thousand Greeks, (after the treacherous murder of their generals,) under the skillful conduct of Xenophon himself, is one of the most interesting pieces of Grecian history.

[3] About a year only had elapsed since the speaking of the first Philippic. Whatever effect that speech may have produced at the time, it seems to have made no lasting impression. The inaction of Philip

dread the king as an enemy terrible to any that he chooses. However, if we are not to oppose the one, because he is contemptible, and yield every thing to the other, because he is formidable, against whom shall we take the field, O Athenians?

There are persons here, men of Athens, famous for advocating the rights of others against you; to whom I would give one little piece of advice—to undertake the defense of your rights against others, that they may set an example of dutiful conduct. It is absurd for any one to instruct you in the principles of justice, without acting justly himself: and it is not just, that a citizen should have considered the arguments against you, and not the arguments in your favor. Look you, I pray! How happens it there is none in Byzantium, who will admonish them not to take possession of Chalcedon,[1] which belongs to the king, and you held it once, and by no manner of title is it theirs?—also that they are not to make Selymbria,[2] a city formerly in your alliance, tributary to themselves, and that Byzantium is not to determine the limits of the Selymbrian territory, contrary to the oaths and the treaties, by which it is declared that the cities shall be independent? And none has there been to advise Mausolus in his lifetime, none since his death to advise Artemisia, not to seize upon Cos[3] and Rhodes and other Grecian

in the two following years relieved the Athenians from any immediate apprehension of danger. They were roused to new alarm by the rupture of Philip with Olynthus.

[1] Chalcedon, founded by the Megarians on the Asiatic coast of the Bosphorus, was called the city of the blind, because the settlers had overlooked the more beautiful spot on the European coast, where afterward Byzantium (site of the modern Constantinople) was built. The fate of Chalcedon, like many other towns similarly situated, was to fall alternately under the dominion of Persia, Athens, and Lacedæmon. It was taken from the Lacedæmonians by Alcibiades, but surrendered to Lysander after the decisive battle of Ægos-Potamos. The peace of Antalcidas restored it to Persia. At this time the Byzantines, who had acquired considerable power since the Social war, were endeavoring to draw it over to their alliance.

[2] Selymbria is on the Propontine coast, between Byzantium and Perinthus.

[3] The island of Cos, celebrated as the birth-place of Hippocrates the physician and Apelles the painter, lies a little off the coast of Caria, not far from Halicarnassus. It is mentioned in the Oration on the Peace, that Cos, Chios, and Rhodes were seized upon by the Carian government. (See p. 80.) Shortly before this time the city of Cos had

cities, which the king their master ceded by his treaty to the Greeks, and for which the Greeks of that period sustained numerous perils and honorable contests. Or, if they have both of them[1] such a monitor, yet seemingly there are none to follow his advice.

I esteem it a just measure, to restore the Rhodian democracy: yet, granting it were not just, when I look at the conduct of these people, I conceive it right to advise the measure.[2] And why? Because, O Athenians, if all men were inclined to observe justice, it would be disgraceful for us alone to refuse; but, when all the rest are seeking the power to do wrong, for us to profess high principle and undertake no enterprise, would in my opinion be not justice, but cowardice. I see that men have their rights allowed them in proportion to their power: of which I can produce an example familiar to you all. There are two treaties between the Greeks and the king; that which our republic made, which is universally praised, and this latter one, concluded by the Lacedæmonians, which is the subject of complaint.[3] And the definition of rights in both the treaties is

been rebuilt on a scale of great splendor, and had become one of the richest and most beautiful in Greece.

[1] *I. e.* the Byzantines and Artemisia.

[2] Demosthenes may seem here to be setting up expediency against right and justice; but his reasoning, properly understood, does not amount to this. He means to say—in the politics of nations it is impossible, that the same rules of justice, which ought to regulate the conduct of individuals toward each other, can be strictly applied. To a great people, in order that they may perform their duty to weaker states and administer justice on a large scale, the maintenance of power is essential. They must not permit their neighbors, because they are nominally at peace with them, to commit aggressions upon neutral states. The end of such acquiescence would be the destruction of their own empire. Such is the principle on which in modern times our own and other governments have frequently gone to war, to preserve the balance of power in Europe. To apply this argument to the present case—Persia has a treaty of peace with Athens: therefore Athens ought not to attack Persia. But Persia has oppressed Rhodes: therefore Athens may break the treaty with Persia, because Persia has committed an injustice, tending (at least in its remote consequence) to ruin Athens. In reality the protection of Rhodes against Persia is not an act of injustice; but granting for argument's sake that it is, Athens has done right in committing it; and the discussion about justice or injustice is nothing but a verbal dispute.

[3] The first of these treaties is supposed to be the peace of Cimon,

not the same. For, although private political rights are granted by the laws impartially to all, the same for the weak as for the strong; the rule of Hellenic right is prescribed by the greater powers to the less.[1]

Since then it is your fixed resolution to pursue a just policy,[2] you must look that you have the means to carry it

according to which the Greek cities on the coast of Asia Minor were made independent, the Persian king was precluded from approaching the coast within the distance of a day's journey on horseback, and from sending any ship of war between the Cyanean islands at the mouth of the Bosphorus and the Chelidonian islands off the Lycian coast. Whether this peace was made after the battle of the Eurymedon, gained by Cimon over the Persians B.C. 466, or after his expedition to Cyprus B.C. 449, has been a matter of controversy; and some historians have doubted whether such a peace was ever made.

The second of the treaties here referred to is the peace of Antalcidas, negotiated by the Lacedæmonians B.C. 387; according to which the Greek cities were to be independent, Sparta retaining her dominions in Peloponnesus, and Athens keeping only Lemnos, Imbrus, and Scyrus; the Greek cities of Asia, and the islands of Cyprus and Clazomenæ were acknowledged to belong to the Persian empire. The Lacedæmonians, by sacrificing the Asiatic Greeks to Persia, detached that monarchy from the Athenian alliance, and were enabled to maintain their own ascendency over the Grecian states.

[1] The argument is thus pursued—In national affairs right follows might. An illustration of this is afforded by the two treaties with Persia. In each case the various claims and questions of right were settled upon a different plan, and according to a different rule. This proves that there can be no fixed principle of international justice, by which the relations of different states to each other can be immutably preserved. The civil law of every free country prescribes a uniform rule of right and justice for all. But there is no such rule in the law of nations, as experience demonstrates.

[2] This observation is in accordance with the argument as above explained. He assumes that his countrymen were sincerely desirous of acting on the principle of justice, but contends that they could not carry out their purposes by abstaining from interference with other nations. If they espoused the cause of the oppressed, they would be looked up to and respected as the patrons of freedom; if they kept aloof, they would be despised, and their allies would gradually fall away from them. Jacobs translates this clause: *Da Euch nun die Kenntniss dessen, was zu thun recht ist, nicht mangelt.* Leland and Francis read *καὶ ποιεῖν*. Leland has: "You assume the character of arbitrators and defenders of justice." Francis: "It becomes the dignity of your character to determine those bounds [of justice] for others, and to act in consequence of that determination." Pabst follows Jacobs; but their version of *ἐγνωκέναι ποιεῖν* is incorrect. Reiske and Schaefer explain it rightly.

out. Such means you will possess, if you are supposed to be the common protectors of Grecian liberty. It is, doubtless, very difficult for you to adopt proper measures. The rest of mankind have one battle to fight, namely, against their avowed enemies: if they conquer those, nothing hinders them accomplishing their desires. You, Athenians, have a double contest; that which the rest have, and also another, prior to that, and more arduous: for you must in council overcome a faction, who act among you in systematic opposition to the state. Since therefore through these men it is impossible for any good measure to be effected without a struggle, the natural consequence is that you lose many advantages. Perhaps the chief cause why so many adopt this line of politics without scruple, is the support afforded them by their hirers: at the same time you are yourselves chargeable with blame. You ought, O Athenians, to hold the same opinion concerning the post of civil duty, as you hold concerning the military. What is that? You consider that one, who deserts the post assigned by his general, should be degraded and deprived of constitutional privileges.[1] It is right therefore, that men who desert the political post received from their ancestors, and support oligarchical measures, should be disabled to act as your counselors. Among your allies you regard those to be the most attached, who have sworn to have the same friends and enemies with yourselves; and yet of your statesmen you esteem those the most faithful, who to your certain knowledge have sided with the enemies of Athens.

However—matter of accusation against these men, matter of censure against the people, is not hard to discover: the difficulty is to know, by what counsels or what conduct our present evils may be repaired. This perhaps is not the occasion to speak of all: could you only give effect to your policy by some useful effort, things in general perhaps, one after another, would go on improving. My opinion is, that you should take this enterprise vigorously in hand, and act

[1] An Athenian who deserted the army in time of war was liable to prosecution by a process called *λειποστρατίον γραφή*. One who deserted his post or rank was liable to a *λειποταξίον γραφή*. A conviction for either of such offenses was followed by disfranchisement, *ἀτιμία*. The Generals were the presiding magistrates, who took cognizance of these matters.

worthily of the state, remembering, that you love to hear men praise your ancestors and recount their exploits and speak of their trophies. Consider then, your forefathers erected these, not that you may view and admire them only, but that you may imitate also the virtues of the dedicators.[1]

[1] The speech of Demosthenes produced no effect. Athens abstained from interference; the Rhodians continued under the government of an oligarchy, and subjection to Caria. (See pp. 80 and 167 of this volume.) Artemisia died soon after the delivery of this Oration, having reigned two years. She is said to have been inconsolable for the death of her husband Mausolus, whose ashes she drank dissolved in scented water, and to whose memory she paid the most extravagant honors. The monument which she erected was so magnificent as to be considered one of the wonders of the world; and from this the name of *Mausoleum* has been applied to all sepulchres built on a grand scale. She invited the most eminent literary men to her court, and offered a reward for the best funeral panegyric. Theopompus the historian, a native of Chios, and pupil of Isocrates, gained the prize. Artemisia was succeeded on the throne by her brother Idrieus, who reigned seven years.

THE ORATION FOR THE MEGALOPOLITANS.

THE ARGUMENT.

Megalopolis was an Arcadian city near the frontiers of Laconia. It was founded in the year B.C. 371, and, being designed for the metropolis of the whole Arcadian people, who then united themselves into one body, it was built on a scale of magnitude corresponding with that purpose, having a circumference of more than six miles, and received the name of the *great city*. Next to Athens, it is said to have been the most beautiful city in Greece. The population was obtained by migration from the existing Arcadian towns, no less than forty of which were required to contribute to it. Most of these were entirely deserted by their inhabitants, others were reduced to the condition of villages dependent on Megalopolis. A supreme council of ten thousand, taken from the whole Arcadian body, held their public deliberations in the capital. About half a century afterward, when it was besieged by Polysperchon, there were found to be fifteen thousand citizens capable of bearing arms in its defense.

The chief object of building this metropolis was, to establish a permanent union among the Arcadians and preserve their national independence. Before that time, the Arcadians as a body had very little influence in the affairs of Peloponnesus, though they occupied a large portion of its territory. They had generally been in the alliance of Sparta, whose armies they strengthened by a brave and hardy race of soldiers. It was therefore the policy of Sparta to keep them feeble and divided among themselves. In the time of the Peloponnesian war Mantinea, then the principal city of Arcadia, formed a small confederacy among her neighbors, renounced her connection with the Lacedæmonians, and joined an offensive alliance with Athens and Argos. But this was soon put an end to. The Mantineans were compelled, by the success of the Lacedæmonian arms, to abandon their confederacy; and at a later period, B.C. 387, paid dearly for their disaffection to Sparta, by having their city dismantled and being dispersed into villages.

The defeat of the Spartans at Leuctra changed the aspect of affairs in Greece. The prestige of ancient victory was gone; and it was soon found that the vast alliance, of which Sparta had been the head, and which had enabled her for many years to give the law to Greece, would crumble almost entirely away. One of the first effects of this change in Peloponnesus was the rebuilding of Mantinea; which was soon followed by the establishment of Megalopolis. But the heaviest blow to the pride and power of Lacedæmon was the loss of her ancient province of Messenia, which for more than three centuries had been the fairest portion of her domain. Whether the Arcadians could have maintained their independence against Sparta without foreign aid, may perhaps be doubted; but this last revolution was wholly due to the arms of Thebes and the genius of Epaminondas.

That general, having assembled a large army in Bœotia, marched across the isthmus and was joined in Arcadia by his Peloponnesian allies. At the head of an overpowering force he invaded and ravaged Laconia. Troops of divers people—who not many years before had followed the Lacedæmonians in their wars, or would hardly have dared to face them in the field—Thebans, Phocians, Locrians, Eubœans, Thessalians, Acarnanians, Argives, Arcadians, Eleans, marched now almost without opposition to the gates of Sparta; and nothing but the shadow of the Spartan name preserved that haughty capital from destruction. Epaminondas did not venture to make a general assault upon the town, but, after continuing his ravages for some time longer, proceeded to execute his well-laid scheme, which he rightly judged would reduce Sparta to the condition of a second or third-rate power in Greece.

The Messenian population had long been, like the Laconian helots, in a state of vassalage to Sparta, but were ripe for insurrection at any favorable opportunity, as they had proved during the Athenian occupation of Pylus. The march of Epaminondas into Laconia was the signal for a universal rising of that people, who were now again to form a nation, and to build a capital city under the protection of the Theban general. But it was not only the existing inhabitants of the country, by whom this task, of reconstituting the nation, was to be accomplished; for which, after their long servitude, they might not have been so well fitted by themselves. Messenian exiles from every quarter, and especially those of Naupactus, who had been expelled after the Peloponnesian war, and migrated to Sicily and Africa, were invited to return to their ancient home, and assist in the glorious restoration. It has been mentioned as a remarkable example of the love of country, that these exiles, during so long an absence, had jealously preserved their ancestral usages and the purity of their original language. They returned in great numbers and formed the nucleus of a Messenian government. The new city was founded on the site of the ancient Ithome, Epaminondas laying the first stone, and received the name of Messene. This was B.C. 369.

The humiliation of Sparta was now complete. She had no power to disturb the new settlement. She was hemmed in by a chain of enemies, who cut off her communication with Peloponnesus; by the Messenians on the west, the Arcadians and Argives on the north. Her war with Thebes continued for eight more years. The succor of Athens and her few remaining allies saved her from further disasters; and the death of her great enemy, Epaminondas, brought on a general peace, B.C. 361.

From the negotiations of this peace the Lacedæmonians kept aloof, refusing to acknowledge the independence of Messenia, which they regarded as a deep disgrace to themselves. Their spirit, though depressed, was not extinguished; and they only waited for an opportunity of recovering their lost dominion. Archidamus, son of

Agesilaus, who had acquired honor in the late war by the *tearless victory*, (in which he defeated the Arcadians and Argives without losing a single Spartan life,) kept alive the ambitious hopes of his countrymen, and continually stimulated them to fresh exertions. He was a man of ardent character; to recover Messenia was the principal object of his desire; in which he had even been encouraged by a pamphlet of Isocrates, entitled Archidamus, and still extant. In the course of seven or eight years events occurred which favored the views of this prince. There had been disturbances in Arcadia. The Sacred war had broken out, in which the principal parties were Phocis and Thebes. An obstinate struggle was yet going on; neither party had gained any decisive advantage, and both were greatly weakened. The Phocian generals had carried the war into the enemy's country; some of the Bœotian towns had been taken; and the Thebans, distressed at home, and burdened with heavy expenses, seemed no longer in a condition to assist their Peloponnesian allies.

Under these circumstances, about the year 353, Archidamus thought the time had arrived to effect a counter-revolution, which should restore the influence of his country. His real aim was the destruction of Megalopolis and Messene. But to avow this purpose, or attempt to execute it without further pretext than the desire to satisfy Spartan ambition, might have drawn on him the hostility of those states which were unconnected with the Theban alliance. Accordingly, he conceived the idea of announcing a principle which would secure certain advantages to the states hostile to Thebes, and induce them to concur in his own scheme of aggrandizement. He gave it out, that ancient rights ought to be resumed; that Athens should have Oropus, the towns of Thespiæ, Platæa, and Archomenus should be restored; Elis and Phlius should have certain claims conceded to them. While he published these declarations, he kept in the background that portion of the scheme in which Sparta was interested, viz., the recovery of Messenia and the dissolution of the Arcadian union.

Notwithstanding all the care which Archidamus took to conceal his views, they could not fail to be apparent; and it was soon understood that the warlike preparations in Laconia were designed against Megalopolis. Two embassies were sent at the same time to Athens, one by the Spartans, and one by the Megalopolitans, each to solicit assistance in the approaching war. The Spartan embassadors reminded the Athenians of their former alliance, and showed what advantage would accrue to them from the plan of Archidamus, by which Thebes their old enemy would be depressed. The Megalopolitan deputies urged the justice of their own cause, and the danger that would result from the revival of Spartan supremacy.

There were many speakers on both sides in the Athenian assembly. Demosthenes espoused the cause of the Megalopolitans, and delivered what Auger pronounces to be one of the most subtle of his orations. He begins by condemning the warmth with which both parties had assailed their adversaries. It became them, (he argues,) without any feeling or prejudice for or against either of the contending states, to decide the question by reference to justice and the good of Athens.

Justice required that no people should be oppressed by another. Their alliance with Sparta had been based on that principle, and they had saved her from ruin; but if Sparta commenced ambitious enterprises inconsistent with the spirit of their alliance, they were justified in breaking it off. It was the interest of Athens, that neither Sparta nor Thebes should be too powerful. The dissolution of Megalopolis would lead to the reconquest of Messenia, and that would destroy the balance of power in Peloponnesus. The advantage offered to Athens might be obtained in a more honorable manner, without sacrificing the Peloponnesians; and as to Thebes, it was better to weaken her by conferring an obligation upon her allies, and attaching them to Athens, than by allowing them to suffer injustice.

It appears to me, O Athenians, that both are in fault, they who have spoken for the Arcadians and they who have spoken for the Lacedæmonians. For as if they were deputies from either people, not citizens of Athens, to which both direct their embassies, they accuse and attack one another. This might be the duty of the envoys; but to speak independently on the question, and consider your interests dispassionately, was the part of men who presume to offer counsel here. I really think—setting aside the knowledge of their persons and their Attic tongue—many would take them for either Arcadians or Laconians.

I see how vexatious a thing it is to advise for the best. For when you are carried away by delusion, some taking one view and some another, if any man attempts to advise a middle course, and you are too impatient to listen, he will please neither party and fall into disgrace with both. However, if this be my case, I will rather myself be thought a babbler, than leave you to be misled by certain people, contrary to my notion of Athenian interests. On other points I will speak, with your permission, afterward; but will begin with principles admitted by all, and explain what I consider your wisest course.

Well then: no man will deny it to be good for Athens, that both the Lacedæmonians and our Theban neighbors should be weak. But things are in this sort of position, if we may form a conjecture from the statements repeatedly made in our assembly—the Thebans will be weakened by the re-establishment of Orchomenus,[1] Thespiæ, and Platæa; the Lace-

[1] The Bœotian cities were at an early period connected by a federal union, each having an independent government. Thebes was at their head, and received a council of deputies from the league. Every state

dæmonians will grow powerful again, if they subdue Arcadia and take Megalopolis. We must mind therefore, that we suffer not the one people to wax mighty and formidable, before the other has become weak; that the power of Lacedæmon do not increase (unremarked by us) in a greater degree than it is well for that of Thebes to be reduced. For we shall hardly say this, that we should like to have Lacedæmonians instead of Thebans for our rivals. It is not this we are anxious for, but that neither may have the means of injuring us: so shall we enjoy the best security.

But granting this ought to be so[1]—it were scandalous forsooth, to take those men for allies, against whom we were arrayed at Mantinea, and then to assist them against the people with whom we shared the peril of that day. I think so too, but with one addition — "provided the others are willing to act justly." If all will choose to observe peace, we

appointed a Bœotarch, who took his share of military command and some other executive duties. In process of time Thebes asserted an imperial authority over the federal cities, and most of them were compelled to submit. Platæa espoused the alliance of Athens, and for a long time enjoyed her protection, but in the Peloponnesian war fell a victim to Theban revenge. The exiles returned and rebuilt the city after the peace of Antalcidas, but it was again destroyed by the Thebans B.C. 373. Thespiæ was destroyed about the same time; having long been suspected of disaffection to Thebes and favor to Athens. The Thebans had dismantled its walls in the Peloponnesian war, though the flower of the Thespian youth had fallen in their cause at the battle of Delium. Orchomenus was taken and depopulated by the Thebans B.C. 368. They had resolved on that measure some years before, but were induced by Epaminondas to change their intention. Afterward, being alarmed by a conspiracy of certain Orchomenian exiles, they fell upon the city, massacred the adult citizens, and sold the women and children for slaves. During the Phocian war, and shortly before or after the date of this Oration, Orchomenus was seized upon by the Phocian general, Onomarchus, and occupied as a fortified post. At the close of that war it was delivered by Philip to the Thebans, who razed it to the ground. After the battle of Chæronea Philip caused all these three cities, Platæa, Thespiæ, and Orchomenus, to be restored.

[1] Viz., that neither Lacedæmonians nor Thebans should be powerful &c. Most of the translators seem to have neglected the word δεῖν in this clause. Jacobs has: *Aber dieses Alles zugegeben.* Auger: "Nous conviendrons peut-être de ce point." Pabst and Francis commit the same error. Leland errs only in giving too much force to δεῖν: "But it will be said—yes! this is indeed a point of utmost moment"

The force of the argument is not impaired by this trifling error. But inattention to minutiæ sometimes leads to considerable mistakes; and I therefore notice it for the sake of the student.

shall not help the Megalopolitans; for there will be no necessity; and thus we shall be in no opposition to our fellows in arms: one people are, as they profess, our allies already, the other will become so now. And what more could we desire? But should they[1] attempt injustice and determine on war—then—if this be the only question, whether we ought or ought not to abandon Megalopolis to the Lacedæmonians, although it would be unjust, I concede the point; let things take their course, don't oppose your former partners in danger: but if you all know, that after taking that city they will march to attack Messene, let any of the speakers who are now so hard upon the Magalopolitans tell me, what in that case he will advise us to do. None will declare. However, you all know, that you would be obliged to support them, whether these men recommend it or not, both by the oaths that we have sworn to the Messenians,[2] and because it is expedient that their city should be preserved. Reflect therefore in your minds, whether it would be more noble and generous, to begin your resistance to Lacedæmonian aggression with the defense

[1] *I.e.* the Lacedæmonians; whom the orator does not expressly name, because they are uppermost in his mind, since the clause ending *τῶν ἑτέρων*.

[2] This engagement was probably entered into at the general peace, which was concluded after the battle of Mantinea, and by which the Athenians, as well as other states of Greece, recognized the independence of Messenia. Pausanias mentions, that at this time, when the assistance of Athens was prayed for by the Messenians, it was promised in the event of a Spartan invasion.

It is quite clear from the argument of Demosthenes, that the claims of Megalopolis upon the Athenians stood upon a different footing from those of Messene, not being grounded upon any former alliance. Yet in the narrative of Diodorus, XV. 94, we read that the Athenians sent a body of troops under Pammenes to quell an insurrection in Arcadia, which broke out in about a year's time after the peace, and threatened to dissolve the Megalopolitan community; that Pammenes reduced the malcontents to submission, and compelled those who had seceded from Megalopolis, and gone back to their ancient homes, to return to the capital. The name of Pammenes, a distinguished Theban general and colleague of Epaminondas, pretty well indicates (as Thirlwall has remarked) that Θηβαίους ought to be read in Diodorus instead of Ἀθηναίους. Besides, (independently of the proof afforded by this Oration,) what could be more improbable, than that the Megalopolitans should so soon after the battle of Mantinea request the assistance of Athens, their opponent? On the other hand, what more probable, than that they should solicit the aid of Thebes, their ally?

of Megalopolis, or with that of Messene. You will now be considered as protectors of the Arcadians, and striving for the maintenance of that peace, for which you exposed yourselves in the battle-field: whereas then it will be manifest to the world, that you desire Messene to stand not so much for the sake of justice, as for fear of Lacedæmon. Our purposes and our actions should always be just; but we must also be careful, that they are attended with advantage.

There is an argument of this kind urged by my opponents, that we should attempt to recover Oropus,[1] and, if we now make enemies of the men who would assist us to gain it, we shall have no allies. I also say, we should try to recover Oropus: but, that Lacedæmon will be our enemy, if we join alliance with the Arcadians who wish to be our friends, they of all men, I consider, are not at liberty to assert, who persuaded you to assist the Lacedæmonians in their hour of danger. The men who argue thus actually persuaded you—when all the Peloponnesians[2] came to Athens and desired to march with you against the Lacedæmonians—to reject their

[1] Oropus was on the confines of Attica and Bœotia, on the coast opposite Eretria in Eubœa. It anciently belonged to Athens, but frequently changed masters. In the twentieth year of the Peloponnesian war it was betrayed to the Bœotians and Eretrians. It became independent at the close of the war; but a few years after, the Thebans took advantage of some internal disturbances to seize upon the city, which they removed nearly a mile from the coast, and annexed to the Bœotian confederacy. A new revolution some time after restored it to Athens. But in the year 366 B.C. Themison, ruler of Eretria, got possession of it by the aid of some exiles. The Athenians marched against him, but, the Thebans also making their appearance with an army, they were induced to leave Oropus under Theban protection, until the dispute could be amicably settled. The Thebans however kept it in their own hands; and so it remained until after the battle of Chæronea, when Philip gave it up to the Athenians.

[2] This statement accords not with the narrative of Xenophon, who makes no mention of such an application to Athens, though he states that the Athenians invited a congress to their own city, which was attended by many of the Peloponnesians. Diodorus however relates, that in the second year after the battle of Leuctra the Spartans sent a force into Arcadia, and took possession of Orchomenus; that they were afterward defeated by Lycomedes of Mantinea, but the Arcadians, still fearing the power of Sparta, even after they had been joined by the Eleans and Argives, sent an embassy for assistance to Athens. The Athenians having refused their request, they applied to the Thebans, who sent an army under Epaminondas and Pelopidas.

overtures, (on which account, as a last resource, they applied to Thebes,) and to contribute money and risk your lives for the safety of Lacedæmon. You would hardly, I think, have been disposed to save them, had they told you, that after their deliverance, unless you suffered them to have their own way and commit injustice again, they should owe you no thanks for your protection. And indeed, however repugnant it may be to the designs of the Spartans, that we should adopt the Arcadian alliance, surely their gratitude, for having been saved by us in a crisis of extreme peril, ought to outweigh their resentment for being checked in their aggression now. How then can they avoid assisting you to regain Oropus, or being thought the basest of mankind? By the gods I can not see.

I wonder also to hear it argued, that, if we espouse the Arcadian alliance and adopt these measures, our state will be chargeable with inconstancy and bad faith. It seems to me, O Athenians, the reverse. Why? Because no man, I apprehend, will question, that in defending the Lacedæmonians, and the Thebans[1] before them, and lastly the Eubœans,[2] and making them afterward her allies, our republic has always had one and the same object. What is that? To protect the injured. If this be so, the inconstancy will not be ours, but theirs who refuse to adhere to justice; and it will appear, that while circumstances change, through people continually encroaching, Athens changes not.

It seems to me, the Lacedæmonians are acting the part of very crafty men. For now they say that the Eleans ought to recover a certain part of Triphylia,[3] the Phliasians Tricara-

[1] He alludes to the war that followed the seizure of the Cadmea, commenced by the invasion of Cleombrotus B.C. 378. See the Historical Abstract.

[2] When the Thebans attempted to get possession of the island. See the Oration on the Chersonese, p. 113.

[3] Triphylia was a small province on the Cyparissian bay, between Elis and Messenia. Concerning this there had been many disputes between the Eleans and the Arcadians. The chief town was Lepreum, which in the Peloponnesian war became the cause of a rupture between Elis and Sparta. The Eleans had assisted Lepreum against the Arcadians, on condition of receiving half the Leprean territory: for which the Lepreans afterward paid a sort of rent or tribute of one talent to Olympian Jupiter. On their refusing to pay this during the war, the matter was referred to Sparta, who decided in favor of the Lepreans;

num,[1] certain other Arcadians their territory, and we Oropus: not from a desire to see us each possessing our own—far from this—it would be late for them to have become generous—but to make it appear as if they helped all to recover their claims, so that, when they march themselves to attack Messene, all these people may readily join and assist them, or be deemed ungrateful, after having obtained their concurrence in the question of their own several claims, for not returning the obligation. My opinion is, first, that our state, even without sacrificing any Arcadian people to the Lacedæmonians, may recover Oropus, both with their aid, if they are willing to be just, and that of others who hold that Theban usurpation ought not to be tolerated. Secondly, supposing it were evident to us, that, unless we permit the Lacedæmonians to reduce the Peloponnese, we cannot obtain possession of Oropus, allow me to say, I deem it more advisable to let Oropus alone, than to abandon Messene and Peloponnesus to the Lacedæmonians. I imagine, the question between us and them would soon be about other matters. However—I will forbear to say what occurs to me—only I think, we should in many respects be endangered.

whereupon the Eleans went over to the alliance of Argos and Athens. In the year B.C. 366, the Arcadians were in possession of Triphylia, when a body of their exiles who had fled to Elis assisted the Eleans to surprise Lasion, one of the Triphylian towns. A war then broke out between Arcadia and Elis, in which the Eleans greatly suffered, though at the close of the war they distinguished themselves by a victory gained over the Arcadians and Argives at Olympia. It was the time of the festival, which the enemy had determined to celebrate under the presidency of Pisa; the games had actually begun, when they were vigorously attacked and routed by the Eleans on the sacred ground.

[1] Tricaranum was a fortress in the Phliasian territory. The city of Phlius was on the confines of Argolis, Achaia, and Arcadia. During the Theban war, when most of their allies had deserted the Lacedæmonians, Phlius continued faithful, and was exposed to the attacks of her neighbors. The Argives fortified Tricaranum, and kept it as a hostile post, making incursions to plunder the Phliasian country, and attack the city, which at one time was nearly surprised by an Argive-Arcadian force, assisted by some exiles. The Phliasians, whose constancy is praised by Xenophon, baffled all the attempts of their enemies. In the year 366, Chares the Athenian was sent to their assistance, and took Thyamia, another hostile fortress occupied by the Sicyonians. Tricaranum, it seems, remained in possession of the Argives. See further as to the history of Phlius, p. 175, note 1.

As to what the Megalopolitans have done against you (as they say) under the influence of Thebes, it is absurd to bring that now as a charge against them, and yet, when they proffer their friendship, with an intention of doing you good instead of harm, to mistrust and look for an excuse to reject them, without considering that, the more zealous they prove this people to have been in the Theban cause, the more will they themselves deserve your anger, for having deprived Athens of such allies, when they applied to her before they applied to Thebes. It looks indeed, as if they wished a second time to turn these people to another alliance.

I am sure—to judge from rational observation—and I think most Athenians will agree with me, that, if the Lacedæmonians take Megalopolis, Messene will be in danger; and, if they take that also, I predict that you and the Thebans will be allies. Then it is much better and more honorable for us, to receive the Theban confederacy as our friends, and resist Lacedæmonian ambition, than, out of reluctance to preserve the allies of Thebes, to abandon them now, and have afterward to preserve Thebes herself, and be in fear also for our own safety. I can not but regard it as perilous to our state, should the Lacedæmonians take Megalopolis, and again become strong. For I see, they have undertaken this war, not to defend themselves, but to recover their ancient power: what were their designs, when they possessed that power, you perhaps know better than I, and therefore may have reason to be alarmed.

I would fain ask the men, who tell us and say, they detest the Thebans and the Lacedæmonians, whether they detest whom they detest respectively out of regard to you and your interests, or detest Thebans for the sake of Lacedæmonians, and Lacedæmonians for the sake of Thebans. If for their sakes, to neither as rational beings ought you to listen: if they say for your sake, wherefore do they exalt either people unduly? It is possible, surely possible, to humble Thebes without increasing the power of Lacedæmon. Ay; and it is much easier too. I will endeavor to show you how.

It is well known, that up to a certain point all men (however disinclined) are ashamed not to observe justice, and that they openly oppose the transgressors, especially where any people suffer damage: it will be found moreover, that what mars every thing, and originates every mischief, is the unwillingness to observe justice uniformly. Therefore, that no such obstacle may arise to the depression of Thebes, let us declare that Thespiæ and Orchomenus and Platæa ought to be re-established, and let us co-operate with their people and call on others to assist us—just and honorable were this, not to regard with indifference the extermination of ancient cities—but let us not abandon Megalopolis and Messene to the aggressors, nor, on the pretense of Thespiæ and Platæa, suffer existing and flourishing cities to be annihilated. If such be your declared policy, every one will desire, that Thebes should no longer hold her neighbor's dominion. If not—in the first place, we may expect to find these men oppose the other scheme, when they see that the establishment of those towns would be their own ruin: secondly, we shall have an interminable business of it ourselves; for where indeed can it end, if we continually allow existing cities to be destroyed, and require those which are in ruins to be restored?

It is urged by the most plausible speakers, that the pillars[1]

[1] It was the practice among Grecian states to inscribe their treaties on pillars of stone or brass, which, so long as the treaties remained in force, were religiously preserved, and exposed to view in temples and other public places. And it was frequently provided in the treaty itself, where the pillars recording it should be deposited. Thus, in the treaty of peace between Athens, Lacedæmon, and their respective allies, in the tenth year of the Peloponnesian war, it was stipulated that pillars should be erected at Olympia, Delphi, and the Isthmus; and also in the Acropolis at Athens, and in the temple of Apollo at Amyclæ. In the treaty between Athens, Elis, Argos, and Mantinea, made in the following year, it was agreed that stone pillars should be set up by the Athenians on the Acropolis, by the Argives in the temple of Apollo in their market-place, by the Mantineans in the temple of Jupiter in their market-place; and that they should jointly erect one of brass at Olympia. This (among many others) was seen by Pausanias in the Olympian temple.

There is some difficulty attending the words that follow: *οἱ δὲ φασί μὲν αὐτοῖς οὐκ εἶναι στήλας, ἀλλὰ τὸ συμφέρον εἶναι τὸ ποιοῦν τὴν φιλίαν.* I have followed the interpretation of Leland and Pabst, which makes good sense and agrees with the tenor of the argument. Jacobs however expresses a doubt whether the words will admit of that interpretation; and Ulpian, whom Reiske follows, explains them, *φασὶ γὰρ μὴ ὑπάρχειν στήλας,* "they say they have no pillars." Now it is impossible to admit this last explanation, when Demosthenes, without denying the truth of the Megalopolitan statement, still insists that the pillars should be taken down. It may also be urged that if this be the true meaning, the latter clause would scarcely harmonize with the former; for if the

of their treaty with Thebes must be taken down, if they mean to be our steadfast allies. These people say, that with them it is not pillars, but interest that binds friendship, and they consider those who assist them to be allies. Granting such to be their views, my notion is this. I say, we should both require of them the destruction of the pillars, and of the Lacedæmonians the observance of peace; if either party refuse to comply, whichever it be, we should side immediately with those that will. Should the Megalopolitans, notwithstanding the maintenance of peace, adhere to the Theban alliance, it will surely be evident to all, that they favor the ambition of the Thebans instead of justice. On the other hand, if the Megalopolitans in good faith espouse our alliance, and the Lacedæmonians do not choose to observe peace, they will surely prove to the world, that they are striving not only for the restoration of Thespiæ, but for an opportunity of conquering Peloponnesus while the Thebans are entangled in this war. One thing in certain men surprises me; that they dread the enemies of Lacedæmon becoming allies of Thebes, and yet see no danger in the Lacedæmonians conquering them; although we have actual experience furnished by the past, that the Thebans always use these allies against Lacedæmon, whereas the Lacedæmonians, while they had the same people, used them against us.

I think further, you ought to consider this. If you reject the Megalopolitans—should their city be destroyed and themselves dispersed,[1] the Lacedæmonians at once become powerful: should they chance to escape, (as unhoped-for events

people of Megalopolis had no pillars, further argument was useless. Besides, it is very unlikely they had none. The doubt of Jacobs is founded upon too minute a view of grammatical nicety. It would have been better had the order of words been, *οὐ στήλας ἀλλὰ τὸ συμφέρον εἶναι*. At the same time, the words as they stand may, according to strict rules of grammar, be literally translated thus: "They say that with them it is not pillars, it is interest that makes friendship,"—the *εἶναι* being repeated twice. The sentence is not so well constructed as in the other case; but we can not always expect from an author the most neat and elegant modes of expression. In this clause lay an emphasis on *οὐκ* and on *στήλας*, but not upon *εἶναι*, and then the reading will express the true sense.

Few persons will approve of Schaefer's conjecture, substituting *κενὰς* for *εἶναι*, or Weiske's far-fetched explanation of—*οὐκ εἶναι* for *οὐδαμοῦ εἶναι*, *i. e.* *οὐδενὸς λόγου*.

[1] Into villages. See p. 76, note 3.

do happen,) they will in justice be steadfast allies of the Thebans.[1] If you accept them for allies, the immediate consequence to them will be deliverance by your means—but passing from their case—let us consider what may be looked for and apprehended with reference to Thebes and Lacedæmon. Well then: if the Thebans be vanquished in war, as they ought to be, the Lacedæmonians will not be unduly great, having these Arcadians for their rivals, living near them. If the Thebans chance to recover and come off safe, they will at all events be the weaker for these men having become our allies and been preserved through us. So that in every point of view it is expedient, that we should not abandon the Arcadians, and that they should not appear (in case they do escape) to have owed their deliverance to themselves, or to any other people but you.

I have spoken, O Athenians, (Heaven is my witness,) not from private affection or malice toward either party, but what I consider advantageous for you: and I exhort you not to abandon the Megalopolitans, nor indeed any other of the weaker states to the stronger.

[1] The event proved the justice of this remark. Demosthenes could not prevail on the Athenians to follow his counsel. They joined the alliance of neither party. Archidamus commenced war against the Arcadians, who were assisted by Argos, Sicyon, and Messene. In the course of the same year, Philip having defeated Onomarchus in the great battle of Pagasæ, the Thebans were enabled to send forces to the succor of their old allies. On the other hand, the Lacedæmonians were reinforced by some Phocian mercenaries; and the war was carried on for two years with various success, and at length terminated by a truce. The Arcadian confederacy, however, were alienated from Athens, and the bad effects of this were discovered some time after, when, alarmed at the designs of Sparta, they applied not to Athens, but to Philip, for assistance, and thus caused Macedonian influence to extend itself in Peloponnesus. See the Argument to the Second Philippic.

ON THE TREATY WITH ALEXANDER.

THE ARGUMENT.

This is one of the Orations which has generally been considered spurious; yet as it is published in Becker's and other editions of Demosthenes, it finds a place in this translation.

It purports to be an address to the Athenian people, rousing them to take arms against Alexander, king of Macedon, and shake off the ignominious yoke to which they were subjected, on account of certain injurious acts committed by that monarch, in violation of his engagements. It appears that in the year B.C. 335, a treaty was entered into between Alexander and the Greek States, according to which a general peace was to be maintained by all the members of the Greek community, both with Macedonia and among themselves, every state enjoying political independence, and Alexander being the common protector of all. It is alleged that Alexander had broken the treaty by sundry acts of interference with Greek cities, more especially Messene, where the sons of Philiades had by his influence regained possession of the government. Another complaint is, that some Athenian ships returning from the Euxine had been seized by Macedonian officers; and that Athens had been insulted by a Macedonian galley sailing into the Piræus without leave.

The date of the speech may have been B.C. 334, after Alexander had crossed over into Asia.

It is right, O Athenians, that those who bid you observe your oaths and engagements should, if they do so from conviction, have your entire concurrence. For I think nothing so becomes a people who enjoy self-government, as to be regardful of equity and justice. The persons then, who are so vehement in urging this course, should not trouble you with declamations on the principle, while their conduct is directly opposite; but should submit to inquiry now, and either have you under their direction in such matters for the future, or retire and leave you to advisers who expound the rules of justice more truly—so that you may either tamely endure your wrongs, and let the aggressor have his way, or, preferring justice to every other consideration, you may be above all reproach, and consult your own interest without delay.[1] From

[1] *I. e.* by taking arms against Alexander, which is a measure of prudence as well as justice.

the very terms of the treaty, from the oaths by which the common peace was ratified, you may see at once who the transgressors are,—in what important particulars, I will briefly explain.[1]

Were you asked, men of Athens, what would most strongly excite your indignation, methinks you would all say, that if you were constrained[2]—I mean, if the Pisistratids were alive at this day, and an attempt were made to reinstate them by force, that you would snatch up your arms and encounter every peril rather than receive them; or, yielding, you must be slaves, like those that are purchased in the market—and far worse,[3] inasmuch as no man will kill a servant wantonly, while the subjects of tyrants are notoriously destroyed without trial, and have outrages also committed upon their wives and children. Well then—Alexander has, contrary to his oath and the express conditions of the general peace, brought back to Messene the sons of Philiades, her tyrants.[4] In so doing has he paid regard to justice—or has he not rather acted on

[1] Reiske explains it differently: "eâ brevitate, quæ locum habet in tantâ argumenti amplitudine;" i. e. "briefly, considering the importance and magnitude of the question."

[2] Schaefer thinks the words *εἴ τις ἀναγκάζοι* ought to be connected with *ἀγανακτήσαιτε*, from which they have been disjoined by an error of the copyist. I connect them with the following clause, and explain it thus:—The orator was intending simply to add *προσδέξασθαι τοὺς Πεισιστρατίδας*, but then it occurring to him that the family of Pisistratus were extinct, he inserts the hypothetical clause *εἰ ἦσαν κ. τ. λ.*, which interrupting the first train of thought, the sentence becomes somewhat irregular. We need not be surprised at examples of loose construction among the orators. At the present day few of our public speakers attend closely to rules of syntax. An Attic audience was more fastidious than an English, yet would tolerate occasional *anacolutha*. Many of these would be retained in the published orations; and some even by design; for now and then a loose mode of speech is more happy than a formal sentence.

[3] Reiske takes *τοσούτῳ μᾶλλον* in connection with *ἁρπάσαντας ἀν—ὑπομεῖναι*. I agree with Pabst and Leland who connect it with *δουλεύειν*.

[4] Philiades was tyrant of Messene in the lifetime of Philip. His sons, Neos and Thrasylochus, were expelled for oppressive conduct, but afterward restored by Alexander. They are mentioned in the Orations on the Crown among the list of traitors by whom, as Demosthenes contends, Grecian liberty was sold to Macedonia. Polybius however maintains that the reproaches of Demosthenes were unjust, and that the connection of these men with Macedonia was for their country's benefit. (XVII. 14.)

his own arbitrary principles, in contempt of you and the common agreement? If then such violence done to yourselves would rouse your utmost resentment, you ought not to remain passive, when it has been committed elsewhere in violation of the oaths taken to you: nor should certain persons here require us to observe the oaths, yet leave to men who have so flagrantly broken them a liberty like this. It can not indeed be permitted, if you mean to do your duty: for it is further declared in the articles, that whoever acts as Alexander has done shall be deemed an enemy by all parties to the peace, himself and his country, and that all shall take arms against him. Therefore, if we perform our engagements, we shall treat the restorer of these exiles as an enemy.

Perhaps these friends of tyranny may say, that the sons of Philiades reigned in Messene before the treaty was made, and therefore Alexander restores them. But the argument is ridiculous—to expel tyrants from Lesbos, who reigned before the treaty, that is, the tyrants of Antissa and Eresus,[1] on the plea that such form of government is oppressive; yet hold that it makes no difference in Messene, when the same nuisance is established!

Besides—the treaty prescribes in the very commencement, that the Greeks shall be free and independent. Would it not be the height of absurdity, that the clause making them free and independent should stand first in the treaty, yet that one who reduces them to servitude should not be deemed to have violated the compact? If then, O men of Athens, we mean to abide by our oaths and covenants, and do that act of justice which they require of you, as I just now mentioned, we must certainly take up arms and march against the offenders with such allies as will join us. Or think ye that opportunity has such force sometimes, as to carry out policy without right[2]—and now, when opportunity and policy meet

[1] Antissa and Eresus are cities in Lesbos.

[2] "Sic construe," says Wolf—*ἰσχύειν πράττειν τὸ συμφέρον καὶ ἄνευ τοῦ δικαίου*—*Ὁ καιρὸς ἰσχύει πράττειν τὸ συμφέρον, τουτέστι, δύναται.* Reiske: "Brevius sic dictum est, quod plenius et planius ad hunc modum dixisset: *οὕτως ἰσχύειν ὥστε βιάζεσθαι ἡμᾶς καὶ ἄνευ τοῦ δικαίου,* &c. *tantum valere ut cogat nos.*"

Schaefer: "tu audi Wolfium."

Reiske explains the indirect meaning of the words, and Wolf their direct meaning. But the point of the matter is intelligible enough

together for the same right, will ye wait for any other time, to assert your own freedom and the freedom of all Greece?

I come to another point under the articles. It is written, that if any persons subvert the constitutions, which existed in the several states when they swore the oaths of ratification, they shall be deemed enemies by all parties to the peace. Now consider, men of Athens: the Achaians of Peloponnesus were living under popular government. Among them, the Macedonian has overthrown the democracy of Pellene, expelling most of the citizens: their property he has given to their servants, and set up Chæron the wrestler as tyrant. We are parties to the treaty, which directs us to regard as enemies the authors of such proceedings. Then must we obey this article of the convention, and treat them as enemies—or will any of these hirelings be impudent enough to say no—these hirelings of the Macedonian, who have grown rich by betraying you! For assuredly they are not ignorant of these proceedings: but they have arrived at such a pitch of insolence, that, guarded by the armies of the tyrant, they exhort you to abide by the violated oaths, as if perjury were his prerogative;[1] they compel you to abolish your own laws, releasing persons who have been condemned in courts of justice, and forcing you into numerous other unconstitutional acts. Naturally enough. It is impossible that men who have sold themselves to oppose their country's interests, should care for laws or oaths: they use their empty names, to cajole people who assemble here for pastime, not for discussion, and who little think that the calm of the moment will lead to strange disturbances hereafter. I repeat, as I declared at the outset—hearken to them who advise you to observe the treaty: unless they consider, in recommending observance of the oaths, that they forbid not the commission of injustice, or suppose, that the establishment of despotism instead of democracy and the

without a paraphrase; and in translating we need not cut down every figurative expression into plain prose. French translators are apt to do this, aiming chiefly at clearness, in which they excel. Auger's version is: "Ou bien, pensez-vous que l'occasion est quelquefois suffisante pour nous faire suivre notre intérêt aux dépens de la justice?"

[1] I have borrowed this expression from Leland. We might say—"he had the privilege of perjury." But Leland's word better suits a monarch. Auger: "comme si ce Prince disposoit du parjure en maître absolu."

subversion of constitutional governments will be felt by none.

But what is yet more ridiculous—it is in the articles, that all members of the congress,[1] all guardians of the public safety, shall see that in the confederating states there be no bloodshed or banishment contrary to the laws established in each, no confiscations of property, nor divisions of land, nor abolishing of debts, nor liberating of slaves for revolutionary purposes. They however—so far from checking any of such proceedings—even help to bring them about. Are they not worthy of death, when they promote such plagues in our cities, plagues which (because they are so grievous) the whole body were commissioned to prevent?[2]

I will show you a further breach of the articles. It is declared, that it shall not be lawful for exiles[3] to make an

[1] Which met at Corinth, where the treaty was made.

[2] The nominative case to ἐπέταξαν is either *αἱ συνθῆκαι* or *αἱ πόλεις*.

[3] From most of the Greek cities there were exiles banished for political causes, and ready to take advantage of any revolution, to return to their country. If these were many in number, more especially if they were connected with a party at home, or supported by a foreign power, they would cause considerable uneasiness to the government. Such for example were the exiles from Elis and Phlius, who have already come under our notice. (See pp. 134, 174, notes.) Such also were the Bœotian exiles, while their country was subject to Thebes. As the treaty of Corinth recognized the independence of the Greek states, and preserved their institutions inviolate, the clause regarding exiles was in the spirit of such arrangement, and introduced as an additional security. Alexander conceded this, being intent on the Persian war, and wishing at that time to conciliate the Greeks; afterward, caring less about their favor, he, or his regent, Antipater, sought to extend Macedonian influence by means of a different kind. Of the facts mentioned here little is known from other sources: but this restoration of the exiles is a measure not only probable of itself, but in accordance with one taken by Alexander at a later period, of which an account is given by Diodorus. About a year before his death, Alexander caused an edict to be published at Olympia, by which the Greek cities were commanded to receive back their exiles, except such as had committed sacrilege or murder. Great consternation was produced by this order, the object of which was to make the Macedonian interest, by means of the returned exiles, preponderant in every state. Demosthenes was sent to Olympia, to remonstrate with Nicanor the Macedonian envoy. Nicanor however had no option but to execute his master's commission. The alarm of the Athenians was increased by the appearance of a large body of their exiles at Megara. They resolved to send an embassy to Alexander to entreat his forbearance. This was done, and the mission was successful: but on Alexander's death,

excursion with arms from any cities included in the peace, to attack any other city comprehended in the peace; if they do, the city from which they start shall be excluded from the treaty. Well! The Macedonian has carried his arms about with so little scruple, that he has never yet laid them down, but still marches wherever he can with arms in hand, and more now than before, inasmuch as by an edict he has restored various exiles in different places, and the wrestling-master in Sicyon. If we are bound then to obey the terms of the convention, as these men declare, the states guilty of such conduct are under treaty with us no longer. I allow, if the truth is to be suppressed, we must not say they are the Macedonian: but when these traitorous ministers of Macedonia never cease urging you to fulfill the conditions of the treaty, let us hearken to their counsel, as it is just, and let us deliberate—putting them under your ban, as the oath requires—how to treat people whose tempers are so imperious and insolent, who are always either forming or executing some designs, and making a mockery of the peace. How can my opponents dispute the propriety of this? Do they require the clauses against our country to be in force, and not allow those which are for our protection? Does this appear to be justice? Will they confirm whatever is against us in the oaths and favorable to our adversaries—yet think proper continually to oppose any fair advantage that is secured to us against them?

To convince you still more clearly that the Greeks will never charge you with infringing any part of the convention, but will even thank you for taking upon yourselves to expose the guilty parties—I will, as the articles are numerous, glance cursorily at a few points.

I believe one article is, that all the contracting parties may navigate the sea, that none shall molest them, that none of them shall force a vessel into port; that whoever breaks this condition shall be deemed an enemy by all parties. Now, men of Athens, you know perfectly well, that this has been done by the Macedonians. They have come to be so lawless,

which followed soon after, a rising of the Greeks took place, which had well-nigh overthrown the Macedonian power. This was the war called the Lamian, in which the Athenians and their allies were at first victorious, but were finally crushed by Antipater.

that they carried into Tenedos all our vessels from the Euxine, and under pretenses refused to release them,[1] until you determined to man a hundred ships of war and launch them immediately, and appointed Menestheus to the command. Is it not absurd, when the wrongs done by others are of such number and magnitude, that their friends here, instead of restraining them the trangressors, should advise us to observe a compact so little regarded? As if it were further declared, that trespass should be allowed to one party, and not even resistance to the other! Were not their acts both lawless and senseless, when they violated their oaths to such an extent, as had well-nigh justly deprived them of their maritime supremacy?[2] And as it is, they have left you this plea beyond a question, when you choose to enforce it: for assuredly they have not the less broken the convention, because they left off committing trespasses: they are only fortunate in profiting by your indolence, that will not even take advantage of a right.

The most humiliating circumstance is this—that while all others, Greeks and barbarians, dread your enmity, these upstarts[3] alone compel you to despise yourselves, either persuading or forcing you into measures, as if they were statesmen of Abdera or Maronea,[4] not of Athens. At the same time they weaken your power, and strengthen that of your adversaries; and yet (without perceiving it) acknowledge our republic to be irresistible; for they forbid her to maintain justice justly,[5] as though she could easily vanquish her enemies, if she chose to consult her own interests. And their notion is reasonable. For as long as we can be indisputably

[1] Schaefer takes ἀφεῖσαν in the sense of ἐπαύσαντο.

[2] Alexander having by the treaty been declared generalissimo of the Greeks, a supremacy both on land and sea was accorded to Macedonia, although that kingdom did not actually possess so large a fleet as Athens. The Athenians furnished twenty galleys to the armament which conveyed Alexander across the Hellespont.

[3] The original νεόπλουτοι (*nouveaux riches*, as the French say,) is noticed by Libanius as a term not likely to be used by Demosthenes. So is βδελυρεύσεται. The former appears to me a very good word. We have none that exactly corresponds with it.

[4] These were cities in Thrace. Abdera was famous for the stupidity of the inhabitants, though it produced Democritus the philosopher.

[5] Because they recommend that the Athenians should observe the treaty, and the Macedonians be allowed to break it.

masters of the sea alone, we may find other defenses for the land, in addition to our existing force, especially if by good fortune these men, who are now guarded by the tyrant's armies, should be put down, some of them destroyed, some proved to be utterly worthless.

So grave an offense (in addition to what I have mentioned before) has the Macedonian committed in the affair of the ships. But the most outrageous and overbearing act of the Macedonians is what has lately occurred—their daring to sail into the Piræus contrary to our convention with them. And you must not regard it as a light matter, men of Athens, because there was only one ship; but[1] as an experiment on our patience, that they may have liberty to do it with more, and a contempt of the agreement, as in the former instances. That they meant to creep along by degrees, and accustom us to tolerate such intrusions, is evident from this only—the commander who put into port, (who ought with his galley to have been instantly destroyed by you,) asked permission to build small boats in our harbors—does it not show that their contrivance was, instead of sailing into port, to be inside at once? And if we allow small boats, we shall shortly allow vessels of war; if a small number at first, very soon a large. It is impossible, you know, to make this excuse,[2] that in Athens there is plenty of ship-timber, (which is brought with trouble from a distance,) and a scarcity in Macedonia (which supplies it at the cheapest rate to all purchasers). No. They looked both to build vessels here, and to man them in the same harbor, although it was expressed in the treaty, that nothing of the kind should be allowed. And these liberties will increase more and more. With such contempt in every way do they treat our republic, through their instructors here, who suggest to them what course to pursue. And such is the estimate which, in common with these men, they have formed of Athens, that she is inexpressibly feeble and imbecile,

[1] I do not, with Schaefer and Pabst, understand *μέγα* before *ὅτι*, but simply take *ὑποληπτέον* to be repeated. The words *οὐκ ἐφρόντισαν κ. τ. λ.* may be literally translated: "They [in so doing] disregarded the common articles, just as they disregarded the articles before-mentioned:" that is: "they disregarded the convention in this particular, as they disregarded those articles which I mentioned before."

[2] Understand *ποιῆσαι τοῦτο*, "to say they did it because," &c.

that she has no forethought for the future, nor takes any account how the tyrant observes the treaty.[1]

That treaty, O Athenians, I exhort you to obey, in such manner as I explained, insisting[2] (under the privilege of my age) that you might at the same time exercise your rights without reproach, and use without danger the opportunities which impel you to your good. For there is a further addition to the articles—"if we will be parties to the common peace." This, "if we will," means also a different thing—"if we ever ought to cease shamefully following others, and forgetting those honors, of which we, beyond all people, have won so many from the earliest time." Therefore, with your permission, men of Athens, I will move, as the treaty commands, to make war upon the transgressors.[3]

1 Wolf has a note on this passage, not very complimentary to the Athenians—"Recte quidem senserunt, nisi Demosthenes ubique mentitur, qui talem nobis depingit Atheniensem populum, ut asino ignavissimo, qui vix contis et fustibus excitari queat, comparandus videatur."

2 I connect διεβεβαιωσάμην with καθάπερ, ἂν with χρῆσθαι. The following sentence I have rendered according to Schaefer's interpretation; but so far agree with Reiske, that I think it is too ill written to be worth a note.

3 Almost all critics, ancient and modern, have pronounced this Oration to be spurious. Lybanius ascribes it to Hyperides, Ulpian to Hegesippus. History affords no confirmation of the fact that such a speech ever was made. And it would also be strange, if Demosthenes had purposed to make war against Alexander, that there should be no allusion to it in either of the speeches on the Crown. Auger makes the following remarks on the inferiority of the style:

"Quoique ce discours se trouve dans les œuvres de Démosthène, tous les critiques s'accordent à dire qu'il n'est pas de Démosthène. Je suis très fort de leur avis. Je n'y trouve point cette véhémence et cette rapidité de style, cette netteté, cette clarté lumineuse, cette profondeur dans les idées, qui caractérisent Démosthène."

Francis says:

"Our editors have preserved to us the Orations upon Halonnesus and Alexander's treaty with Athens, even while they hold them written by other authors, and unworthy of our orator's character. The translator therefore hopes to be forgiven his not attempting to preserve what in themselves are confessedly spurious, and, if they were genuine, would be injurious to the reputation of his author. A painting would do little honor to the cabinet of the curious, merely because ignorance and false taste had once given it to the divine Raphael."

The only commentator that I have seen, who maintains the genuineness of this Oration, is Leland. It is but fair to hear his reasons:

"Critics seem willing to ascribe this oration to Hegesippus, or to

Hyperides. It is observed that the style is diffuse, languid, and disgraced by some affected phrases; and that the whole composition by no means breathes that spirit of boldness and freedom which appears in the orations of Demosthenes. But these differences may possibly be accounted for, without ascribing it to another author. Dejection and vexation, a consciousness of the fallen condition of his country, despair and terror at the view of the Macedonian power, might have naturally produced an alteration in the style and manner of the orator's address. A great epic genius, when in its decline, is said by Longinus to fall naturally into the fabulous. In like manner, a great popular speaker, when hopeless and desponding, checked and controlled by his fears, may find leisure to coin words, and naturally recur to affected expressions, when the torrent of his native eloquence is stopped. Nor is the Oration now before us entirely destitute of force and spirit. It appears strong and vehement, but embarrassed. The fire of Demosthenes sometimes breaks forth through all obstacles, but is instantly allayed and suppressed, as if by fear and caution. The author, as Ulpian expresses it, speaks freely, and not freely: he encourages the citizens to war, and yet scruples to move for war in form; as if his mind was distracted between fear and confidence. In a word, I regard this Oration on the Treaty with Alexander as the real work of Demosthenes, but of Demosthenes dejected and terrified, willing to speak consistently with himself, yet not daring to speak all that he feels. It may be compared to the performance of an eminent painter, necessarily executed at a time when his hands or eyes labored under some disorder, in which we find the traces of his genius and abilities obscured by many marks of his present infirmity."

APPENDIX I.

OLYNTHUS.

The taking of Olynthus was one of the turning points of Philip's success, and merits particular attention.

Olynthus was the chief city of the Chalcidic peninsula, which is separated from the inland part of Macedonia by a range of mountains, crossing from the Thermaic to the Strymonic gulf. The peninsula itself runs out into three smaller peninsulas or tongues of land, the eastern of which is overshadowed by Mount Athos, and was called Acte; the central was named Sithonia, and the western Pallene. The whole district was called Chalcidice, on account of the numerous colonies planted there by the Chalcidians of Eubœa. In early times, and long before Athens took a prominent part in Grecian affairs, Chalcis and Eretria, the chief cities of Eubœa, had acquired considerable eminence, and sent out colonies not only to the northern parts of Greece, but to Sicily and Italy. Of their Macedonian colonies the most ancient was Methone, founded by the Eretrians in Pieria. In the Chalcidic region there were established upwards of thirty towns, many of Euboic origin. The principal among them were, Apollonia, Stagira, Acanthus, Cleonæ, Argilus, Mende, Scione, Torone, Mecyberna, Anthemus, Sane, Æneia, Spartolus, Potidæa. This last city, so important in Athenian history, was founded by Corinth.

Olynthus, which stood at the head of the Toronaic gulf, was originally inhabited by a Bottiæan tribe; but having been taken by Artabazus, the Persian satrap, who massacred the population, it was repeopled by Chalcidians.[1] At the close of the Persian war, the Greek cities on that coast became attached to the general confederacy, of which Athens was at the head. But Potidæa and many of the Chalcidian cities were induced to revolt from Athens, B.C. 432, chiefly by the persuasion of Perdiccas, king of Macedonia, and under promise of assistance from Peloponnesus. Perdiccas at the same time advised, that the inhabitants of the smaller towns on the

[1] Herodotus, vii. 127.

coast should remove to Olynthus, and concentrate their power in that city, which, on account of its position, a little inland, was less exposed to an attack from the sea. This was done, and by such means Olynthus became the capital of the Chalcidic population.[1]

During the Peloponnesian war, although Potidæa was taken, the members of the Chalcidian league maintained their independence against Athens. In the third year of the war they defeated the Athenians near Spartolus. It was partly at their invitation that Brasidas was sent to attack the Athenian possessions in the neighborhood; and it was their jealousy that in a great measure prevented the restitution of Amphipolis, after the peace of Nicias. In the eleventh year of the war, the Olynthians took Mecyberna, which was defended by an Athenian garrison. This place, which is near Olynthus on the Toronaic gulf, they afterwards made the port of their own city.[2] A truce followed between Athens and Olynthus; and the misfortune of the Athenians in Sicily prevented them from making any further attempt to restore their empire in this quarter.

At the close of the Peloponnesian war, when the power of Athens was annihilated, a new prospect was opened to the ambition of the Olynthians. Potidæa and many other towns joined their confederacy. A large military force was kept on foot, and they began to turn their thoughts to the establishment of a navy, for which their peninsular situation and the abundance of ship-timber in the country were eminently favorable. It might have been better for them, had they confined their attention (at least for some time) to the acquisition of maritime power; but the weakness of their neighbors tempted them to make inland conquests in Thrace and Macedonia, which led to a combination against them before their strength was sufficiently consolidated. History is silent as to any operations in Thrace, but we are informed, that they had acquired considerable influence among the independent Thracian tribes, who inhabited the country stretching eastward of the Strymon towards Rhodope; and it is probable that they coveted possession of the mine district of Pangæus. But the hostilities in which they engaged with Amyntas king of Macedonia led to most important results. At first they were completely successful: they either took or seduced from his allegiance a great number of Macedonian towns. They even got possession of Pella, which afterwards became the capital of Macedonia; and Amyntas, who had about the same time suffered a great defeat from the Illyrians, appeared to have lost all his dominions. Diodorus says, that he surrendered Pella to the Olynthians in the

[1] Thucydides, i. 58. The war in the Chalcidic is related in divers parts of his history. See particularly iv. 79; v. 21, 38, 39, 80; vi. 7.

[2] Fragment from the end of Strabo's seventh book, τῆς Ὀλύνθου ἐπίνειόν ἐστιν.

time of his distress, and they refused to restore it when his affairs were retrieved. However this be, it was certainly in their hands shortly before the year B.C. 383, when Sparta commenced the war, which I am about to mention.[1]

Amyntas applied to Sparta for aid; but it was not his solicitation so much, as one from another quarter, that induced the Lacedæmonians to interfere. Apollonia and Acanthus, the two greatest (next to Olynthus) of the Chalcidian cities, had sent an embassy to Sparta for the same purpose, to implore her protection against the Olynthians, who threatened them with war, unless they would join their confederacy.

It may seem surprising, that people situated as these were, exposed to aggression from powerful states and monarchies, should not have perceived the advantage of a federal union such as that of which Olynthus was the head. But this was the feeling of Greek states in general; they preferred independence to safety. The same jealous feeling had overthrown the Athenian empire; it was destined to work the ruin of Olynthus, and lead ultimately to the subjugation of Greece. Apollonia and Acanthus had never joined the league which had been formed under the advice of Perdiccas; the conditions of which, though liberal, involved a submission to Olynthus as the ruling state. Appollonia had once been the most considerable city of the district; it lay far inland, about twelve miles from Olynthus, at the foot of the Cissæan mountains. Acanthus was a coast-town on the Strymonic gulf, north of the isthmus of Mount Athos, across which the famous canal was cut for Xerxes. The Acanthians were the first people that revolted from Athens, when Brasidas came into their country. Their jealousy of Athens was now transferred to Olynthus.

The embassadors from these two cities were introduced by the Ephors to the Spartan assembly, which was attended by deputies from the Peloponnesian allies. The Acanthian envoy addressed to them an elaborate speech, in which he set forth the growing power and ambitious projects of Olynthus, her military force and resources, the towns that she had wrested from Macedonia, the extreme weakness of Amyntas, and the danger that threatened themselves. He stated that he had left embassadors from Thebes and Athens at Olynthus, and that the Olynthians had passed a resolution to negotiate alliance with those cities. Many of the Chalcidians were ready to revolt, he said, if the Lacedæmonians would send them assistance.

The Spartans and their allies were prevailed on by these arguments, and it was resolved that an army of ten thousand men should be raised in Peloponnesus, to carry on the war. The Acan-

[1] The history of these events is related by Xenophon, Hellen. lib. v. c. 2, 3. Diodorus Siculus, lib. xv. c. 19—23.

thian embassadors requested that a Spartan general with a smaller force should be at once sent off; and accordingly Eudamidas was dispatched with two thousand men, to be followed by his brother Phœbidas with reinforcements.

Eudamidas marched to Thrace, and put garrisons in the towns that were friendly to him. Potidæa immediately revolted, and there he established himself, and commenced hostilities against Olynthus. Phœbidas, who was sent after him, stopped on his road at Thebes, and seized the Cadmea, a measure, which had the immediate effect of bringing Thebes under subjection to Sparta, though it ultimately led to the overthrow of the Spartan empire. Teleutias, brother of Agesilaus, followed with the bulk of the Peloponnesian army, and passing Thebes on his way, received a contingent of horse and foot from that city. Amyntas had been ordered to join him with as large a force as he could collect, and Derdas, prince of Elymia, was solicited for aid on behalf of Amyntas his kinsman.

When Teleutias arrived at Potidæa, he was joined by these auxiliaries, and marched directly against Olynthus. According to Xenophon, the first campaign was favorable to Teleutias; the Olynthians, after a battle which they had very nearly gained, were shut within their walls, and the Spartans ravaged the country; though, after the dismissal of the Macedonian and Elymian troops, the Olynthians made destructive incursions into the hostile states, and plundered their territories. Diodorus relates that the Spartans were defeated in several battles, and mentions no victory won by Teleutias. But both he and Xenophon agree in the result, which Xenophon assigns to the second campaign, viz. that Teleutias fell in a hard fought battle under the walls of Olynthus, in which his army was completely routed and dispersed.

The Lacedæmonians, on receiving intelligence of this defeat, felt the necessity of making still greater exertions. A large army, chiefly of volunteers, was raised in Peloponnesus, and put under the command of Agesipolis, one of the kings. He marched through Thessaly, which supplied him with a troop of cavalry; and being joined by Derdas and Amyntas, whose zeal in the cause was nowise abated, he marched straight against Olynthus. His force was so overpowering, that the Olynthians dared not meet him in the field, but confined themselves to the defence of the city, which they had well stored with provisions against a siege. Agesipolis ravaged the country, and took Torone, soon after which he was seized with a fever, and died. Polybiades was sent out as his successor, and commenced the siege of Olynthus with great vigor. The Olynthians were defeated in various sallies, and the siege was turned into a blockade; yet they held out till the following year, B.C. 379, when they submitted to Sparta, on the terms of becoming her dependent allies. This involved the necessity of following the Lacedæmonians in all their wars; and accordingly, we find a body of Olynthian cavalry serving afterwards under the Spartan general against Thebes.[1]

In ten years after this event important changes had taken place in Greece. The power of Sparta was broken by the Theban war; Epaminondas had been at her gates, and threatened her very existence. Her navy had been beaten by the Athenians in the Ægean and Ionian seas. Athens had regained her maritime supremacy; most of the Ægean islands, besides Corcyra and Byzantium, had again become her allies. Thebes was the only state that appeared to be her rival.

In another ten years events had happened of more immediate concern to the Olynthians. During a long peace they had risen again to prosperity, and seem to have resumed in a great degree their sway or influence over the Chalcidian peninsula. It is not stated either by Xenophon or Diodorus, that all the dominion which Olynthus exercised in the peninsula was taken away by the Lacedæmonians. We may rather suppose that her willing allies were left to be subject to her as before; for so long as Olynthus was subservient to Sparta, it was even better for Sparta that she should be at the head of a respectable confederacy. Certain it is that the influence of Olynthus greatly revived after the humiliation of Sparta. Demosthenes[2] gives us to understand that she had become at a much later period more powerful than she was before the Spartan war. But at the time that we are now speaking of a new enemy appeared. Athens, having become mistress of the sea, had turned her attention to the coasts of Macedonia and Thrace, with a view to recover the towns and dependencies which formerly belonged to her. Many expeditions were sent for that purpose, especially against Amphipolis, the possession of which was greatly coveted by the Athenians. These measures necessarily brought them into conflict with the Olynthians, who saw with alarm the revival of an empire which threatened their own independence. A war ensued, of which we have no full or clear account, but the general result was to the disadvantage of Olynthus; for many cities near her coast were taken by the Athenians, and especially Methone, Pydna, Potidæa, and Torone, the two last of which had probably been re-annexed to the Olynthian alliance. Such things had occurred, and the relations between Athens and Olynthus were still of a hostile character, when, at the close of this last decennial period, B.C. 359, Philip ascended the throne of Macedon.

[1] Xenoph. Hellen. lib. v. c. 4, s. 64.

[2] De Falsâ Leg. 425. He also represents the terms of peace with Sparta to have been more favorable to Olynthus: *δπως ἠβούλοντο τὸν πόλεμον κατέθεντο.* But we must make allowance for exaggeration in this passage, where the orator is drawing a contrast between two periods.

In order that the position of things at this time may be understood, it is necessary to state more particularly what had passed in the interval.

Amyntas, ever since the restoration of his kingdom by the aid of the Lacedæmonians, had remained firmly attached to that people, and his friendship was extended afterwards to Athens, when the Athenians had entered into a treaty of peace and alliance with Sparta. In the year B.C. 371 a congress was held at Athens, attended by the Spartans and their allies, to settle the affairs of Greece. A deputy of Amyntas was there, who publicly declared that Amphipolis belonged to Athens, and that he would support her in the assertion of her claim.[1] With such encouragement, the Athenians conceived hopes of recovering their ancient colony; and Iphicrates was selected as the most suitable person to accomplish that object, on account of his personal friendship with Amyntas, who had adopted him for a son. It does not distinctly appear when the first expedition was sent against Amphipolis. Amyntas died in the year B.C. 370, and the opportunity for obtaining his assistance was gone. The Amphipolitans themselves were averse to the alliance of Athens, from which they had been entirely alienated ever since the revolution effected by Brasidas. However, in the year B.C. 368, Iphicrates was sent to the coast of Thrace on an exploring expedition, with a small armament.

It happened soon after this, that Alexander, who succeeded Amyntas, was murdered, and Pausanias, a pretender to the crown, having gained a large party in Macedonia, and collected some force, invaded the country, and took various towns on the coast. Eurydice, the queen-mother, sent for Iphicrates, who was still cruising in the neighborhood, and reminding him of his former attachment to Amyntas, implored his protectlon for her children, Perdiccas and Philip, the latter of whom was then about fifteen years of age. Iphicrates espoused the cause of the queen, judging it, doubtless, the best policy for Athens. Turning then his arms against Pausanias, he expelled him from the kingdom; after which, being at liberty to prosecute his main design, he took into his service Charidemus of Oreus, with a body of mercenary troops, and commenced operations against Amphipolis.

Charidemus, a native of Oreus in Eubœa, who from this time began to make a figure in Athenian warfare, was a soldier of fortune, who had first been a slinger, and afterwards set up a pirate vessel, with which he infested the Ægean sea. Having contrived to draw together a band of needy adventurers like himself, he became the

[1] Συνεξαιρεῖν μετὰ τῶν ἄλλων Ἑλλήνων, is the expression said to have been used by the deputy. Æschines, De Falsâ Leg. 33; from whom we get most of our information concerning these transactions. Compare Demosth. contra Aristoc. 669. Corn. Nepos in vit. Iphic.

leader of a mercenary force, ready to engage himself in the service of Athens, or the Persian king, or any other government that would employ him. Iphicrates at this period was glad to engage such a man; and Charidemus was retained in his service for upwards of three years.

Of the operations of Iphicrates we have no detailed account. We learn that he was completely disappointed in his expectations of Macedonian aid. After the expulsion of Pausanias, the government fell into the hands of a man named Ptolemy, suspected to be the queen's paramour, and even to have been the murderer of Alexander. So far from assisting Iphicrates to recover Amphipolis, he exerted his influence[1] the other way, probably through fear of the Thebans.[2] Iphicrates for three years kept up a sort of blockade on the coast, and at length prevailed on the Amphipolitans to negotiate for the surrender of their city. Matters had gone so far, that hostages were given to him for the performance of the agreement. But an unaccountable event occurred, which baffled all the calculations of the commander. Iphicrates, having been recalled home, left the hostages with Charidemus; who, on receiving an order from the Athenians to bring them to Athens, sent them back to Amphipolis. Mitford conjectures, (and possibly he is right,) that the hostages had been intrusted to the faith of Iphicrates; that Charidemus, being under an engagement to Iphicrates, did not consider himself bound to obey orders from Athens. The Amphipolitans might regard the Athenian decree as a breach of faith, and as evidence of a treacherous design. Under some such impression, they broke off all further negotiation.

The Athenians then appointed Callisthenes to command the fleet. But now Perdiccas, who had killed the regent and assumed the government of Macedonia, appeared as their enemy, and declared war. Callisthenes defeated him in battle, and compelled him to solicit an armistice. But that general, from some unexplained reason, was recalled to Athens, and put to death. Timotheus was his successor; who so ably managed affairs, that in a few years he effected many important conquests for his country.

Timotheus, on taking the command, engaged the services of Charidemus, it being desirable to strengthen his armament by the mercenaries of that officer; for the Athenians had got into the practice

[1] The words ἀντέπραττε τῇ πόλει do not warrant us in supposing that Ptolemy made war against Iphicrates, especially when it is said of Perdiccas immediately after, ἐπολέμησε τῇ πόλει. Æschin. ib. 32.

[2] Pelopidas, invited into Macedonia by the nobles, compelled Ptolemy to give hostages for his good conduct, with a view to preserve the crown to the heirs of Amyntas. Philip himself is said to have been one. But the date and circumstances of this transaction are matters of controversy. See Plutarch in vit. Pelop. Thirlwall, Grecian Hist. v. 164. Leland's Life of Philip, i. 41.

of sending out vessels without a proper complement of men,[1] trusting to their generals to supply the deficiency. Charidemus, however, obtaining what he thought a more profitable employment under Cotys, king of Thrace, broke his promise to Timotheus, and carried away his own troops with some of the Athenian vessels. Timotheus, left to his own resources, vigorously prosecuted the war; and then it was that Olynthus, as the principal protector and ally of Amphipolis, came into serious conflict with the Athenians.[2]

Whether this proceeding on the part of Olynthus was the cause, or the effect, of a change in the policy of Macedonia, we can not tell. Perdiccas abided by his engagement with Callisthenes, and not long afterwards entered into an alliance with Athens, and co-operated with Timotheus against the Olynthians.[3] The result was that Timotheus captured Potidæa and Torone, and divers other towns on the Chalcidian coast, by which the power of Olynthus was seriously impaired. If we could implicitly adopt the statement of Isocrates,[4] he reduced the whole of Chalcidice; but this would have increased the power of Athens, and the weakness of Olynthus, to a degree which is not reconcilable with the events that followed. All that we can fairly gather from the words of Isocrates is, that the influence of Athens was greatly extended in the Chalcidian peninsula, and that some of the cities joined her alliance, perhaps without receiving an Athenian garrison. Isocrates might be disposed to exaggerate the merits of Timotheus, who had been his friend and benefactor. Yet history furnishes strong testimony to the abilities of that general. He appears to have had more capacity for operations on a great scale than either Iphicrates or Chabrias. The good discipline which he kept among his troops, and the uprightness and moderation of his character, were greatly instrumental to his success. Æschines says, that he added seventy-five cities to the dominions of Athens: Isocrates mentions only twenty-four, referring perhaps to such only, as were actually taken by arms. His reputation for success was so great, that a picture represented him sleeping in a tent, whilst Fortune was catching cities for him in a net.

The operations of Timotheus against Olynthus began about the

[1] Κενὰς ναῦς, with no more than the bare nautical crew. Demosth. Ol. xxix.

[2] The words of Demosthenes, contra Aristoc. 669, are not referable, as Thirlwall intimates, to the time of Iphicrates, but to the time when Timotheus was commander. But it is very probable that the Olynthians, though not openly at war with Athens, had secretly aided the Amphipolitans against Iphicrates.

[3] Demosth. Ol. ii. 14.

[4] *On the Exchange*, 119. Χαλκιδεῖς ἅπαντας κατεπολέμησεν. These words agree with the literal expression of Cornelius Nepos, *Olynthios subegit.* (Vit. Timoth.) Compare Demosth. Philipp. i. 41. Εἴχομεν—πάντα τὸν τόπον τοῦτον οἰκεῖον κύκλῳ. Dinarch. cont. Demosth. 91.

year B.C. 364. Two years after that we find him making war in the Hellespont, where he took the cities of Sestos and Crithote in the Chersonese. He was occupied for eleven months in the siege of Samos, which ultimately capitulated. Isocrates boasts of his friend, that with a fleet of thirty sail and eight thousand targeteers, and without any cost to the state, he had reduced an island, for the conquest of which Pericles had employed two hundred galleys and spent a thousand talents of the public money.

During all this time, Amphipolis had, with the aid of the Olynthians, successfully defended herself. But in the year B.C. 360 Timotheus resolved to make another effort for the conquest of that important city. The Olynthians, in close alliance with the Amphipolitans, prepared to defend them, and engaged the services of Charidemus, who set sail from Cardia, but was captured on his way by the Athenian fleet, and compelled to unite his forces to those of Athens. Timotheus sailed up the Strymon, and landed his troops to attack the city; but here his fortune failed him. He was attacked by an army superior to his own, and compelled to make a disastrous retreat. This was the last attempt which the Athenians made to recover Amphipolis by arms.[1]

In the following year Perdiccas was slain in battle by the Illyrians, and Philip ascended his throne. At this time the king of Macedonia possessed not a single maritime town of importance.[2] Athens had Pydna and Methone, Potidæa and some other towns of Chalcidice, besides possessions in the Chersonese. She was in alliance with Byzantium and other Propontine cities. Thasos, Lemnos, and Imbrus belonged to her; and also the group of islands off the coast of Thessaly. She had thus the means, with her powerful navy, of infesting all the northern continent of the Ægean, and making a sudden descent where she pleased for the purposes of war or conquest. Olynthus seemed the only power capable of opposing her in that neighborhood; but Olynthus had been much weakened; and there can be little doubt, that, had the affairs of Athens been conducted by a Pericles, Olynthus and the whole of Chalcidice must soon have fallen under Athenian dominion. Yet in the space of a twelve-month from this time the position of things became so totally changed, that we find Olynthus, the old enemy of Athens, courting her alliance, and even Amphipolis doing the same, not from any fear of Athenian armaments, but from dread of a more formidable power. That power was Philip; whose extraordinary successes and rapid movements had already excited alarm in his own neighborhood.

[1] Thirlwall, v. 189.

[2] Anthemus was perhaps on the sea, but had no importance except from its vicinity to Olynthus. Perdiccas had probably taken it from the Olynthians in the late war.

Never did any king succeed to his throne under greater disadvantages than Philip. He was only twenty-three years of age. His kingdom was threatened on all sides. In the west the Illyrians, flushed with recent victory, were preparing for a new inroad. The Pæonians made an incursion from the north, and ravaged his country. At the same time there appeared two pretenders to the crown; Pausanias, the ancient rival of Perdiccas, who was now assisted by Cotys, king of Thrace; and Argæus, who was supported by the Athenians. Argæus had made them his friends by promising to forward their designs against Amphipolis and Olynthus;[1] and accordingly an Athenian armament, under the command of Mantias, was sent to Methone, with directions to advance from thence, and support his cause in Macedonia.

Meanwhile Philip, doubtful on which side to defend himself, made terms for the present with the Pæonians, bribed Cotys to abandon the cause of Pausanias, and proceeded to attack Argæus and the Athenians. They had marched from Methone thirty miles into the interior of Macedonia, to Ægæ, the ancient capital of the kingdom, where they expected to find a party in their favor. In this hope they were disappointed, and made a hasty retreat, but were overtaken and attacked by Philip. Their general Mantias had remained at Methone, and the troops, after suffering a severe loss, retreated to a hill, where, having no means of escape, they capitulated and were allowed to depart on giving up the Macedonian exiles. Philip carried his lenity so far, that he restored to the Athenians all the booty which he had taken; and being anxious at this time to conciliate them, he sent embassadors with a letter to

[1] Diodorus, xvi. 3. The following words respecting Amphipolis, *ἐξεχώρησε τῆς πόλεως, ἀφεὶς αὐτὴν αὐτόνομον*, may seem perhaps to imply, that Philip at this time possessed the city, but there is more than one difficulty in the way of such a supposition. In the first place, there is no historical evidence that Amphipolis had at this time been taken or occupied by Macedonian troops. Perdiccas had very lately been in alliance with Athens, nor is there any reason to suppose that he had turned against her at the last, when Timotheus attacked Amphipolis. Even if he did so, it does not follow that the Amphipolitans received a Macedonian garrison. In the next place, it is not very likely that Philip would have given up Amphipolis if he really possessed it; especially at the time indicated by Diodorus, when he was about to attack the Athenian forces. He would hardly be desirous of conciliating the Athenians at that moment. On the other hand, it would be his interest to conciliate the Olynthians and Amphipolitans, and confirm them in their hostility to Athens. With such view it would have been a wise measure to declare that Amphipolis should be independent both of Athens and Macedonia. *'Εξεχώρησε* then may signify nothing more than *παρεχώρησε*, "he withdrew all claim to dominion over the city." See Thirwall, v. 173.

Athens, proposing peace and amity with the republic, and renouncing all claim of his own to Amphipolis. The proposal was joyfully accepted.[1]

No sooner was this danger averted than Philip hastened to chastise the Pæonians. It so happened, their king Agis had just died. Philip invaded their country, overthrew them in battle, and reduced them to entire subjection. Immediately afterwards he marched into Illyria, and rejecting the offers of peace made by the old king Bardylis, defeated that veteran warrior in a hard-fought battle, in which more than seven thousand Illyrians were slain. Bardylis then obtained peace, on condition of ceding to Macedonia all the country that lay to the east of Lake Lychnus.

The next step taken by Philip was one yet bolder, and pregnant with more momentous consequences. Without any delay, and apparently without any ground of quarrel, he advanced and laid siege to Amphipolis. We are told by Diodorus, that the Amphipolitans had afforded him some pretext for war. But we need look for no further cause or pretext, than Philip's own interest and ambition. Great must have been the surprise and alarm of the Olynthians, to see their old enemy, the king of Macedonia, at the head of a powerful army flushed with conquest, besieging a city scarcely less considerable than their own, and connected by close alliance with themselves. A semi-barbarous continental monarch, with a large standing army, was a power far more to be dreaded than even Athens, the mistress of the sea. Perhaps they began to see, that a union on liberal terms with Athens was the best protection for the Greek cities on the coast. At all events they resolved to apply for Athenian aid, and an embassy was sent for that purpose.

But whatever sensation the attack upon Amphipolis might produce at Olynthus, it created neither alarm nor surprise among the Athenians. They were quite prepared for the event. Philip had by vague promises deluded them into a belief, that he meant to take Amphipolis for them. No distinct engagement to that effect seems ever to have been made; but after the receipt of Philip's letter, in which he had given a hint of his friendly intentions, Antiphon and Charidemus[2] were sent from Athens to conclude terms of alliance, and especially to treat with him on the subject of Amphipolis. They did so, and an understanding was come to, that Philip, if he got possession of that city, should surrender it to Athens, and the Athenians should, as a recompense, deliver up Pydna to him. Pydna was strictly a Macedonian town, and formerly belonged to the kingdom, while Athens had, on more than one account, a strong claim to Amphipolis; so that there appeared nothing objectionable

[1] Diodorus, xvi. 4. Leland's, Life of Philip, i. 86. Demosth. contra Aristoc. 660.

[2] Not Charidemus of Oreus, but an Athenian of the same name.

in this arrangement, nor any great difficulty about carrying it into effect.

There was indeed no formal treaty to bind the parties; but such a contract, from its very nature, could not safely be reduced to writing; and therefore, when the embassadors communicated the result of their negotiation to the Athenian magistrates, it was considered perfectly satisfactory, and the people were given to understand that Amphipolis would soon be theirs.[1]

Under this persuasion, the people of Athens not only spurned the application of the Olynthians, but at a later period, when the Amphipolitans themselves, pressed by the besieging army, sent a deputation to Athens and offered to surrender their city, the offer was refused.[2]

We can hardly wonder at this conduct on the part of the Athenians. To have entered into terms with Olynthus or Amphipolis after their engagement with Philip, might well have been considered not only a breach of faith, but an unwise policy at that time. There appeared no reason to distrust Philip. The kings of Macedonia had frequently been allies of Athens, ever since the time of the second Perdiccas. Their friendship had certainly been precarious, but their hostility had not been very violent or very mischievous. Philip himself had merited the gratitude of the Athenian people by his generosity. On the other hand, Olynthus had for a long time past been the enemy of Athens. The Amphipolitans had exhibited a malignant hostility ever since their revolt in the Peloponnesian war, and their repudiation of the treaty with Iphicrates caused their promises to be suspected.

Philip sent a letter to the Athenians, renewing his assurances,[3] and meanwhile the siege of Amphipolis was pressed with vigor. Diodorus says, it was taken by storm; Demosthenes, that it was betrayed. It is likely enough, that there was an Amphipolitan party favorable to Macedonia, and that, after the siege had continued for some time, and their appeared no prospect of relief, this party induced the citizens to capitulate.

To hold out long would have been impossible; for not only had Athens refused assistance, but even the Olynthians had abandoned the cause of their ally. Had the Olynthians taken the same vigorous measures against Philip, which they did against Timotheus, the issue might perhaps have been doubtful. But Philip, anxious to get speedy possession of Amphipolis, and not to be embarrassed at so critical a time by a war with the Olynthians, bought off their opposition by the cession of Anthemus, a town in their neighborhood,

[1] Thirlwall, v. 192. Leland's Philip, i. 96. This was the *τὸ θρυλούμενον ἀπόῤῥητον*. (Olynth. ii. 19, page 48 in this volume.)

[2] Olynth. i. 11; ii. 19.

[3] Contra Aristoc. 659. De Halonn. 28.

which had formerly belonged to them.[1] Having thus disarmed the two opponents, from whom he had most to fear, Amphipolis became an easy prey.

But Philip had now to consider, whether he should keep his promise to the Athenians, and offer to deliver up Amphipolis in exchange for Pydna. He appears to have made up his mind with very little hesitation; for immediately after the capture of the one city, he appeared with his army before the walls of the other. Here also he found a party in his favor. Whether he had concerted any plans with them beforehand, does not appear; but by their assistance he was admitted into Pydna without difficulty; and it soon became apparent, that he intended to keep both cities on his own account, and set the Athenians at defiance.

The Athenians, as might have been expected, were not slow to express their resentment of such treachery; but how to avenge themselves on the deceiver, was a more difficult matter. Whether Philip was able at this time to cope single-handed with the power of Athens, may be doubted; but he was too prudent to venture on such a chance. An opportunity was open to him, for obtaining an important ally, and he hastened to seize it. Experience had proved, that a combination between two of the three powers, (Athens, Olynthus, and Macedonia,) would turn the scale against the third. Philip proposed to the Olynthians to join them in an offensive war against Athens, to expel the Athenians from their possessions on the Macedonian coast, and to share the spoils. This offer was accepted. The war that followed was called the Amphipolitan war, and, as far as Philip and the Athenians were concerned, it lasted till the year B.C. 346, when peace was concluded by the Embassy of Ten. On the part of Athens, the war was prosecuted with neither skill nor vigor. She incurred a large amount of expense in fruitless expeditions, and hardly obtained a single advantage.[2] Her efforts were indeed, during a part of this time, distracted by the Social war, and by the affairs of Eubœa and the Chersonese. The loss of Byzantium and the confederate islands, followed by that of Corcyra, crippled her power, and greatly reduced her revenues;[3] nor was the cession of the Chersonese by any means a sufficient compensation.

The most important achievement by the united arms of Philip and the Olynthians, was the reduction of Potidæa. An Athenian garrison, stationed here, and holding considerable property in the town, was obliged to surrender. Philip, to whom the merit of the conquest was principally due, seized the Athenian possessions, and

[1] As to the position of Anthemus, see Thirlwall, v. 194.

[2] Olynth. iii. 36. Tamynæ and Thermopylæ were creditable affairs, but brought no permanent advantage to Athens.

[3] Philipp. iv. 141.

gave them up, together with the town itself, to the Olynthians: the garrison he treated kindly and sent back to Athens.[1]

Philip does not appear to have taken an active part in any other military operation in favor of Olynthus. It can not however be doubted, that the war was carried on in Chalcidice between Athens and Olynthus for several years, and that divers of the Chalcidian towns were again wrested from the Athenian alliance, and brought back to the Olynthian; among others, Torone, which was taken by Philip from the Olynthians at a later period.[2] We read of an expedition sent by the Athenians against Olynthus somewhere about this time,[3] which turned out a failure. Philip might well leave Athens and Olynthus to fight it out by themselves, when he knew that the Athenians had their hands so full; and the Chalcidians were easily persuaded to desert the cause of Athens, when not controlled by a garrison. Leland sagaciously observes,[4] that Philip saw the advantage of keeping his own army undivided, while he left Potidæa and other places to be garrisoned by the Olynthians.

Philip indeed was turning his attention to another quarter, where he had an important conquest to make on his own account. This was the mine district of Mount Pangæus, which commenced on the left bank of the Strymon, and extended eastward as far as Scapte Hyle, where lay the property of Thucydides the historian. From the Pangæan hills flowed the Hebrus with its golden sands. There were mines here both of gold and silver. The Thasians, who had mines also in their own island, had planted various colonies for mining purposes on the adjoining continent. The principal of these was Datus. They had lately formed a new settlement more inland, called Crenides, in a beautiful spot, watered by numerous mountain rivulets, and abounding with veins of gold. The Thasians were

[1] Diod. xvi. 8. Dem. cont. Aristoc. 656. De Halonn. 79.

[2] Demosthenes more than once enumerates the towns taken by Philip from the Athenians, apparently in historical order, thus—Amphipolis, Pydna, Potidæa, Methone, (Olynth. i. 11, 12; Philipp. i. 41.) Had any other important town been taken by him during the same period, Demosthenes would hardly have forborne to mention it. On the other hand, he was not so likely to speak in these orations of conquests made by the Olynthians alone, towards whom he desired his countrymen to have none but friendly feelings. In the Oration de Chers. 105, Philip is said to have given to the Olynthians Ποτίδαιον καὶ πόλλ' ἕτερα. His assistance, no doubt, enabled them to get other places. In the Oration of Demosthenes on the Embassy (426), it is represented that all the Chalcidian cities had again become allies of Olynthus. Compare Æschines De Falsâ Leg. 37.

[3] Contra Midiam, 566, 578. The date of this expedition was probably the year B.C. 355.

[4] Life of Philip, i. 105.

subject to Athens; and Philip had no hesitation in expelling them from their possessions, and seizing upon the whole district. At Crenides he established a Macedonian colony; the place was soon enlarged into a considerable city, and called from the founder Philippi. A new method of working the mines was adopted, the waters being drained off into canals; and in a short time they yielded to the king of Macedonia such an amount of revenue, as enabled him not only to maintain a large standing army, but to extend his influence among the Greek states by corruption. A gold coin was struck, called Philippeum, which quickly circulated over Greece; and from this time Philip owed his success as much to his gold as to his arms, according to the general tradition of antiquity,[1] as expressed in the well known lines of Horace—

> Diffidit urbium
> Portas vir Macedo, et subruit æmulos
> Reges muneribus.

The last mentioned conquest was effected B.C. 356, not long after the reduction of Potidæa. In the same year his son Alexander was born. For the two following years Philip was (comparatively speaking) inactive; that is, in a military point of view; for we can not doubt that he was actively engaged in the affairs of his kingdom, directing its internal administration, improving the revenue, fortifying and embellishing his towns,[2] training his army, collecting mercenary soldiers, stores and materials. He commenced at the same time (what no Macedonian king had done before) the establishment of a navy, for which the coast-towns that he now possessed, and especially Amphipolis (whose situation was like that of the modern Antwerp), afforded him abundant facilities. He was busy with his negotiations in foreign states, sending emissaries wherever he was likely, either by corruption or otherwise, to promote Macedonian influence. The effects of this were soon visible in Eubœa, where in the year 354 his intrigues fomented the quarrel between Callias and Plutarch, and drew the Athenians into the perilous battle of Tamynæ.

In the year 353 Philip laid siege to Methone, a city on the Thermaic Gulf, about five miles from Pydna. It was held by the Athenians, and strongly fortified. To them it was useful as a sallying place into the interior of Macedonia, as had been seen in the case of Argæus, as well as on former occasions.[3] Philip was therefore ex-

[1] Demosth. cont. Lept. 476. Diodorus, xvi. 8. Leland's Life of Philip, i. 110. Thirlwall, v. 202.

[2] Justin, viii. 3, where it is related that he defrauded the contractors of their money. But this is not credible.

[3] Thucydides, vi. 7.

tremely anxious to take it. The Methonéans defended themselves with the utmost obstinacy, and the siege lasted for nearly a twelvemonth.

While Philip was eagerly pressing the attack, he was wounded in the eye by an arrow shot from the walls. The arrow being extracted was found to have this inscription: "Aster to Philip's right eye." It is said that Aster, being a skillful archer, had offered his services to Philip, assuring him that he could kill any birds flying. "Well!" said Philip, "I will employ you when I make war upon starlings." Aster, in revenge for the slight, threw himself into Methone, and shot this arrow which deprived Philip of the sight of one eye. Philip ordered the arrow to be shot back with another inscription: "If Philip takes Methone, he will hang Aster," a threat that was afterwards executed.

The city was open to relief from the sea, and a blockade would have been unavailing. The Athenians were actually sending fresh succors, when Philip ordered a general assault. A large number of besiegers had mounted the battlements, when, to cut off their retreat, Philip ordered the scaling ladders to be removed, leaving his men to conquer or to perish. They fought with desperation, and carried every thing before them. The besieged laid down their arms. Philip accepted their surrender on these conditions, that they should be suffered to depart with one suit of apparel only, that the city and all within it should be given up to pillage. Methone was razed to the ground.[1]

Immediately after this followed the campaign in Thessaly, the defeat and death of Onomarchus, the expulsion of the tyrants of Pheræ, the capture by Philip of Pagasæ and Magnesia, his march to Thermopylæ, and his retreat on finding the pass occupied by Athenian troops. From Thessaly he marched into Thrace. In the interior of that country were various tribes, ruled by divers princes. One at least of these had not long before conspired with the Illyrians and Pæonians to make war against Macedonia.[2] Philip resolved to avenge this insult, and at the same time to establish his own influence among the barbarous tribes, who were able to furnish useful recruits to his armies.[3] Here Philip was occupied for some time, establishing friendly princes in their dominions, and expelling others;[4] after which he suddenly marched to the Propontine coast, and attacked Heræum, a fortress near Perinthus, held by the Athe-

[1] Diodorus, xvi. 34. Demosth. Philipp. i. 50. Leland's Life of Philip, i. 194.

[2] Diodorus, xvi. 22.

[3] The Thracian Peltastæ made excellent light troops, and had often been employed by the Athenians. See Thucydides, vii. 9, 27, 30.

[4] Τοὺς μὲν ἐβαλών, τους δὲ καταστήσας τῶν βασιλέων. Demosth. Olynth. i. 13.

nians, and important to them for the protection of their corn trade. The alarm which this excited at Athens, the vigorous resolutions and dilatory measures of the people are particularly mentioned by Demosthenes.[1] The siege was begun in the latter end of the year 352, nor does it clearly appear whether or not Heræum was taken. Philip however, fatigued by his long marches and incessant toil, fell dangerously ill; and for a time his military operations were suspended. No sooner had he recovered, than he quitted Thrace, and marching towards Chalcidice, early in the year 351, surprised the Olynthians by making a hostile inroad into the peninsula.[2]

Why or on what pretense he took such a step, is doubtful. It appears however, that some time before this the Olynthians had broken off their connection with Philip, and made friendly overtures to the Athenians.[3] They had discovered soon after the capture of Potidæa, that Philip would do nothing more for them, that he was beginning to make conquests on his own account in their neighborhood, and acquiring power of a formidable character. They were acquainted with the value of the mine district, and saw the great advantages that he was deriving from it. To them, living on the confines of Macedonia, all his plans and proceedings, his naval and military preparations, became speedily known. The fall of Methone, one of the strongest fortresses of Greece, revealed to them, that few cities would be protected by their walls from the assault of the Macedonian army. The late occurrences in Thessaly and Thrace must have greatly increased their apprehensions. Philip had defeated in a pitched battle the veterans of Onomarchus, and made the Thessalians his allies. Olynthus was surrounded by his power on every side. For even the sea was now open to Philip. He had not indeed such a navy as could meet the Athenians in a fair sea-fight; but he sent out piratical expeditions to infest their commerce and plunder their allies.[4] His cruisers had lately made a descent upon Lemnos and Imbrus, captured a fleet of merchantmen off the Eu-

[1] Olynth. iii. 29. Demosthenes intimates, that if the armament first decreed had sailed in time, they might have surprised Philip during his illness and destroyed him, *οὐκ ἀν ἠνώχλεί νυν ἡμῖν σωθείς.*

[2] Olynth. i. 13. *Εὐθὺς 'Ολυνθίοις ἐπεχείρησεν.* "He made an aggression (or an attack) upon the Olynthians." The words themselves are ambiguous, not denoting any particular mode of aggression; and it is probable, that if Philip had committed any decided act of hostility, Demosthenes would not have mentioned it so slightly.

[3] Demosth. contra Aristoc. 652. That speech was delivered in the year 352. The orator assigns no cause for a rupture between Philip and the Olynthians, except their alarm at his growing power. Athens and Olynthus were at that time friends, but not allies: *ὑμᾶς φίλους πεποίηνται.φασὶ δὲ καὶ συμμάχους ποιήσεσθαι.*

[4] Justin, viii. 3. "Piraticam exercere instituit." Ib. ix. 1.

bœan coast, and even sailed into the bay of Marathon and carried off the Athenian state galley.[1]

The time when the Olynthians began to change their policy was about the year 353, perhaps before the siege of Methone. Overtures were soon afterwards made to Athens for peace; and they were joyfully accepted.[2] Yet, although the two cities had resumed their friendly intercourse, it does not appear that an offensive alliance had been formed between them against Macedonia, and certainly the Olynthians had taken no hostile measures, at the time when Philip, as above mentioned, crossed the Chalcidian frontier. It is likely enough that Philip considered, or chose to consider, the revival of their connection with Athens an act of hostility towards himself; and undoubtedly from that time he looked with an evil eye upon Olynthus.[3] But another cause of offense is alleged by Justin.[4] Philip had three half-brothers, Archelaus, Aridæus, and Menelaus. One of these, Archelaus, he had put to death for treason; the other two escaped, and found refuge in Olynthus.

Whatever may have been Philip's pretext, he now appeared in the character of an enemy; though what overt act of hostility he committed, is not disclosed to us. From the loose language of the orator I should infer, that Philip at this time showed his teeth without biting; he infringed (as we should say) the law of nations by some aggressive act, but his enterprise, whatever it was, did not succeed. He may have crossed the mountains and attempted to surprise some towns, or seduce them from the Olynthian confederacy; not succeeding in this, he retired, like the lion who has missed his spring, to wait for a better opportunity.

This view is confirmed by the subsequent conduct of Philip. It was nearly two years before war actually broke out, by his invasion of Chalcidice.[5] He had little else meanwhile to engage his attention. The Sacred war was left to run its course without his interference. Athens had a breathing time allowed her. A few murmurs were heard from the Thessalians, for his holding Pagasæ and

[1] This happened after his Thessalian campaign: and, as Thirlwall observes, he probably made use of the ships which he found in the harbor of Pagasæ. Vol. v. 284. Æsch. De Fals. Leg. 37.

[2] Olynth. i. 11; iii. 30.

[3] Olynth. iii. 30.

[4] Justin, vii. 4; viii. 2, 3.

[5] Thirlwall (Hist. v. 289) conjectures that Apollonia was taken soon after Methone. But the reason which he assigns is unsatisfactory, namely the mention which Demosthenes makes of the three cities, Olynthus, Methone, and Apollonia, in the third Philippic, p. 117. They are only mentioned together on account of their importance, and the similarity of their fates. If Apollonia had then been taken, it would have brought on a war earlier, and probably Demosthenes would have spoken of it.

Magnesia; but them he pacified by promises, and in the year 350 conferred a new obligation upon them by the expulsion of Pitholaus from Pheræ. But all this while he was silently and secretly preparing for the destruction of Olynthus, which he saw was essential to the accomplishment of his further objects. Therefore he suspended his operations against Athens, and lulled her into a false security. She had been roused by the first Philippic in 352. Little more than a year had passed, when all the alarm had died away, and Philip was talked of as a person from whom nothing was to be feared.[1] This was just what the king of Macedon desired. He had rightly judged, that the Athenians would not make a good use of the respite which he allowed them. He feared that, if he attacked the Olynthians at once, he might have to encounter the whole force of the Chalcidian body, a formidable conjunction, when the Olynthians alone could bring into the field ten thousand infantry and a thousand horse; and still more difficult to overcome, should they be reinforced by Athenian auxiliaries. His safest course was, to divide his enemies and cripple their means of subsistence. How was this to be done?

Philip had discovered by experience, if he had not learned by his residence at Thebes, that in most Grecian cities there were different parties contending for the upper hand; that the influence of faction was strong; that corruptible citizens were always to be found, and that the laws gave equal liberty of speech to the patriot and the traitor. Acting on this persuasion, he sent his emissaries to the Chalcidian towns, and in each of these, by dint of artifice and intrigue, established a Macedonian party. Gold was lavished without stint. He had now ampler means than before; since, in addition to the resources of his own kingdom, and what he had gained by plunder, he was receiving a large portion of the revenues of Thessaly.[2] Bribery he judged to be the best economy; it would save him expense in the end, by rendering his conquest more easy; and the price of corruption would be reimbursed by the spoils of the vanquished.[3]

In none of these towns was Macedonian gold more efficacious

[1] Demosth. de Rhod. lib. 197. It may be thought that even Demosthenes was not then fully alive to the real state of things, as he quotes what was said of Philip without contradicting it. But it was not his business to mix two questions together. He may well have thought, that it would strengthen Athens to gain Rhodes for an ally, and that to keep the Athenian forces in active employment was a means of preparing them for war with Macedonia. It might not be prudent to tell the people all his reasons. I think, however, that Demosthenes was not yet sensible of the danger to be apprehended from an extensive system of corruption.

[2] Olynth. i. 15.

[3] Diodorus, xvi. 54. Hence *callidus emptor Olynthi.* Juvenal, Sat. xii. 45.

than in the capital itself. Olynthus beheld many of her citizens grow suddenly rich; their stock of possessions was increased, no one knew how; they improved their houses and displayed an unusual magnificence.[1] Yet were the people so blinded, they withheld not their confidence from such men. It was studiously disseminated, that Philip had been their benefactor, that he would be still, and that Macedonian protection was their best security. Thus, instead of preparing for their defense betimes, instead of throwing themselves into the arms of Athens, and soliciting her immediate co-operation against the common enemy, they left him to choose the moment of attack, and began to prepare when it was too late.

Towards the end of 350 B.C., Philip at the head of a powerful army marched into Chalcidice, determined to effect its final conquest. He made no declaration of war, but summoned town after town, as he advanced, to surrender. Which first opened its gates to him, is uncertain. Diodorus, who does not profess to give the details of the campaign, relates that he laid siege to Stagiri[2] and razed it to the ground. Apollonia[3] shared the same fate. Other towns, intimidated or corrupted, hastened to make terms with the conqueror. After reducing the whole, or nearly the whole, of the peninsula, he marched against Olynthus.

What were the Olynthians doing all this time? On the first intelligence of Philip's invasion they sent to Athens, imploring succor. They sent to Philip also, to demand an explanation; he assured them positively, that he was not at war with them, and still continued his progress. They sent again, and received the same answer; Philip affecting to treat the Chalcidians as independent, and refusing to hear any remonstrance on their behalf. It was not till he had approached within five miles of the capital, that he threw off the mask, and told them plainly, that either they must quit Olynthus, or he Macedonia.[4]

On the arrival of the Olynthian ambassadors at Athens, an assembly was immediately called to consider what should be done. The feeling was almost universal, to send assistance to Olynthus. Demades[5] alone opposed it; but on what grounds we are not informed.

[1] Demosth. De Fals. Leg. 426. Mitford contends that these were only innocent presents. Hist. Gr. iv. p. 432.

[2] Such is the true reading, instead of Γεῖραν, xvi. 52.

[3] Demosth. Philipp. iii. 117. From this passage it might perhaps be inferred, that thirty-two Chalcidian cities were actually destroyed by Philip. The number is probably exaggerated. I can imagine that his jealousy of the Chalcidian race would prompt him to take severe measures. Potidæa he preserved. Or, de Halonn. 80.

[4] Demosth. Philipp. iii. 113; iv. 147.

[5] Suidas in v. Δημάδης. He was a man of natural wit and eloquence, but of a coarse mind and profligate character. Throughout his whole

Probably he enlarged on the difficulty of contending with Philip in Chalcidice, and the want of sufficient funds to carry on the war. He was the first Athenian orator in the pay of Macedonia. Philip had calculated on a burst of popular enthusiasm at Athens, and a warlike vote in favor of Olynthus; but he calculated also on confusion and delay, and, to augment these, a clever and reckless man like Demades was exceedingly useful. The debate seems to have turned on questions of ways and means—how the troops were to be provided, when to be dispatched—what number—whether citizens or mercenaries, &c. Demosthenes, who rose after many speakers had been heard, breaking at once into the subject, contended that an Athenian force should be sent off immediately, that the crisis was important, they ought to take arms in person, and contribute to the expenses of the war. He had little difficulty in procuring a vote for a considerable armament.

Some days elapsed before any troops could be got ready, and in the meantime Demades and his party were busy creating obstacles, and disheartening the people. They had, for the last two years, without any formal truce, been enjoying a respite from war, and were now called upon to make new exertions. The first excitement caused by the Olynthian embassy had a little cooled. It was thought necessary to convene another assembly; Demosthenes made a second speech, in which he encouraged the Athenians, showed the precarious nature of Philip's power, and the importance of prosecuting the war. At length succors were shipped off; not such a force, however, as the urgency of the case required, and probably not all that had been decreed, but only two thousand mercenaries, commanded by Chares. Hardly had they gone, when the misgivings of the people were exchanged for an overweening confidence; such was the fickle temper of the people. It was imagined that Athens and Olynthus would be more than a match for Macedonia, and the general talk was about punishing Philip for his perfidy. In this state of the public feeling, another assembly was held; the cry was for war; the orators spoke in a tone of exultation, as if what was to be done had been done already. Demosthenes himself, perhaps, not fully alive to the danger, yet appreciating it far better than the others, reminded his countrymen that the question was not about punishing Philip, but about saving Olynthus. He saw that very inadequate succors had been sent; the citizens were reluctant to serve in person; there was difficulty about providing for the expenses; no one had dared to propose an application of the surplus revenue, though Demosthenes had hinted the expediency of such a measure. He ventured now to press this point more openly, urged the neces-

life he was in opposition to Demosthenes, and quite his match on some occasions. Many anecdotes are told of him in Plutarch's Lives of Phocion and Demosthenes.

sity of making a great sacrifice, and concluded with an eloquent appeal, calling upon the Athenians to maintain the ancient honor of their country.[1]

Chares meanwhile had sailed to the Chalcidian coast. There he made a sudden descent, and cut off a body of stragglers from Philip's army. Content with this achievement, and not finding himself strong enough to attempt a more serious diversion, he returned to Athens, and, in honor of his victory, gave a public entertainment, which cost no less than sixty talents. The money, it seems, was obtained from the spoils of Delphi, given by the Phocians to Chares, for some service that he had done. While the Athenians were amused with this piece of vanity, and little thinking of the serious nature of the case, a second embassy came from the Olynthians and their confederates, imploring immediate succor, representing that their country was overrun by the Macedonian army, and they were in the greatest distress. The Athenians sent off directly a body of

[1] The notion, that the three Olynthiac orations were connected with the three Olynthian embassies, though derived from the respectable authority of Dionysius, and assented to by Leland and many other critics, is wholly unsupported by the internal evidence of the Orations themselves, in whatever order we like to arrange them. The arguments are all of a general character. The necessity of assisting the Olynthians, and assisting them vigorously and effectively, is urged over and over again; but there is no reference to that extremity of danger, as to which Demosthenes could not have been silent, if he had spoken on the occasion of the third embassy. In not one of the speeches is there the slightest mention of a second or third embassy, or any allusion to the operations of Chares, or Charidemus, or Philip. Neither history nor probability confirms the fancy of Dionysius. It is likely that there would be several debates upon the original resolution, to embark in the war: Philochorus says that on the occasion of the first embassy, *οἱ Ἀθηναῖοι συμμακίαν τε ἐποιήσαντο καὶ βαήθειαν ἔπεμψαν*, whereas on the two second embassies there is no mention by him of any formal vote. And this view agrees with the arguments of Libanius. When the second message—and still more when the third—arrived from Olynthus, there was no need of debate; the principle had been agreed to; every one saw that the case was pressing; and succors were sent off without any opposition. It may be gathered from Philochorus, that embassadors came on the second occasion from the Chalcidian body, so that the deputation being more imposing, and the emergency more critical, one need not be surprised that the Athenians did not wait for a speech from Demosthenes, before they sent off their reinforcements. Besides, it is likely that the Athenians were preparing reinforcements in the interval between the first and second expedition, never intending the troops of Chares to be their only succors. I fully assent to what is said by Jacobs on this point in the introduction to his translation of the Olynthiacs.

four thousand mercenaries, of the middle-armed kind, with a hundred and fifty horse, and appointed Charidemus to the command.[1]

Charidemus, who was in the Hellespont when the armament sailed from Athens, as soon as he received notice of his appointment, hastened to Olynthus. Philip had by this time reduced a considerable part of Chalcidice, and had sent some of his forces into Pallene, probably to summon Potidæa. Charidemus put himself at the head of his troops, in conjunction with those of Olynthus, attacked the Macedonians in Pallene, and took some prisoners. Afterwards, to make a diversion, he sailed to Bottiæa, where he landed and ravaged the country. Returning to Olynthus, instead of pursuing his instructions, or concerting any plan with the people whom he was sent to protect, he gave himself up to vicious pleasure, indulging his licentious humor so far at to offer a gross insult to the Olynthian magistrates.[2] This was not to be tolerated; nor was his military services any compensation for his misbehavior. The Olynthians had no confidence in his abilities as a general, and not much in the valor of his troops, who were mercenary adventurers like himself. In the extremity of their alarm, they sent once more to Athens, praying for a reinforcement of native Athenians. This was granted. Two thousand heavy-armed citizens, and three hundred cavalry, were shipped off, and Chares, who was then in Athens, had influence enough to procure his own reappointment as general.[3]

Philip, little disturbed by the proceedings of Chares or Charidemus, had been steadily pursuing his object. Having entered the Sithonian peninsula, and received the submission of Torone, he marched to Mecyberna, whose gates were opened to him by the same treachery. He was now within a few miles of Olynthus, and it was here that he made the terrible denunciation, which left to the Olynthians no hope of mercy. They marched bravely to meet him with all the forces they could muster, and were defeated. They hazarded a second battle with no better success, and were shut up within their walls.[4] Philip immediately commenced the siege, and made bold efforts to carry the place by assault; for he knew the importance of time, and feared the arrival of fresh succors from Athens. Yet, so obstinate was the defense, that all his efforts were

[1] Philochorus, apud Dyonis. Epist. ad Amm. ix. Theopompus, apud Athen. xii. 43. Leland (in the Life of Philip, ii. 13) states that Chares was sent for by the Athenians; but the passage of Æschines (De Fals. Leg. 37) refers to a different time.

[2] Theopompus, apud Athen. x. 47. *Εἰς τοσοῦτον προῆλθεν ἀκρασίας, ὥστε μειράκιόν τι παρὰ τῆς βουλῆς τῆς τῶν Ὀλυνθίον αἰτεῖν ἐπεχείρησεν, ὃ τὴν μὲν ὄψιν ἦν εὐειδὲς καὶ χάριεν, ἐτύγχανε δὲ μετὰ Δέρδου τοῦ Μακεδόνος αἰχμάλωτον γεγενημένον.* The name of Derdas, the Elymian prince, may seem to suggest that this Derdas was a person of rank.

[3] Philochorus, l. c.

[4] Diodorus, xvi. 53.

baffled, and he was repulsed from the walls with considerable loss. The prompt arrival of Chares might have saved Olynthus. But now began to be seen the effects of Macedonian bribery. One of the most eminent Olynthians, and the commander of their forces, was Apollonides, who had served his country with zeal and fidelity. As long as he was intrusted with the conduct of affairs, there was little hope that treason would prosper. The Macedonian party accused him before the people, as the author of their misfortunes. It is the nature of men who are in trouble to lay the blame somewhere. The Olynthians were unhappily persuaded to deprive Apollonides of his command, and to confer it upon Euthycrates and Lasthenes, the paid agents of Philip. From that moment the doom of Olynthus was sealed.[1]

Meetings were now held in the city to propose negotiations with Philip; but the people were not yet prepared for submission. The Athenians were expected; their soldiers, though outnumbered, were brave; they had a fine body of five hundred horse, which had greatly distinguished itself in the field. It was resolved to try the effect of a sally. But the design was betrayed to Philip. Lasthenes, who commanded the horse, led them into an ambuscade, where they were surrounded by the Macedonians, and made prisoners of war.[2]

This consummate piece of treachery threw the whole city into consternation. No man any longer could trust his neighbor. The besieging army surrounded the walls. If Chares had arrived, it would have been too late now.[3] Olynthus was not on the sea, so that he could throw his forces into the town; and he was not strong enough to attack Philip in his lines. All hope of raising the siege was gone; and the Olynthians, in utter despair, were driven to surrender. The only terms which they could obtain were, that their lives should be spared.

Thus, in less than a year from the time that he invaded Chalcidice, Philip terminated the war, and entered Olynthus in triumph. He kept his promise to the inhabitants, and spared their lives, putting to death only his fugitive brothers, Menelaus and Aridæus:[4] but the whole body of the Olynthian people, without distinction of sex, age, or rank, were put up to sale by public auction, and reduced to

[1] Philipp. 67, 79. It is true, as Thirlwall (Hist. Gr. v. 314) observes that ἐκβαλεῖν does not necessarily signify that Apollonides was expelled, but it may signify that, and there is no reason to think that it does not. So Leland takes it; (Life of Philip, ii. 22.)

[2] Demosth. De Fals. Leg. 426.

[3] What Chares did with himself, does not appear. Probably finding he could not relieve Olynthus, he did nothing, and attempted nothing. Some Athenians were taken in Olynthus by Philip, as we learn from Æschines, (De Fals. Leg. 30) but clearly not Chares or his troops.

[4] Justin, viii. 3.

slavery.[1] The walls, the houses, the whole city of Olynthus was demolished; and the lands distributed as a reward among the officers of Philip.[2]

The total destruction of this great city, which had once defied Lacedæmon in the plenitude of her power, excited a feeling of dismay throughout the whole of Greece. "Has Philip destroyed Olynthus?" said one; "he himself never raised such a city!" But nowhere was it felt so deeply as at Athens. The grief and indignation of the people were mingled with shame and fear. The words of Demosthenes were recollected,—that unless they saved Olynthus, the war would soon be on their own frontiers. In the first moment of their anger, they passed a vote of outlawry against the traitors who had sold their country, making it lawful to slay them wherever they could be found. Chares came in for his share of their resentment, yet contrived, by means of his influence, to escape any public censure.[3] What became of Charidemus is unknown: whether he was slain in battle, or whether he saved his life and liberty. No more is heard of him in Athenian history.

Euthycrates and Lasthenes received the recompense of their treason, though not exactly in the way that they expected. Philip maintained them at his court, but only as servile dependents and parasites. The Macedonian courtiers held them in contempt, the soldiers reviled them for their baseness. On one occasion they complained to Philip. "Never mind," said he; "the Macedonians are a blunt people; they call a spade a spade."[4]

The conquest of Olynthus was of the utmost importance to Philip. It secured his dominions from being attacked by Athens or any other maritime power. The Chalcidian peninsula had separated one part of his kingdom from the other, and, while it remained subject to Olynthus, gave an access to his enemies into the heart of Macedonia. Now it became a province of his own; and the severe measures which he resorted to, in rooting out the hostile population, prove how anxious he was to prevent all disturbances in that quarter for the future. A glance at the map will show us what progress Philip had made in the ten years since he ascended the throne. From the bay of Pagasæ to the mouths of the Nestus in Thrace, all the coast of Northern Greece had been brought under his power. Thessaly was devoted to him. His territories were extended on the Illyrian and Pæonian frontiers; and he had made an impression

[1] Diodorus, xvi. 53. Dinarchus cont. Dem. 93. Demosth. De Fals. Leg. 439.

[2] Thirlwall, Gr. Hist. v. 316, citing Theopompus.

[3] Aristotle, Rhet. iii. 10. The interpretation of this passage is doubtful. See Mitford, Gr. Hist. iv. Leland's Life of Philip, ii. 30.

[4] Demosth. de Chers. 99; de Coron. 241. Leland's Life of Philip, ii. 31.

upon Thrace. In the north he menaced the Athenian dominions in Chersonesus; while on the south he came in contact with Eubœa, and alarmed Athens for her own safety.

While the Athenians were lamenting the disasters of the late war, and preparing to send embassies among the Greek states, to raise up a new confederacy against Macedonia, Philip had given orders for a solemn festival in honor of the Muses to celebrate his triumph. Archelaus, one of his predecessors, had instituted this festival at Ægæ, after the model of the Olympian. It was held by Philip at Dium in Pieria, a district of his own kingdom, on the borders of Thessaly, sacred from the earliest time to the goddesses of song. It was solemnized with extraordinary pomp, with games, sacrifices, banquets, and theatrical exhibitions, and continued for nine days. Nor was this intended by Philip for an idle display. A concourse of visitors flocked from all parts of Greece, to enjoy his hospitality; and while all were dazzled with the grandeur of the spectacle, and impressed with admiration of the king's fortune and power, many eminent men from foreign states were won over to his friendship: military adventurers were lured by his gifts and promises, and led to believe that the camp of Philip was the place to look for honor and reward.[1]

It is pleasing to record one or two acts of clemency and generosity on the part of the conqueror. At the sale of Olynthian citizens, at which Philip himself was present, one prisoner, who was about to be put up to auction, loudly demanded his liberty, declaring that he was a friend to the king, and desiring to be brought near him, that he might prove his word. This having been allowed by the king, the man begged him in a whisper to let fall the skirt of his robe, as he was exposed in an indecent manner. Philip entered into the joke, and said: "Yes: this man is my friend: let him be set at liberty."[2]

At a banquet given during the festival, Philip, observing the melancholy countenance of Satyrus the actor, and that, while other artists and performers claimed a recompense for their services, he alone asked for nothing, inquired the cause. "I am indifferent," replied Satyrus, "to what the others desire; there is one favor I would gladly ask, and one that Philip could easily grant, but I fear he would refuse it me." Philip pressed him to speak out, and declared that he would deny him nothing: on which Satyrus preferred his request as follows:—"Apollophanes of Pydna was my friend. When he was murdered, his relations sent his two daughters, then children, to Olynthus, as a place of security. They are among the captives of the fallen city, and are now of marriageble age. I pray and beseech you to give me them. But I would have you know what is the nature of the boon I ask, It is one for which I seek

[1] Diodorus, xvi. 55.

[2] Leland, l. c.

no personal advantage. If you deliver them to me, I shall give them each a marriage portion, and they shall be treated in a manner worthy of me and of their father." This speech was received with a tumult of applause from all the company: Philip was greatly affected, and set the girls free, although Apollophanes their father had been one of the murderers of his brother Alexander.[1]

Diodorus adds, that there were numerous other instances in which Philip displayed a similar generosity.

APPENDIX II.

ATHENIAN MONEY AND MINES.

Phidon, an ancient king of Argos, said to have lived in the eighth century before Christ, was the first person in Greece who established a system of weights and measures, and also a coinage in silver and copper. It acquired the name of the Æginetan, because the people of Ægina, by their commercial intercourse with other parts of Greece, brought it into general use. There was another system called the Euboic, introduced to the Greeks by the people of Chalcis and Eretria, who at an early period were celebrated for their commercial activity, and who worked mines of silver and copper in their own island.[2]

In fact however, both these systems were derived from the East, having been invented in very ancient times by the Chaldees of Babylon, and brought into Greece by the commerce of the Phœnicians. The standard of weights, which became known as the Euboic, was one used in Asia for gold. Herodotus expressly informs us, that in the reign of Darius I. the silver tribute collected from the satrapies of the Persian empire was estimated by the Babylonian talent, the gold tribute by the Euboic.[3] Whether Herodotus means that the term *Euboic* was adopted by the Persian government, or only the weight so called by the Greeks, does not appear.

The denominations under both these systems were the same, although the scales were different; viz. the talent, the mina, the

[1] Demosth. De Fals. Leg. 402. Diodorus, l. c.

[2] For more full information upon this subject the reader is referred to the Archæological Dictionary, titles *Nummus* and *Pondera*.

[3] Herod. iii. 89.

drachm, and the obol; which bore the following invariable relation to each other:

A talent	=	60 minas.
A mina	=	100 drachms.
A drachm	=	6 obols.

The word *talent* originally signified *weight*, that is, any weight, or weight in general; and was also used to signify a pair of scales. In such sense it is used by Homer. Afterwards the term was applied to a specific weight, and became the principal standard in the Greek systems. *Mina* was a term of oriental origin. *Drachm* and *obol* are Greek words. Drachm is said by the lexicographers to signify *a handful*, that is, as much coin as could be held in the clenched hand.[1] Obol takes its name from *a spit*, which it somewhat resembled in figure.[2]

The weights under each system were as follows:

Æginetan talent	about	96 lb.
Euboic talent	"	80 lb.

The denominations of money in Greece were the same as those of weight, and the proportions the same likewise. Money (as is well known) has always been founded on a system of weight. In process of time the coinage ceases to represent the original standard, although the name is preserved. For example *a pound*, in our own country, formerly represented a pound weight of metal; now it signifies a sum of twenty shillings. So in Greece an Euboic talent (in a pecuniary sense) anciently denoted eighty pounds of silver—that being the metal generally current in Greece—afterwards its value would be measured by the number of draehms that were paid for it; and, if the drachm-piece had fallen below the ancient standard of weight, so would the talent.

The Æginetan system was adopted in Peloponnesus and most of the Dorian states. The Euboic prevailed in the Ionian settlements, and in Attica. Solon however, for certain political reasons which will be noticed elsewhere, lowered the standard of money, and the Attic talent, according to his regulation, was reduced about twenty-seven per cent.[3] The money computed on the Solonian scale is that which we have generally to deal with in perusing the Attic

[1] As if it were *δραγμὴ*, from *δράσσω*.—It must then have been a copper coin, when it received that name.

[2] 'Οβελὸς is a spit or broach. Scopula says in his Lexicon of the Obol: " Ah *ὀβελὸς* derivatum putatur, quod *ὀβελοῦ* figuram haberet, ita tamen ut non in acutum desineret."

[3] The Euboic scale still continued in use at Athens for merchandise, though the scale for money was altered. See Grote's Hist. of Greece, iii. 228.

writers. Judging from the ancient coins which have been preserved, the value of the Attic money has been thus estimated in English:

		£	s.	d.
An obol	=	0	0	1½
A drachm	=	0	0	9
A mina	=	3	15	0
A talent	=	225	0	0

The value however has been put by others both higher and lower.

It must be observed that the talent and the mina are sums only, the drachm and the obol are coins also. And it will be found in perusing the orators, that the Athenians generally made their computations in drachms, so that, when no specific sum is mentioned, drachms are understood.

The coinage at Athens was principally silver, consisting of drachms and obols, with fractions and multiples of those pieces. The obol and half-obol were small coins, like our silver penny. There were also copper coins, as the quarter-obol, the chalcus.[1] The following is a table of Attic coins:

		s.	d.	
The four-drachm piece	value	3	0	
The two-drachm piece.......	"	1	6	
The drachm	"	0	9	
The four-obol piece	"	0	6	
The three-obol piece.........	"	0	4½	
The two-obol piece	"	0	3	
The obol	"	0	1½	
The half-obol..............	"	....	3	farthings.
The quarter-obol...........	"	....	1½	farthings.
The chalcus................	"	....	¾	farthings.
The lepton	"	....	⅜	farthings.

Thus the lowest Attic coin was pretty nearly equal to the French centime.

There was no gold coined at Athens before the time of the Macedonian empire. But there was gold in circulation, the coinage of other countries, chiefly the stater and the daric.

The gold stater was equal in value to twenty drachms, or fifteen shillings. It was first coined by Crœsus king of Lydia, or at least first became known to the Greeks as a Lydian coin. There were various other staters brought into Greece from Asia Minor and the islands; for example, from Smyrna, Cyzicus, Phocæa, Samos, Siphnos, Thasos.

The daric, named after the first Darius, who reformed the Persian currency, was of the same value as the stater. This coin, which

[1] So its name imports. Χαλκὸς is copper.

had an extensive circulation, was retained by the Macedonian kings, who melted down all the gold coinage of Greece, and had their own image stamped upon it.

There were also half-staters and half-darics in circulation, which are mentioned by Greek writers.

The daric was stamped on one side with the figure of an archer, which gave rise to a good saying of Agesilaus, related by Plutarch. While the Spartan king was overrunning the provinces of Asia Minor, Tithraustes the satrap, to get rid of so formidable an enemy, sent Timocrates of Rhodes with fifty talents of gold into Greece, to stir up war against Lacedæmon. This money was distributed in Thebes, Argos, and Corinth—Xenophon says the Athenians had no share of it[1]—and the effects were quickly seen. The Spartans, alarmed at the confederacy against them, recalled Agesilaus; whereupon he declared "that a thousand Persian archers had driven him out of Asia."

There was but a scanty supply of the precious metals in Greece at an early period, while the eastern monarchs collected the treasures of Cholcis, Lydia, Phrygia, Armenia, and India. The wars of Xerxes opened a more extensive intercourse with Asia, and enriched the Greeks by commerce and by plunder. Thus, and by an increase in the produce of their native mines, money became more plentiful among them; and in the time of Demosthenes its value was five times less than in the days of Solon. The relative value of gold to silver, in the time of Herodotus, was thirteen to one, in the time of Demosthenes, ten to one.

The Greek islands that most abounded in precious metals were Samos, Siphnos, and Thasos, in which there was both gold and silver. The mines of Thasos were anciently worked by the Phœnicians, to whom the Greeks were at an early period indebted for their supply of metal in general. They brought the common metals from Spain and Arabia, tin[2] from Britain, and probably taught the art of mining to the Greeks. The Thasians found gold and silver on the adjacent continent of Thrace. But when the island was conquered by Cimon, their settlements also fell into the hands of the Athenians, who worked the mines until the close of the Peloponnesian war. The gold, which they obtained from this district, they used not for coinage, but for commercial purposes. Philip afterwards took possession of these mines, and worked them, as we have already seen, with great advantage.[3]

There were silver mines also in Thessaly. But the most valuable

[1] Hell. iii. 5. 1.

[2] They purchased it in the Cassiterides Insulæ (Scilly Islands) so called anciently from the Greek *κασσίτερος*, *tin*. The islanders are supposed to have obtained the tin from the mainland of Britain.

[3] See p. 240 of this volume.

in Greece were those of Laurium in Attica, to which Xenophon has devoted a long chapter of his treatise on the Athenian revenues, and on which in modern times a dissertation has been written by Böckh, the celebrated author of the *Staatshaushaltung der Athener*, or Public Economy of Athens, from whom English scholars have derived most of their information upon these subjects.

The mines of Laurium were the property of the Athenian people, but were worked by private speculators, to whom the state granted allotments, receiving a certain sum by way of premium or purchase-money, and receiving a perpetual rent of a 24th part of the produce. These persons were thus in point of law tenants of the state; but for most purposes might be regarded as the absolute owners. Many wealthy citizens embarked their capital in the mining business, which they carried on by means of agents or sub-tenants. Nicias had several mines, with a thousand slaves at work in them, for each of whom he received from his lessee a clear rent of an obol a day. Thus was Laurium an important source of revenue to Athens. When Decelia was occupied by the Lacedæmonian army, she suffered greatly by losing the profit of the mines. They had yielded a considerable income in the time of Themistocles, who persuaded his countrymen to apply the money to ship-building, instead of distributing it among themselves. In the time of Demosthenes, though he speaks in high terms of the value of this property,[1] the quantity of silver obtained was diminished; and Strabo tells us, that in the first century of the Christian era the Laurian mines were exhausted.

Foreigners in Attica were allowed equal privileges with citizens in the renting of the mines:[2] so anxious was the state, that they should be let. To prevent frauds on the revenue, every mine in work was required to be registered, and an indictment lay against any person who evaded this regulation.[3]

Xenophon, who seems to have thought that the riches of Laurium were inexhaustible, recommended that his countrymen should improve their finances by abolishing the middle-men, and letting the mines, together with mining-slaves, to the working tenants, in the same way that other revenues were let to farm. He advised that they should buy slaves gradually, until they had got three slaves to every citizen; and he calculated that the mines would afford profitable employment for all, and the revenue would be immensely increased.

The trade of Athens was much promoted by the purity of her silver coin, which was every where exchanged with advantage, while

[1] See the Oration *de Chersoneso*, p. 100; the fourth Philippic, 135.

[2] Xenophon, de Vectig. iv. 12. The student should peruse this treatise.

[3] This was called ἀγράφου μετάλλου γραφή.

that of other states would only pass at home. One instance only is recorded of her issuing a debased gold coinage; but this was in a time of distress, at the close of the Peloponnesian war.[1] The right of coining money was (no doubt) vested in the state, and forgery was a capital crime.[2]

The Attic coins were generally stamped with a head of Pallas on one side, and an owl (her sacred bird) on the other. Hence the point of the story told by Plutarch, in his life of Lysander—That general sent Gylippus with a bag of money to Sparta. Gylippus unsewed the bottom of the bag, took out a portion of the money, and sewed it up again. But unfortunately for him, the bag contained a paper which gave an account of the sum sent home. The magistrates, finding the money short, were surprised, and made inquiries. Gylippus had concealed the stolen coins, which were Athenian with the owl-stamp, under the tiles of his house; but his servant, who was in the secret, betrayed him by declaring, that he had observed a great many owls roost in the Ceramicus.[3] The theft was thus discovered, and Gylippus tarnished the good name which he had acquired by his victories at Syracuse.

Although the Attic money has been reduced into terms of our own, to give the reader some notion of its value, it is plain enough, that the relative values of Attic and English money could only be fully determined by a comparison of the quantities of the precious metals, the different modes of living in the two countries, and many other considerations of the same kind. For these reasons, besides the awkwardness of making Demosthenes talk of pounds, shillings and pence, I have, in the translation, adhered to the Attic terms for money. The following particulars will help to throw some light on the subject.

An Athenian could live respectably on the interest of a talent,—that is, on seven or eight minas a year. In the speech written by Demosthenes against Bœotus, the plaintiff[4] says he had been supported and educated out of such an income. Isæus speaks of an estate of fifty minas as sufficient to live comfortably, but not to perform public services. The expenses of Demosthenes, his mother and sister, during his minority, amounted to seven minas annually, exclusive of house rent. His father, who was a merchant,[5] left to his family an estate of fourteen talents, and is represented as a person of considerable property. But we read of larger fortunes than his at

[1] But even this instance is questioned by Grote. Hist. of Greece, iii. 153.

[2] Demosth. cont. Lept. sub fin.

[3] A pun on the Ceramicus at Athens and κέραμοι, *tiles*.

[4] The person for whom Demosthenes composed the speech, pp. 1014, 1023.

[5] Thirlwall's Hist. v. 247.

Athens. Conon possessed forty talents; Nicias one hundred; Alcibiades still more. One of the richest men was Callias, son of Hipponicus, whose property was valued at two hundred talents, partly acquired by the plunder of the Persian war. He had a son Hipponicus (who was killed at the battle of Delium) who gave his daughter in marriage to Alcibiades, with a portion of ten talents, and a promise of ten more after the birth of a son; the largest portion ever given by a Greek.

I have spoken of seven or eight minas as being the interest of a talent; that is, about twelve or thirteen per cent. per annum. Such in fact was a common rate of interest at Athens, but it was considered low; eighteen per cent. being frequently paid for loans on good security. There was no laws against usury; and although usurious money-lenders were regarded, as they have been in all ages, with an evil eye by the people, much higher rates than those above mentioned were exacted from needy borrowers, and wherever the risk was considerable. Thus, we read of thirty per cent. being paid on a bottomry contract for one summer. The lowness of personal credit, frequency of wars, instability of governments, and imperfection of national law, besides other causes of risk, would render all mercantile adventures perilous. The chief money-lenders at Athens were bankers; who kept the cash of their customers pretty much in the same manner as bankers of the present day, and made a profit by lending it out to others. They were serviceable to their customers in various ways; as the depositaries of important documents; as referees; as witnesses to payments and other transactions between them and third persons; and generally by extending their credit. They were usually men of high repute in the commercial world. Isocrates[1] tells us that money was lent to them without witnesses; and this need not surprise us, when we consider that writing materials were not so plentiful or easy to be had, and men were obliged to place more reliance on their agents.

The interest above referred to has been calculated, after the English fashion, by the year; but it must be remembered that it was usually reserved at Athens by the month, which makes it really higher.

[1] Trapeziticus, 358.

APPENDIX III.

THE THRACIAN CHERSONESE.

The peninsula known anciently by the name of the Thracian[1] Chersonese is washed on its eastern coast by the Hellespont, on its west by the Ægean sea. It stretches about fifty-two miles in length from its most southern point to the isthmus where it joins the continent of Thrace. The isthmus was between four and five miles long, being the same length as the isthmus of Corinth. It contained in Xenophon's time eleven or twelve cities. There were many good harbors on the coast, and the land was generally fertile both for corn and pasture. We read in Thucydides, that in the time of the Trojan war this land was cultivated by the Greek army for their subsistence. It was here, according to the legend, that Polydorus, the son of Priam, was murdered by the treacherous king Polymnestor.[2]

The southernmost town was Elæus opposite Sigeum in the Troad. Here was a tomb and temple of Protesilaus, the first of the Grecian warriors who leaped ashore at the siege of Troy, and who was slain by Hector, according to the prediction of the oracle.[3]

> Sors quoque nescio quem fato designat iniquo,
> Qui primus Danaûm Troada tangat humum.

The temple was conspicuous on the shore, and held in great veneration. It contained valuable treasures in gold and silver, which were seized by Artayctes, the Persian satrap, during the invasion of Xerxes; for which the people of Elæus were so incensed against him, that afterwards, when he fell into the hands of the Athenians, they caused him to be crucified, and his son to be stoned to death before his eyes.[4]

Erom Elæus the land curves eastward to the promontory of Cynossema, or Dog's-tomb, so called from Hecuba, the queen of Priam, who was fabled to have been changed into a dog and buried there.[5]

[1] The student must not confound this with the Tauric Chersonese, (the modern Crim Tartary,) which projects into the Euxine sea beyond the Borysthenes; the ancient name of which is preserved in the present town of Cherson.

[2] Xenophon. Hell. iii. c. 2, s. 10. Thucydides, i. 11. Herodotus, vi. 36. Virgil, Æn. iii. 49. Euripid. Hecuba, 8.

[3] Ovid, Epist. Laodamiæ, 93.

[4] Herod. ix. 116, 120. Thucyd. viii. 102.

[5] Euripid. Hecuba, 1265. Ovid, Metamorph. xiii. 560. Diodorus Siculus, xiii. 40.

The projection at this point is sharp and angular.[1] Afterwards it bends inward, and forms a deep bay, on which are the towns of Madytus and Sestus.

Sestus stood at the northern corner of the bay, nearly at the point where the strait is narrowest, so as to command the entrance. It was an Æolic city, of ancient foundation, famous both in history and in song. The story of Leander is familiar to all readers. Hero with her torch in the Sestian watch-tower lighted him over the deep, as he swam from Abydos. Their love-tale is the theme of two epistles of Ovid; and in modern times the feat of Leander was imitated by Lord Byron, who swam across the Hellespont at the same point. The classic lines in the Bride of Abydos have added a further interest to the spot:

The winds are high on Helle's wave,
As on that night of stormy water,
When Love who sent forgot to save
The young, the beautiful, the brave,
The lonely hope of Sestos' daughter.
Oh! when alone along the sky
Her turret torch was blazing high,
Though rising gale, and breaking foam,
And shrieking sea-birds warn'd him home;
And clouds aloft, and tides below,
With signs and sounds forbade to go,
He could not see, he would not hear,
Or sound or sign foreboding fear;
His eye but saw that light of love,
The only star it hail'd above:
His ear but rang with Hero's song,
"Ye waves, divide not lovers long!"
* * * *
Oh yet—for there my steps have been;
These feet have press'd the sacred shore;
These limbs that buoyant wave hath borne—
Minstrel! with thee to muse, to mourn,
To trace again those fields of yore,
Believing every hillock green
Contains no fabled hero's ashes,
And that around th' undoubted scene
Thine own broad Hellespont still dashes,
Be long my lot! and cold were he
Who there could gaze denying thee!

The stream of the Hellespont flows rapidly toward the Ægean, and gave the Greeks the idea of a river rather than a sea; whence

[1] Thucyd. viii. 104. As to the situation the reader may consult Goeller's note.

probably was derived Homer's epithet of *broad*, which has been the subject of much controversy,[1]

The sea of Helle is the sea where Helle, the sister of Phryxus, was drowned, falling from the golden ram; according to the ancient legend:[2]

> Et satis amissâ locus hic infamis ab Helle est;
> Utque mihi parcat, crimine nomen habet.
> Invideo Phryxo, quem per freta tristia tutum,
> Aurea lanigero vellere vexit ovis.

Her tomb was at the Isthmus. The modern name of the strait is the Dardanelles, apparently a compound of her name and the Asiatic city of Dardanus.

It was to a rugged part of the coast between Sestus and Madytus, that Xerxes carried his double bridge of boats across the strait, about a mile in length from Abydos. The army was seven days in crossing. Then it marched right up to the isthmus, and turning off to the left passed along the shore of the Sinus Melanis, and arrived at Doriscus on the Thracian coast, where the king held a grand review of his forces.[3]

The bridge was afterwards broken by a storm, and when Xerxes arrived at the Hellespont on his retreat, he carried his troops over in sailing vessels to Abydos. Herodotus mentions another story, of which he declares his own disbelief; that Xerxes crossed over to Asia in a single vessel from Eion on the Strymon, and was only saved from shipwreck by causing his Persian followers to jump overboard.[4] To this last story, as it would seem, Juvenal alludes in the following lines:[5]

> Ille tamen qualis rediit Salamine relictâ,
> In Corum atque Eurum solitus sævire flagellis,
> Barbarus, Æolio nunquam hoc in carcere passos,
> Ipsum compedibus qui vinxerat Ennosigæum,
> Sed qualis rediit! nempe unâ nave cruentis
> Fluctibus, ac tardâ per densâ cadavera prodâ.

Further to the north was the little stream called Ægos Potamos, or Goat's River, near to which the great fleet of the Athenians, through the negligence of their commanders, was captured by Lysander in the last year of the Peloponnesian war. It was exactly opposite the Mysian Lampsacus, which was given by the Persian king to Themistocles, to supply him with wine; as Magnesia for his

[1] Ἐπὶ πλατεῖ Ἑλλησπόντῳ. Iliad, vii. 86; Odyssey, xxiv. 82.
[2] Ovid, Leand. Epist. 141.
[3] Herod. vii. 33, 56, 59.
[4] Ib. viii. 117, 118.
[5] **Juv. Sat. x. 178.**

bread, and Myus for his meat.[1] This city was long famous for its wealth and luxury, and also for the worship of the god Priapus, who had a temple there. To this Virgil alludes in the line:[2]

Hellespontiaci servet tutela Priapi.

Further on was the city of Crithote, and a little beyond was Pactya.

The terminus of the Chersonese at an early period was a supposed line drawn from Pactya to Cardia, where the wall was afterwards built. Cardia was a Milesian settlement, and stood at the head of the Melanis Sinus. In later times it became a city of importance, and was considered the key of the peninsula; its possession giving facility for a hostile inroad from the interior of Thrace.[3]

For the better understanding of that part of Athenian history which relates to the occupation of the Chersonese by Athens, it will be needful to give a brief account of the Thracian kingdom.

The people inhabiting the country that lay between the Ægean sea and the Danube, the Strymon and the Euxine, where known generally to the Greeks by the name of Thracians. They consisted of numerous tribes. Could they have been united (says Herodotus) under a single monarch, they would have been invincible.[4] The more warlike and ferocious among them were the mountaineers who dwelt on the ridges of Hæmus and Rhodope. Those who lived in the plain were more peaceable, especially those who came into contact with the Greek colonies on the Ægean and Propontine coasts. They were devoted to the worship of Mars and Bacchus.[5] With their warlike character was mixed a wild religious enthusiasm; and down to a very late period they were notorious among the nations for quarreling over their cups: Horace says,

Non ego sanius
Bacchabor Edonis.

And again,

Natis in usum lætitiæ scyphis
Pugnare Thracum est.

In the time of the Peloponnesian war the most considerable of

[1] Thucyd. i. 138. Cornelius Nepos in vit Themist.

[2] Georgics, iv. 111. See Pausanias, ix. 31. For the artifice by which Anaximenes the orator saved Lampsacus from the wrath of Alexander, see Pausanias, vi. 18.

[3] Demosth. contra Aristoc. 681.

[4] Herod. v. 3, 7.

[5] Ὁ Θρῃξὶ μάντις Διόνυσος, Euripid. Hecuba, 1267. He was the god of the Orphic mysteries, perhaps derived from Egypt. Herod. ii. 81, 103.

the tribes were the Odrysæ, who occupied the centre of the country below Mount Hæmus. The sway of their king Sitalces extended from the city of Abdera to the Euxine and the mouths of the Danube. He was in alliance with Athens, and in pursuance of his engagement with her led an innumerable host to attack Perdiccas and the Chalcidians. His invasion excited the utmost terror all through Macedonia and Thessaly; but the Athenians derived little advantage from it; for Sitalces, after ravaging the enemy's country for some time, entered into a negotiation with Perdiccas and returned home. Thucydides expresses the same opinion with Herodotus as to the formidable character of the Thracian people, if they could all have been united.[1]

The first connection of the Athenians with the Thracian Chersonese took place in the following way. The story is somewhat romantic.

In the time of Pisistratus the Chersonese was inhabited by a Thracian tribe called Doloncians. They, pressed by a war of the Absinthians, sent their princes to Delphi to consult the oracle; which directed them to invite the first person who offered them hospitality to come and settle among them as their chief. The princes passed through Phocis and Bœotia and came to Athens. There, as they walked through the town, their strange dress and arms were observed by Militiades, the son of Cypselus; who invited them to his house and entertained them. They told him of the oracle, and entreated him to comply with it. Miltiades was a man of good family and wealth, and not very well satisfied with his position in Athens, were Pisistratus held the supreme rule. He was therefore not indisposed to accept the offer of the strangers. He took the precaution, however, to consult the oracle in person, and having received a favorable answer, proceeded with the Doloncians and a body of Athenian emigrants to the Chersonese, where he was made ruler of the country, and building a wall from Pactya to Cardia repressed the incursions of the Absinthians.[2]

Divine honors were paid to Miltiades after his death by the Chersonesites, who looked upon him as the founder of a colony.[3] He was succeeded by his nephew Stesagoras, son of Cimon; who having been soon after assassinated, his brother Miltiades was sent by Hippias from Athens, to take possession of the government. This happened B.C. 518. The young Miltiades commenced his reign by seizing the persons of the Chersonesite princes, whom he suspected probably of being concerned in his brother's murder; he

[1] Thucyd. ii. 95—101.

[2] Herod. vi. 34—39. The Athenians had at an early period occupied Sigeum in the Troad, and so became known in the Chersonesite region before the migration under Miltiades.

[3] Οἰκιστής. See Thucyd. v. 11. Cornelius Nepos confounds the elder Miltiades with the younger.

then established a body of mercenaries, and strengthened his connection by marrying the daughter of a Thracian king.

About three years after, viz. B.C. 515, Darius invaded Scythia. He crossed by a bridge of boats over the Thracian Bosphorus, and marched through the eastern part of Thrace to the Danube, where the Ionians, who commanded the fleet, had prepared a bridge for his passage. Many Thracian chiefs joined his army, and among others, Miltiades; for the Chersonese, though ruled by the Athenian prince, was tributary to the Persian empire. Miltiades remained with the Ionians who guarded the bridge, while Darius was in the enemy's country. He advised them to break it up, after the expiration of the sixty days which Darius had prescribed for his return; but this advice was overruled, and Darius re-crossed the Danube in safety. Megabazus the satrap was left in Thrace to complete the subjugation of the country. Miltiades returned to the Chersonese, where for many years he reigned without disturbance, except for a short period, when he was driven out by a Scythian invasion.[1]

At length, however, after he had reigned about twenty-four years, Miltiades was compelled to fly from his kingdom for fear of Persian hostility. After the suppression of the Ionian revolt, B.C. 494, Darius sent his Phœnician fleet to chastise the cities on the European side of the Hellespont and Propontis, which had assisted his rebellious subjects. Miltiades, conscious of having merited the king's displeasure, either for his treacherous counsel on the Danube, or by some other act of disloyalty, prepared for flight. He set sail from Cardia with five ships, while the Phœnician fleet was anchored at Tenedos. One of the ships, containing his eldest son Metiochus, was captured by the Phœnicians, who sent him a prisoner to Susa. Darius, instead of visiting the father's crime upon the son, treated him with the utmost generosity; gave him a Persian lady in marriage, and an estate with her. Miltiades escaped to Athens, where he was again admitted to the rights of citizenship. He was reserved for a more glorious destiny than the government of a Thracian prin-

[1] Herod. iv. 89—98, 137; vi. 40. Thirlwall, in an appendix to the second volume of his history, contends that the counsel imputed to Miltiades at the Danube was a fiction, and that his second flight from the Chersonese was occasioned by his having taken Lemnos from the Persians. The arguments which he advances in support of this view are exceedingly strong. Grote, on the other hand, in his History of Greece, vol. iv. 368, maintains that the story of Herodotus, as to the advice given by Miltiades, is correct; but that Herodotus ascribed the first flight of Miltiades from the Chersonese to the wrong cause; viz. to his fear of the Scythian incursion; whereas the real cause was the fear of Persia. The dates of Herodotus can scarcely be made to agree with this latter view. Miltiades was a man very likely to have invented the story.

cipality. In a few years afterwards he was the hero of Marathon. The cities of Chersonesus, all excepting Cardia, were brought under subjection to the Persian king.[1]

So things remained till after the defeat of the second Persian invasion. The united fleet of the Greeks sailed then to the Hellespont, where finding the bridge of Xerxes broken, the Peloponnesians returned home; the Athenians, under Xanthippus, stayed to recover the dominion of Miltiades. All the Persian troops in the neighborhood were drawn from the different towns into Sestus, which was strongly fortified. The Athenians laid siege to that city, and took it after a long resistance, putting Artayctes the satrap to death, as we have already seen. Among other spoils which fell into their hands were the cables of the famous bridge, which they carried home to be deposited in the temples of Athens.[2]

It was Cimon, the son of Miltiades, who completed the conquest of Chersonesus. After the departure of the Athenian fleet from Sestus, the Persians came over again, and recovered their possessions. Cimon sailed against them with only four galleys, defeated a much larger squadron, and chased the Persians out of the peninsula, together with a body of continental Thracians, whom they had invited to their assistance.[3] To this period we may refer the following story related by Plutarch:[4]—

The Athenians and their allies having taken a great number of barbarians prisoners in Sestus and Byzantium, Cimon, being chosen to divide the booty, put the naked prisoners in one lot, and the rich attire and jewels in another. The allies complaining of this as an unequal division, he said they might take which lot they pleased, and the Athenians would be content. Herophytus of Samos advised the allies to take the ornaments, and leave the slaves to the Athenians. This was done, and Cimon at first was laughed at for his liberality; but soon after, the parents and kinsmen of the prisoners came from Lydia and Phrygia, and paid a high price for their ransom; whereby Cimon collected money enough to maintain his fleet for four months, and even to reserve something for the Athenian treasury.

At a later period, when Pericles held the administration at Athens, it being his policy to extend the influence of his country by establishing numerous colonies, he sent out a thousand Athenians to take allotments of land in the Chersonese, and caused the wall across the isthmus, which had been damaged by hostile inroads, to be repaired.[5]

[1] Herod. vi. 33, 41.
[2] Herod. ix. 114—121. Thucyd. i. 89.
[3] Plutarch. in vit. Cimon.
[4] Ibid.
[5] Plutarch in vit. Pericl.

In the last six years of the Peloponnesian war the Hellespont and Propontis became the scene of most important military operations, which it will be sufficient briefly to notice;—viz. the battle gained by the Athenians off the headland of Cynossema[1]—the action off Abydos, where they defeated the Poloponnesian fleet under Mindarus[2]—the victory of Alcibiades at Cyzicus in the Propontis[3]—his successful sieges of Chalcedon and Byzantium. The importance of the struggle in these seas will be apparent, when we consider that they were the great thoroughfare of the corn-trade, on which Athens was entirely dependent for the subsistence of her people. Eubœa, once the granary of Athens, had revolted.[5] Attica was virtually in the hands of the enemy, by means of the garrison at Deceleia. Yet it was impossible to starve out the Athenians whilst they possessed a navy which protected their commerce, and enabled them to import corn from the shores of the Hellespont and the Euxine. This had forcibly struck Agis the Spartan king, who commanded at Deceleia, as from that fortress one day he espied a multitude of corn-ships sailing into the Piræus. It was no use, he said, to exclude the Athenians from Attica, unless they stopped the passage of corn by sea: and accordingly he advised that measures should be taken to cut off their commerce. His advice was followed; and on this in fact the issue of the war ultimately turned.[6]

Hitherto the Athenians had been victorious in the northern seas; but in the year B.C. 405, Lysander, already famous by his victory at Notium, sailed with a considerable fleet to Abydos, then in alliance with the Peloponnesians. From hence he sailed to Lampsacus, a few miles north of Abydos, which he attacked by sea, while the Abydenes, under Thorax the Lacedæmonian, besieged it from the land side. That city had just been taken by storm, when the Athenian fleet, consisting of 180 ships, arrived at Elæus. It was commanded by six generals, Conon, Philocles, Adimantus, Menander, Tydeus, and Cephisodotus. Hearing that Lampsacus was taken, they sailed up the channel, and, putting in at Sestus for provisions, proceeded to Ægos Potamos, just opposite Lampsacus, where the enemy still lay at anchor. The width of the channel at this point was fifteen furlongs; the two fleets were in sight of each other, and a decisive battle was expected.[7]

Early the next morning the Athenians crossed the Hellespont, and drew up in order of battle opposite the harbor of Lampsacus. Lysander, whose fleet seems to have been inferior in number, had given strict injunctions to his men to make every preparation for a

[1] Thucyd. viii. 104.
[2] Xenoph. Hellen .i. c. 1, s. 5.
[3] Ib. s. 16.
[4] Ib. c. 3, s. 2, 14.
[5] Thucyd. viii. 95.
[6] Xenoph. Hellen. i. c. 1, s. 35.
[7] Xenoph. Hellen. ii. c. 1, s. 16—29.

sea-fight, but not to stir from their position. The Athenians continued offering battle till late in the afternoon, when, finding that the enemy would not move, they sailed back to Ægos Potamos. Lysander ordered two or three of his swiftest ships to follow them, and see what they did after landing: his own troops he kept on board till the messengers returned. These operations on both sides were repeated for four days. The Athenians each day, after returning to their station, dispersed themselves to Sestus and other places to seek provisions.

It so happened, there was one vigilant eye which discerned the stratagem of the Spartan general. Alcibiades, in disgrace and exile since the affair of Notium, had retired to an estate which he possessed in the Chersonese, not far from Pactya; there he had fortified three castles, to serve him, in case of need, for places of refuge. From one of these, which stood near the coast, he descried the manœuvres of the hostile fleets. Seeing the peril of his countrymen, he rode on horseback down to the Athenian camp, and pointed out to the generals two important oversights which they had committed,—first, that they had stationed their fleet on an open beach, without cover or shelter; secondly, that they were too far removed from Sestus, to which they were obliged to resort for a market, and which was nearly two miles off. He advised them to sail to Sestus immediately, where they would enjoy the convenience of the town and harbor, and have it in their power to fight when they pleased. He reproved them also for their negligence in suffering the crews to be dispersed, when the enemy was so near. This wise counsel was utterly disregarded. Tydeus and Menander reminded him, they were the generals, not he, and ordered him to be gone. He told the few friends who accompanied him out of the camp, that if the generals would put themselves under his directions, he could bring to their aid a body of Thracians, and that he would force Lysander into a battle by attacking him on land. This was looked upon as an idle boast; but very likely it was no more than the truth, for it appears that Alcibiades during his sojourn in the Chersonese had made excursions beyond the isthmus, and ingratiated himself with some of the princes in the interior of Thrace. All he could say, however, had no effect.[1]

On the fifth morning the Athenians advanced to Lampascus, and returned as before, looking with contempt on the Peloponnesians for their cowardice; and landing again, they dispersed themselves with still greater carelessness over the country. The captains that followed them were ordered by Lysander to watch the moment of their dispersal, then to row back, and, when they were half-way, to hoist a shield. He himself kept his whole fleet in readiness. The

[1] Plutarch in vit. Alcib. Id. in vit. Lysand. Diodorus Siculus, xiii. 105. Cornelius Nepos in vit. Alcib.

shield was raised, and the Peloponnesian galleys, with Thorax and his land forces on board, were soon crossing the channel at full speed. Conon saw their advance, and gave the signal to his men to come on board; but it was too late; they were scattered too far; and of the whole fleet only eight ships besides his own could be manned and put to sea. One of these was the Paralus or state-galley, which sailed off to Athens, to bear the melancholy tidings. Conon with the other eight escaped from the enemy, and found refuge in Cyprus; from which, some years after, he issued forth to be the restorer of his country. Meanwhile, the rest of the fleet became, without a struggle, the prize of Lysander. The few Athenians who had run down to their ships were put to the sword; the rest were pursued over the country, and nearly the whole body of them were made prisoners, and massacred in cold blood in the streets of Lampsacus.[1]

Thus, by the extraordinary negligence of the Athenian commanders, Lysander acquired the glory of terminating the Peloponnesian war.

The Chersonese, together with the rest of her empire, was lost to Athens; and it was more than forty years before she recovered any of her dominion in this quarter. The Spartans did not seize the vacant possession for themselves, but, content with having destroyed the Athenian empire, and established their own preponderating influence, left the inhabitants to a nominal independence. Lysander indeed, having taken Sestus, gave up the whole town as a property to his troops; but the Spartan government were displeased at his conduct, and restored the Sestians to their rights.[2] We may presume that many Athenian colonists were compelled to migrate. Alcibiades, deeming it unsafe to remain in the neighborhood, departed, with all the treasure that he could carry away, into Bithynia, where, having been plundered by Thracian robbers, he sought the protection of the satrap Pharnabazus, who assigned him a dwelling in Phrygia, and for a time treated him kindly, but afterwards, at the instance of Lysander, caused him to be treacherously murdered.[3]

The Chersonesite Greeks, no longer under the protection of a powerful empire, were again exposed to the inroads of their continental neighbors, insomuch that it was almost useless to cultivate the land. In the year B.C. 398 Dercyllidas, the Spartan general, who was then with his army at Lampsacus, was informed by some commissioners from home, that a deputation of the Chersonesites had been at Sparta, praying to have the isthmus fortified against the

[1] According to Pausanias, ix. 32, four thousand prisoners were massacred, and their bodies left unburied.

[2] Plutarch. in vit. Lysand.

[3] Diodorus xiv. 11. Plutarch and Cornelius Nepos in vit. Alcibiad.

barbarous Thracians. It seems that little or none of the old wall was then remaining. Dercyllidas marched into Thrace, and after passing some time at the court of Seuthes, king of the Odrysæ, arrived at the isthmus, where he first chased away the marauders, and then set his troops to work at the fortification, dividing the ground among them in portions, and stimulating them by rewards. The new wall was completed in half a year.[1]

The great kingdom of the Odrysæ, after the death of Sitalces, who was slain by the Triballi B.C. 424, was inherited by his nephew Seuthes. He enjoyed a long and prosperous reign. His revenues are said to have amounted to four hundred talents a year, besides presents to an equal amount in gold and silver, which it was usual for the kings of Thrace to receive.[2] Towards the end of the fifth century B.C. this kingdom had devolved upon Amadocus or Medocus; but it was divided and greatly weakened. A prince named Mæsades ruled the southern and eastern parts, extending to the lower shores of the Euxine and the Propontis, as far as the city of Ganus. The tribes subject to him were named Melanditæ, Thyni, and Tranipsæ. But he was expelled from his kingdom, and his son Seuthes was brought up at the court of Amadocus. Seuthes, when he arrived at man's estate, endeavored, with the assistance of the Odrysian monarch, to recover his dominions, but was unable to do more than live by plunder.[3] Alcibiades had made friends of both these princes in the year B.C. 405, but what position Seuthes then held we are not informed.[4] Indeed, we have so little historical information about the Thracian people, except when they are brought into contact with the southern Greeks, that it is difficult to make out the geography of the country reigned over by their kings, or the boundaries of the various tribes that composed the nation. We read occasionally of incursions made by particular tribes into the territories occupied by Greek colonies; and it appears clear enough that the mountaineers of Hæmus and Rhodope always maintained a rude independence against the Thracian monarchs of the plain.[5] When Xenophon and his Cyrean troops, on their return from Persia, arrived on the coast of the Bosphorus, in the year B.C. 400, Seuthes applied to him for assistance against his rebellious subjects. This, after some delay, was granted. Xenophon marched from Perinthus into the interior of the country, defeated the rebellious mountaineers, and re-established the power of Seuthes, from whom he with some difficulty obtained the promised reward for his sol-

[1] Xenoph. Hell. iii. c. 2, s. 8. Diodorus, xiv. 38.
[2] Thucyd. ii. 97; iv. 101.
[3] Xenoph. Anab. vii. c. 2, s. 32—38.
[4] Diodorus, xiii. 105.
[5] Thucyd. ii. 96. Xenoph. Hell. v. c. 2, s. 17. Diodorus, xiv. 12; xv. 36.

diers.[1] It has already been mentioned that Dercillidas the Lacedæmonian was hospitably entertained at the court of Seuthes. We read that in the year B.C. 392 Thrasybulus, then commanding an Athenian fleet in the Ægean, visited the Chersonese, and brought over Amadocus and Seuthes to the alliance of Athens.[2] A few years later, Seuthes was again disturbed by insurrection, and in his distress applied for the aid of Iphicrates, who had rendered himself famous by the success of his peltastæ or targeteers. By the arms of that general he recovered his dominion.[3]

In the year B.C. 382 Cotys succeeded to the monarchy of Thrace; but whether to the kingdom of Amadocus as well as that of Seuthes does not appear. The latter he certainly possessed; and it is not unlikely that he enlarged his power by conquest of the former. The long sojourn of Iphicrates in Thrace—for since the peace of Antalcidas he had no employment for his troops in the south—had brought him into connection with Cotys, to whom, after the death of Seuthes, he transferred his services. Cotys, to reward and attach him more closely to his own interests, gave him his daughter in marriage, and assigned to him for his domain a Thracian town called Drys, situated near the mouth of the Hebrus, which Iphicrates strengthened by fortifications, and by the introduction of a Greek colony.[4] Thus, says Grote,[5] "Iphicrates became a great man in Thrace, yet by no means abandoning his connection with Athens, but making his position in each subservient to his importance in the other. While he was in a situation to favor the projects of Athenian citizens for mercantile and territorial acquisitions in the Chersonese and other parts of Thrace, he could also lend the aid of Athenian naval and military art, not merely to princes in Thrace, but to others even beyond those limits; since we learn that Amyntas, king of Macedonia, became so attached or indebted to him as to adopt him for his son."

Here it is convenient to notice the loose and irregular practices of which the Athenian generals of this period were so frequently guilty, but which scarcely drew upon them any rebuke or censure

[1] Xenoph. Anab. vii. c. 1, s. 5—c. 7, s. 55.

[2] Diodorus, xiv. 94.

[3] Cornelius Nepos in vit. Iphicrat.

[4] Suidas, s. v. Κότυς and Δρῦς. Anaxandridas apud Athen. iv. 6, where there is an amusing description of the wedding feast. A good saying of Menestheus, the son of Iphicrates, is related by Cornelius Nepos: "Is cùm interrogaretur, utrum pluris patrem matremve faceret; matrem inquit. Id cùm omnibus mirum videretur; at ille, meritò inquit facio. Nam pater, quantum in se fuit, Thracem me genuit; contra mater Atheniensem." The absence of Iphicrates in Thrace is mentioned by Isæus, de Menecl. Hered. s. 7.

[5] History of Greece, x. 146.

from their own people. I allude to their constant residence abroad, their roaming in quest of adventures, their service under foreign princes, forming connections with them by marriage and otherwise, receiving gifts of cities and fortified posts, and acting independently without the order or permission of the state. Much of this may be traced to the consequences of the Peloponnesian war. A large number of men accustomed to warfare were thrown out of employment, and glad to find any service where pay and plunder could be got. The march of the ten thousand Greeks into Persia was one of the first demonstrations given of the importance of this class of men. The remnant that returned under Xenophon were employed in Asia Minor by the Lacedæmonians. Athens owed her restoration to the foreign troops commanded by Conon. Mercenary soldiers began to be necessary for her wars. Her generals, if successful, acquired an influence over them, and in proportion as the soldiers were attached to the general, he was less under the control of the state. Thus was the power of the state weakened, and a change wrought in the temper and feelings of the people. Necessity itself prevented the Athenians from scrutinizing the conduct of their generals too nicely. They were compelled to send them out unprovided with the sinews of war; and the generals had no choice but to get money in irregular ways, by contributions from allies, by plunder, or by foreign service. When Athens began to recover her maritime empire, she ought to have established a better rule of discipline. But she did not; the people imagined that they could make foreign conquests in the same scrambling way that they had extricated themselves from their difficulties. Hence, not only did they allow such men as Iphicrates and Timotheus to use their armaments on expeditions that were not immediately connected with the interests of Athens, but they tolerated, if they did not encourage, the mischievous irregularities of such men as Chares and Charidemus. It is true, the Athenians sometimes profited by these irregularities, but they lost by them in the long run. We shall see presently what damage was done to the affairs of Athens in the Chersonese by the adventurer Charidemus. And even Iphicrates, greatly as he had served his country on former occasions, was induced by his alliance with Cotys to commit open treason.[1]

These remarks are quite distinct from another charge, which has been brought against the Athenian people both in ancient and modern times, viz. that their leading men resided abroad, because, owing to the jealousy of their fellow-citizens, they could not live in comfort and security at home. Theopompus was the original author of such accusation, which has been repeated by Cornelius Nepos in the Life of Chabrias:—

[1] See pages 51, 105, 189, 232, of this volume. Also Thirlwall, Gr. Hist. v. 209—212.

"Non enim libenter erat ante oculos civium suorum, quod·et vivebat laute, et indulgebat sibi liberalius quam ut invidium vulgi posset effugere. Est enim hoc commune vitium in magnis liberisque civitatibus, ut invidia gloriæ comes sit, et libenter de his detrahant, quos eminere videant altius; neque animo æquo pauperes alienam opulentam intuentur fortunam. Itaque Chabrias, quoad ei licebat, plurimum aberat. Neque vero solus ille aberat Athenis libentur, sed omnes ferè principes fecerunt idem, quòd tantum se ab invidiâ putabant abfuturos, quantum a conspectu suorum recessissent. Itaque Conon plurimum Cypri vixit, Iphicrates in Thraciâ, Timotheus Lesbi, Chares in Sigeo."

Grote, who has given proof of a clearer insight into the spirit of Greek history, and especially of Athenian character, than any English historian who has preceded him, successfully refutes the sweeping charge of Theopompus and Nepos. I can not do better than quote his own words:[1]

"That the people of Athens, among other human frailties, had their fair share of envy and jealousy, is not to be denied; but that these attributes belonged to them in a marked or peculiar manner, can not (in my judgment) be shown by any evidence extant, and most assuredly is not shown by the evidence here alluded to.

"Chabrias was fond of a life of enjoyment and luxurious indulgence. If, instead of being an Athenian, he had been a Spartan, he would undoubtedly have been compelled to expatriate, in order to gratify this taste; for it was the express drift and purpose of the Spartan discipline, not to equalize property, but to equalize the habits, enjoyments, and personal toils, of the rich and poor. This is a point which the admirers of Lycurgus—Xenophon and Plutarch—attest not less clearly than Thucydides, Plato, Aristotle, and others. If then it were considered a proof of envy and ill temper, to debar rich men from spending their money in procuring enjoyments, we might fairly consider the reproach as made out against Lycurgus and Sparta. Not so against Athens. There was no city in Greece where the means of luxurious and comfortable living were more abundantly exhibited for sale, nor where a rich man was more perfectly at liberty to purchase them. Of this the proofs are every where to be found. Even the son of this very Chabrias—Ctesippus—who inherited the appetite for enjoyment, without the greater qualities, of his father—found the means of gratifying his appetite so unfortunately easy at Athens, that he wasted his whole substance in such expenses. (Plutarch, Phocion, c. 7; Athenæus, iv. p. 165.) And Chares was even better liked at Athens in consequence of his love of enjoyment and license—if we are to believe another fragment (238) of the same Theopompus.

"The allegation of Theopompus and Nepos, therefore, is neither

[1] History of Greece, x. 147.

true as matter of fact, nor sufficient, if it had been true, to sustain the hypothesis of a malignant Athenian public, with which they connect it. Iphicrates and Chabrias did not stay away from Athens because they loved enjoyments or feared the envy of their countrymen; but because both of them were large gainers by doing so, in importance, in profit, and in tastes. Both of them loved war and had great abilities for war—qualities quite compatible with a strong appetite for enjoyment; while neither of them had either taste or talent for the civil routine and debate of Athens when at peace. Besides, each of them was commander of a body of peltasts, through whose means he could obtain lucrative service as well as foreign distinction; so that we can assign a sufficient reason why both of them preferred to be absent from Athens during most part of the nine years that the peace of Antalcides continued. Afterwards, Iphicrates was abroad three or four years in service with the Persian satraps, by order of the Athenians: Chabrias also went, a long time afterwards, again on foreign service, to Egypt, at the same time when the Spartan king Agesilaus was there; (yet without staying long away, since we find him going out on command from Athens to the Chersonese in 359—358 B. C.—Demosth. cont. Aristoc. p. 677;) but neither he, nor Agesilaus, went there to escape the mischief of envious countrymen. Demosthenes does not talk of Iphicrates as being uncomfortable in Athens, or anxious to get out of it: see Orat. cont. Meidiam, p. 535."

The case of Conon residing at Cyprus, as Grote justly remarks, is far from being an illustration of Athenian jealousy or ill temper. It is not a case at all in point, as from any common history may be gathered.

But I must return from this disgression.

Events that occurred somewhere about the year B. C. 362 brought Cotys into collision with the Athenians.

Towards the close of the year B. C. 363 Timotheus, who then commanded the Athenian fleet in the Ægean, was sent to the coast of Asia Minor to assist Ariobarzanes, satrap of Phrygia. Ariobarzanes about five years before had sent an agent to Delphi, named Philiscus, who held a congress for the pacification of the Greek states. The Thebans thwarted his views, upon which Philiscus threatened them with war, and began to levy troops against them.[1] The Athenians, then in alliance with Lacedæmon against Thebes, conferred the honor of citizenship on Ariobarzanes and his deputy;[2] and the connection thus formed with the satrap apparently led to the mission of Timotheus. What were the precise objects of the Athenians, we are not informed. It appears however that in the same year the Thebans sent a naval armament under the command of Epaminondas

[1] Xenoph. Hell. vii. c. 1, s. 27.
[2] Demosth. contra Aristoc. 666, 687.

to the Hellespont and Propontis, which defeated a small force under Laches at Byzantium. Epaminondas was well received at that city, and exerted himself (not without effect) to detach it from the Athenian alliance.[1] After scouring the seas for some time, he was obliged to return home to attend to more pressing affairs, but his appearance in the Ægean had greatly alarmed the Athenians; and it is probable that they desired the aid of the Persian satrap, (especially in money,) to counteract the efforts of the Thebans in that direction. Ariobarzanes had views of his own, which caused him to need the assistance of an able general like Timotheus. In fact, he was meditating revolt from his master Artaxerxes, and wanted men and officers. The Athenians had some suspicion of his intention; and therefore,[2] while they permitted their general to co-operate with the satrap, to save appearances, they inserted a clause in their decree, forbidding any infringement of their treaty with the king of Persia. Agesilaus was allowed by the Spartans to go out on the same mission, but without any such limitation of his powers. The result of the expedition—as far as concerns our present inquiry—was, that Timotheus, in requital of the services which he rendered, was assisted by Ariobarzanes to get possession of Sestus and Crithote; and the Athenians, having thus again got a footing on their ancient territory, were encouraged to claim the whole dominion of the Chersonese.[3]

Cotys, who considered the peninsula as rightly belonging to his own kingdom, by no means acquiesced in this claim. He had already made an attempt on the town of Sestus, which was defeated by Agesilaus,[4] and he now prepared for war with the Athenians. He engaged in his service Iphicrates, who being at this time out of employment, and in some disgrace on account of his bad success at Amphipolis, did not scruple to assist his father-in-law against his country.[5] Timotheus nevertheless took Elæus, carried the war into Thrace, and acquired a considerable amount of plunder. But he had not much leisure for operations in the Chersonese; for he was now called off to the siege of Samos, where he was occupied for nearly a twelvemonth, until some part of the year B.C. 361. At the end of that year he went on his last disastrous expedition against Amphipolis; and we do not find him again employed as general until the occasion of the Social war.[6]

Meanwhile Cotys had been greatly alarmed by a rebellion which broke out in his own kingdom. A Thracian chieftain, named Mil-

[1] Diod. xv. 79. Isocr. Phil. 59.

[2] Demosth. de Rhod. Lib. 192, 193.

[3] Isocrates, *On the Exchange*, 115, 119. Cornelius Nepos in vit. Timoth.

[4] Xenoph. Agesil. ii. 26.

[5] Demosth. contra Aristoc. 663.

[6] See page 234 of this volume.

tocythes, at the close of the year 372, rose in arms, and seized upon the Sacred Mountain.[1] He sent off an embassy to Athens, proposing alliance and offering to give up to her the Chersonese. Ergophilus, then commanding on that coast, prepared to support him: but Cotys, probably under the advice of Iphicrates, sent a submissive letter to the Athenians, which induced them to suppose they should gain more by the friendship than by the punishment of that monarch; and accordingly they sent out a new general, Autocles, with a commission which gave him discretionary power to act according to circumstances. The result of this double-faced policy was, that Miltocythes, having no assurance of support, and rather supposing the Athenians were against him, abandoned his stronghold, and withdrew: Cotys, being relieved from danger, soon gave the Athenians to understand that they had merited no recompense from him. They vented their anger upon Autocles, whom they brought to trial for having permitted the rebellion to be quashed; and sent out Menon as his successor. Menon in a short time was superseded by Timomachus. Neither of them gained any success in their warlike operations against Cotys. He on the contrary was able to annoy the Athenian commerce: and the presence of a naval force in the northern seas became necessary for the protection of the corn-trade, not only against Cotys, but also against the Byzantines and others who detained the Athenian vessels and intercepted their supplies.[2]

Towards the end of the year B.C. 361 Cotys led an army into the Chersonese, and contrived, with assistance from Abydos, which had generally been hostile to Athens, to take Sestus. In this enterprise he was no longer aided by Iphicrates, who, either drawing a distinction between offensive and defensive measures, or repenting of his past conduct, or for some other cause dissatisfied with his father-in-law, would serve no longer against Athens. He had, as Demosthenes represents, saved Cotys from ruin—referring probably to the rebellion of Miltocythes—and expected from his gratitude, that he would change his policy towards Athens: but instead of this, his own service was required for further hostilities. Refusing to comply with this demand, and fearing the resentment of the king, he retired to Antissa, and afterwards to Drys.[3] The Athenians over-

[1] A district about fifteen miles north of the Chersonese, stretching west of the river Zoralus, nearly down to the sea above Ganus.

[2] Demosth. contra Aristoc. 655, 658; contra Polyclem. 1207, 1210, 1211, 1213.

[3] Demosth. contra Aristoc. 663, 664. It is possible that a feeling of rivalry against Timotheus influenced the conduct of Iphicrates. Timotheus threatened him with a γραφὴ ξενίας, but they were afterwards reconciled, and joint commanders in the Social war. See Demosth. contra Timoth. 1204. Cornelius Nepos in vit. Iphic. and Timoth.

looked his treasonable conduct, and employed him at a later period in the Social war. Cotys, deprived of his ablest officer, engaged in his stead Charidemus.

Of this adventurer's character I have already spoken. After the defeat of Timotheus, under whom he had served by compulsion, at Amphipolis, he had passed over to Asia, and, breaking an engagement which he had entered into with Memnon and Mentor, brothers-in-law of the satrap Artabazus, took forcible possession of Scepsis, Cebren, and Ilium, in the Troad. These being inland towns, he had no means of maintaining himself against the power of the satrap, who soon collected his forces for a siege. Charidemus, in his distress, wrote a letter to Cephisodotus, then the Athenian commander in the Hellespont, begging the loan of some ships to convey him and his troops from Asia, and promising in return to reduce the Chersonese under Athenian dominion. He was lucky enough to escape without such help; for Mentor and Memnon, hearing of the design, persuaded Artabazus to let him go. Charidemus, having crossed over to the Chersonese, instead of performing his promise to Cephisodotus, joined the army of Cotys, from whom probably he expected a more ample reward, and proceeded with him to besiege Elæus and Crithote.[1]

The siege of these places had continued for some time without success, when the Athenians were relieved from further peril by the violent death of Cotys, who was assassinated by two natives of Ænus, Python and Heraclides. The alleged motive of the deed was revenge for some insult which Cotys had offered to their father. Cotys with much energy and strength of character united the rude ferocity common among his people. He was addicted to hard drinking and licentious habits, and it not unfrequently happened, that the courtiers and companions of the king were the victims of his intemperance. Strange stories are told of him by Theopompus —that he used to make excursions over his kingdom, and wherever he found pleasant spots, well wooded and watered, he established places of entertainment, to which he resorted with his generals and officers, and gave himself up to sensual enjoyment. Sacrifices to the gods formed a part of these festivities, until the habit of unrestrained indulgence overcame his piety as well as his discretion, and he conceived the idea that he was beloved by the goddess Minerva. Full of this belief, he actually ordered a wedding-feast, and fitted up a nuptial chamber for his bride. In a state of intoxication he awaited her arrival; till at length, becoming impatient, he sent one of his guards to see if the goddess had come. The guard informed him that there was no one in the chamber, and for this unwelcome news was shot by the king with an arrow. A second messenger shared the same fate: a third, more prudent, told him,

[1] Demosth. contra Aristoc. 670—672.

the goddess had been waiting for him some time. Another story is, that, being jealous of his queen, he killed her in a most brutal manner, cutting her up the middle with his own sword. Such was the man, who now, for some outrage upon a Greek citizen, fell a victim to filial vengeance.[1]

The murderers fled to Athens, and were well received. The Athenians were weak enough to pass a vote, conferring on them the honor of citizenship and crowns of gold. Nothing could justify this step. It would have been wrong in the Athenians to have murdered Cotys themselves, whether as a tyrant or an enemy; and if so, it could not be decent to reward others for doing such a deed. I mention this, because some writers speak loosely about tyrannicide, as if the Greeks were excusable for encouraging it. Python, one of the brothers, did not regard the honor bestowed on him as in any way binding him to the interests of Athens; for not long afterwards he passed over into the service of Philip.[2]

Another instance of the same folly, on a more memorable occasion—when the Athenians, on the news of Philip's death, offered sacrifice to the gods, and voted a crown to Pausanias, his murderer—is thus animadverted on by Plutarch in the life of Demosthenes:—

"For my part, I can not say that the behavior of the Athenians on this occasion was at all decent or honorable, to crown themselves with garlands, to sacrifice to the gods, for the death of a prince, who in the midst of his success and victories, when they were a conquered people, had used them with so much clemency and humanity. It was a practice both unworthy and base, to make him free of their city, and honor him while he lived; and yet, as soon as he fell by treason, to set no bounds to their joy, to insult over his death, and sing triumphant songs of victory, as if by their own valor they had conquered him."

The death of Cotys occurred B.C. 358. Three princes claimed the succession, to the whole, or to different parts of his kingdom; Cersobleptes, Berisades, and Amadocus. Cersobleptes was the son of Cotys; the other two were either sons, or more distant relatives. They were all very young, and sought the aid of Greek generals to make good their pretensions. Charidemus espoused the cause of Cersobleptes, whose sister he had married: Berisades was supported by Athenodorus, a citizen of Athens, with whom he had formed a

[1] Aristotle, Polit. v. 8, 12. Theopompus apud Athen. xii. 42.

[2] Demosth. contra Aristocr. 659, 662. Whether this Python was the same as the Byzantine Python, who at a later period distinguished himself as an orator and embassador of Philip, is a matter of doubt. See Thirlwall, Gr. Hist. v. 221, (note), who assigns good reasons for believing them to be the same. Jacobs' Dem. 319.

nuptial alliance; Amadocus by Simon and Bianor, who were similarly connected with him.[1]

Meanwhile Cephisodotus, the Athenian commander, ignorant of the plans of Charidemus, arrived at Perinthus with ten ships to claim the fulfillment of the promises which he had made in the Troad. Charidemus with some cavalry and light troops, watching his opportunity, attacked the Athenian soldiers while they were on shore taking their meal, and slew a considerable number of them. He continued his hostilities for seven months, and the Chersonese again became the scene of war. Cephisodotus sailed with his squadron to Alopeconnesus, a promontory on the south-west coast of the Peninsula, lying over against Imbrus, where a band of pirates had established themselves; but Charidemus, marching across the country, attacked the Athenians, and forced Cephisodotus into a disadvantageous convention. As soon as this was known at Athens, it was indignantly repudiated. Cephisodotus was recalled, and sentenced to a fine of five talents. Athenodorus was appointed to take his place.[2]

No war had hitherto broken out between Cersobleptes and the other two princes; nor does it exactly appear over what parts of the kingdom they respectively reigned, except that Cersobleptes must have held the country north of the Chersonese and the Propontine coast; Amadocus seems to have had dominion west of the Hebrus.[3] It happened that about this time Miltocythes made a new attempt to get the crown, but was betrayed, and delivered into the hands of Charidemus. That general was at Cardia, which city had at his special desire been reserved to him by the terms of the convention. Knowing that it was the custom of the Thracians not to put their prisoners to death, he gave up Miltocythes, not to Cersobleptes, but to the Cardian people; who, to gratify Charidemus, took the captive and his son out in a boat, slew the son before his father's eyes, and then threw the father into the sea. This act of cruelty roused the anger of the Thracians. Berisades and Amadocus united their forces against Cersobleptes, who was charged as the author of the crime; and concluded an alliance with Athenodorus, who was now upon the coast. The object of the princes was to enlarge their dominions, or secure themselves in what they already possessed; that of the Athenians was to obtain a cessiou of the Chersonese. Cersobleptes, assailed by a superior force, was driven into a treaty, whereby it was agreed that the kingdom of Cotys

[1] Demosth. contra Aristoc. 623, 624, 661, 674. Isocrates, De Pace, 164. Grote, Hist. of Greece, x. 518. Thirlwall, v. 222.

[2] Demosth. contra Aristoc. 675, 676. The pirates were sent probably by Alexander of Pheræ. See Thirlwall, l. c. Reiske thinks differently. See his Index in Demosth.

[3] Demosth. contra Aristoc. 681.

should be equally divided among the three princes, and the Chersonese should be ceded to Athens. This occurred in the beginning of the year 357. Chabrias, who had been appointed to succeed Athenodorus, came with a single ship only to the coast of Thrace, expecting to receive a formal surrender of the Chersonese. But Athenodorus had in the meantime been compelled for want of money to disband his troops; Charidemus then persuaded Cersobleptes to renounce his engagement; and Chabrias, entirely destitute of means, was in his turn forced into a convention more humiliating than that of Cephisodotus. It was soon reported to the Athenian assembly, where, after an angry debate, the act of Chabrias was repudiated, and ten commissioners were chosen with instructions to go out to Thrace, and either procure a ratification of the treaty, or take measures for war. The commission was dispatched, but, being unprovided with force, it produced no result but evasion and delay on the part of Cersobleptes and Charidemus, while Berisades and Amadocus sent letters of complaint to Athens. There seemed no prospect of bringing the affairs to a desirable issue, unless the Athenians could send an armament strong enough to overawe their opponents. This was not accomplished till the conclusion of the war in Eubœa.

During the above-mentioned operations in Thrace, the Athenians were for about a month engaged in a harrassing war in Eubœa, to expel the Thebans, who had made an attempt to establish their power in the island. Great exertions were made on that important occasion, although the finances of the state were in a low condition. A body of mercenaries was raised, who together with the citizen troops were put under the command of Chares and Diocles. After various skirmishes, in which sometimes the Athenians and sometimes the Thebans had the advantage, an armistice was agreed upon, and the Thebans evacuated Eubœa.[1] The troops were then at liberty to be sent elsewhere, and accordingly they were shipped off to the Hellespont under the command of Chares. It was no longer in the power of Charidemus to resist the demands of the Athenians; and at length he made, on behalf of Cersobleptes, an actual surrender of all the territories of the Chersonese. There was one exception however, which, though not deemed of importance at the time, led to serious disputes at a later period. That was the city of Cardia; which by a special clause, at the instance of Charidemus, was declared to be independent; on the ground, as it would seem, that it lay without the boundaries of the Peninsula. Thrace was partitioned among the three princes; and this was supposed to be an additional security to the Athenian power.[2]

[1] Diodorus, xvi. 7. Demosth. contra Mid. 570. De Cherson. 103. Æsch. contra Ctesiph. 65.

[2] Demosth. contra Aristoc. 676—679, 681, 623.

While their ancient dominion of the Chersonese, its territory and its revenue,[1] were thus recovered by the Athenians, events had occurred elsewhere, which greatly counterbalanced the advantage;[2] and new disasters were at hand. In this very year, B.C. 357, the Social war broke out. Byzantium, Chios, Cos, and Rhodes revolted from Athens, and waged against her a successful war until their independence was acknowledged B.C. 355. Corcyra had also thrown off her allegiance. Potidæa was taken by Philip B.C. 356. The Olynthians were wresting from Athens her dominion in Chalcidice.[3]

These misfortunes appear to have encouraged the Sestians, notwithstanding the compact entered into by Cersobleptes, to dispute the sovereignty of Athens and assert their own independence. It was not till the end of the Social war, that the Athenians were able to chastise them. Chares then besieged and took Sestus. The importance of the place, which from its position, commanding the passage of the Hellespont, was called the corn-bin of the Piræus,[4] was thought to justify a rigorous punishment. Chares massacred all the adult population, and reduced the others to slavery. Soon afterwards the Athenians, imitating the policy of Pericles, sent out a body of their own citizens to take possession of the vacant land in Chersonesus, and thereby to strengthen and consolidate the empire of Athens.[5] Such resumption of their ancient rights appears to have given cause of offence. Isocrates, who about this time wrote a pamphlet, in the form of an oration, recommending his countrymen to maintain an equitable peace with their allies, and to give up a useless struggle for empire, condemns these colonial acquisitions as impolitic and unjust.[6]

Philip of Macedon had not hitherto taken any part in the contests of the Thracian kings, either among themselves or with the Athenians. Cotys had, after the death of Perdiccas, espoused the cause of the pretender Pausanias, but had been induced by presents or promises to abandon it.[7] Philip, occupied elsewhere, remained at peace with Cotys, and for some years made no attempt to encroach upon Thracian ground beyond the bank of the Nestus. But about the year B.C. 353 he conceived the idea of forming an alliance with Cersobleptes, and attacking the Athenians in the Chersonese. How far Cersobleptes himself encouraged this design,

1 As to the amount see Demosth. contra Aristoc. 657.

2 The capture of Amphipolis and Pydna by Philip, and his offensive league with the Olynthians. See Appendix I. pp. 236—238.

3 Appendix I. 239.

4 Τηλία τοῦ Πειραιέως. Aristotle Rhet. iii. 10.

5 Diodorus, xvi. 34. Æschines, De Fals. Leg. 37.

6 Isocrates, De Pace, 159. Compare Aristotle, Rhet. ii. 6.

7 Diodorus, xvi. ii. 3.

is not very clear. Since the treaty, by which he finally surrendered Chersonesus to the Athenians, he had apparently been on amicable terms with them. An Athenian fleet was constantly stationed in the Hellespont, ready to act if occasion required; and the partition of the Thracian kingdom among three princes restrained the ambitious projects of each.[1] The death of Berisades disturbed this peaceful arrangement, and led to new combinations. He died somewhere about the year B.C. 353, leaving children under the guardianship of Athenodorus. That Cersobleptes meditated war against both Amadocus and the sons of Berisades, is distinctly asserted by Demosthenes.[2] Philip took advantage of these occurrences, to propose an alliance with Cersobleptes, for the conquest of Thrace and the expulsion of the Athenians from Chersonesus. In furtherance of this purpose he marched to Maronea, and had an interview with Apollonides, an envoy of the Thracian king. At the same time a negotiation was opened with Pammenes the Theban general, who some time before had been sent to Asia to assist Artabazus against the Persian satraps. It does not appear from the language of the orator, that Pammenes had any direct communication with Philip; but rather that he communicated only with Cersobleptes. The project however was disconcerted by Amadocus, who refused to the king of Macedon a passage through his territory; and for the present the designs of Philip upon Thrace were suspended.[3]

Then followed an extraordinary measure on the part of the Athenians, which we must attribute partly to the weakness of their government, partly to financial embarrassment, and the difficulty which they experienced in finding troops and money for the support of their empire. Charidemus, as we have seen, had been one of their most active opponents in the recovery of the Chersonese. Yet no sooner had he been brought to reason by the arrival of Chares in the Hellespont, than the Athenians passed a decree bestowing on him the franchise of their city and a golden crown.[4] His military skill and his influence in Thrace were highly extolled at Athens, where he contrived to secure a party in his favor; and it was said that he was the only person capable of recovering Amphipolis. The report of an intended alliance between Philip and Cersobleptes, of which it seems Chares had informed his countrymen by letter,[5] excited alarm at Athens; and the partisans of Charidemus deemed it a favorable opportunity to promote his advancement.

[1] Demosth. contra Aristoc. 623, 680.
[2] Ibid. 624.
[3] Ibid. 681.
[4] Aristoc. Rhet. ii. 23. Libanius in Argum. Or. Demosth. contra Aristoc.
[5] Demosth. contra Aristoc. 682.

It was necessary, they said, to keep on good terms with Cersobleptes, and for that purpose they should secure the attachment of Charidemus, his favorite minister. It was contended also, that he had rendered signal service to Athens in the surrender of the Chersonese. One Aristocrates now moved a decree, making it a capital crime against the laws of Athens to kill Charidemus. The people were persuaded to pass this decree; but the mover was afterwards prosecuted by Euthycles, for whom Demosthenes composed an elaborate speech, showing that the measure of Aristocrates was not only contrary to the spirit of the Athenian law, but was fraught with danger to the country; that Charidemus was a profligate and treacherous person, who had always been the enemy of Athens; that the effect of the decree would be to deter Athenodorus and the other Greek commanders in Thrace from opposing Charidemus; that by his aid Cersobleptes would crush the rival princes, and, once master of the whole Thracian kingdom, would drive the Athenians from Chersonesus. It is from this oration that we get most of the historical materials relating to Athenian affairs in Thrace. The trial took place in the year B.C. 352. Notwithstanding all the exertions of the orator, Aristocrates was acquitted, and the decree confirmed.[1]

Strange as it was to pass such a decree in favor of this man, the event in some measure accorded with the declarations of his party. Cersobleptes from this time became the firm friend of Athens, while Amadocus, seeing his cause abandoned by the Athenians, espoused the alliance of Philip, and assisted his projects in Thrace.[2]

In was in this same year that Philip, after gaining his great victory in Thessaly, made an expedition into Thrace, which is said by Thirlwall to be one of the most obscure parts of his history. It does not appear that he made at this time any attack upon Cersobleptes, although he approached so near as to alarm the Athenians who had settled in the Chersonese.[3] His invasion was at first directed to the interior, and perhaps to the central and northern parts of the kingdom, where he was engaged for a considerable time, chastising hostile tribes, and establishing his own dependents in authority and power. He may very likely have assisted Amadocus in pushing his conquests over the territory of his neighbors. It is vaguely stated by the Athenian orators, that he made what kings he pleased, and we know not enongh of Thracian history to get more precise

1 The whole of this speech should be perused, to obtain a proper insight into the events of the period. See Thirlwall, Gr. Hist. v. 290—293.

2 Harpocration s. v. Ἀμάδοκος. Demosth. de Chers. 105. Philipp. iv. 133.

3 Æschines, De Fals. Leg. 37.

information.[1] No certain account of Philip's movements reached the Athenians, until they heard that he had marched eastward to the Propontine coast, and laid siege to Heræum.[2] The importance of this place, which was held by an Athenian garrison for the protection of the corn-trade, was well understood by the people. They instantly convened an assembly, voted an armament of forty galleys, to carry out all the citizens under forty-five years of age, and ordered sixty talents to be raised by general contribution. It was then the month of November in the year 352. Notwithstanding the energetic resolutions of the people, nine months were consumed in preparation. Reports came to Athens, that Philip was dead or ill, and this served as an excuse for delay. At length, in the autumn of 351, ten galleys were dispatched with the bare crews only, and a sum of five talents. Charidemus, who was then at Athens, and had probably been sent by Cersobleptes to warn the Athenians of the danger, was appointed to the command. Such a force would hardly have been sufficient to check the progress of Philip, had he been inclined to pursue it. But it was then considered by the Athenians, that the danger was past. And so in fact it was. For Philip had been seized with a severe illness, and returned to his own kingdom.[3]

For above four years Philip abstained from any further aggression in that quarter. But in the year B.C. 347, having consolidated his power by the reduction of Olynthus and Chalcidice, he prepared himself for new schemes of conquest. His most formidable enemies were the Athenians. It was necessary to humble them. Two methods of doing so presented themselves: first, to put himself at at the head of the Amphictyonic confederacy, invade Phocis, terminate the Sacred war, and acquire a preponderating power in southern Greece; secondly, to invade the Chersonese, drive the Athenians from the coast of the Hellespont and Propontis, and starve them out, as the Lacedæmonians had done, by stopping their importation of corn. For this last purpose it was necessary to subdue the kingdom of Cersobleptes, which lay between him and the Chersonese, and protected the Greek cities on the northern shore of the Propontis. To accomplish his objects more easily, Philip had recourse to stratagem.[4]

It may seem to us, reading history after the event, that Philip might with ease have overrun the kingdom of Cersobleptes and the

[1] Isocrates, Philipp. 86. Demosth. Olynth. i. 13. See p. 241 of this volume. In Athenæus, xiii. 557, mention is made of Cothelas, a Thracian prince, who submitted to Philip, and gave his daughter Meda to be one of his wives or concubines.

[2] As to its situation near Perinthus, see Herodotus, iv. 90.

[3] Demosth. Olynth. iii. 29.

[4] Demosth. de Cor. 254. De Fals. Leg. 367, 397.

Chersonese in spite of any resistance which the Athenians could have offered and that afterwards he might have led an overpowering army into Phocis, and beaten down all opposition. Such, however, was not the view which he himself took of the matter. It was a maxim with that politic prince, not to employ force, where he could succeed as well by negotiation or intrigue; nor to let his enemies combine, but to separate and beat them one after another. Nor were the difficulties in his way so inconsiderable. The Athenians, driven from the Macedonian and Chalcidic shores, having fewer garrisons to maintain, and fewer objects to distract their attention, might concentrate all their naval power for the defence of the Hellespont, which they felt to be so important. The commerce of Macedonia had already suffered greatly by the presence of their cruisers. Again, they might with the Lacedæmonians send troops to the assistance of Phalæcus, and occupy the pass of Thermopylæ, as they had done some years before. In such case the issue of the war in Phocis might be doubtful, even with the forces of Thebes and Thessaly at his disposal. It was well known how Demosthenes had exerted himself to rouse his countrymen against Macedonia. Defeat would be greatly injurious to Philip's reputation and prospects; and he saw a way of gaining his ends without incurring any such risk.[1]

He caused a negotiation for peace to be opened with the Athenians, and so contrived matters, that the first formal proposal came from the Athenians themselves. His wishes were made known at Athens by some Eubœan embassadors, and by other indirect communications. The Athenians, weary of an unprofitable war, were not indisposed to accept his overtures. A motion was then made by Philocrates, that he should have liberty to send a herald to Athens. The motion was carried; and Philocrates, having been prosecuted for it, was successfully defended by Demosthenes, who appears at this time to have been in favor of a peace. Aristodemus the actor was sent to Macedonia, to treat for the ransom of the Athenian prisoners, who had been taken at Olynthus; and on his return reported, that Philip was desirous not only of peace, but of alliance with Athens. Thereupon Philocrates moved and carried another decree, to send embassadors to Philip with full powers to negotiate a treaty. Ten embassadors were appointed accordingly —Æschines, Demosthenes, Aristodemus, Philocrates, Ctesiphon, Phrynon, Iatrocles, Nausicles, Dercylus, Cimon. Another was added, to represent the Athenian confederacy; Aglaöreon of Tenedos. They started for Macedonia in the beginning of the year 346 B.C.[2]

[1] Demosth. Olynth. ii. 20. De Cherson. 105. De Cor. 276. De Fals. Leg. 442. Diodorus, xvi. 54. Pausanias, viii. 7.

[2] Æschines, De Fals. Leg. 29, 30. Demosth. de Cor. 232. Æschines contra Ctes. 62.

The transactions of this embassy are revealed to us by the two principal embassadors, Æschines and Demosthenes, in their celebrated speeches on the trial which took place a few years after, on which Æschines was charged by his rival with corruption and treason. The speeches must be perused with the closest attention by any one who desires to gain full information; and even this will not be satisfactory; for the speeches so abound in contradictions, and have so little the appearance of fairness and candor, that it is difficult even to form an opinion of the truth.[1] Here it will be sufficient to notice what concerns the subject before us.

Parmenio, Philip's general, was besieging Halus in Thessaly; Philip himself was at Pella, preparing for a new invasion of Thrace, when the embassadors arrived. They were admitted to an audience, and addressed the king in order of seniority. Æschines made a long speech about the ancient connection between Iphicrates and Amyntas, and the rightful claims of his countrymen to Amphipolis. Demosthenes, either abashed in the presence of a man against whom he had so fiercely declaimed at home, or feeling that no arguments of his could have any effect on this occasion, after speaking a few words, stopped suddenly short, and made an abrupt ending. Neither of them said a word about the terms or conditions of the proposed treaty. It was known to them, that Philip was about to march against Cersobleptes; yet, although that prince was an ally of Athens, no remonstrance was made on his behalf. Philip promised only, that he would make no attack upon the Chersonese pending his negotiation with the Athenians. He made a formal reply to the statements of the embassadors, invited them to supper, and afterwards dismissed them with a letter to the people of Athens, in which he assured them of his pacific intentions, and sincere wish to become their ally and benefactor. It was arranged that his own ministers should speedily follow the embassadors to Athens, where the conditions of peace were to be decided on.[2]

The embassadors, on their return, made a report of their proceedings to the senate and people, and delivered Philip's letter. On the motion of Demosthenes, two special days, the seventeenth and eighteenth of Elaphebolion (March,) were appointed to consider the offers of peace and alliance. Before that time the ministers of Philip arrived; three distinguished men, Parmenio, Antipater, and Eury-

[1] See Thirlwall, Gr. Hist. v. 338. Mitford, Gr. Hist. iv. c. 39, s. 4; c. 40, s. 2. Leland's Life of Philip, ii. 56.

[2] Æsch. De Fals. Leg. 31—33, 38, 39. Demosth. De Fals. Leg. 353, 354. De Halonn. 85. Plutarch, in the Life of Demosthenes, gives a different account of his address to Philip on the embassy. He represents, that Philip took more pains to reply to Demosthenes than to the other embassadors, though in other respects he treated him with less kindness and civility.

lochus. They were hospitably entertained by Demosthenes himself, who showed them marked attention, and from first to last displayed an earnest desire to press the conclusion of the treaty. A congress of deputies from the Athenian allies was then sitting at Athens, who passed a resolution, that, as the envoys sent to rouse the Grecian states to the defence of their freedom had not returned, it was better to wait for their return before debating the question of peace. Æschines condemns Demosthenes for having frustrated this resolution by his decree, which fixed an arbitrary day for the discussion. Demosthenes probably thought that, as things had gone so far, it was better to terminate the war as soon as possible, and prevent Philip's designs upon the Chersonese. On the first day of the assembly there was a stormy debate, of which we have no clear or consistent account. There was much discussion, whether peace only, or peace and alliance should be agreed upon. Various proposals were made about the restoration of Amphipolis, the Phocians, and other matters. The Macedonian envoys would not hear of Amphipolis being given up; nor would they permit the Phocians to be treated as allies of Athens. Of Cersobleptes they did not condescend to speak, but insisted on the recognition of Cardia as an independent state in alliance with Macedonia. Philocrates supported them in all their claims, but met with much opposition, and even from Æschines himself, if we can trust the assertion of Demosthenes, who charges him with having espoused different sides on the first and second days, as if he had been brought over in the meantime. Æschines denies this, and alleges that it was impossible he could have spoken on the second day, as Demosthenes prevailed on the presidents to put the question without debate. However this be, certain it is, that on the second day the treaty with Philip was concluded almost in the very terms proposed by his ministers.[1]

Before the ministers of Philip had departed, there came to Athens a representative of Cersobleptes, one Critobulus, a citizen of Lampsacus; who demanded, on behalf of the Thracian king, that he should be included in the treaty as one of the allies of Athens. This, if Æschines is to be believed, was opposed by Demosthenes, but carried by the people in spite of him; whereas Demosthenes asserts, that Critobulus was afterwards prevented from taking the oath by Æschines. A different account is given by Philip himself, in his letter to the Athenians, viz. that Cersobleptes desired to make a separate treaty with him, but was prevented by the Athenian generals, who represented him to be an enemy of the Athenians. It is not indeed clear, that what Philip alleges took place at Athens, or had any connection with the proceedings of which we are now speaking. That Cersobleptes, however, was exclnded from the treaty

[1] Æsch. De Fals. Leg. 34—36, 39. Demosth. De Fals. Leg. 345. Æsch. contra Ctes. 62, 63.

is certain; and the probability is, that Philip's ministers at Athens would not permit his name to be inserted.[1]

An embassy was now appointed to proceed immediately to Macedonia, to receive Philip's oath in ratification of the treaty. The same embassadors were chosen as before. While they were yet preparing for departure, a letter was brought from Chares, who commanded the Athenian fleet in the Hellespont, announcing that Cersobleptes had lost his kingdom, and Philip had seized the Sacred Mountain. The senate, in alarm, passed a decree, ordering the embassadors to set out instantly upon their mission. This was on the third of Munychion, or April.[2]

Philip had in truth been making the best use of his time, while the Athenians were deliberating about peace and alliance with him. In the very month (Elaphebolion) when his embassadors were sent to Athens, he was overrunning the kingdom of Thrace. Myrtium, Ergisce, Serrium, Doriscus, cities on the Ægean coast, yielded to his arms. He seized upon the fortresses of the Sacred Mountain, defeated Cersobleptes in divers battles, and compelled him to deliver up his son as a hostage, and engage to pay tribute to Macedonia. No attempt was made by the Athenian general Chares to check the progress of Philip. How far he may have been guilty of neglect, as Æschines insinuates he was, it is impossible, in the absence of historical evidence, to determine. Athenian troops are said to have been stationed at Serrium, and on the Sacred Mountain, and to have been driven away by Philip. We may presume they were not strong enough to offer any resistance to his arms.[3]

The Athenian embassadors proceeded to Oreus in Eubœa, from whence they were to be conveyed by sea to the nearest place where they could find the kiug of Macedon. Notwithstanding this injunction of the senate, they lost some time at Oreus, and then took a circuitous route to Pella, by which they consumed twenty-three days. At Pella they had to wait nearly a month, while Philip was in Thrace. He returned with the son of Cersobleptes, and the

[1] Æsch. De Fals. Leg. 38, 39; contra Ctes. 63, 64. Demosth. De Fals. Leg. 395, 398. Epist. Philipp. ad Athen. 160.

[2] Æschin. De Fals. Leg. 40. Demosth. De Fals. Leg. 389. De Coron. 235. The decree set forth in this last passage is manifestly incorrect. See Jacobs' note (20) to his translation of the Oration on the Crown.

[3] Diodorus, xvi. 71. Justin, viii. 3. Demosth. de Coron. 234, 235. De Fals. Leg. 390, 447, 448. Æsch. de Fals. Leg. 37, 38. It is here stated, that Antiochus was sent to find Chares, and inform him, that the people of Athens were astonished, that, while Philip was marching against the Chersonese, they did not even know where their general or his armament was. It is not quite clear, whether the story has reference to this period. Compare Or. de Chers. 105. Philipp. iii. 114; iv. 133. Æsch. contra Ctes. 65.

reports of his conquest were confirmed. Meanwhile embassies from divers parts of Greece had arrived at Philip's court, the most important being those from Thessaly, Thebes, and Lacedæmon. Warlike preparations were going on. It was easy to see that Phocis was their object, and that Philip was about to take some decisive step for the termination of the Sacred war. What were the Athenian embassadors to do? They had no power to interfere with Philip's designs. Their business was simply to receive Philip's oath and signature to the treaty, the terms of which had already been drawn up. It is true, there was a clause in their instructions, empowering them generally to consult the interest of the commonwealth. But it might be dangerous to construe this with too much latitude, and, unless it authorized them to break off the treaty altogether, any mere remonstrance of theirs against the proceedings of Philip would be disregarded by him. The result may be briefly stated. Philip preserved silence as to his intentions, and induced the Athenian embassadors to accompany him as far as Pheræ, on the pretext that he desired their mediation between the Pharsalians and the people of Halus. The signature of the treaty was delayed until their arrival at Pheræ. Here he demanded, that both Halus and the Phocians should be expressly excepted from it, and the colleagues of Demosthenes, in opposition to his opinion, allowed the clause to be introduced. This first excited the suspicions of Demosthenes, according to his own account; yet, although a letter was sent by his colleagues to Athens, misrepresenting the position of affairs, he took no step himself to warn his countrymen or counteract the danger. The embassadors returned to Athens, where they arrived on the thirteenth of Scirrophorion (June), while Philip set out on his march for Thermopylæ. The success of his schemes was complete. An assembly was held at Athens on the sixteenth, when Æschines and Philocrates buoyed up their countrymen with hopes of advantage to be derived from Philip's expedition. The capitulation of Phalæcus, the occupation of Phocis and Thermopylæ, the delivery of the Bœotian cities to Thebes, and the election of Philip into the Amphictyonic council, awakened them from their delusion.[1]

Among the many perplexing questions which suggest themselves to the historian concerning these transactions, the most interesting are those which arise upon the conduct of Demosthenes himself. How came it that he allowed the peace to be concluded, without having Cersobleptes and the Phocians comprehended in its provisions? He complains himself of their exclusion. He complains of the delay on the second embassy, which enabled Philip to conquer

[1] Æsch. De Fals. Leg. 40, 41, 44. Demosth. de Coron. 236, 237. De Pace, 59. Philipp. ii. 74. De Fals. Leg. 355, 359. Diodorus, xvi. 60, 64.

Thrace before the peace was ratified. But, assuming that Æschines has not answered this charge, it does not appear how Philip could have been prevented from completing his conquest, if the embassadors had caught him during his progress; for he would still have contended, that Cersobleptes, not being named in the treaty, was not entitled to its benefits. Demosthenes indeed might argue, that, as the peace was made with Athens and her allies, Cersobleptes, being an ally of Athens, was virtually included in it. But if so, Philip was to blame for violating the treaty, rather than Æschines and others for having sanctioned it: and all parties were in some measure to blame, for having left so important a question open to dispute. But if we look at the circumstances, it can hardly be thought that Philip committed any breach of faith by pursuing his Thracian campaign. The embassadors, on their first visit to Pella, were distinctly apprised of his intentions; and therefore, if it had been intended to give protection to Cersobleptes, there ought to have been an express clause to that effect. It may be that Demosthenes, never having been friendly to Cersobleptes, or regarding the success of Philip in a Thracian war as doubtful, or thinking the danger remote, did not think it worth while to require such a clause; or perhaps he considered that peace was desirable for the security of the Chersonese. With respect to the Phocians, it did not appear at the time when the peace was first made, what the designs of Philip were. It might be open to the Athenians, notwithstanding the treaty, or even the rather on that account, to insist that Philip should not pass the Straits of Thermopylæ for the purpose of any hostile invasion. And it might well seem, that there was plenty of time for the consideration of any future question concerning Phocis. When, however, Demosthenes was the second time at Pella, when he found that Cersobleptes had been subdued, and vast preparations made for an invasion of Phocis, then his eyes were opened to the danger; he saw that the peace was a delusion; that the Phocians would be overwhelmed, unless his countrymen came to their assistance; and that there was no security against Philip's ulterior projects. The danger was augmented, in his opinion, when Philip had prevailed on his colleagues to exclude the Phocians expressly from the benefits of the peace; and then, it seems, he first suspected that Æschines was a traitor. His true course then was, to return instantly to Athens, to call a special meeting of the people, and urge them to take arms and march with the Lacedæmonians to the defence of Phocis. But for this his courage or presence of mind was not sufficient, and he let things take their course. Afterwards, when Æschines and Philocrates, playing the game of Philip, amused the Athenian people with reports of his friendly intentions, Demosthenes raised a warning voice: but it was too late; the people, thinking that his colleagues were in the secrets of Philip, believed them rather than him; and Demosthenes himself did not then assume that confident tone, either as counsellor or accuser, which was likely to gain credence to his assertions. In the speech which he delivered three years afterwards on the subject of the embassy, having a case to make out against Æschines,—and there was a very good one as far as regarded his conduct upon the second journey to Pella,—he overcharges it by imputing blame to Æschines for mistakes, in which Æschines was either not implicated at all, or no more implicated than others: and he may have been partly induced to do so by the consciousness, that he himself was to some extent duped and deluded in common with the rest of his countrymen, and had neglected to provide those guarantees and securities for his country, which were indispensable in a negotiation with so crafty a monarch as Philip.

The general result of the whole proceedings was, that Philip had made a conquest of Thrace; he had acquired the honor of terminating the Sacred war, by which he greatly increased his influence and ascendancy in Greece; he had conferred obligations upon the people of Thebes and Thessaly, and been elected a member of the Amphictyonic council; he had got possession of Nicæa, Thronium, and Alponus, which commanded the pass of Thermopylæ, and gave him admittance into Phocis and Bœotia. The only advantage which Athens had gained by the peace, was the security of Chersonesus; and even that, as Demosthenes justly observed, was in reality weakened by the augmentation of Philip's power.[1] It was at this time that Isocrates, struck with admiration at the achievements of Philip, composed a pamphlet in the form of an address to that monarch; in which, eulogizing his good fortune and magnanimity, he exhorts him to effect by his influence a pacification of all the Greek states, and then to unite them under his own standard for a war against the Persian empire.

For the chain of events which followed, but which can not here be enlarged upon—such as the debate on the embassy of Amphictyons to Athens; the negotiations in Peloponnesus; the intrigues of Philip at Megara; his invasion of Epirus and Ambracia; the establishment of his partisans in Eubœa—the reader is referred to the Historical Abstract in this volume, and the arguments and notes to divers Orations.[2]

In the year following the peace, that is, B.C. 345, the Athenians sent a body of their citizens to take allotments of land in the Chersonese. The object was, not so much to make a provision for a poor class of emigrants, as to establish an army of obversation, to strengthen their position in that important peninsula. At the head

[1] De Fals. Leg. 365, 366.

[2] See the Argument to the Oration on the Peace, p. 73. Argument to the second Philippic, p. 81. Argument to the Oration on Halonnesus, p. 89. Text and notes in pp. 96, 119, 123, 134, 157.

of them was Diopithes, a man of considerable military ability. The colonists in taking possession of their lands, (allotted to them in the neighborhood of the Isthmus, where it was peculiarly necessary to establish a protective force, and where probably they occupied the ancient fortresses of Alcibiades,) came into collision with the Cardians, between whose domains and those of Athens the boundaries were not very well defined. No immediate rupture took place; but the grounds were laid of a quarrel which afterwards became serious.[1] Philip meanwhile was extending his power in the north and north-west. He attacked the Triballi, with whom his Thracian conquests had brought him into contact. He invaded Illyria, and, after ravaging the country and taking many towns, returned home laden with spoil.[2] It was perhaps during his absence on this expedition that an embassy arrived from Artaxerxes, and was received by Alexander, then only twelve years old, who astonished the Persian envoys by the questions he put to them concerning the state of the Persian empire, the army, the roads, and the character of their king.[3] About the same time Philip, to secure and consolidate his power in Thrace, began to found new cities in different parts of the kingdom, peopling them either with Macedonian colonists, or with the inhabitants of countries which he had conquered and depopulated. One of these was Cabyla, situated on the river Taxus, among the tribe of the Asti below Mount Hæmus. Another was Philippopolis, on the river Hebrus, between the ridges of Hæmus and Rhodope, which, from the vile character of the population transported to it, received the nickname of Poneropolis, or Rogue-town.[4] Returning from his northern expeditions, Philip marched into Thessaly, where a new revolution at Pheræ called for his interference; and he was for some time occupied in settling the government of the Thessalian provinces on a new basis, calculated to secure Macedonian ascendancy.

Demosthenes and his party watched all the movements of Philip with anxiety. In the second Philippic, which was spoken in the

[1] Libanii Argumentum in Demosth. Or. de Cherson.

[2] Diodorus, xvi. 69. Justin, viii. 6. Demosth. de Coron. 240.

[3] Plutarch in Vit. Alexand. v. Leland's Life of Philip, ii. 149. Thirlwall assigns this story to a later period: Gr. Hist. vi. 91.

[4] Diodorus, xvi. 71. Justin, viii. 5. Strabo, vii. 320. Leland's Life of Philip, ii. 147. Thirlwall, Gr. Hist. vi. 32. Demosthenes de Cherson. 100. Philipp. iv. 135. It is doubtful, whether the orator is there speaking of places conquered by Philip, or settlements founded by him. His own knowledge of the facts was probably imperfect. Nor can the date of these settlements be determined accurately.

[5] Diodorus, xvi. 69. Demosthenes, Philipp. ii. 71; iii. 119. De Coron. 241. Thirlwall, Gr. Hist. vi. 13, 14.

year B.C. 344, we find a particular allusion to Philip's proceedings in Thessaly. But during the same year an event occurred, which induced the Athenians to send envoys to Philip, with a formal complaint against him for infraction of the peace. This was the seizure by him of the island Halonnesus, which had a short time before been wrested from the Athenians by Sostratus a pirate. Sostratus, having committed plunder on the Macedonian coast, was expelled by Philip, who, regarding the island as a fair conquest, kept it for himself. The Athenians, taking a different view of the matter, resolved to demand restitution; and an embassy having been decreed for that purpose, it was thought proper at the same time to speak of other grievances, arising out of the late treaty of peace. Philip thereupon sent Python to Athens; who, in a speech made before the people, which was heard with applause, gave them strong but vague assurances of his master's desire to settle their disputes amicably, and to amend the treaty in any way that was reasonable.[1] This led to another embassy from Athens, at the head of which was Hegisippus, instructed to demand such concessions as from the language of Python it was imagined they could obtain. Among them were an alteration of that article in the treaty, which declared that both parties should retain what they possessed. It was proposed to substitute a clause, "that each should have his own;" the Athenians having especially in view the restoration of Amphipolis.[2] Another amendment was, that Greek states not included in the treaty should be free and independent. This was demanded, in order to prevent Philip's making new conquests, or extending his influence in Greece; and it had particular reference to his aggressions in Thessaly and Epirus.[3] A third proposal was, that those places which Philip had taken after the peace should be restored; meaning in particular the towns and fortresses in Thrace which he had got possession of since the negotiation had begun: for the Athenians had now discovered their mistake in not insisting that hostilities should be suspended on both sides during the progress of the treaty, and they sought to rectify it by an equitable construction, that the peace was to be reckoned as having commenced before the final ratification.[4] A complaint was also preferred on the subject of Cardia and the Chersonese, which will be presently explained.

Philip was so incensed at these demands, that he could hardly treat the embassadors with common civility, and even ordered the poet Xenoclides to quit his dominions, because he had received

[1] Or. de Halonneso, 77, 78, 81, 82, and Liban. Argument.
[2] Ib. 83. Confer Epist. Philipp. 165.
[3] Or de Halonneso, 84. Confer Philipp. iii. 118, 120.
[4] Ib. 85. Confer Philipp. iii. 114. De Coron. 233, 234.

them with hospitality.[1] Nevertheless he sent a letter by them to Athens, in which he discussed the various questions which had been raised. Halonnesus, he said, was his own by right of conquest, but he was willing to make a present of it to the Athenians: an offer which roused the indignation of the orators.[2] With regard to Amphipolis he asserted with perfect justice, that the treaty, which took the basis of the *uti possidetis*, had confirmed his title;[3] and he said the Athenians had misconstrued the language of his ministers. He agreed to introduce a clause providing for the independence of the Greek states, and offered to refer the dispute concerning Cardia and the Thracian towns to arbitration.[4]

A debate was held on this letter in the Athenian assembly, where Demosthenes and his party declaimed against it with vehemence. The oration on Halonnesus, which is printed among the works of Demosthenes, is ascribed by the best critics to Hegesippus.[5] That their arguments prevailed, and that the offers of Philip were rejected, we may infer from the events that followed. Halonnesus was not given up. Shortly afterwards the Peparethians made a descent on the island, and surprised the Macedonian garrison. Philip sent fresh troops to recover his conquest, and then revenged himself by ravaging the island of Peparethus; for which the Athenians again demanded satisfaction, but in vain.[6]

The dispute about the Chersonese was a question of boundary. The Cardians had applied to Philip for assistance against the encroachments of the Athenian settlers; and Philip, as their ally—as such he was acknowledged by the late treaty of peace—had engaged to support them.[7] Cardia was (no doubt) included within the ancient wall across the Isthmus; so that its territories, or most of them, lay within the Peninsula. The Athenians, dissatisfied with the treaty which declared Cardia independent, were anxious at all events to straiten its limits, while the Cardians contended that they, as residents, had a much better title to land in Chersonesus than Athenian colonists, who came to a country which was not their home, still retaining their rights as citizens of Athens. Another question arose about the boundary of the Chersonese itself. The old wall must have been destroyed, in or before the time of Cotys: for there had been a talk of cutting a canal through the Isthmus,

[1] Demosth. De Fals. Leg. 447.
[2] See p. 90 of this volume, notes 2 and 3.
[3] See p. 95, note 1.
[4] Or. de Halonn. 87. Confer Philipp. Epist. 161.
[5] Æschin. contra Ctes. 65. Jacobs' Introduction to the Oration on Halonnesus, p. 298, et seq. Ib. note 3, p. 314.
[6] Philipp. Epist. 162. Demosth. de Coron. 248. Plutarch in Vit. Demosth.
[7] Demosth. De Fals. Leg. 396. Philipp. Epist. 161.

and a promise held out that Philip would do it at his own expense.[1] The intended line of the canal was not in the direction of the wall, but further on, perhaps making a shorter cut, from Pteleum to Leuce Acte.[2] Midway between these two places stood an altar of Jupiter, erected apparently to mark their boundaries. Hegesippus contended that this altar was the land-mark of the Chersonese. And his argument was a little helped by the circumstance of the projected canal. Philip, conceiving that the town of Agora,[3] which stood midway between Pactya and Cardia, in the line of the old wall, marked the extreme limit of Chersonesus, had taken possession of a tract of land which lay between it and the altar. This, according to Hegesippus, was an act of injustice to Athens; and the offence was not diminished by his having given a portion of the land to Apollonides of Cardia. Philip disdained to make any answer to this complaint, but, with respect to the boundary question between the Athenians and his allies, he repeated his proposal of an arbitration. The Cardians made the same offer; but it did not suit the Athenians, who, while they asserted their own title to Cardia itself, knew that it could not be supported by international law in derogation of their own compact, and that there was an unrepealed decree at Athens which distinctly acknowledged the rights of the Cardians. To find an impartial umpire would have been almost impossible; and neither party could seriously have entertained the project.[4]

The remonstrances on neither side having produced any result, Philip, in the year B.C. 343, sent troops into Chersonesus to assist the Cardians.[5] Diopithes, unable with his Athenians only to resist this accession of force, collected a body of mercenaries, and then, returning to the attack, drove the Macedonians out of the Peninsula. Not content with this advantage, he roused Cersobleptes and the Thracians to take arms to recover their independence. It has been remarked by Pausanias, that none but the Romans ever effected a complete conquest of Thrace.[6] Philip, absent at this time in Epirus, found it necessary on his return to march with a powerful army against his rude eastern neighbors, to protect his infant settlements, and re-establish his power in the country. But this time it was not quite so easy a matter. Besides Cersobleptes, an Odrysian prince named Teres, who had formerly been Philip's ally, had now risen in arms against him; and Diopithes seized every op-

[1] Philipp. ii. 73.
[2] This place is mentioned by Lysias, contra Alcib. 142.
[3] Herodotus, vii. 58.
[4] Or. de Halonn. 86, 87. Philipp. Epist. 161.
[5] Demosthenes, De Coron. 274. De Cherson. 104. Philipp. iii. 114; iv. 147.
[6] Pausanias, i. 9.

portunity to make diversions in their favor. While Philip was engaged in the interior, Diopithes attacked the adjoining parts of Thrace, which were subject to Macedonia. Two cities, Crobyle and Tiristasis—probably on or near to the Sacred Mountain—he took by storm, and made the garrisons prisoners. Amphilochus, a Macedonian, who came to demand their release, was himself cast into prison, and forced to pay a heavy ransom.[1]

The length of time, that Philip was occupied in Thrace, proves the great difficulties which he encountered. After nearly a twelvemonth's campaign he was obliged to send for large reinforcements from Macedonia and Thessaly; and not being at leisure to turn his arms against Diopithes, he sent a letter to Athens, to complain of his conduct.[2] The charge was, that Diopithes by attacking his allies, and assisting his enemies, had violated the treaty of peace The manifest object was to gain time, and to cripple the efforts of an active general, by setting his countrymen against him. Philip knew that the Macedonian party at Athens would second his endeavors; and so in fact they did. A clamor was raised against the general, not only for making war against Macedonia, but for divers irregularities of which he had been guilty. Diopithes, being at the head of a troop of mercenaries, unprovided for by any supply from home, had adopted the same methods of raising money, which Chares and others before him had done; that is to say, he had begged, borrowed, or extorted it from merchants, from the islands, or cities on the coast of Asia. The orators opposed to him declaimed loudly against these practices, and pressed for his recall.[3] They were answered by Demosthenes in one of the most powerful speeches which he ever addressed to the Athenian assembly.

The true question for the people to consider was (said he), not the conduct of Diopithes, but the safety of Athens. If Diopithes had raised troops and money by improper means, it was the fault of the Athenians themselves, who had not supplied him with the materials of war. There would be time enough to punish him hereafter: to recall him now, and leave the Hellespont and the Chersonese unguarded, was what Philip and his partisans most most desired, but what no friend of his country could advise. It was not Diopithes who had first broken the peace, but Philip himself, by his proceedings in Thrace, in Epirus, and elsewhere. If Philip might attack the allies of Athens, why might not Diopithes defend them? Philip was virtually attacking Athens in Thrace: all his plans and operations were directed against Athens. If their armament was with-

[1] Philipp. Epist. 159, 160. Demosth. de Cherson. 92. Liban Argument.

[2] Demosth. de Cherson. 90, 93. Liban. Argument.

[3] Demosth. de Cherson. 95, 96. Olynth. ii. 26. Compare Isocrates de Pace, 164, 165, 167, 168

drawn from the Hellespont, there would be nothing to prevent him from besieging the Propontine cities or invading the Chersonese. Unless they found employment for him where he was, he might attack Megara or Eubœa, or even march against Attica. Instead of discouraging Diopithes, they ought to support him; instead of disbanding their forces, they ought to increase them. It was idle to wait until Philip declared war: this he would never do until he was at their gates. They should exert themselves in every possible way; shake off their indolence, submit to pecuniary contribution and to military service; send embassies among the Greek states and excite them to arms; for not Athens only, but all Greece was in peril. Finally, they should denounce and punish the corrupt statesmen who sold their interests to the enemy, and prove to men of a different stamp that they could serve their country with honor and advantage.

Such was the substance of this oration. The arguments were sound and just,[1] and produced the desired effect on the hearers. Philip's complaint was disregarded; and the Athenians not only retained Diopithes in his command, but prepared to give him vigorous support.

Philip however was not deterred by any resolution of the Athenian assembly from prosecuting his designs. It may be gathered from his extant letter, that the Athenians had sent a message informing him that Teres and Cersobleptes were allies and citizens of Athens, and requiring him not to meddle with their dominions.[2]

[1] Other writers however have expressed a different opinion. I am surprised to read the following remarks in Thirlwall, Gr. Hist. vi. 36:—"Diopithes retained his command, and it may be presumed, after such a mark of his sovereign's approbation, was not much more circumspect in his conduct. There can be no doubt that he had given cause for such complaint, and that in his invasion of Thrace, at least, if not in his hostilities with Cardia, he had violated both the letter and the spirit of the treaty with Philip. The wisest, as well as the most honorable course would have been, to disavow his proceedings, and remove him from his command. Demosthenes, we may be sure, would have been very willing that an armament should have been sent under another general to supply his place. But he knew that a decree to this effect would probably be only so far executed as to disarm Diopithes, and to leave the Athenian interests near the seat of war unprotected. How far he was misled by the fallacy of his own reasoning, which appears to a modern reader flagrantly sophistical, we can not determine. His view however of the perilous position of his country is not the less sound, and may be admitted as an excuse for some indistinctness of ideas as to the precise line of separation between offensive and defensive measures. Compare Leland's Life of Philip, ii. 201—210. Jacob's Introduction to his translation of the speech. Mitford, iv. 521.

[2] Philipp. Epist. 160.

At such an intimation the King of Macedon would only smile. He was determined, if possible, to crush the rebellious princes of Thrace, and knowing by experience how lightly they regarded the observance of treaties, and how easily they repaired the disasters of a short campaign, he encamped himself in their country during the winter of 1842–1841, with the intention of completing his conquest in the spring, and then proceeding to those ulterior measures, for which his war in Thrace was paving the way.[1] Demosthenes had rightly conjectured, that, although the Byzantine people were in alliance with Philip, he would not hesitate to attack them, if they presumed in any manner to thwart his purposes, or even refused to co-operate with him.[2] He saw how important the possession of the Propontine cities would be to Philip; that it would enable him to intercept the commerce of Athens with the Euxine and the Hellespont, and in a short time to deprive her of Chersonesus. The long continuance of the campaigns in Thrace, while it created in the minds of other men a doubt of Philip's success, caused uneasiness to Demosthenes, who saw in it an indication of Philip's perseverance in his plans. What Philip was exactly about, was unknown to Demosthenes himself; as we may infer from the vague manner in which he speaks of Drongilus, Mastira, and other places which Philip was either taking or fortifying.[3] It was enough for him that a Macedonian army was advancing to the neighborhood of the Greek coast: and the very uncertainty augmented his alarm.

In this state of suspense, an assembly was held at Athens, and Demosthenes deemed it necessary to animate his countrymen to fresh exertions. He delivered the oration which is known by the name of the Third Philippic, which in substance repeats the arguments already urged in the oration on the Chersonese. The Athenians, had not done their duty. They had not sent sufficient reinforcements to the Hellespont. Clitarchus and Philistides, partisans of Philip, had been suffered to establish themselves in Eubœa. The peril was imminent. He urges them to reinforce Diopithes both with men and money; to apply for succor to Peloponnesus, to Rhodes and Chios, the ancient allies of Byzantium, and also to the king of Persia. This is memorable as the first occasion on which Demosthenes advised an alliance with Persia. He was justified by the necessity of the case; and it shows how critical the position of affairs had in his opinion become.[4]

Philip, having completed the overthrow of Teres and Cersobleptes,[5]

[1] Demosthenes, de Cherson, 101. Philipp. iv, 135.

[2] De Cherson. 93. Philipp. iii. 118, 120; iv. 149. De Coron. 254.

[3] De Cherson. 100.

[4] Philipp. iii. 111, 125, 126, 129. Compare Philipp. iv. 139, 140.

[5] Philipp. Epist. 161. I have referred the passage in Diodorus, xvi. 71, to the first and not the second war with Cersobleptes, notwith-

and settled other affairs in the interior of Thrace, suddenly marched southward, and appeared in the neighborhood of Chersonesus. His immediate purpose was, not to attack the Athenian general, but to protect the passage through the Hellespont of a Macedonian fleet, which he had ordered to sail to the Propontis. He was preparing to besiege Selymbria, a city which stood on the Propontine coast between Byzantium and Perinthus; and, that the siege might be brought to a speedy issue, he resolved to invest it both by land and sea. Speed was of great importance to him on this occasion. Selymbria was an ally, or subject, of Byzantium.[1] It might receive aid from that powerful city. Its capture might determine the submission both of Byzantium and Perinthus, which had hitherto refused to join him in any offensive measures against the Athenians.[2] Once master of the whole Propontine coast, it would not be difficult for him to bring the Athenians to terms; and the command of the Bosphorus would facilitate that which had become the great object of his ambition, the invasion of Persia.[3] His intentions were a profound secret. He knew that the Athenian forces in the Hellespont were ready to attack him, if they could find an opportunity, and would certainly, unless he took precautions, intercept the advance of his fleet. Accordingly, while his vessels were sailing up the Hellespont, he himself, making a sudden irruption into Chersonesus, marched along the coast for their protection. The presence of a land force on the shore was often of great service in the maritime warfare of the Greeks:[4] and Philip very likely desired, not only to strike terror into the Athenians, but also to mask his real design with respect to Selymbria. It does not appear that any actual hostilities took place between the troops of Athens and Macedonia. Diopithes was probably not strong enongh to meet Philip in the field, though his naval and military force would enable him to protect the Chersonesite cities. Philip still affected to be at peace

standing the date which he assigns, because it agrees better with his facts. He states that the Propontine cities, which had been attacked by Cersobleptes, became allies of Philip after his defeat. But this can not apply to the second war, after which they became hostile to Philip, and in which they probably rendered secret assistance to Cersobleptes and the Athenians. (Philipp. Epist. 159, 163. Diod. xvi. 74.) It does apply to the first war, after which Byzantium undoubtedly became Philip's ally. (Dem. Philipp. iii. 120. De Coron. 254.) Nor is it likely that Cersobleptes, after being so humbled in 346 B.C., and giving his son as a hostage to Philip, would have ventured to attack the cities on the Greek coast on his own account.

[1] Demosthenes, de Rhod. Libert. 198.

[2] Demosthenes, de Coron. 254.

[3] Polybius, iii. 6.

[4] Thucydides, ii. 86, 90; vii. 53.

with Athens, and complains in his letter, that the warlike measures of Diopithes and the Chersonesites had placed him under the necessity of entering their territories. He alleges also, that it was in his power, if he had chosen, to capture the fleet and fortresses of the Athenians; an assertion to which we can hardly give credence, more especially as it is not consistent with his previous complaint.[1]

When his fleet had passed through the straits, Philip marched rapidly to Selymbria, which was soon blockaded on all sides. The Greek cities were so surprised by this movement, that they had no time to send relief, and Selymbria, in the course of the year, was forced to capitulate. An incident occurred during this time which marks the dubious character of the relations between Athens and Philip. Twenty Athenian corn-ships, passing from the Propontis to the Hellespont, were seized by Amyntas, the Macedonian admiral, and carried away as prize. Messengers were sent from Athens to demand restitution, who brought back the following letter:[2]—

"Philip, king of Macedon, to the senate and people of Athens, greeting:—Your embassadors, Cephisophon, Democritus, and Polycritus, have been with me, and conferred about the restoration of the ships which Laomedon commanded. I must indeed regard you as very simple, if you imagine I do not see, that your ships were dispatched under the pretense of conveying corn from the Hellespont to Lemnos, but really to assist the Selymbrians whom I am besieging, and who are not comprehended in our treaty of peace. These orders were given to your commander, without the sanction of the people of Athens, by certain magistrates and other persons not now in office, who are urgent for the people to break off the treaty and begin the war again, and are far more anxious to accomplish this than to assist the Selymbrians. And they suppose that such an event will be a source of profit to them. I do not think it will be advantageous either to you or to me. Accordingly, I restore the vessels which have been carried into my ports, and for the future, if you will not permit your statesmen to pursue their malignant policy, but rebuke them for it, I will, on my part, endeavor to maintain the peace. Farewell."

The correspondence was a piece of coquetry on both sides. Philip had made a lucky prize of some merchantmen, but was well aware that he might be greatly embarrassed in his operations by the ships of war, which the Athenians could send against him. The Athenians, in order to obtain restitution of their squadron, had condescended to use the language of peaceful negotiation. Philip adopted the same artifice, hoping that possibly, by a small sacrifice, he might

[1] Philipp. Epist. 163. The ravaging of the Chersonese mentioned in Demosth. de Coron. is not referable to this occasion.

[2] Demosthenes, de Coron. 249—251.

purchase their neutrality in his contest with the Propontine cities. He soon found himself mistaken.

Selymbria having been surrendered, Philip laid siege to Perinthus. There can be little doubt that the Perinthians and Byzantines had not only attempted to relieve Selymbria, but had been concerting measures of defence with Diopithes and the Athenians. It was enough for Philip that they had refused to join him in an offensive war; and he had no more hesitation in attacking them, than he had formerly in besieging Olynthus. Succor, however, was promptly sent from Byzantium, and the Propontine fleet, assisted by the Athenian, was more than sufficient to protect Perinthus from blockade. Philip resolved to take it by storm. The Macedonian army was thirty thousand strong, and well provided with all the materials for a siege. The usual methods were resorted to, of battery, scale, and mine. Movable towers were advanced against the wall, and the besieged were driven from their ramparts by a storm of missiles. A breach was effected, but the citizens rushed to the opening and defended it obstinately, until it was repaired by a new wall. At length, after a hard struggle, which was continued by night as well as by day, the whole outer circle of defence was carried by the besiegers. But their difficulties had still to begin again. Perinthus was built on a sloping isthmus: the houses stood close together on a succession of terraces; and the passages were blocked up by the inhabitants, so that each terrace formed a new rampart, on which a more desperate resistance had to be encountered. The numbers and discipline of the Macedoniaus might still have prevailed, had not a powerful reinforcement been sent into the town by Arsites, Satrap of Phrygia. A negotiation had, under the advice of Demosthenes, been opened with the Persian king,[1] who, alarmed at the ambition and victorious progress of Philip, ordered his satraps to render every possible assistance to the Perinthians. A large body of mercenaries came to their relief, with all kinds of provisions and military stores. They were commanded by Apollodorus, an Athenian. Philip, seeing that all his efforts to take the city were unavailing, withdrew from the attack; and, leaving one half of his army before Perinthus, marched with the other half to surprise Byzantium, which, weakened by its efforts to relieve the Perinthians, he hoped to find unprovided for defense.[2]

Before he left Perinthus, or perhaps shortly before he commenced

[1] Demosthenes, Or. ad Epist. 153. Philipp. iv. 139, 140. The orator and his countrymen were both reproached for this, but unjustly. Demosthenes has also been censured for receiving money from Persia; but the real question is, for what purpose he received it, and how he used it. See Philipp. Epist. 160. Plutarch in Vit. Demosth. Æschines contra Ctes. 88, 90.

[2] Diodorus, xvi. 74—76. Pausanias, i. 29.

the siege, he had sent a letter to the Athenians, which is still extant, and is a remarkable document. It is a letter of reproof and menace. In style it is clear and forcible, in argument weak, except where it confutes the false points made by his adversaries. He complains of various breaches of treaty, and violations of international law, committed by the Athenians; referring particularly to the operations of Diopithes in Thrace. He denounces their embassy to Persia as an offense against the Greek community. He defends his own conduct with respect to Cardia and the Thracian princes, and declares that his march into Chersonesus was necessitated by the hostilities of the Athenian general and the Chersonesites themselves. His own pacific intentions had been manifested by the Amphictyonic embassy after the peace, when the Athenians spurned every proposal made to secure the safety of Greece. For this the orators were chargeable, who consulted their own interests rather than the advantage of their country. In every respect the Athenians were the aggressors: he had given them no provocation; he had shown the utmost forbearance: but as this had produced no effect, he must decide the quarrel by arms.[1]

Such arguments might have come well from a king who remained quietly at home, and interfered not with his neighbors. But coming from the conqneror of Olynthus, the invader of Epirus and Thrace, the dictator of Thessaly, the plotter in Eubœa and Megara, they appear somewhat ludicrous, until one reflects what the real object of Philip was—viz. to encourage his own party at Athens, including not only his paid advocates, but all who were afraid of war, or selfishly attached to mercantile pursuits, or to a life of idleness and amusement. He might distract the counsels of the Athenians, impede their warlike preparations, and so create a diversion in his own favor. There is a current of ill humor in the letter, arguing that he had been annoyed by the Athenian operations in the Hellespont, and that he discerned symptoms of more than usual vigor in their administration.[2]

Demosthenes, at this time all-powerful at Athens, replied to the letter by an animated speech, in which, repeating the old arguments, he urged his countrymen to redouble their exertions in the war.[3] They had been greatly encouraged by the success of their arms in Eubœa, from which, at the close of the year B.C. 341, they expelled the tyrants Clitarchus and Philistides. It was the generalship of

[1] Philippi Epistola. See p. 156 of this volume.

[2] Mitford praises the energy of Demosthenes at this period. Hist. of Greece, iv. c. 41, s. 1.

[3] Demosth. Oratio ad Epistola. See p. 149 of this volume. Whether we have this oration in an entirely genuine state, may perhaps be doubted.

Phocion, the counsel of Demosthenes, that secured this important victory; and the latter was rewarded with a golden crown.[1]

The Byzantines, on the approach of Philip, sent an embassy to Athens to solicit succor; and such was the state of public feeling, that the Athenians were easily induced to forget former injuries, and pass a decree in their favor. It was resolved, on the motion of Demosthenes, that the pillar, on which the treaty with Philip was inscribed, should be taken down, and an armament sent instantly to the Propontis.[2] He himself went beforehand to encourage the people of Byzantium, and conclude a treaty of alliance.[3] It seems there was a party in that city who preferred submission to Macedonia. Demosthenes silenced their opposition, confirmed the waverers, and animated the people to resistance.[4] The Athenian armament arrived; but great was the disappointment of the Byzantines when they found that Chares was in command. Chares was the man whose rapacious exactions had brought on the Social war; who had caused the revolt of Corcyra; who had massacred the Sestian population.[5] He was generally feared and detested throughout the Ægean and the Hellespont. The citizens refused to receive his fleet into their harbor, so that he was forced to cruise about the Euxine, committing piracy, and subsisting by plunder. An attack which he made on the Macedonian fleet was disgracefnlly repulsed. When the news of this came to Athens, it excited indignation among the people, who regarded the disrespect shown to their general as an insult to themselves. Demosthenes had not returned; and the people in their angry mood were about to take some rash step; when Phocion addressed them in a calm speech, showing that the fault lay in the character of their general, and not in the fickleness of their allies. A vote was then carried to send reinforcements, and Phocion himself was put in command. He sailed immediately to the Bosphorus, and, landing his forces on the beach, encamped outside the walls. He had an intimate friend in Byzantium, one of the principal statesmen, named Cleon, who had formerly been his fellow-student in the Academy at Athens. Cleon pledged his own responsibility for the good behavior of his friend; and Phocion was at once admitted into the city, where both he and his soldiers ex-

[1] Demosthenes, De Coron. 253. Diodorus, xvi. 74.

[2] Philochorus apud Dionys. Epist. ad Amm. i. 11. (This, according to him, was the first formal breaking of the peace.) Plutarch in Vit. Demosth.

[3] He had advised this course in the case of Olynthus, *πρεσβείαν πέμπειν ἥτις ταῦτ' ἐρεῖ καὶ παρέσται τοῖς πράγμασι.* Olynth. i. 10.

[4] Demosth. de Coron. 308. Æschines contra Ctes. 90, sneers at his rival's boast.

[5] Diodorus, xv. 95. Argument. Isocr. De Pace. Compare pp. 189, 281, of this volume.

cited the esteem and admiration of the Byzantines by their zeal, their valor, and their sobriety.[1]

Philip had, in the meantime, been vigorously carrying on the siege; but Byzantium was not only strong by its position and its fortifications,[2] but had received considerable succors from Cos, Chios, Rhodes, and other states of Greece. On Phocion's arrival, the aspect of affairs was so greatly changed, that Philip deemed it prudent to abandon his enterprise. He raised the siege both of Byzantium and Perinthus, and after ravaging the territory that lay between those cities, retired to his own kingdom.[3] That on his way he made an attempt to surprise the cities of Chersonesus, is indeed very probable; and that his failure was owing partly to the courageous resistance of Diopithes and the inhabitants, partly to the activity of the gallant Phocion. Plutuarch relates, that Phocion, after expelling Philip from Byzantium, captured some of his ships, and recovered places which Philip had taken and garrisoned; that then he made incursions into the enemy's territory, and levied contributions; but, being at length wounded in a battle with the Macedonians, was forced to return. From this vague narrative it may be collected, that Phocion sailed with his fleet to the Chersonese, to protect it against Philip's inroad; that having chased him from thence, he pursued his victory into the continent of Thrace, and recovered some of the fortresses which Philip had there taken. This is more reasonable, than to suppose that Phocion invaded Macedonia; and it partly agrees with the statement of Justin, and with that of Demosthenes, which implies that the Chersonese had been in danger.[4]

Such was the issue of this memorable campaign; the first in which Philip suffered defeat and loss of reputation. Perinthus and Byzantium testified their gratitude to the Athenians by a joint decree, which is preserved to us in the oration of Demosthenes on the Crown. By this it was resolved, that the rights of citizenship, intermarriage, and other honorable privileges, should be conferred on their allies—that three colossal statues should be erected in the harbor of Byzantium, representing the people of Athens crowned by the Byzantines and Perinthians—and that a religious deputation should be sent to the Isthmian, Nemean, Olympian, and Pythian

[1] Plutarch in Vit. Phoc. s. 14. Leland's Life of Philip, ii. 257.

[2] Pausanias, iv. 31.

[3] Diodorus, xvi. 77. Justin, ix. 1, 2. Plutarch, l. c. Demosthenes, de Coron. 255.

[4] It may be presumed that the Chersonesites would not have passed the decree cited by Demosthenes, had not their country been in danger of conquest. The statement of Justin, (l. c.) *multas urbes Chersonensium expugnat*, is an exaggeration of the truth. Compare Leland's Life of Philip, ii. 267.

festivals, to proclaim these well-earned honors to the Grecian world. Nor were the Chersonesites behindhand in their acknowledgments. The inhabitants of Sestus, Eleus, Madytus, and Alopeconnesus, honored the senate and people of Athens with a golden crown, and built an altar consecrated to Gratitude and the Athenian people, in requital for the preservation of their country, their laws, their liberty, and their sanctuaries. Demosthenes justly boasted, that these glories were in a great measure attributable to his own counsels and exertions.[1]

Of Diopithes, whose able measures contributed so much to the discomfiture of Philip, history says nothing further. We may infer that he died shortly afterwards; for Aristotle mentions a present having been sent to him from the King of Persia, which arrived after his death. The exact date, however, is uncertain.[2]

Within two years after these occurrences, the liberties of Greece were extinguished at Chæronea. The Athenians were still permitted to retain their possessions in Chersonesus, though their real independence was gone. In the year 334 B.C., twenty Athenian galleys assisted in the transportation of Alexander's army from Sestus to Abydos. At a somewhat later period the Chersonese itself fell under Macedonian dominion. Lysimachus built a town at the Isthmus, between Pactya and Cardia, which was named after him Lysimachia.[3]

During the reign of Philip, the Thracian Chersonese gave birth to one great man—Eumenes of Cardia—concerning whom Plutarch writes as follow:[4]—

"Duris reports that Eumenes the Cardian was the son of a poor wagoner in the Thracian Chersonese, but liberally educated, both as a scholar and a soldier; that, while he was very young, Philip, passing through Cardia, amused himself with seeing the youth of the place perform their gymnastic exercises; and, being struck with the cleverness and activity of Eumenes, took him at once into his service. But the more credible story is, that Philip promoted him on account of the friendship which he bore to his father, whose guest he had often been."

Eumenes accompanied Alexander into Asia as his principal secretary, and after his death played a conspicuous part in the theatre of the world.

[1] Demosthenes, De Coron. 255—257.
[2] Aristotle, Rhet. ii. 8, 11.
[3] Strabo, Excerpta ex lib. sept. fine, 26. Polybius, xviii. 34.
[4] In Vit. Eumen. init.

APPENDIX IV.

THE PROPERTY TAX.

We frequently read in Demosthenes of *contributions*[1] for the service of the state, of the reluctance of the Athenians to pay *contributions*, the necessity of *contributing*, &c. These expressions almost always relate to an extraordinary tax, in the nature of a property or income-tax, which was levied at Athens in times of danger and necessity, to defray the expenses of war.

In ancient times there was no such thing as a standing army in any Grecian state, and little occasion to employ a military force for any length of time at a distance from home. The citizens formed a national militia for the defense of their country, and were bound to serve for a certain period at their own expense. Afterwards, when wars became long and frequent, not only was it necessary to pay to citizens who performed military duty, but large bodies of mercenary soldiers had to be maintained at the public cost. For this purpose the Athenians resorted to the extraordinary tax above mentioned, when the proceeds of their ordinary revenue were found insufficient.

The first instance that we know of this tax being levied was in the fourth year of the Peloponnesian war, when two hundred talents were raised to carry on the siege of Mitylene. The principle of its assessment, however, was established long before, according to the classification of the people by Solon, which I am about to explain.

Solon distributed all the citizens of Athens into four classes, according to the amount of their property, which he caused to be assessed and entered in a public schedule. The highest class were those whose land yielded an annual income of five hundred measures (medimni) of corn, and hence they were called Pentacosiomedimni.[2] The second class consisted of those whose income amounted to three hundred measures; they were therefore called Triacosiomedimni; and also Knights, because they were reckoned able to keep a war-horse. The third class were those whose income amounted to two hundred measures:[3] they were called

[1] The expressions are εἰσφορά, *contribution* or *payment of property-tax:* εἰσφέρειν, *to contribute, to pay, &c.:* sometimes εἰσφέρειν χρήματα, εἰσφέρειν εἰς τὸ δημόσιον.

[2] The μέδιμνος was about a bushel and a half. The estimate might also be made in liquid produce, and then it was calculated by the με-τρητής, or nine gallon measure.

[3] I have here followed Grote's view in preference to Böckh's. See his History of Greece, iii. 157.

Zeugitæ, or yeomen, because they were able to keep a yoke of oxen. The fourth and most numerous class comprised all whose income was below the last amount. They constituted the free laboring population.

These classes had their respective duties and privileges. The highest honors of the state, that is the offices of the nine Archons and Senate of Areopagus, were reserved for the first class. They also took the principal military commands. Posts of inferior distinction were filled by the second and third classes, who were bound to military services, the one on horseback, the other as heavy-armed soldiers on foot. Among these three classes—besides direct taxation—there were distributed, according to certain rules, the honorable but expensive duties that bore the name of *Liturgiæ*.[1] The members of the fourth class were disqualified to hold any office of dignity. They served as light troops in the army, and manned the ships; but were exempt from the expensive duties and all direct taxation.

Solon thus introduced a new feature into the constitution of Athens, viz. a property qualification. His classes were distinctions not of caste, nor of birth, but of wealth only. The scale is stated as if none but landed property were taken into account. This was to be expected in the infancy of a state not yet enriched by commerce. Perhaps, however, as Grote supposes, property of other kinds was intended to be included, since it served as the basis of every man's liability to taxation.

As the state became more democratical, the distinctions between the four classes were gradually abolished, and the highest offices of the republic were thrown open to all. But the principle, according to which they were assessed to the public taxes, was preserved from first to last.

The members of the first three classes were entered in the state-schedule as possessed of a certain taxable capital, which was estimated by reference to their income, but in a proportion diminishing according to the scale of such income; and they paid taxes according to the sums for which they were respectively rated in the schedule. The rateable property of the first-class man was calculated at twelve years' purchase of his income; that of the second-class man at ten years' purchase; that of the third-class man at five years' purchase. The medimnus then being taken as worth a drachm; the first-class man, whose income was exactly 500 drachms, the minimum qualification of his class, stood rated in the schedule for a capital of 6,000 drachms, or one talent; or, if his income were larger, for a capital proportionally increased. The second-class man, whose income was exactly 300 drachms, the minimum qualification of his class, stood rated for 3,000 drachms, and so on, in proportion, for any income

[1] *Public Offices.* See Appendix V.

between 300 and 500 drachms. The third-class man, whose income was exactly 200 drachms, the minimum qualification of his class, stood rated for 1,000 drachms, and so on, in proportion, for any income between 200 and 300 drachms. The members of the fourth class were not taxed, as we have already mentioned.

If therefore a property-tax had been levied of one per cent., the poorest man of the first class would have paid, upon 6,000 drachms, 60 drachms; the poorest of the second class, upon 3,000 drachms, 30; the poorest of the third class, upon 1,000 drachms, 10. Thus the mode of assessment established by Solon was, in some measure, like a graduated income-tax.

With the advance of wealth and power pecuniary contributions became more frequent; and then there is no doubt that the personal property of Athenians formed a considerable part of their rateable capital. Also, while the Solonian principle of graduation was maintained, the scale of assessment must have been altered, and the number of classes was probably increased.

In the year B.C. 377, in the Archonship of Nausinicus, when the Athenians had joined the alliance of Thebes against Sparta, a new valuation was made of the whole taxable capital of the country, which amounted, as Demosthenes states in round numbers, to 6,000 talents, and according to Polybius, who perhaps gives the exact estimate, to 5,750 talents.[1] This, it must be understood, was the capital estimated for the purpose of taxation, not the whole capital of the people, which was (as Böckh supposes) five or six times that amount.

At the same time, for the better management of the property-tax, the following method was introduced. From each of the ten Attic tribes were selected 120 of the wealthiest citizens, making a body of 1,200, from whom again were selected the wealthiest 300, 30 from each tribe, to exercise a general superintendence. To this select body of 300 the State looked for immediate payment of the tax, in case of need. They might be called upon to advance the whole sum required; and then have to be reimbursed by contributions from the rest. To facilitate this, the 1,200 were divided into 20 *Symmoriæ*, or Boards, of 60, two for every tribe, whose business it was to collect the taxes from the members of their respective tribes, a certain number of whom were assigned to each Board. The course then was, that the 300 advanced the tax; they obtained contribution from the 900 by means of the Boards; and the Boards exacted contribution from the general body of rate-payers. Every Board had its Chairman,[2] and subordinate officers to collect the rates, summon defaulters, &c.

It appears that in the year referred to a property-tax was imposed. Demosthenes, then an infant of seven years, his father

[1] See p. 183 of this volume.

[2] Ἡγεμών.

having just died, was returned by his guardians as possessing an estate of fifteen talents. He was assessed by the state at three talents, and this was the highest scale of assessment, as he himself expressly tells us in his oration against Aphobus.[1] It seems also, that the tax extended as low as to estates of twenty-five minas. Böckh has supposed, that there were four classes of rate-payers; the first having estates which amounted to twelve talents; the second, estates amounting to six talents; the third, estates amounting to two talents; the fourth, estates amounting to twenty-five minas; —that these classes were assessed at one fifth, one sixth, one eighth, and one tenth of the value of their estates, respectively. If we adopt this hypothesis, which, whether exact or not, is equally good for the purpose of illustration; and if we further assume, that a tax of five per cent. was at that time levied;[2] the following tables will serve to exhibit specimens of the entries in the Athenian rate-book:—

FIRST CLASS.

Name of Person,	*Value of Property.*	*Taxable Value.*	*Tax.*
Onetor	30 talents	6 talents	18 minas.
Timotheus	25 talents	5 talents	15 minas.
Demosthenes	15 talents	3 talents	9 minas.
Phænippus	12 talents	2 tal. 24 min.	720 drachms.

SECOND CLASS.

Name of Person.	*Value of Property.*	*Taxable Value.*	*Tax.*
Timocrates	10 talents	1 tal. 40 min.	5 minas.
Philo	9 talents	1 tal. 30 min.	450 drachms.
Menestheus	8 talents	1 tal. 20 min.	4 minas.
Antidorus	6 talents	1 talent	3 minas.

THIRD CLASS.

Name of Person.	*Value of Property.*	*Taxable Value.*	*Tax.*
Strepsiades	5 talents	3750 drachms	187 drachms, 3 obols.
Nausicrates	4 talents	30 minas	150 drachms.
Phanias	3 talents	2250 drachms	112 drachms, 3 obols.
Euphron	2 talents	15 minas	75 drachms.

[1] Contra Aphobum, 815, 816.

[2] Böckh thinks that a tax of five per cent. was actually imposed at that time, and that the amount which it produced was three hundred talents. He relies upon the words of Demosthenes, cont. Androt. p. 606. Grote contends that he is wrong. See the note to his History of Greece, p. 158, vol. x.

FOURTH CLASS.

Name of Person.	*Value of Property.*	*Taxable Value.*	*Tax.*
Archippus	1 talent, 30 minas	9 minas	45 drachms.
Stratocles	1 talent	6 minas	30 drachms.
Tisias	30 minas	3 minas	15 drachms.
Mantitheus	25 minas	250 drachms	12 drachms, 3 obols.

Many of the details connected with the Athenian property-tax resembled those which we have become familiar with in our own country, and which serve to make the tax generally odious. Every citizen had to make a return of the value of his property, to be entered in the register; and his return was open to cavil and dispute. Examples of such disputes were common; the officers being often induced, from motives of personal dislike, to surcharge the rate-payer. Thus numerous inequalities crept into the register from time to time. The process called the *Exchange* was allowed in respect of this tax, as well as in respect of the *Liturgiæ*.[1] Any citizen who believed himself to be overcharged, while his neighbor, as rich or richer than himself, bore not his fair share of the burden, might call upon the other to take his place, or submit to an exchange of property. This was designed as a measure of relief, like our own right of appeal against an unequal rate; but it must have been attended with a vast deal of trouble and annoyance. The Generals held a court for the decision of all disputes relative to the rating, collecting, &c., and also to the process of the *Exchange*. The whole affair was under their control and superintendence; and it was their business particularly to see, that the richest citizens were included in the select body of three hundred.

The tax could never be imposed without a decree of the people, which fixed the amount, the number of classes, the estates included in each, the scales of assessment, &c. It is clear from many passages in Demosthenes,[2] that there was great reluctance on the part of the people to impose this tax, and that it required some special necessity to make it tolerable. Demosthenes himself, during his minority, paid eighteen minas property-tax to the state, on a capital of fifteen talents;[3] so that in ten years he paid one-fiftieth part of his property. This (says Böckh) can not be deemed an unreasonable tax, when we consider that the capital of Demosthenes might in that time have been doubled by good management on the part

[1] See Appendix V.

[2] See particularly the first Olynthiac, p. 44 of this volume; second Olynthiac, p. 52; on the Chersonese, p. 104; on the Navy Boards, pp. 184, 185.

[3] Contra Aphobum, 825.

of his guardians; and more especially, when we consider the low rate of the custom duties, and the cheapness of the necessaries of life at Athens. The graduated scale of assessment, (according to Solon's plan of taxing the rich in a higher proportion than the poor,) though contrary to the English principle of taxation, appears to me to have been exceedingly fair. And it must be observed in favor of the untaxed Athenian multitude, that they showed no disposition to impose the burden unnecessarily or too often.

When the tax was granted, there could be no exemption from it, on personal or any other grounds. The mines, being public property, were not included in the assessment. Aliens resident in Attica were subject to the tax, but were included in a distinct register from the citizens, and were rated on a higher scale.

APPENDIX V.

THE TRIERARCHY.

Athens owed her glory and her empire to her navy. Until she turned her attention to the sea, she was but a second or third-rate power among the states of Greece. The character therefore, of her naval establishment, and the provisions made by law for its maintenance, are matters of considerable interest to the reader of Athenian history.

The situation of Attica was eminently favorable for maritime enterprise; being a kind of peninsula, with most commodious harbors, in the centre of the Grecian world. Solon perceived these natural advantages, and laid the foundation of a navy, by imposing on each of the forty-eight divisions,[1] into which the country was then distributed, the charge of providing a ship. But it was not till after the first Persian war that the importance of a national marine came to be fully understood; and the person who first enlightened the Athenians on the subject was Themistocles. It has already been mentioned, that he persuaded them to apply the rent of the Laurian silver-mines to ship-building.[2] This was in the year B.C. 483. Athens had been at war with Ægina, and had been compelled some years before to borrow Corinthian galleys to meet her enemy at

[1] *Ναυκραρίαι.* "The name seems to have nothing to do with navigation, but to be derived from *ναίω*. *Ναύκραρος* is another form of *ναύκληρος*, in the sense of a householder, as *ναῦλον* was used for the rent of a house." Thirlwall, Gr. Hist. ii. 52.

[2] Page 254. Herodotus, vii. 144.

sea. Peace had not yet been established, and the navy of Ægina was still greatly superior. Themistocles prevailed on his countrymen to increase theirs to two hundred ships; and soon afterwards he procured a law to be passed, that twenty triremes, or ships of war, should be built every year. The wisdom of these measures was proved by the victories of Artemisium and Salamis.[1] I subjoin the comment of Grote:[1]—

"In recommending extraordinary efforts, to create a navy, as well as to acquire nautical practice, Themistoklês displayed all that sagacious appreciation of the circumstances and dangers of the time, for which Thucydides gives him credit. Not only was there the struggle with Ægina, a maritime power equal or more than equal, and within sight of the Athenian harbor,—but there was also in the distance a still more formidable contingency to guard against. The Persian armament had been driven with disgrace from Attica back to Asia; but the Persian monarch still remained with undiminished means of aggression and increased thirst for revenge; and Themistocles knew well that the danger from that quarter would recur greater than ever. He believed that it would recur again in the same way, by an expedition across the Ægean, like that of Datis to Marathon; against which the best defence would be found in a numerous and well-trained fleet. Nor could the large preparations of Darius for renewing the attack remain unknown to a vigilant observer, extending as they did over so many Greeks subject to the Persian empire. Such positive warning was more than enough to stimulate the active genius of Themistocles, who now prevailed upon his countrymen to begin with energy the work of maritime preparation, as well against Ægina as against Persia. Not only were two hundred new ships built, and citizens trained as seamen, —but the important work was commenced, during the year when Themistocles was either archon or general, of forming and fortifying a new harbor for Athens at Piræus, instead of the ancient open bay of Phalerum. The latter was indeed somewhat nearer to the city, but Piræus, with its three separate natural ports, admitting of being closed and fortified, was incomparably superior in safety as well as in convenience. It is not too much to say, with Herodotus, that the Æginetan war was the salvation of Greece, by constraining the Athenians to make themselves a maritime power."

After the second Persian war, Athens became the head of a great naval confederacy, comprising all the Ægean islands and a great number of sea-port towns on the continent. It was arranged which of the allied states were to find money, and which of them ships. Treasurers were appointed by the Athenians to receive the contributions, which at first amounted to 460 talents. These began in a short time to fall into arrear, and were exacted by compulsion.

[1] Thirlwall, Gr. Hist. ii. 269. [2] History of Greece, v. 69.

Many of the allies, being reluctant to perform military service, agreed to contribute money instead of ships; and thus, while the fleet of the Athenians was augmented out of the general fund, their citizens, by a system of laborious training, and by constant and regular employment, became decidedly the best seamen in Greece.[1]

To be mistress of the sea was necessary for the safety as well as for the pre-eminence of Athens. Her enemies, the Lacedæmonians and their allies, could bring into the field a land-force which she was unable to encounter; and by ravaging Attica, or occupying it with their armies, could deprive her people of all the ordinary means of subsistence. But having the command of the sea, she could import the necessaries of life from a distance, while her own ramparts protected her against all assaults from land, and the long walls which connected her city and harbor gave her the advantages of an island. It was Themistocles who formed the design, but it was Pericles who brought it to the test, and fully proved its wisdom. To use our own expression, the wooden walls of Athens were her real security. At the commencement of the Peloponnesian war, she had three hundred galleys fit for service. A hundred of the best were laid by, and captains appointed for them, to be employed only on extraordinary occasions.[2]

The duty of providing ships, which in Solon's time had been distributed among the 48 divisions of the people—which number was increased by Clisthenes to 50—devolved afterwards upon the state at large. Ship-building was superintended by the Council of Five-hundred. Each ship of war was the property of the state; and in general also the furniture and stores. Pay and provisions for the crew and the marines[3] were found by the public. On the Sicilian expedition every sailor received a drachm a day from the treasury.[4]

The command of a ship, or the trierarchy, was one of those public duties,[5] which were imposed upon wealthy citizens without further reward than the honor of the service. Each appointment was made by the generals according to a scale of property; and the ships were assigned to the different captains by lot.

It was a duty attended with expense, as well as personal responsibility. The captain had to find the crew, to keep his galley in repair, and to restore it, together with the tackle and furniture, in as good a condition as he received them, making allowance for ordinary wear and tear and inevitable contingencies. But a crew was not always readily to be got, and the captain frequently found it necessary to allure men to the service by bounties or extra pay.

1 Thucydides, i. 96, 99.
2 Thucydides, i. 93; ii. 13, 24, 65.
3 Ἐπιβάται.
4 Thucydides, vi. 31.
5 Λειτουργίαι.

Again, the ship and stores might not be in a good condition when the captain first received them; and divers captious questions might arise on the subject of repairs, mismanagement, &c. To repair an old ship might cost as much as to build a new one. Heavy liabilities might thus fall upon the captain; and therefore Cleon, in the Knights of Aristophanes, threatens his rival, that he will get him appointed to an old ship with a rotten mast. There were Admiralty officers,[1] whose business it was to see to the equipment of the vessels and to expedite their sailing. On one occasion we find them empowered by a special decree to imprison those captains who had not left the pier by a certain time; while, on the other hand, a reward of a crown was given to the man who first brought his vessel off the stocks.[2]

The command lasted for a year, at the end of which a successor was appointed, and it became his duty to enter upon the office immediately. If the ship was absent, he was compelled to join it under a severe penalty, and also to reimburse his predecessor for any expenses which he had incurred beyond the legal period. An action might be brought to recover such expenses; of which we have an example in the speech written by Demosthenes for Apollodorus against Polycles.[3]

The expense varied from forty minas to a talent. During his year of service the captain enjoyed an immunity from all other offices of burden; nor could he be required to serve again for two years.

Personal exemption from the trierarchy was very rarely granted, and only as a special honor. Leptines passed a law to prohibit all exemptions, against which, as being unjust to the few persons who enjoyed the privilege, and useless as a measure of public economy, Demosthenes made one of his best early speeches, and procured its repeal. There were however certain classes of persons exempted by the general policy of the law. Thus, the nine archons could not be called upon to command ships, as being incompatible with their magisterial duties. Orphans were not liable to serve any office till a year after the expiration of their minority. As to the other cases mentioned in the speech on the Navy Boards, I may refer to my note on the passage.[4]

Notwithstanding the inconveniences and hardships to which the captains were exposed in the performance of their duty, there was no reluctance to undertake it in the early times of Athenian great-

[1] Ἀποστολεῖς.

[2] See the Oration of Demosthenes, De Coron. Trierarch. 1228, and the Argument.

[3] Or. contra Polyclem. 1206. There are many details in this speech, which make it useful for the student to peruse.

[4] Page 181.

ness. Those who could afford it were glad of the opportunity to display their public spirit, their patriotism, and their valor. To command the best ship, or to have the best outfit, was an object of emulation. There were occasions when wealthy men made presents of ships to the state. Thus Clinias, the father of Alcibiades, brought his own galley to the battle of Artemisium. And if the best seamen were not to be had without additional cost, the captain would willingly defray it out of his own purse. Of this a splendid example is furnished by Thucydides in his description of the armament which sailed against Syracuse.[1] "This," says he, "was the most costly and magnificent which had ever been sent from Athens. It was fitted out at a vast expense both on the part of the captains and the state. For the treasury gave a drachm a day to every seaman, and provided empty galleys, sixty men-of-war, and forty transports; while the captains found the crews for them, and gave gratuities, in addition to their pay, to the officers and superior rowers. Their ensigns and equipments were of the most expensive kind; for every commander was anxious that his own ship should be remarkable for its speed and beauty." He then notices the rivalry between the land and naval forces; the immense outlay incurred by private citizens for their own arms and accoutrements; and the provision which the captains must have made for their future expenditure during the campaign. He then describes the launching of the fleet, after a solemn libation and prayers to the gods for success, in which an immense concourse of spectators on shore, citizens and strangers, all joined. The galleys, having first sailed out in line, kept up a race as far as Ægina. Such was the spirit of that day, when Athens had risen to the meridian of her glory.

At a later period things had greatly changed. After the disasters in Sicily, neither the state nor private citizens had the same means at their disposal. As a measure of relief, two captains were frequently appointed to one ship; each of whom took the command alternately, or one paid the other a sum of money to take the whole command. This led afterwards to the practice of providing deputies, which was found highly injurious to the naval service; for the deputy was generally a person who took the office for the lowest price, and sought to make a profit of it. Having such purpose only in view, he would be disposed to neglect his duties, to curtail the time of public service, to attend to his own business rather than the business of the state, and to reimburse himself for his outlay by plunder, piracy, and extortion.[2] Of the irregularities committed by Athenian officers in the period subsequent to the

[1] Thucydides, vi. 31, 32. Plutarch, in the Life of Alcibiades, makes the fleet to consist of nearly a hundred and forty sail.

[2] Thirlwall, Gr. Hist. v. 215.

Peloponnesian war, and the mischievous consequences which resulted from them, so much has already been said in this volume, that it will be unnecessary to recur to the subject. The appointment of deputies was, no doubt, illegal, and subjected the real servant of the state to a penalty; but having been permitted in times of distress and difficulty, it grew into a custom, and was connived at, except where any actual mischief occurred. Thus, after a sea-fight in which the Athenians were defeated by Alexander of Pheræ, the captains who had delegated their command were brought to trial by Aristophon, and convicted of a treasonable desertion of duty.[1] "Had not the jury been merciful," says the orator, "nothing could have saved them from capital punishment."

Other abuses also crept into the management of the trierarchy. The burden was not always equally distributed. The appointments, which ought to have been made according to a scale of property, were often capricious and unfair; and when public virtue had decayed, and citizens were not easily found, who were willing to sacrifice their private interests to their country, an unjust appointment was regarded as an act of oppression. Jacobs truly observes, that individual patriotism, although it may do wonders on extraordinary occasions, ought not to be made the basis of a legal ordinance; and that the Athenians discovered their mistake in placing too much reliance upon it.[2] Little can be expected from the self-sacrifice of private citizens, where the state does not perform its own part honestly and well. Demosthenes complains, that the commanders were often nominated on the spur of the moment, when the armament ought to have been ready to sail; and that, while they were contesting their liability, and the people were inquiring how the ways and means were to be provided, the time for action had slipped away.[3] The captains, thus suddenly appointed, were put to extreme hardship; since it might be difficult, or even impossible, to procure a crew by the time of departure; and we read that, in order to escape the imprisonment, to which they were liable by law for neglect of duty, they would fly to the temple of Diana, which was a kind of sanctuary, at Munychia, or appeal as suppliants to the popular assembly.[4]

An attempt was made to rectify the injustice of unfair appointments by a method called the Exchange, which is said to have been introduced by Solon. The course was as follows:—If a man charged with the command of a ship thought that another, who was not charged, was better able to bear the burden, he might propose to

[1] Demosthenes, De Coron. Trierarch. 1230.
[2] Introduction to his translation of the speech, De Symmoriis, p. 9.
[3] Philipp. i. 50. Page 69 of this volume.
[4] Demosthenes, De Coron. 262.

transfer the office to him, or to make an exchange of estates. If the other declined these terms, he might be summoned before the Generals, who exercised a jurisdiction for the decision of all disputes relating to the naval appointments. If the case could not be settled by them without a formal trial, it had to be brought into court before a jury; and the main question for the jury was, whether under all the circumstances the complainant was entitled to the relief he prayed for. If they decided in his favor, the defendant was forced to choose, whether he could take the office or the exchange. If he took the office, there would be no further trouble. But if the exchange was accepted, a complication of difficulties might arise. Each of the parties was obliged to give to the other an inventory of his property within three days after the making the demand; and, to prevent any fraudulent concealment, a summary power was given to each to enter and make search upon the house and land of his opponent, and to seal up every chamber, closet, barn, outhouse, or other place where his effects might be deposited. An oath was also taken by each that he would make a full disclosure of all that he possessed, and a fair and complete transfer. For the whole property of a man, real and personal, together with all claims and obligations attached thereto, was at once in point of law transferred by the exchange; except, indeed, property in the Laurian mines, the ownership whereof was vested in the state, and the occupant was a mere lessee.[1] Here was another fertile source of litigation. Whether each party had made a *bona fide* disclosure; whether any effects had been concealed or removed; whether any false or fraudulent claims were put in; these and a multitude of similar questions were likely enough to spring out of such an arrangement. It was a clumsy contrivance altogether.[2]

In the year B. C. 358 an attempt was made to improve the naval service and lighten the burden of the trierarchy, by putting it under the management of Boards, much in the same way as the property-tax had been some years before.[3] This was by the law of Periander. The ships required at any time were equally divided among the Boards, who again apportioned the burden among their own members, so that a single ship was assigned to five or more persons, and commonly to sixteen.[4] The trierarchy so constituted was no longer a personal service, but a sort of pecuniary obligation imposed upon the associated members. There was of course a real captain—in the natural sense of the word—who might either be one of the managing

[1] See p. 254.

[2] The speech of Demosthenes against Phænippus gives us some account of these proceedings. Also the speech against Aphobus, 840, 841; and that against Midias, 539, 540.

[3] See the last Appendix, p. 301.

[4] Called συντελεῖς—*joint contributors.*

trierarchs, or a deputy appointed by them; but the name of trierarch was still given to them all. Their duties, with respect to the equipment of the vessels, keeping them in repair, &c., were the same as under the previous system. But it seems, the wealthier members abused their trust by letting out the command for the lowest price, and making a profit by the contributions of the other members.[1] And in other respects the arrangements were defective, which caused Demosthenes, in the year B. C. 354, to propose the reforms set forth in the Oration on the Navy Boards. His principal objects were, to insure the full complement of serviceable members, by adding eight hundred to the twelve hundred whose names were on the navy list—to divide the boards into sections, each having about the same average of property, and then to apportion the ships, the stores, and the allowance made by the state, equally among them; to make also a commodious arrangement of the docks, so that the captains might always know where to find their own ships, and that when the time came for sailing there might be no confusion or delay.[2]

The reform of Demosthenes was not carried; nor does he appear even to have brought it forward as a motion before the assembly. And for many years he did not recur to the subject.

But after the year B.C. 346, it became apparent that the naval service had been greatly neglected. Miscarriage and defeat had attended almost all the Athenian expeditions. This was partly owing to the want of proper regulations in the war department at home. The expense of the trierarchal office was shirked by those who could best afford it, while, falling on men of moderate and small fortunes, it greatly abated their zeal in the performance of public duties. But from the time last mentioned Demosthenes had been gradually rising to the head of the Athenian administration. He saw more than ever the necessity for an improvement, and especially for such a regulation of the trierarchy as would distribute the burden fairly among all classes. In the year B.C. 340, about or before the time when war against Philip was formally decreed, he procured the passing of a law, by which the burden of the trierarchy was made to fall more equally upon property. It provided that every man whose estate was valued at ten talents should take charge of one galley; at twenty talents, two galleys; at thirty talents, three galleys; but no man should be charged with more than three galleys and one boat: while men whose estates were estimat-

[1] A talent was a common price, as we learn from Demosth. contra Mid. 564.

[2] See pp. 181—184 of this volume. On the whole of this subject, as well as that of the last Appendix, the reader, if he has time, should consult the admirable work of Böckh.

ed at less than ten talents should contribute in a fair proportion to the expense of one galley. The result was that the poorer citizens were greatly relieved, while men, who had under the old system borne but a sixteenth part of the cost of a single ship, were charged with two ships under the amended law. Demosthenes boasts of the important advantages which resulted from his plan. There was no longer any complaint of oppression or unfairness; the duties were cheerfully undertaken; the ships punctually sailed; and none were lost or captured during the whole of the war. That the author of such a law should have made enemies among the wealthy few, who profited by the old abuses, and especially of those who were opposed to war with Macedonia, was a thing to be expected. He was indicted for having proposed it, but triumphantly acquitted, the prosecutor not obtaining a fifth part of the votes.[1]

That the Athenians were greatly indebted to Demosthenes for their success at Byzantium, has been already shown;[2] and it is possible that this very law may have contributed to the result. Such is the opinion of Thirlwall, who writes on the subject as follows:[3]—

"It seems probable that the success of the expedition was in a great measure due to Demosthenes, not only as the mover of the decree which ordered it, but still more on account of a law which he procured to be passed nearly at the same time, and which effected a most important reform in the naval service of Athens. Down to this time a regulation had subsisted, which affords a remarkable instance how, even under the most purely democratical institutions, the grossest injustice may be authorized by the laws in favor of the wealthy. The citizens who were liable to the charge of the trierarchy were distributed into classes, each of sixteen members, without any respect to difference of fortune. By the existing law these sixteen were made to contribute equally to the expense of one galley. Demosthenes had attempted at an earlier period to remedy this abuse, which was of course cherished by many powerful patrons. We do not know whether his proposal was rejected, or whether means were found to evade the execution of it. The evil seems at least to have been as crying as ever, when the necessity of a vigorous effort in behalf of Byzantium enabled him to carry his plan. Its object was to distribute the whole burden of the trierarchy with reference not to persons, but to property: so that the part which fell on each contributor should be in exact proportion to

[1] Demosthenes, De Coron. 260—262.

[2] Page 303 of this volume.

[3] History of Greece, vi. 51. Demosthenes himself does not claim for his law any credit on this account. It had perhaps not been long enough in operation.

his means. Demosthenes himself spoke with exultation of the success of his measure; and the charges, by which his adversaries endeavored to detract from his merit, are hardly intelligible, and are the less deserving of notice, as they do not seem to impeach the equity and utility of the reform."

END OF VOL I.

www.ingramcontent.com/pod-product-compliance
Lightning Source LLC
LaVergne TN
LVHW020220110826
845151LV00003B/769

* 9 7 8 1 4 2 5 5 3 3 0 0 7 *